The true interest and political maxims of the Republick of Holland and West-Friesland. In three parts. ... Written by John de Witt, and other great men in Holland. ...

Pieter de la Court

The true interest and political maxims of the Republick of Holland and West-Friesland. In three parts. ... Written by John de Witt, and other great men in Holland. ...
Court, Pieter de la
ESTCID: T105638
Reproduction from British Library
Wrongly attributed to Jan de Witt; in fact by Pieter de la Court. A translation of 'Aanwissing der heilsams politike Gronden en Maximen van de Republike van Holland', 1669, a revised and enlarged edition of 'Interest van Holland' published in 1662 withou
London : printed in the year, 1702.
lvi,492p. : ill.,port. ; 8°

Eighteenth Century
Collections Online
Print Editions

Gale ECCO Print Editions

Relive history with *Eighteenth Century Collections Online*, now available in print for the independent historian and collector. This series includes the most significant English-language and foreign-language works printed in Great Britain during the eighteenth century, and is organized in seven different subject areas including literature and language; medicine, science, and technology; and religion and philosophy. The collection also includes thousands of important works from the Americas.

The eighteenth century has been called "The Age of Enlightenment." It was a period of rapid advance in print culture and publishing, in world exploration, and in the rapid growth of science and technology – all of which had a profound impact on the political and cultural landscape. At the end of the century the American Revolution, French Revolution and Industrial Revolution, perhaps three of the most significant events in modern history, set in motion developments that eventually dominated world political, economic, and social life.

In a groundbreaking effort, Gale initiated a revolution of its own: digitization of epic proportions to preserve these invaluable works in the largest online archive of its kind. Contributions from major world libraries constitute over 175,000 original printed works. Scanned images of the actual pages, rather than transcriptions, recreate the works *as they first appeared.*

Now for the first time, these high-quality digital scans of original works are available via print-on-demand, making them readily accessible to libraries, students, independent scholars, and readers of all ages.

For our initial release we have created seven robust collections to form one the world's most comprehensive catalogs of 18th century works.

Initial Gale ECCO Print Editions collections include:

> ***History and Geography***
> Rich in titles on English life and social history, this collection spans the world as it was known to eighteenth-century historians and explorers. Titles include a wealth of travel accounts and diaries, histories of nations from throughout the world, and maps and charts of a world that was still being discovered. Students of the War of American Independence will find fascinating accounts from the British side of conflict.

Social Science
Delve into what it was like to live during the eighteenth century by reading the first-hand accounts of everyday people, including city dwellers and farmers, businessmen and bankers, artisans and merchants, artists and their patrons, politicians and their constituents. Original texts make the American, French, and Industrial revolutions vividly contemporary.

Medicine, Science and Technology
Medical theory and practice of the 1700s developed rapidly, as is evidenced by the extensive collection, which includes descriptions of diseases, their conditions, and treatments. Books on science and technology, agriculture, military technology, natural philosophy, even cookbooks, are all contained here.

Literature and Language
Western literary study flows out of eighteenth-century works by Alexander Pope, Daniel Defoe, Henry Fielding, Frances Burney, Denis Diderot, Johann Gottfried Herder, Johann Wolfgang von Goethe, and others. Experience the birth of the modern novel, or compare the development of language using dictionaries and grammar discourses.

Religion and Philosophy
The Age of Enlightenment profoundly enriched religious and philosophical understanding and continues to influence present-day thinking. Works collected here include masterpieces by David Hume, Immanuel Kant, and Jean-Jacques Rousseau, as well as religious sermons and moral debates on the issues of the day, such as the slave trade. The Age of Reason saw conflict between Protestantism and Catholicism transformed into one between faith and logic -- a debate that continues in the twenty-first century.

Law and Reference
This collection reveals the history of English common law and Empire law in a vastly changing world of British expansion. Dominating the legal field is the *Commentaries of the Law of England* by Sir William Blackstone, which first appeared in 1765. Reference works such as almanacs and catalogues continue to educate us by revealing the day-to-day workings of society.

Fine Arts
The eighteenth-century fascination with Greek and Roman antiquity followed the systematic excavation of the ruins at Pompeii and Herculaneum in southern Italy; and after 1750 a neoclassical style dominated all artistic fields. The titles here trace developments in mostly English-language works on painting, sculpture, architecture, music, theater, and other disciplines. Instructional works on musical instruments, catalogs of art objects, comic operas, and more are also included.

The BiblioLife Network

This project was made possible in part by the BiblioLife Network (BLN), a project aimed at addressing some of the huge challenges facing book preservationists around the world. The BLN includes libraries, library networks, archives, subject matter experts, online communities and library service providers. We believe every book ever published should be available as a high-quality print reproduction; printed on-demand anywhere in the world. This insures the ongoing accessibility of the content and helps generate sustainable revenue for the libraries and organizations that work to preserve these important materials.

The following book is in the "public domain" and represents an authentic reproduction of the text as printed by the original publisher. While we have attempted to accurately maintain the integrity of the original work, there are sometimes problems with the original work or the micro-film from which the books were digitized. This can result in minor errors in reproduction. Possible imperfections include missing and blurred pages, poor pictures, markings and other reproduction issues beyond our control. Because this work is culturally important, we have made it available as part of our commitment to protecting, preserving, and promoting the world's literature.

GUIDE TO FOLD-OUTS MAPS and OVERSIZED IMAGES

The book you are reading was digitized from microfilm captured over the past thirty to forty years. Years after the creation of the original microfilm, the book was converted to digital files and made available in an online database.

In an online database, page images do not need to conform to the size restrictions found in a printed book. When converting these images back into a printed bound book, the page sizes are standardized in ways that maintain the detail of the original. For large images, such as fold-out maps, the original page image is split into two or more pages

Guidelines used to determine how to split the page image follows:

- Some images are split vertically; large images require vertical and horizontal splits.
- For horizontal splits, the content is split left to right.
- For vertical splits, the content is split from top to bottom.
- For both vertical and horizontal splits, the image is processed from top left to bottom right.

The Interest of *Holland*.

THE
True Interest and *Political Maxims*
OF THE
REPUBLICK
OF
Holland and West-Friesland.

In Three Parts.

The First Treating of

Liberty in General.	A General Naturalization.
Of Manufactures.	
Fisheries.	Freedom from Imposts.
Traffick.	Impartial Justice;
Navigation.	and
Toleration of Religion.	Settling of Colonys.

Part II. and III.

Of a Free Navigation, and clearing the Seas.	Of the natural Strength and Fortifications of *Holland*. And
Of War and Peace	
Of Treatys of Peace and Alliances, particularly with *England, France* and *Spain*.	Of its Interest in all Respects as to the Government of a Single Person.

Written by JOHN De WITT,
and other Great Men in *Holland*.

Publish'd by the Authority of the States.

LONDON,
Printed in the Year MDCCII.

The Preface.

'TIS now full ten Years, since the infinitely wise and good God in the course of his overruling Providence was pleased to visit me with Afflictions which produced such melancholy thoughts in me, that if they had continued might have proved fatal to my Health. But because things past cannot be amended by sorrow or complaint, I accounted it a part of wisdom to compose the disorder of my Mind, by applying my thoughts to things more agreeable. And whereas from my tender Years I had been delighted with nothing more than the study of History, Philosophy and Political Government, I soon concluded that one of these would be very much conducing to my present purpose and recreation. And whilst I was deliberating with my self about the choice, I was desired by some good Friends to set down in writing such Political Thoughts as I had at several times communicated to them. Partly therefore for my own sake, and partly for the satisfaction of those to whom

whom I ow'd the greatest deference, I undertook among other things to consider the Fundamental Maxims of the Republick of *Holland* and *West-Friesland*.

These Thoughts drawn up in haste, and without the least Ornament of Language, I caused to be transcribed for the use of those Friends who had prevailed with me to write them, and of some others who having a part in the Government of our Native Country, stand obliged to promote the Publick Welfare, and consequently to inquire into the means conducing to that end. And I doubted not that if any thing set down in those Papers should be esteemed serviceable to my Country, they would upon occasion offer'd, make use of it to advance the Publick Interest.

But, contrary to my expectation, a Copy of this rough and imperfect Draught fell into the Hands of those, who without my knowledg gave it to a Printer in order to be published to the World.

And this I found to be done by Persons of an eminent Character, who not only condescended to peruse my Papers, but also to strike out some things, and to add divers others, in particular the 29*th* and 30*th* Chapters of that Edition, treating of *the Reasons why the Liberty injoyed in* Holland *since the Death of the Prince*

Prince of Orange *hath produced no more good; and what Publick Advantages have already risen from the Free Government.* And indeed the Stile of these Additions as well as the Subject, plainly discovers, that whatever had been altered, added or diminished, was done by Persons of so great and profound knowledg of all Affairs relating to the United *Netherlands* and Government of *Holland*, that they seem to have transacted all those things themselves, or at least to have been the principal Persons concern'd in them.

But when the Printer in hopes of more profit had surreptitiously reprinted this imperfect Work, which was never designed for the Press, I resolved carefully to review it, to make divers additions, and to reduce the whole into a better order; and having kept it by me about nine Years (the full time prescribed by one of the most judicious among the * Antients) to print and publish it to the World.

And because the Additions abovementioned have been highly esteemed by many, and are accounted by me to be of great moment, I shall incorporate them without alteration in this Impression, which I own exclusive of all other, and insert

---
* Nonumq, prematur in annum. *Hor.*

them in the fifth and sixth Chapters of the Third Part. I shall likewise omit all such matters as were expunged, out of the singular deference I ow to the Judgment of those who did me that Favour.

To the truth of this I think my self obliged to add, that I was never disobliged by any Monarch, Prince, or Great Lord, much less by any of the Family of *Orange*. Neither have I ever received any particular favour from the Governours of any free State, or desire any. So that it would be an apparent deviation from truth to affirm, that this Work was undertaken with a design either to flatter the Governours of this great and powerful Commonwealth, or to dishonour the Memory of the Princes of *Orange*, who were formerly Captains General and Stadtholders of these Provinces. As if my intention had been only to shew that the Monarchical Administration of those Princes was more prejudicial to *Holland*, than that of any other could have been.

On the contrary, the Service of my Country, which I value above all human concernments, was the only thing I had in view when I wrote these Papers. I am no slavish Courtier, who can be unconcerned for the Welfare of his Country, and learns to speak or be silent as best

plea-

pleases his Master. I am a true *Hollander*, who always calls a *Spade* a *Spade*, and hates all indirect paths. That I might therefore be in some measure serviceable to my Country and Friends, and like a good Citizen instruct such as perhaps have less experience, I have endeavoured to inquire into the true Interest and Maxims of our Republick, and to follow the thred of Truth to the utmost of my Power.

And since all Men know that the preservation and prosperity of a Country depends upon such a Government as is consistent with it self; and Reason informs us that the welfare of *Holland* is founded upon Manufactures, Fishery, Trade and Navigation, I think my self obliged particularly to consider those means of subsistance and Pillars of the State, with some Observations upon the late Government of a Stadtholder and Captain-General, which some ignorant and mistaken *Hollanders* still desire.

This did at first bring me under some uneasiness, because these United *Netherlands*, and particularly the Province of *Holland* and *West-Friesland*, having had no other Stadtholders and Captains General except the Princes of *Orange* and *Nassau*, I doubted not that many ignorant and disaffected Persons, more inclined to the

increase

increase of a Prince's Power, than to the freedom and prosperity of their Country and themselves, would not fail to say, that I had written this Treatise with no other design than to traduce and calumniate those Illustrious Houses. But when I considered that no Difficultys ought to discourage a Man from performing his duty, and that ill Men as well as ill Things were to be * resisted, I resolved to go on, without any regard to those who had always opposed the Liberty of this Country, and to write for the Common Good, tho Great Names should happen to be concerned.

At least I may justly say, that in all that I have written either for my self, or my Friends of the Magistracy and others, touching these weighty matters, I have always avoided and abhorr'd the flatteries of some Writers, which I think not only destructive to Nations, but to Reason it self, and could never offer violence to my Judgment, or slavishly lay a side my Pen. For a good Man ought in due time and place to speak the Truth in the cause of his Country, tho with the hazard of his Life.

I conceive the publication of these Papers cannot be blamed, unless by those,

---

* Tu ne cede malis, sed contra audentior ito. *Virg.*

who maintain the Monarchical Power of the Princes of *Orange* to have been so great in *Holland* and *West-Friesland*, that the shadow of it still remaining among us, ought to be sufficient to deter all Men from writing any thing against the Interest of that Power, or to the disadvantage of any Persons of that Family, tho in other respects highly tending to the Publick Service.

But if this were our case, we might confess, that no Country ever fell into greater Slavery than *Holland* lay under during the Service and Government of those Princes. Which I conceive our greatest admirers of Monarchical Government will not allow, because they used *to extol the said Princes for assisting the States* to resist the King of *Spain* in order to deliver this Country from Oppression, and not to exalt themselves into his place; comparing them to *Virginius Rufus*, who having suppressed the Tyranny of *Vindex*, desired only the following words to be engraven on his Monument;

Here lies Virg. Rufus *who expell'd the Tyrant, not for himself but for his Country.* Plin.

Prince *William* and his Son might in like manner have commanded their Heirs to cause this their Immortal Atchievement to be engraven on their Tomb,

Here lies ..... who assisted to defend his Country against our Earl Philip 2d *King of* Spain, *in order to deliver us from Servitude, and not to be our Master,*

If the States General had not order'd more words to be added, tho to the same effect, which may be seen upon a marble Monument erected at *Delft* 1620.

But because I trust my Country will not suffer her self to be brought under the like intolerable Servitude, at least not in this Age, I have presumed to speak of the true Interest and Maxims of *Holland* as far as I thought necessary. And this after the consideration and mature deliberation of divers Years, I have delivered to be printed, not without the Knowledg and Allowance of my Natural Superiors, the States of *Holland* and *West-Friesland*.

I have always been and still continue to be a lover of the Princes of *Orange*, both as they were Men, and as far as their Actions might tend to the advantage of *Holland* and the rest of the *United Provinces*. I willingly acknowledg that Prince *William* the First, with his Sons *Mau-*

-ice and *Henry*, have generally been esteemed in these Countrys as Men endued with Noble and Princely Virtues, and blemished with few Monarchical Vices.

For History informs us that Prince *William* I. in the 11*th* Year of his Age, by the last Will of *Rene de Chaalons*, became Heir to all his vast Possessions: That at twelve he was placed by his Father in the Service of the Emperor *Charles* the 5*th* as his Page, in order to secure that great Inheritance to himself, by complying in the point of Religion, and getting the favour of the Emperor. By this means he became so acceptable to *Charles*, that he found no difficulty to take possession of those great Revenues in due time. We are also told that he carried himself with much prudence and evenness of Temper as well in adversity as prosperity; that he had a good Understanding, a tenacious Memory, and a magnanimous Spirit; was not at all insolent, but rather modest, affable and of easy access; by which he gained the good will of all sorts of Men. In short, we are inform'd that he was a Person of few words, and knew very well how to conceal both his thoughts and his passions, tho he design'd to pursue them with the utmost constancy. He is said to have been neither cruel nor covetous,

La Pise.
Bentivoglio.
Van Rheid.

vetous, not wasting his time in Gaming or Hunting, but on the contrary, fre[e] from most of those Vices that reign in th[e] Courts of Princes.

Concerning Prince *Maurice* the Hi[storians] of that time say, that his elde[r] Brother *Philip* then living, and by vir[tue] of the Will of *Rene de Chaalons*, a[s] well as in the right of his Mother, an[d] that of Primogeniture, claiming the Inhe[ritance] of his Father, as necessarily de[volved] to him, he so acquainted himse[lf] during the Troubles of the *Netherland*[s] with all Manly and Princely Exercise[s] that he became a Person of great abilit[y] And tho at the Death of his Father [he] exceeded not the Age of 17 Years, ha[d] no Sums of Mony in stock, saw his F[a]ther's Estate encumbred with many a[nd] great Debts, and his own Affairs as w[ell] as those of these Countrys in a very lo[w] condition; yet being naturally of gre[at] penetration and sagacity, prudent, frug[al] and laborious, he overcame all the[se] Difficultys, and was not blemished wi[th] many Court Vices; not delighting [in] Musick, Dancing, Hunting, Glutto[ny] or Drinking.

As to Prince *Henry*, his elder Broth[er] *Philip* and *Maurice* were Heirs to the [Pa]ternal Estate and Lordships which [his] Father left, and the latter possessed great Offices of Prince *William* in this Country (except the Stadtholdership of *Friesland* and *Groningen*, which fell to his Nephew *William Lodowick*) so that there was little appearance during his Youth, that he should ever have been advanced to those Honours he attain'd to, and therefore it must be acknowledged, that the Courtiers had little reason to corrupt him in his Education.

This Prince was forty Years of Age before he was advanced from the Command of Colonel of the Horse, to take possession of the great Offices, or rather Monarchical Power that had been introduced by ways of Violence into the Government of *Guelderland, Holland, Utrecht* and *Overyssel*, and might have learned by the Conspiracy which had been formed against his Brother upon those alterations, that the Sovereign Power of these Provinces might be sooner and more certainly obtained by real or at least seeming Virtues, than by open Force and avowed Vices, because the Legal Magistrates and the Inhabitants of these Countrys had not yet been accustomed to commend all the Vices and Blemishes of Princes for Virtues. 'Tis therefore said in praise of Prince *Henry*, that he was affable and courteous, of a good understanding and great application to Business; and used not to misspend

pend his time in the Pleaſure and Luxury ſo common in Courts. And theſe three Princes having had a better Education and a more free and uſeful Converſation with Men than other Monarchs and Princes uſually have, they became more commendable and better Monarchs and Princes, than they would otherwiſe have been.

And if, notwithſtanding all this, any one will go about to aſperſe the Lives Services and Government of theſe deſerving Monarchs, as if they were common and maintain that Prince *William* the Firſt was much addicted to Drinking after the *German* manner; if they ſhould accuſe him of Incontinency, and Riot in keeping ſuch a Court as very much impaired his Eſtate in order to procure Creatures to favour his Ambitious Deſigns, whilſt preſſed by Ambition on one ſide and Want on the other, he uſed all kind of Arts to make himſelf Lord of theſe Provinces, in prejudice to the King of *Spain*, whoſe Right he who was his Stadtholder ſtood obliged to maintain, or elſe to lay down his Commiſſion, fomenting our inteſtine diſorders, that he might render himſelf Sovereign of all the *Netherlands*, and more eſpecially of thoſe Parts which were under his own Government.

Hoofd.
Strada.
Rheid.

The Preface.

And tho this might be excused by saying, that * *Illustrious Ambition, accompanied with Poverty, may violate Laws and Equity:* Yet his three Sons *Philip*, *Maurice* and *Henry*, can hardly be justified, who mutually engaged in the Year 1609 to take possession of their Paternal and Maternal Estates, and to divide them equally, with the exclusion of all their Sisters and Creditors, who had any just pretences upon their Father's Estate.

Neither can these hardships be excused or removed, by alledging that at the instance of these Princes, the States of the *United Provinces* were moved to allow their Sisters an annual Pension, and the Creditors of the Father recommended to the same States for payment. For we cannot from hence infer any great Virtues of these Princes, but only the Goodness, Generosity and Bounty of the States General, and especially of the States of *Holland* and *West Friesland*.

But to return, if it be said that Prince *Maurice* was not only scandalously Incontinent, but withal so Ambitious, that forgetting what he ow'd to the Province of *Holland*, and to the Best Patriots in the *Leicestrian* Times, who next under God was the principal cause of his

---

* Si violandum est jus, regnandi causa violandum est. *Eurip.*

Safe-

sent and future Greatness, he took away his Life in a most unwarrantable manner, and contrary to the Laws of that Province.

Lastly, If any Man shou'd accuse Prince *Harry* of shameful Lewdness, and affirm that when he had inherited the vast Possessions of his two Brothers, and been advanced to all those great and profitable Offices which Prince *Maurice* had enjoyed, he had notoriously profuse and extravagant in his Expences: That he manifested his insatiable Ambition on many occasions, by assuming much more Power than ever had been conferred on him, intruding himself into the Stadtholdership of *Groningen* in the Year 1640, and wresting the Stadtholdership of that of *Friesland* from his own Nephew Count *William*; more especially by taking the Field for so many Years together with vast Armys at a prodigious expence, to make his own Name famous by Conquest, tho to the prejudice and oppression of *Holland*; and this in order to make himself or his Son Sovereign of these Provinces. I say, if such things should be said, some Men would return the following Answer.

Such Accusers ought to know that the Princes of *Orange*, who are Men and not Angels, should not be blamed for such Faults as are common to all Men, or at least

least to those of great Birth, together with all such as are advanced to the greatest Dignities. Inferior Lords usually and without scruple take possession of their paternal Estates without paying any Debts; and all young and healthy Men are violently inclin'd to Women. Besides, 'tis not just to require Moderation in the Sons of Princes; and indeed two of these having either never married at all, or not till they arrived to a considerable Age, could not be guilty of so great a Crime as if they had been engaged in Marriage.

As to the Profusion and Excess of Drinking used in their Court, to the great diminution of the Revenues, 'tis a thing so universally practised, especially in the *Northern* parts, that none of these Princes ought to be so much blamed for it, as Prince *Maurice* deserves to be commended for the Frugality and Sobriety of his Family.

And we have no reason to wonder at the ingratitude of the said Prince, but on the contrary ought rather to wonder that any wise Man, after he has obliged Princes in the highest manner, should expect any better recompence, since Reason and Experience, with all the Historys of Antient and Modern times, do unanimously teach us, that no other Rewards are to be expected from Kings and Princes for extraordinary Services. For Princes being perswaded that their Inferiors are always bound to do them much more service than they perform, 'twould be a rare and unexampled thing to find one who should think himself oblig'd to any. And if by chance a Prince of such understanding were found, he would hardly like such a Benefactor, and for that very reason send him out of the World upon the first fair opportunity.

And therefore if the words of *Lowise* Princess of *Orange*, may be taken for true, " That the Services and good Offi-
" ces performed by the Advocate *Barne-*
" *felt* to the House of *Orange* and *Nassau*
" were so great, that he had acted not
" only like a Friend but a Father, and
" that the Family was obliged to ac-
" knowledg all they had received from
" those of *Holland* to have been procured
" by his means, then, according to the usual course of things of this nature, neither he nor the Province of *Holland* ought to have expected any other reward than they received.

Lastly, Concerning the Ambition of these Princes, 'tis well known that all Men spread the sails to a fair Wind. Ambition in Princes meets always with Applause; and when they either encroach upon a

free

free People, or advance their Conquests by fuccefsful Wars abroad, they are exalted to the Heavens, ftiled *always Auguft*, Enlargers of their Empire, and the moft glorious of Monarchs. And many will be ready to fay that the Princes of *Orange* deferve as much Praife for increafing their Authority in the Government of thefe Countrys, as induftrious Merchants for their Ingenuity in augmenting their Eftates by Navigation and Trade. For the whole Bufinefs and Employment of Princes confifts in endeavouring to increafe their Power.

If any Man fay, that as fraudulent Merchants are to be abhorred with all their Profits and ill-gotten Goods, fo deceitful and Tyrannical Princes ought not to be commended for their fuccefsful Frauds and Violences; 'tis anfwered, that Princes are not ufually efteemed for their Truth, Juftice and Integrity, like other Men, but for their Power, and Knowledg how to exert both Force and Fraud upon a Happy Conjuncture.

For an inftance of this, *Philip* the Second of *Spain* by fixing his Refidence in that Kingdom, and calling home 4000 *Spaniards*, who were the only Military Force he had in thefe Provinces, gave a fair opportunity to *William* Prince of *Orange*, who was then in the Vigor of his Years,

Years, and about 30, possessed of a vast Estate, and by the King made Stadtholder of *Holland, Zealand* and *Utrecht*, to engage the States, together with the inferior Magistrates and other Inhabitants in his Party. On the other hand, the said Prince had great opportunitys to make himself Master of these Countrys, because the States themselves, as well as the inferior Magistrates and Commonalty, had been for many Years oppress'd under their Lords of the Houses of *Burgundy* and *Austria*; none had experienced the Happiness enjoyed under a free State, and few understood the Advantages of a Republick above the Government of a single Person. So that he had great cause to hope he might not only withdraw himself from the Obedience he ow'd to his Masters, but bring the States themselves under his Power, together with all the inferior Governours and Inhabitants of these Provinces, which would certainly have hapned in the Year 1584, if the Hand of a Murderer had not put an end to his Life.

However the Princes of *Orange* have understood so well how to manage their own Affairs, as to obtain an increase of Power to be conferr'd upon them from time to time under colour of necessity, or this failing, to break through all Rights,

Privileges and Laws, and yet deserved not so much Blame, as the States and inferior Magistrates, who were intrusted with the Government of these Countrys, and who by making four of those Princes Captains General for Life, so ill maintained and preserved the Free and Legal Government, that nothing could be denied to them, without hazarding that Liberty, or rather shadow of Freedom, which they seemed yet to possess. Unless perhaps one might say, and prove by former experience, as well as by latter complaints of our Inhabitants, that the Power of the Captains General and Stadtholders has been so great, even from the beginning of our Troubles, by reason of their numerous Adherents, together with the common People and standing Army, that Men may more reasonably wonder, how the States of *Holland* and *West-Friesland* have so often adventured to shew their Zeal to maintain their Legal Government and Libertys, with the apparent hazard of their Lives and Estates.

If these things are true, the Reader may conclude, that if the States of *Holland* and *West-Friesland*, with the Inhabitants, Manufactures, Fishery, Trade and Navigation, have been intolerably burdened, and yet greatly neglected and dis-

discouraged during the Power of those Officers, whilst *Holland* in the mean time was left without defence either by Sea or Land, tho necessitated to take up incredible Sums of Mony at Interest to carry on their ambitious Designs. I think I have to my Power declined to publish the defects of the Princes of *Orange*, since I make no other than a general mention of their insatiable desire of Dominion, which has exhausted our Treasure, and weakned the Frontiers as well as the inland Citys of the Province of *Holland*.

Besides, it is hoped a prudent Reader will easily conceive what pernicious effects might be expected from a succession of such Princes in the Government of *Holland*, and at the same time consider, whether the late Prince *William* would not have proved another Monarch both in his Life and Government, if God, who is our Deliverer, had not taken him away before the 25*th* Year of his Age, since he being the eldest Son of his Father, was to inherit his vast Possessions and Princely Dignitys: And to this end in the Year 1631, before he had attained the Age of five Years, he was placed among the Governours of the *United Provinces*, who seemed unwillingly willing to give up the Liberty of their Country, and in all respects to

be

be able, willing and necessitated to bear an Universal Slavery, by granting and promising to a Child the future Succession of all his Father's Offices; and whether the said Prince *William* the 2d, who was continually conversant with Foreigners and other Slavish Courtiers, had any better Education or Conversation with Men than other ordinary Monarchs use to have: Or whether, after the reversion of the Stadtholdership of *Friesland* had been taken from Count *William*, in order to qualify the Prince to obtain the eldest Daughter of the King of *Great Britain* in Marriage, this Prince would not of necessity have been Sovereign of these United *Netherlands*.

An understanding Reader will also consider, whether our late Stadtholder of *Holland* and *West-Friesland* had not spent his time in such a manner, tho he died before the 25th Year of his Age, as to furnish me with abundant matter of Writing, if I were inclin'd to publish the blemishes of his Life and short Government; and whether I have not spoken of him with as much regard and temper, as my design of explaining the Interest of *Holland* would permit: And I conceive on this Subject I have fully manifested my Moderation.

But

But to return from this long Digression; the Reader is desired impartially to read this Book, which was written by me not only with a composed and sedate Mind, but with a sincere affection to Truth and to my Country: and by weighing and considering what is here said concerning the true Maxims and Interest of *Holland*, he will be able to judg whether I have effected my design. And if he thinks otherwise, I desire him however to believe that I have used the best of my endeavours to that end, and contenting my self to have done what I could, think I cannot but deserve thanks from my Native Country, for exciting by this Attempt some abler Hand to rectify my Mistakes, and finish the Work.

And tho the matters treated in this Book have been carefully weighed and considered since the Year 1662, and indeed so much altered and enlarged, as to make the whole Composition to seem new, yet I would not have any Reader think that I believe it must of necessity please him, since in some respects I my self am not contented with it, and particularly because it fell too hastily at first from my Pen: And tho afterwards it was maturely considered and review'd; yet many pieces were inserted, accommodated and fitted

ted to several parts, as well as my leisure would give me leave, whilst I wanted either time or application to peruse the whole, as if it had not been composed by me, or to invent and write with more Order and Method.

So that there is reason to believe that divers accidents may give occasion to review this Subject, which concerns the Prosperity of the most Powerful Republick at this day in the World. Which that it may be done successfully, may our Gracious God grant us such happy times, as may encourage Men both in publick and private to conceive and write whatever shall tend to the Service of our Native Country.

The Contents.

PART I.

Chap. 1. Wherein are laid down the General Political Maxims which tend to the Prosperity of all Countrys. And some Reasons to make it evident, that the same do aptly agree to Holland and Westfriesland Page 1.
The true Interest of all Countrys consists in the Prosperity of all the Inhabitants, 2. 'Tis the Interest of Monarchs to weaken the Subject, that they may assume what Power they please, 3. But of Republican Rulers, to procure rich and populous Citys, 6. Holland's Interest consists in promoting Manufactures, Fishing, Traffick, &c. 7. The Interest of Courtiers and Soldiers, directly against them, 8. 'Tis dangerous for the wiser sort to declare against the Government of single Persons, 9. Whether People naturally are to be govern'd by one Person. Whether the Dutch are so peevish that they cannot be govern'd otherwise, or would be happier under a Stadtholder than formerly under Earls, 10. Whether they are too stupid to be govern'd by a Commonwealth, 12.

Chap. 2. That the true Interest and Political Maxims of Holland may be well understood, it must not be consider'd as *in Speculation it should be, but as it stands at present.* P. 15.

Holland *may be improv'd to the most perfect Republic,* 15. *In Affairs of Polity we must strike the Ball as it is found lying,* 16. *What is understood by* Holland's *Interest,* 17. *The Prosperity of the Rulers of* Holland *depends on the Subjects, which formerly consisting of divers Republics, could not have the same Interest,* 18. *But inasmuch as they now center in one, the Interest of* Holland *is made evident,* 19.

Chap. 3. *Of* Holland's *natural Burdens and Hindrances* P. 20.

Its Situation: the Inconveniences thence arising in time of Peace, by the Seasons, by the propinquity of the Sea, lowness of the Country, poorness of Land, and smallness of Territory, 21, 22, 23. *The Mischiefs caus'd by War are intolerable, the Inhabitants paying yearly to the State by the ordinary Taxes about* 14 *Millions of Guilders,* 23. *What in time of War,* 24.

Chap. 4. *Of the natural Product and Advantages of* Holland. P. 24.

Chap. 5. *That the Inhabitants of* Holland *cannot be fed by its own Product.* P. 25.

Chap. 6. *That* Holland *lies very commodiously to fetch its Provision out of the Sea, and to provide it self by other Arts and Trades: and how great a means of Subsistence the Fisherys may prove to us.* P. 26.

The

The Contents.

The great means of Inhabitants, a powerful means to the Traffick in Holland, 27. *How considerable the Fisherys of Holland are,* 28.

Chap. 7. *That no Country in Europe is fitter for Traffick than Holland; and how great a means of Subsistence Commerce is to it.* P. 30.

Of the Traffick of Holland, its convenient situation for Trade, 30. *Its Advantage would be much greater, if the Trade to the Indys were free,* 32, 33. *Low Interest of Mony a furtherance to Trade,* 33. *Chargeable Living in Holland a spur to its Merchandizing,* 34.

Chap. 8. *Holland by Fishing and Traffick his acquir'd Manufacturys and Navigation, how great a means of Subsistence Manufactury, and Ships let out to Freight prove to them.* P. 34.

Traffick depends on Fishing and Manufacture, Manufacture on Fishing and Traffick, 34. *Navigation on Manufactures, Fisherys, and Commerce,* 35. *Climate of Holland proper for Manufacture. A free Government invites all to get Estates,* 36.

Chap. 9. *That the Inhabitants of Holland, being in a state of Freedom, are by a common Interest wonderfully linked together; which is also shen'd by a rough Calculation of the Number of Inhabitants, and by what means they subsist.* P. 37.

The greatest Traders in Fish, makers of Manufactures, and owners of Ships depend one upon another, 37, 38. *Husbandmen, &c. a necessary consequence of other Inhabitants,* 38. *Our Rulers Prosperity depends on the Success*

of

The Contents.

of all their Subjects. 'Tis calculated how the People in Holland *are maintain'd,* 39, 41. *How many Inhabitants there are,* 40. *'Tis* Holland's *happiness to have her Inhabitants link'd together,* 43. *But the greatest unhappiness that she may be ruin'd by advancing a single Person,* 44.

Chap. 10. *Why the heavy Taxes occasioned by War, have not driven Fishing, Trading, Manufactury, and Shipping out of* Holland P. 45.

Chap. 11. *The antient State of Manufacturys, Fisherys, and Navigation in* Europe. P. 46.

Above 700 *Years ago there were few Merchants in* Europe; *Inconveniences thence arising,* 46. *The* Flemings *first traded in Manufactures here, next the* Brabanders, 47. *Lastly the* Hollanders *and* English, 48. *When and how the Association of the* Hans Towns *was erected: How the Trade fell to* Bruges, Antwerp, *and* Amsterdam, 49.

Chap. 12. *It is particularly shewn, that Fishing and Traffick must entirely settle in* Holland, *and Manufacturys for the most part, and consequently Navigation, or sailing upon Freight.* P. 51.

How the Trade of Antwerp *remov'd to* Amsterdam, 50, 51. *And not to the* Zealand *Islands, nor to* France, England, *nor any Eastern Citys,* 52. *Why all Manufactures did not leave* Flanders, *and fix in* Holland, 53.

Chap. 13. *That* Amsterdam *is provided with better means of Subsistence, and is* a greater City of Traffick, and Holland a richer Merchandizing Country, than ever as is the World. P. 55.

How Amsterdam by its Scituation is become the greatest Trafficking City in the World, 55. A List of its imported Goods, &c. from abroad, 56. The Hollanders the onely Navigators of the Sea, the causes thereof, --

Chap. 14. That Freedom or Toleration in and about the Service and Worship of God, is a greater means to preserve many Inhabitants in Holland, and to allure Foreigners to dwell amongst us. P. 58.

The Cruelty amongst other Nations persecute those that differ from the publick Sentiments, 59. That our Authority is onely to teach and exhort, &c. Many to escape that Persecution, fly into Holland. Persecution detrimental to the State, 62, 63. Hinders the Conversion of the Erring, 63. Toleration especially needful in Holland, particularly for Roman Catholicks. The Wars against Spain grounded on that like Basis, 65.

Chap. 15. A second means to keep Holland populous, is a plenary Freedom for all that will cohabit with us, to follow any Occupation for a Livelihood. P. 66.

Such a Freedom is more beneficial in Holland than in most other Countrys, but to a few old Inhabitants it is detrimental, 68. 'Tis likewise profitable to the Rulers, 70.

Chap. 16. That Monopolizing Companys and Guilds, excluding all other Persons

The Contents. xxxiii

sions from their Societys, are very prejudicial to Holland. P. 70.

Wherein select Companys are hurtful, 70. *Out of their Abundance they become wasteful and slothful,* 71. *They cause the Inhabitants of other Countrys to seek other means of Subsistence to those. Whereas if all Countrys have an open Trade, it tends properly to one Traffick,* 72. *Companys trading by Charter have often ruin'd Trade and Navigation,* 73. *Prov'dly the* Greenland *Company* 74.

Chap. 17. *That Fishers, Manufacturers, Merchants, and Owners of Freight Ships, ought not as such to be charged, by paying any imposition to the Country, under any pretext whatsoever.* P. 76.

The ignorance of such as are for Impositions on Fishery, Manufactures, &c. illustrated by a Fable, 78. *The building of Shipping, and Drapery, do manifest, that what the other Inhabitants pay to the Government, is drawn from the Fisherys, Traffick, &c.* 79, 80.

Chap. 18. *That Freedom of Religion is, contrary to all Reason, obstructed in* Holland P. 80.

Toleration was formerly more obstructed, by Placaets against the Remonstrants *and* Papists. *The Reasons of those Placaets now cease,* 81.

Chap. 19. *That the Freedom of Fishery and Traffick in* Holland *is in some measure unjustly restrain'd.* P. 83.

A Monopoly Charter sometimes useful to settle a Trade, 81. *Prov'd by the* East-India *Company: Yet that Trade, when settled, if manag'd by a select Company, thwarts the Pub-*

b *lic*

be Good, 84. Land-Conquests carried on by Merchants, are not tenable against all Enemys, 89.

Chap. 20. *That Manufactures, and other Mechanic Works, are imprudently neglected.* P. 87.

Chap. 21. *That the heavy and manifold Imposts will at length destroy the Prosperity of this Country.* P. 88.

Chap. 22. *The Grounds and Reasons upon which the greatest Caution is to be us'd in laying the Tax of Convoy-mony, or Customs.* P. 92.

'Tis possible some Goods and Ships may be brought to the profit of Holland, yet there ought to be great caution as to prohibited Goods, &c. 92. Last mony, as now laid, is very ill managed, 93. As appears by Inland Production, West-India, and raw Silk, 94. The charging such Goods as come by Land-carriage, more than Navigation, 95. As will appear by the charging of some foreign Shipping, and foreign made Wines. Raw imported foreign Goods ought to be charg'd little; such as come by Rivers, more, 96. We ought to ease imported unwrought Goods, of which our Manufactures are made, and to ease our own, and charge Outlandish Manufacture. These Maxims better observ'd by the English than Dutch, 97.

Chap. 23. *That in levying Convoy-mony, even Holland deviates in many particulars from these Maxims, and in many things contradicts themselves.* P. 98.

The

The prohibiting the Exportation of Gold and Silver, has bin detrimental to Holland, 98. The not charging of Fisherys, and the Eastern Trade, is well order'd, but not the Corn-Trade. How much Holland is concern'd to have the Staple of Corn, 99. Manufactures are too much charg'd, 100 As also our Husbandmen. The Interest of Merchants has been much neglected by paying 1 and 2 per Cent. on Goods imported and exported, as appears by raw Silk and Grograin Yard, 101. That the Sea must maintain it self, is a detrimental Maxim for Holland, and why, 104.

Chap. 24. *What Professions of the Inhabitants of Holland ought to be more or less burden'd with Taxes, or favour'd by the Politick Magistrate.* P. 105.

The best way of raising Taxes, is to charge all Wares consum'd at home; to make all Inhabitants pay equally, but especially such as have any public Imployments, and why, 107. And after that all that live upon others, and those that live on the Lands, 108. Also all immoveable Holland Goods, 109. In cases of necessity all moveable and immoveable Goods jointly, tho that is very hard and unequal, 110. Caution to be us'd in weakning the four Pillars of the State, viz. Manufactures, Fisherys, Traffick, and Freight-Ships, 111. Yet in an urgent necessity they may be charg'd something, 112 How much is shown, 113, 114, 115. And as they may be more or less charg'd, so the Rulers ought to favour them proportionably, 116. In what respects is shewn, 117, 118. Colleges should be erected of such as are interested in Manufactures and Fisherys,

fore it, 117. *That in case of more Interest* *it be paid to Proprietors*, 118, 119. *As also of the Duties of the Levant Trade*, 120. *That the East-English Seas are than Holland Seas better*, *and other things relating to a different Levant trade*, 121, 122.

Chap. 25. *The Ancient State of Justice in Holland, and West-Friesland being related, it is further shewn, that the Laws and Orders of Justice ought to be made for the greatest advantage of Trade.* P. 124.

The present defects are ... *the State of Justice arising from the Earls of Holland*, 125. *Disputes on the naming of Judges, and other* ... *Service as the Earls, &c. related*, 126. *What little amendment has been made, especially as to Trade, is shewn*, 127. *By what provision made against designing Bankrupts*, 128. *What Orders ought to be taken against them*, 129. *Settlements before Marriage prejudicial to Creditors. A Debt-book under Oath ought to be a sufficient ground for an immediate Execution*, 130. *Vindications and Evictions prejudicial. Present Justice only by a Court-Merchant very necessary, but the* Beneficium Inventarii *determined*, 131. *As are likewise Letters of Cession, or Attermination*, 132. *What Preservatives are necessary against designing Bankrupts*, 133. *The Advantages of the foregoing Method*, 136. *A reasonable Allowance should be given to an honest, tho insolvent Merchant*, 137. *Our Courts of Justice ought to consist of many Counsellors, and why*, 138.

Chap

The Contents.

Chap. 26. *That the settling of Dutch Colonys in Foreign Countrys, would be very advantageous for the Rulers and People of Holland, and for Traffick and Commerce as well as Navigation.* P. 139.

In all Countrys will be found many distressed Persons; the Reasons of it, 139, 140. *Who being discontented, may occasion great Evils: How it happens to be so,* 141. *'Tis therefore necessity to give them some Vent by Colonys: Holland has had fair Opportunitys for it, and still would have if the Indian Companys would make use of them,* 142, 143. *Who cannot trade in all the Countrys under their District, while the Holland Merchants want more Countrys to trade in,* 144. *But are not incovrag'd by those Companys,* 145. *Such Foreigners as yield to the hard Slavery of those Companys, are not fit for Colonys,* 146. *These matters elucidated by the yearly Placaet published at Batavia, which is exhibited at large,* 147—153. *The Hollanders are naturally inclin'd to erect Colonys,* 153. *And fitter for it than any other Nation,* 154.

PART

PART II.

Of the Interest of *Holland* in relation to Foreign Princes and States.

Chap. 1. THAT *a free Navigation ought to be carefully kept, and defended, against all Pirates and Enemys. How this may be put in practice; and after what manner it has been heretofore done or omitted.* P. 156. *Most Merchandize being imported from, and exported to Foreign Parts, and our Ships being of no defence, it is necessary to scour the North Sea from Pirates, and to keep the Mediterranean clear by Convoys,* 157—159. *This will be done, as the Rulers are well or ill affected,* 160. *This Maxim confirm'd both by Reason and Experience. Before the Year* 1300. *our Earls and Gentry neglected Navigation; but afterwards, when the Citys were concern'd, they took more care of it,* 161—165. *Prince* William *took care to scour the Seas, because he could not subsist but by the Prosperity of our Inhabitants,* 166. *The clearing of the Seas intrusted to Count* Maurice, *and the Earl of* Leicester *jointly,* 168. *But the said Earl neglected it, and greatly prohibited our Navigation,* 170. *After, in regard of Pr.* Maurice's *minority, it was devolv'd on the States and Princes concern'd therein. In* 1593, *to please the Prince, the Seafaring Inhabitants*

were

were neglected, 171 *In* 1597, Holland *lost much of its Strength at Sea, and how,* 172. *The Prince of* Orange, *and the Inland Provinces, tho little or nothing concern'd, were vested with a Power in Sea affairs,* 173. Zealand *by a majority of Commissioners prevents any good from being done in the Maritime Affairs of* Holland, 175 *All which is detrimental to* Holland 176 *A remarkable Instance of the Perfidiousness of the* Zealand *Capers,* 177 *Their Commissioners being permitted for Life, or a long term of years, are too hard for our* Holland *Commissioners, who are settled but for 3 years,* 178. Holland *and its Citys having so little Authority for scouring the Seas, the* Dunkirkers *began to infest them,* 179. *In* 1602, *the States prohibited Traffick beyond the Cape of* Good Hope, *but incourag'd Free-booting at Sea,* 180. *The* Hollanders *in the Straits much plagu'd by Pirates,* 181. *Our Whale-fishers much damaged by the* English. *To redress which, the desperate Polity of pardoning Criminal Pirates was made use of,* 182. *As likewise that of rooting out the* Turkish *Pirates,* 183. *After Pr.* Maurice *would allow of no prolongation of the Truce, and the Scans of* Mardike *was built, the* Dunkirkers *infested us much by Sea,* 185. *The States General prohibited our Inhabitants to trade in* America *and* Africa, *by erecting a* West-India *Company,* 186. *And the* East-India *Company had their Charter prolong'd,* 187 *To the great detriment of our Inhabitants,* 188. *The Commonalty of* Holland *loaded more than ever with extraordinary Subsidys for scouring the Seas, still as much infested as before,* 189. *This was more evident*

b 4 *dent*

The Contents.

Sir Henry had the Administration, 180. *The Treaty, concerning the War be-tween Holland and* ... *many years af-ter* ... *Sea-men and Soldiers,* 191. ... *and their Subsidys,* 192. ... *Sir Henry* ... *in the Office of the* ... *Prince of Orange* ... *States* ... 6—19... ... *a great Order is given out,* 19... ... *and why,* 200. ... *Convoys were reduc'd* ... *whereupon those of Zealand chose new Admiral,* 201. ... *States made Com-plaint against Courses of Affairs, to both which Sir Henry reply'd. The Rulers of Amsterdam would have fcour'd the Seas with 10 Men of War, but were prevented,* 202. *The Prince of Orange, and the Deputys of the Generality shew'd some Zeal to recess Affairs,* 203. ... *On which the States Council desir'd the payment of* ... *Land-Forces might be postpon'd,* ... *the Seas clear,* 204. *Such Ships of Norway, &c. had Convoys* ... *upon hard Conditions:* ... *the Generality devolv'd* ... *of clearing the Seas on Pr. Hen-ry,* 205. *Notwithstanding the Inhabitants* ... *oppos'd to the Dunkir-kers,* 206. *At last some Privateers being* ... *to go out, it was pretty discern'd* ... *the Seas ought to scour'd,* 207. *But*

long

being ill paid, it appear'd that the Pr. of Orange, &c. would not keep the Seas clear, 208. Their ill Conduct particularly seen about the West-India Company, 209. Making the Subscribers poor, and then deserting them; while they chose rather to keep up the War by Land, which run the Treasury of Holland 120 Millions in debt, 210. All which Sums were mostly imply'd to aggrandize France, while the Sea was neglected, 212. The design of the Cabinet Lords was to advance the Prince, and to lessen Holland, 213. Admiral of Holland perceiving how things were manag'd, laid down his Commission, 214. The K. of England pretended to the Dominion of the Seas, 215. When the poor Inhabitants complain'd of their Losses, &c. it was little regarded by Pr. Henry, 216. The Losses by Sea continuing, the States of Holland complain'd, that the Mony collected for the Seas was converted to Land-service, 217. The Dunkirkers took our Ships before our Ports, even after our Victory in the Downs, 218. Which the Deputys, and Pr Henry proposing to secure by new Expedients, the States of Holland, especially the Magistrates of Amsterdam, set themselves stoutly against it, 219, 220. Whereupon they proceeded no further, the Sea being still as much neglected as afore, 221. A great number of Bankrupts was hereby occasion'd. The States of Holland again threat-ned not to pay the Land-Forces, but had not Courage to stand to it, 222. Instead of redressing Complaints, their Mony was applied to assist Portugal, 223. And the Officers of the Army paid to the full, and liberally reward-ed.

ed New Taxes propos'd to defend the West-India Navigation, 224. As if the other Taxes ought not to be applied to the maintenance of our Trade by Sea, 225. After we had Peace with Spain, France began to prey upon us, which caus'd a vast number of Bankrupts, 227. The new Treaties lasted till after the Death of Pr. William. Objection answer'd, That these Provinces flourish'd under the Government of the said Princes, 228. Our Thriving proceeds from the Wars of our Neighbours, our own Situation, and shadow of Liberty, &c. 229.

Chap. 2. *Above all things War, and chiefly by Sea, is most prejudicial, and Peace beneficial to* Holland. *P*. 230.

This appears, in that our Debts are confiscable in an Enemies Country, and our Navigation and Trade entirely destroy'd, 231. A Calculation of the Different Product of the Customs and Convoy-money, in a time of War and Peace, 231, 232. Land Conquests will hasten Holland's Ruin, 232. This well known to the Prince's Party, and likewise to Pr. Maurice, 233. Several Citys have been taken by us which tho they yield but one Million yearly, require 4 Millions to keep. All Offensive War ought to be forborn 234.

Chap. 3. *That* Holland *has antiently receiv'd these Maxims of Peace* P. 235.

This demonstrated by the Intercursus magnus, which was sign'd by all the trafficking Citys, 236. It appears also by the Earls of Holland's having no standing Force, especially in times of Peace, likewise by Phil. de Comines. Duke Charles of Burgundy the first
whe

who kept standing Forces, 237. *The Union of Utrecht shews how careful these Netherlands were to avoid a new War*, 238.

Chap. 4. *Some Cases laid down, in which it seems advisable for* Holland *to ingage in a War; and yet these being well weighed, it is concluded, that* Holland *nevertheless ought to seek for Peace*. P. 239.

Whether we should make War to free our selves from foreign Taxes, 239. *Or to hold the Ballance of Europe. We must first grow strong and healthful*, 240. Holland's *Interest, since the Weakness of the* Spaniard, *is alter'd*, 241. *Whether an uncertain Peace be worse than a War*, 242. *No such thing as a certain Peace*, 243. *That 'tis unadvisable to stand only on one's Defence, answer'd*, 244. *'Tis true of Monarchs, not of free Republics; because they are single, and oppress their Subjects, whereas the Rulers of a Republic are many, and govern more gently, and are naturally shy of a War*, 245. Holland, *tho she defended her self stoutly against* Spain, *rather to be compar'd to a Cat than a Lion*, 246. *Tho by bearing Impositions, she might be compar'd to an Ass, in the times of our Stadtholders*, 247. *What has been discours'd, illustrated by certain Fables: First of the Lion and Huntsman. By gaining time many Evils may be avoided*, 248. *The Fable of a wise Man and a Fool: For Peace sake we ought to yield somewhat*, 249. *This confirm'd by the Fable of a Frog and a Crab*, 250. *The Fable of a Fox, Wolf, and Bear*, 251. *Of the Fox, Cat and Huntsman*, 252. *Small Business*

The Contents.

fairs with neighbours, is better than much Corresp. with great Courts, 253

Chap. 5. *Inquiry is made whether and for the Welfare of any Country may be preserv'd by Treatys of Peace.* P. 255.

To comprehend what a Treaty of Peace, or an Alliance is, we must consider that all Actions look either at the future, or the present, 255. *And what care must be taken in making of mutual obligatory Contracts, which ought to the present to future*……*and Sovereigns,* 256……*How*……*these Contracts are to be kept, especially with Monarchs,* 257. *Who seldom know what is just and fit, as the Civil Rules do. In Treatys of Alliance men are apter to be* ……*than by Treatys of Peace,* 258……*then most, especially when they are not civil Sovereigns, without*……*Superiority any over Religions. Why*……*these*……*little,* 259. *It is unusual to in the Princes considerable Presents. The*……*tures to Favorites may be advis'd,* 260. *Who are compar'd to hungry Dogs. The general Causes of all Contractions and Treatys are, Peace, Hope, and Vain-glory,* 251. *No Alliance with a Great*……*good, unless he first perform his Contract,* 262.

Chap. 6. *Some Considerations particularly relating to Alliances between* Holland *and Islamic Powers.* P 263.

All Alliances……*jest detrimental to* Holland, *as also for*……*Trade, if made with Republics,* 263, 264. *The Union of* Utrecht *has been misused, to the prejudice of* Holland. *Other Republics, whether* German

The Contents.

& Italian, would be much less serviceable to us, 265. What Alliances are to be made with lesser Monarchs, 266. Who hating Republicks, especially ours, we must always be upon our guard. We may more safely make Alliances with Weaker than with Stronger, 267.

Chap. 7. *Some Considerations touching the Alliances which* Holland *might enter into with mightier Potentates than themselves; and first with* France. P. 269.

France *did formerly subsist wholly by Agriculture, not so now,* 269. *List of Manufactures and Commoditys exported out of* France, *of which there is yearly transported above 30 Millions, whereof* Holland *takes off the greatest part,* 271. France *formerly took off many* Holland *Goods, but not now, cannot hurt us by Land, and by Sea is not considerable,* 272. *But in the Mediterranean she may hurt us. Our Naval Forces may keep* France *in a continual Alarm, so that we may compel them to a Peace,* 273. *And pursue our own Interest against them,* 274.

Chap. 8. *Considerations concerning* Holland's *entering into Alliances with* Spain. P. 275.

Spain *subsists by its Commerce with the* West-Indys: *yields Wool, and takes off more of our Manufacture; has no Ships nor Mariners; its Dominions much dispers'd,* 275. *Our Naval Power can hinder their Communication.* Spain *stands in fear of* France, *has had Pretensions upon* Holland, *bounds upon it,* 276. *Being in a good condition for a defensive War, we may pursue our Interest against* Spain, 277.

Chap.

Chap. 9. *Considerations touching Holland's entering into Alliance with England.* P. 278.

England formerly subsisted by Husbandry, … Naval Strength; and is some measure … does the Destiny of the Netherlands … at all, and why, 278. Is … form due to all the Princes of Europe, … 279. By its convenient Situation, is … for the Dominion of the Sea, 280. How … England may be benefited by Peace … Holland, or damaged by a War, 281. A War by Sea too chargeable for England, … have a great Naval Strength, … 282. And is unserviceable to the Commons, 283. England *may be … Landward, but* Holland *not. All Monarchs, especially the* English, *… of their Treasure, and Thievish, 284. All Republicks, especially* Holland, *are Frugal. A War with* England *will be detrimental … 285. We ought to give the* English *good words, notwithstanding a War … 286. Above all we ought not to … them by altering our free Government, 287. But to preserve it sound and intire, and to have … Alliances with them, 288. But a … Alliance with them against* France *may … 289.*

Chap. 10 *Some General and Particular Inferences drawn from the foregoing Considerations touching all our Allies.* P. 289.

General Maxims against the three most Potent Monarchs, France, England, *and* Spain, *290. In matters of Polity relating to an Enemy,* my, none ought to be fainthearted. Contracts with lesser States are the best, 291. A good Alliance with a Republic is better than with a King. Alliances with France, Spain and England, are dangerous, yet rather than have France for our Neighbour, almost all Alliances are good, 292. We ought to make no Alliance with England made against France, 293. Benefit of Alliances consists in never performing first, and why, 294. Princes trifle with Oaths. The Conclusion illustrated by a Fable of an old and rich Man, and a young Country Fellow, 295. Weak States, improving their natural Strength, do commonly defend themselves against a bold aggressing Neighbour, 296.

Chap. 11. That Holland heretofore under the Government of a single Person was in continual Tumults and Broils: And that under a Free Government it can defend it self against all Foreign Power better than formerly. P. 297.

In order to consider whether Holland can stand against all Potentates, we must not regard what flattering Courtiers have given out, 297. A Ruler that governs as if his State could not be secure, acts like a Monk, 298. Holland hath stood of it self 700 years together: it had Tumults under its Earls, because in those Divisions they fought their own disadvantage, 299, 300. It was antiently much weaker than it is now; yet hath at all times defended it self well, 301. Even against the King of Span, tho he was very formidable, who was not only beat off, but other United Provinces in the mean time fortified by Holland,

302. What the other Provinces contributed to it, its value, 303. Holland in the mean time is compell'd to groan under the Yoke of the Captain General. Most of the other Provinces were troubl'd with the Mony, 304. Holland has cast off the Yoke of all her Lords, and that of her Ministers, 305. The States of Holland never so much oppress'd under the Earls of Burgundy or of Austria, as under the Stadtholders of Orange, 307. Holland now is better surrounded with the Sea and Rivers, and provided with great and populous Citys, 308. And with a Free Government; while at the same time the Burgundian and Spanish Princes remain in Spain, and their Power is every way diminish'd, 309. Holland is now better able than ever to defend her self. Against which 'tis objected, that Land-ward she is no so fortified than ever, and the adjacent Provinces and Citys are very strong, and that she has not kept her Right of giving Commissions to her Officers without the Province, 310. How this hapned against the Rules of good Government, 311. While our Fleets and Merchant Ships are taken at Sea, 312.

Chap. 10. *That* Holland *during its Free Government cannot be ruin'd by any Intestine Power.* P. 314.

If any way whatever Holland may be ruin'd by Factions, in case one Province should take the Prince of Orange for their Head, 314. 'Tis answer'd in the Affirmative, but else not: Much less could the Deputys of the Generality, depriv'd of such a Head, be able to cause Commotions, 315. Whether the free Holland Rulers

The Contents.

Rulers are likely to bring in the Trojan Horse, 316. This happen'd a part in these Netherlands, because the Earls, Stadtholders, &c. were not to be contradicted, 317. 'Tis not probable it will happen so now, and why, 318. The States of Holland have express'd their Sentiments of this Matter in their Deduction, 319. They will not easily forget the Violence of their own Captain General, 320. Nor lose their Free Government, but with the loss of their Lives, 321. In 1667 they made a perpetual Edict to preserve their Government, forbidding the Election of any Magistrate, &c. 322. And excluding all Stadtholders of any Province from being Captain-General, 323. Swearing over to suffer any thing repugnant thereto, and that all Captains General swear to maintain the Free Government, 324. Whether one free City, at variance, could ruin each other. All Republicks, having Governours for Life, will come to it, 326. Those without such Heads, never will, as it appears in Germany and Switzerland, 327. Who are envious of chusing a Political or Military Head, while our Head has caused almost all our Divisions, 328. Holland without a Head can never be inwardly troubled, 329.

Chap. 13. That Holland during its Free Government is very well able to resist all Foreign Power. P. 330

What is to be suppos'd, that Holland may repel all Foreign Force, 331. It can easily stand against the other United Provinces, and why, 332. Groningen and Friesland are now, both by Interest of Government and Situation, separated from Holland, 333. Over-Yssel being without a Head, can never make War upon Holland, and being a free Republic, will probably never chuse a Head, 334. Guelderland may make War upon us, yet with greatest Damage to it self, 335. This is not confuted by the Incursion of Martin van Rossem, 336. Guelderland lies perfectly open to Holland: The Province of Utrecht is wholly indefensible,

The Contents.

...Holland,... 338. ...
...Zeeland... of Noble...
Holland... Security...
...Zeeland, 330. Who...
...Holland... Zealand's...
...

...Forces at for...
...Utrecht...
...self against...
P. 342
...
...
...
...
...occupied from...
...
...force for all, 346
...would help to be...
...Bolduke, Bergen, and Breda..., 347. Utrecht is especially...
...Holland... and Government...
... 348
...City in Holland,... is able to defend... almost P. 350
...Haerlem's Siege, 350. ...Cities be not fortified, yet they may... Forts, 352. This appears by the Example of the Free Imperial Citys of Germany, the Cantons of Switzerland, Ragousa, and Lucca, 353. The Cities of Holland can... those, 354. The Example of Haerlem taken by the Spaniards does not disprove it, 355. The Rivers should not suffer Suburbs... 356 They should keep vacant Places... 357 They should fortify their Citys

The Contents.

Citys, and provide all Necessaries against an Enemy, 358. Constantly exercise the rich Citizens in Arms, and have some Mony in store, 359. But not much, and why, 360. Little concern needful for good Alliances, 361. The Sum and Conclusion of the Two first Parts of this Book, presenting at one view all that is necessary to Holland's Interest both at home and abroad, 362——365.

PART III.

Chap. 1. IN which Inquiry is made in what the Interest of the Free Rulers of Holland, as to all the Particulars by which the People may live happily, consists. P. 366 The Power of making or changing a League is in the Magistrate, 367. Most Rulers seek the common Advantage no otherwise, 368. 'Tis of dangerous that a Republic and a Monarchy really are, not observe the Name, nor where the Right and the Name is, but there the Power likewise is, 369. The Right and Name vanish by degrees before the Power and Effect, 370. This seen by shewing of what importance the Love of the People is, or that of the Soldiery, 371. The Rulers as well as People use to be swayed by the Soldiery, 372. As appears by the Roman Republic, which could not preserve its Freedom under the Heads of the Soldiery, 373. The Public Freedom of Holland cannot subsist under a perpetual Head over its Forces, 374. Fisherys, Manufactures, &c. depend upon having free Rulers, 375. The Magistracy yielding little Profit here, they oft breed up their Children to Merchandizing, 376. Whatever is necessary for the Prosperity of the Country, is profitable to the Rulers, 377. Freedom of Religion not hurtful to free Rulers, and why, 378. The Heads of the Seditious use the Tongues and Pens of Preachers as the Cat's Paw, 379. Prudent Toleration of the Romish Religion would not be hurtful, 381 Coercion in Religion would prove hurtful, and wherein, 382. As happened in the Roman and German Empire, 383. Heathen Priests and Jews have not caused so many Seditions as the Christians have, 384, 385. The Christian Priests almost able to influence their Hearers, especially in Monarchys, where there is but one Religion, 386 Why it ought to be feared in Holland, 387 A free Burgership would advance the Interest of Rulers, by causing populous Citys, 388. They would thereby have an easy Government, and be better secured against Foreign Power, 389 Select Companys, &c prejudicial to free Rulers, and wherein, 390. They ought to be cautious in raising Controversy, 391. Free Rulers to regulate Courts of Justice, settle Colonys, 392 And keep the Seas clear from Pirats, 393 They ought especially to aim at Peace, and why, 394, 395. To make good Alliances, 396. And to fortify their Cities, 397.

Chap. 2. Wherein is consider'd the Interest of the Monarchical Government in Holland as to all the foregoing Matters, by which the Commonalty may thrive or prosper. P. 397.

Monarchical Government would be very chargeable in Holland, 398. Would lessen and weaken great Citys, 398. Amsterdam would especially be in that danger, 399 Favourites and Courtiers will rise and drain the People, 400 They will drive no Trade, but to the prejudice of others, 401. Hollanders having an Aversion to Court Flatterers, a Dutch Prince will entertain Foreigners, 402, 409. Church-Government consisting of Councils and Classes, will offend Monarchs, 403. A Prince by making Bishops acquires a Power over his Subjects, 404. Bishops are intolerable in Republicks, but much desired in Monarchical Governments, 405 They are Enemies to Toleration, 406. Princes will easily change the preach-

ing of Sermons into reading of Homilies,&c. as was begun in England, and practised in Transylvania, &c. 407, 408. *They promote Monopolies. Under a single Person Customs would be heightned,* 410. *To lessen the Greatness of Cities, while the Customs are put into their own Coffers,* 411. *Justice would be thereby corrupted,* 412. *As* Culenburg, Vyanen, *&c. do evidence. Few Colonies settled by Monarchs,* 413. *This is not confuted by the Spanish and English Colonies, and why. Our Indian Companies have hindred the settling of Colonies,* 414. *The Sea would not be at all cleared, and why,* 415. Holland *would be always falling into Wars, make bad Alliances, and continue unfortified,* 416. *This proved by what we suffered under our Earls,* 417, 418.

Chap. 3. *Wherein is examined whether the Reasons alledged in the two preceding Chapters, receive any Confirmation from Experience.* P. 419.

Traffick has thriven little in America, Asia *and* Africa, *and not at all but in Republics,* 420. *As first at* Sidon, *when it was a free Government; which lost all its Trade by Sea when it fell under a Monarch,* 422. Tyrus *flourished in Traffick and Navigation so long as it kept its free Government,* 423. *After which it lost all its Traffick,* 425. Tyre *and* Sidon *kept their Freedom under the* Phenician *Kings, and the* Romans, 428. *The Inhabitants of* Banda *and* Amboyna *great Merchants during their Free Government,* 429. *But are now under a miserable Subjection. The City of* Carthage *kept its Trade and Navigation under its Freedom,* 431. *But lost both by War, and the Slavery thereupon following,* 432. Milan, Florence, *&c. have lost their Liberty and Traffick; while* Genua, Lucca, Venice, *and the* Hans Towns *retain theirs,* 433. *In the* Netherlands *Merchandize and Navigation have been both advanced and ruined,* 434. *Manufactures throve in* Holland *whilst the Earls were weak,* 435.
The

The Contents.

The Stadtholders would have driven Traffick out of Holland, but were prevented, 436.

Chap. 4. *Reasons why the Inhabitants of Holland were no more damnified under the Government of the Captains General or Stadtholders.* P. 437.

This occasioned by the ill Government of the Neighbouring Countries, and the Shadow of our Republican Government, 438. *The time when the Captains General did good or harm, ought to be considered; and first as to Prince* William *I. who placed his Safety in some measure in Holland's Prosperity,* 439. *The Earl of* Leicester *did not so. Prince* Maurice *being young, and obedient to the States, did much good,* 440 *But afterwards, following bad Counsel, did much harm,* 441 *Under* Henry's *Government, all Merchant Ships and Fishers were a continual Prey to the Dunkirkers: He sought to continue a chargeable War on us,* 442. *Making clandestin Covenants of several Lordships for himself of the King of* Spain's, 443. *And is known to the States, the King of* Spain *was promised that the Romish Religion should be maintained in several Places,* 446. *The Ruin of Holland was designed by our last Stadtholder,* 447. *Who domineered extremely over Holland,* 448 *And had the Thanks of the other Provinces for it,* 449.

Chap. 5. *The Reason why the General Liberty in* Holland *hath caused no more Benefit since the Death of the Prince of* Orange, *the last Stadtholder of* Holland, *and Captain General during Life.* P. 450.

Why there was no easing of the Imposts, 451. *Because* Holland *was in Debt* 140 *Millions, &c. The* English *and the* Eastern *Wars were likewise Occasions of it,* 452. *Our Captains General have been the Cause of our dreadful Taxations, the Sums taken up being mispent for the Conquest of Cities, and thereby to keep* Holland *in Slavery, whic*

The Contents.

is illustrated by a Similitude, how much the Country thrives better now than under the Stadtholders, 453. Then Money was taken up at Interest to consume and wast, but now we husband it to pay off the Debts contracted by them, 454. The French and English Depredations by Sea hapned by means of the late Government, 456. The War with England was brought on us for the sake of the House of Orange, 457. The English sought our Friendship first. Some Rulers still remaining Slaves to the House of Orange, oppos'd themselves against the Alliance with England, 458. The English Ambassadors suffered great Contempt, which the States of Holland could not prevent; on which they parted discontented, 459. This was the real Cause of the first English War. The Remainders of the former Government, the Cause of the Eastern War, 460. The Duke of Brandenburg, &c. wheedl'd Holland into it, first getting us into an Allyance with him, who having got a good Sum of us, broke from it, and join'd the Swede, 461. Which caus'd the Treaty of Elbing for us, the Advantages of which are reckon'd up, 462, 463. Why the same was not ratified. The D. of Brandenburg, to obtain the Electoral Prussia, fell again from the Swede, and join'd the Polander, 464.

Chap. 6. *What good Fruits the Beginnings of a Free Government have already produc'd, from the Death of the last Stadtholder, to the Year 1662.* P. 465.

First, the not taking up Money at Interest, and the reducing of 5 to 4, in order to discharge the Capital taken up, 466. This is not comprehended by many of our People, 467. Who understand not that the Country's Guardians should give no higher Interest for the Orphans Use than for their own. How great the Fruits of this Discharge are, is set forth by a Similitude, 468. The Benefit of this Reduction under the Stadtholders was converted to the levying of many Soldiers, 469. The third Fruit

The Contents.

Enemies of a Free Government, A great part of the Christian World is surrounded, whereby Holland has possessed... which... The fourth... That Contests, Cares and Provisions... which yet are nearly carried on... Society, 472. Whereas the State would not be troubled with any Difference... 1651, 473. And the King of Denmark... Overruled, which... 474. What happened... Observation, where the State was to be... desired the States to... Differences, 475. Which they did... Places, 476. To the Body... the Free Government... the Powers of Holland... New Forces, 477. The good Effects... particularly shewn, 478—480.

Chap. 7. The third and last Part concluded with this, That all good Inhabitants ought to defend the Free Government of Holland and West-Friesland with their Lives and Estates. P. 480

Chap. 8. The Conclusion of the whole Book, with a Declaration of the Author's Design, and a Caution both to the ill and well affected Readers. P. 487

ERRATA.

PAG... read... Line p. 32 l. 32. dele f p. 39 marg. depends. p. 223 marg. dele comma... p. 373 marg. l. 11 r. could not preserve. p. 378 marg. l. 5... p. 435 dele the last marginal Note. p. 449 marg. l. 3. l. r. title. p. 453 marg. l. 9 for... p. 462 marg. l. 11. r. take up. p. 474 marg. l. 5 r. title &c.

The True Intereſt, and Political Maxims of the Republic of *Holland* and *Weſt-Frieſland.*

PART I.

CHAP. I.

Wherein are laid down the General Political Maxims which tend to the Proſperity of all Countrys: And ſome Reaſons to make it evident, that the ſame do aptly agree to Holland and Weſtfrieſland.

THAT we may not abruptly ſpeak of the true Intereſt and Political Maxims of *Holland* and *Weſt-Frieſland,* nor yet ſurprize the Reader with unknown Matters, I judg it neceſſary to begin with a general Diſcourſe of the Univerſal and true Political Maxims of all Countrys: That the Reader being inlightned by ſuch Reaſoning, may the better comprehend the true Political Maxims of *Holland* and *Weſt-Frieſland.* And ſeeing that almoſt all the People in *Europe,* as the *Spaniards, Italians, French,* &c. do expreſs the ſame by the word *Intereſt,* I ſhall often

often have occasion to use the same likewise here for brevity sake, in the same sense that they do. Seeing the true Interest of all Countries consists in the joint Welfare of the Governors and Governed, and the same is known to depend on a good Government, that being the true Foundation whereon all the Prosperity of any Country is built, we are therefore to know, that a good Government is not that where the well or ill-being of the Subjects depends on the Virtues or Vices of the Rulers, but (which is worthy of observation) where the well or ill-being of the Rulers necessarily follows or depends on the well or ill-being of the Subjects. For seeing we must believe that in all Societies or Assemblies of Men, Self is always preferred, so all Sovereigns or Supreme Powers will in the first place seek their own Advantage in all things, tho to the prejudice of the Subject. But seeing on the other hand true Interest cannot be compassed by a Government, unless the generality of the People partake thereof, therefore the Publick Welfare will ever be aimed at by good Rulers. All which very aptly agrees with our *Latin* and *Dutch* Proverb, that, *Tantum de publicis malis sentimus, quantum ad privatas res pertinet*; i. e. We are only sensible of publick Afflictions, in so far as they touch our private Affairs; for no body halts of another Man's Sore.

Whereby it clearly follows, that all wise Men, whether Monarchs, Princes, Sovereign Lords, or Rulers of Republicks, are always inclined so to strengthen their Country, Kingdom, or City, that they may defend themselves against the Power of any stronger Neighbour. The Rulers Welfare therefore

does

does so far necessarily depend on the Welfare of the Subject, else they would soon be conquer'd by stronger neighbouring Princes, and be turn'd out of their Government. Those Monarchs and Supreme Powers, who by bad Education, and great Prosperity, follow their Pleasures, suffer their Government to fall into the hands of Favorites and Courtiers, and do commonly neglect this first Duty, the said Favorites in the mean time finding themselves vested with such Sovereign Power, do for the most part rule to the Benefit of themselves, and to the Prejudice, not only of such voluptuous and unwary chief Magistrates, but also of their Subjects, and by consequence to the weakning of the Political State, so that we have often seen Revolutions of such Monarchies by the ill Government of Favorites. But such Princes as are wise, and do not entrust their Power in other Mens hands, will not omit to strengthen their Dominions against their Neighbours as much as possible. But when Monarchies, or Republicks are able enough to do this, and have nothing to fear from their neighbouring States or Potentates, then they do usually, according to the opportunity put into their hands by the Form of their Government, take Courses quite contrary to the Welfare of the Subject.

For then it follows as truly from the said General Maxims of all Rulers, that the next Duty of Monarchs, and Supreme Magistrates, is to take special care that their Subjects may not be like generous and metalsom Horses, which, when they cannot be commanded by the Rider, but are too headstrong, wanton, and powerful for their Master, they reduce, and keep so tame *Whence 'tis the Interest of Monarchs to weaken and impoverish the Subject, that they may assume to themselves what Power they please.*

and

and manageable, as not to refuse the Bit and Bridle, I mean Taxes and Obedience. For which end it is highly necessary to prevent the Greatness and Power of their Cities, that they may not out of their own Wealth be able to raise and maintain an Army in the Field, not only to repel all Foreign Power, but also to make Head against their own Lord, or expel him. And as little, yea much less may Prudent Sovereign Lords or Monarchs permit that their Citys, by their strong Fortifications, and training their Inhabitants to Arms, should have an opportunity at all, if they pleas'd, to discharge and turn off their Sovereign. But if herein a Sovereign had neglected his Duty, there's no way left for him, but to wait an Opportunity to command such populous Citys and Strongholds by Citadels, and to render them weak and defenceless. And tho *Aristotle* says that it very well sutes an Oligarchical State to have their Citys under command of a Castle, yet this is only true of a great and populous City, that hath a Prince over it, and not of a City that governs it self, or hath a share in the Supreme Government; for in such a Republick, the Governour of that Citadel would certainly be able to make himself Master of that City, and to subjugate or overtop his Rulers. And we see that this Reason is so strong and clear, and confirm'd by Experience, that the History of all former Ages, as well as the Age we live in, teach us, That the Rulers of Republicks, whatever they are, have wisely forborn erecting Citadels, and do still continue to do so. So that it appears that the said Maxim tending to the overthrow of great and populous Cities, may be attributed

Chap. 1. *General Maxims.*

tributed to Monarchs and Princes at all times, but never to Republicks, unless when they have inconsiderately subdued great Cities; and tho not willing to demolish them, yet are willing to keep them distinct from the Sovereign Government. But if the inconsiderate Reader be so far prepossess'd in favour of Monarchy and against Common Freedom, that he neither can nor will submit himself to this way of Reasoning, nor to the venerable and antient Lessons of old and renowned Philosophers, then let him know, that the Christian and Invincible Monarch *Justinian* has for ever established the said Monarchical Maxim by form of Law in the *Corpus Juris*, now become the common Law-book of all Civiliz'd People, and especially of Christians. * For the said Emperor having by his Captain General of the East, *Belisarius*, reconquer'd from the *Goths* that part of *Africa* which he had formerly lost, and brought it under his subjection, gave him no order that the Inhabitants of great Citys should be better disciplin'd and provided with Arms, or strengthned by good Walls, that they might jointly with ease defend themselves, and their great and populous Citys, against the Assaults of those Barbarous People: But on the contrary, he commands the said Captain General *Belisarius* (and consequently, according to the *Roman* Laws, all his other Governours of Provinces) to make such provision, that no City or strong

As the Emp. Justinianus in his Corpus Juris, in form of a perpetual Law, has establish'd it.

---

* *Belisario Magistro militum per Orientem, &c. Interea vero si aliquas Civitates seu Castella per limites constituta providerit tua Magnitudo nimiæ esse Magnitudinis, & propter hoc non posse bene custodiri ad talem modum ea constitui disponat, ut possint per paucos bene servari, &c.* Cod. l.1. Tit 27. par 14.

Hold lying on the Frontiers be so great as it could not be well kept; but in such Cases so to order them to be built, that they may be well defended with few Soldiers, and particularly such as were in pay, and depended only on the Emperor of *Rome.*

And tho weak, voluptuous, dull and sluggish Monarchs neglect all these things, yet will not the Courtiers who govern in their stead, neglect to seek themselves, and to fill their Coffers whether in War or in Peace; and thus the Subjects Estates being exhausted by Rapine, those great and flourishing Cities become poor and weak. And to the end that the Subject should not be able to hinder or prevent such Rapine, or revenge themselves, those Favorites omit no Opportunities to devest those Populous Cities of all Fortifications, Provision, Ammunition of War, and to hinder the exercising of the Commonalty in the use of Arms. Since it appears from the said Maxims, that the Publick is not regarded but for the sake of private Interest; and consequently that is the best Government where the Chief Rulers may best obtain their own Welfare by that of the People: It follows then to be the Duty of the Governours of Republicks to seek for great Cities, and to make them as populous and strong as possible, that so all Rulers and Magistrates, and likewise all others that serve the Publick either in Country or City, may thereby gain the more Power, Honour and Benefit, and more safely possess it, whether in Peace or War: And this is the reason why commonly we see that all Republicks thrive and flourish far more in Arts, Manufacture, Traffick, Populousness and Strength, than the Dominions and Cities of

The Interest of Republican Rulers, is to procure rich and populous Cities. Arist. Pol. l. c. II. l. 5. c. 11.

Monarchs: * for where there is Liberty, there will be Riches and People.

To bring all this home, and make it sute with our State, we ought to consider that *Holland* may easily be defended against her Neighbours; and that the flourishing of Manufactures, Fishing, Navigation, and Traffick, whereby that Province subsists, and (its natural Necessities or Wants being well considered) depends perpetually on them, else would be uninhabited. I say, the flourishing of those things will infallibly produce great, strong, populous and wealthy Cities, which by reason of their convenient Situation, may be impregnably fortified: All which to a Monarch, or one Supreme Head, is altogether intolerable. And therefore I conclude, that the Inhabitants of *Holland*, whether Rulers or Subjects, can receive no greater mischief in their Polity, than to be governed by a Monarch, or Supreme Lord: And that on the other side, God can give no greater temporal Blessing to a Country in our Condition, than to introduce and preserve a free Commonwealth Government.

Holland's true Interest consists in promoting Fishing, Manufacture, Traffick, &c.

But seeing this Conclusion opposeth the general and long-continued Prejudices of all ignorant Persons, and consequently of most of the Inhabitants of these *United Provinces*, and that some of my Readers might distaste this Treatise upon what I have already said, unless somewhat were spoken to obviate their Mistakes, I shall therefore offer them these Reasons.

Altho by what hath been already said, it appears, That the Inhabitants of a Republick are infinitely more happy than the Subjects of a

---

* *Quippe ubi Libertas, ibi & Populus & Divitiæ.*

8 *General Maxims.* Part I.

Land governed by one supreme Head; yet the contrary is always thought in a Country where a Prince is already reigning, or in Republicks, where one Supreme Head is ready to be accepted.

The Interest of Courtiers and Souldiers to cry up Monarchy.

For not only Officers, Courtiers, idle Gentry, and Souldiery, but also all those that would be such, knowing, That under the worst Government they use to fare best, because they hope that with Impunity they may plunder and rifle the Citizens and Country People, and so by the Corruption of the Government enrich themselves, or attain to Grandeur, they cry up Monarchical Government for their private Interest to the very Heavens. Altho God did

1 Sam. 1.8. &c. at first mercifully institute no other but a Commonwealth Government, and afterwards in his Wrath appointed one Sovereign over them.

Yet for all this, those Blood-suckers of the State, and indeed of Mankind, dare to speak of Republicks with the utmost Contempt, make a Mountain of every Molehill, discourse of the Defects of them at large, and conceal all that is good in them, because they know none will punish them for what they say. Wherefore all the Rabble (according to the old *Latin Verse) being void of Knowledg and Judgment, and therefore enclining to the Weather or safer side, and mightily valuing the vain and empty Pomp of Kings and Princes, say *Amen* to it; especially when kept in Ignorance, and irritated against the lawful Government by Preach-

---

* —— *Sed quid ?*
Turba Remi sequitur Fortunam, ut semper, & odit Damnatos. Juven.

Chap. 1. *General Maxims.*

ers, who aim at Dominion, or would introduce an independent and arbitrary Power of Church-Government; and such (God amend it) are found in *Holland,* and the other United Provinces, insomuch, that all vertuous and intelligent People have bin necessitated to keep silence, and to beware of disclosing the Vices of their Princes, or of such as would willingly be their Governors, or of Courtiers and rude Military Men, and such ambitious and ungovernable Preachers as despise God, and their Native Country.

Nay there are few Inhabitants of a perfect Free state to be found, that are inclinable to instruct and teach others, how much better a Republick is than a Monarchy, or one Supreme Head, because they know no Body will reward them for it, and that on the other side, * Kings, Princes, and great Men, are so dangerous to be conversed with, that even their Friends can scarcely talk with them of the Wind and Weather, but at the hazard of their Lives; and Kings with their long Arms can give heavy blows. And altho all intelligent and ingenuous Subjects of Monarchs, who have not, with lying Sycophantical Courtiers, cast off all Shame, are generally by these Reasons, and daily Experience, fully convinced of the Excellency of a Republick above a Monarchical Government; yet nevertheless, many vertuous Persons, lovers of Monarchy, do plausibly

And how dangerous it is for the wiser sort to declare themselves to the prejudice of Governments by single Persons.

Which yet out of love to my Native Country, I have here performed, and exquired,

---

* —— *Sed quid violentius aure Tyranni,*
Cum quo de pluviis aut æstibus aut nimboso
Vere locuturi Fatum pendebat amici? Juven.

maintain,

maintain, that several Nations are of that Temper and Disposition, that they cannot be happily governed but by a single Person, and quote for this the Examples of all the People in *Asia* and *Africa*, as well as *Europe*, that lie Southerly. They do also alledg, that all the People who lie more Northerly, are more fit to be governed by a single Person, and with more Freedom, as from *France* to the Northward, all absolute Monarchical Government ceaseth, and therefore maintain or assert, with such ignorant Persons as I mention'd before, that the *Hollanders* in particular are so turbulent, factious, and disingenuous, that they cannot be kept in awe, and happily governed, but by a single Person; and that the Histories of the former Reigns or Government by Earls, will sufficiently confirm it.

But on the other side, the Patriots, and Lovers of a Free-state will say, That the foregoing Government by Earls is well known to have bin very wretched and horrid, their Reigns filling History with continual Wars, Tumults, and detestable Actions, occasioned by that single Person. And that on the contrary, the *Hollanders*, subsisting by Manufacture, Fishing, Navigation, and Commerce, are naturally very peaceable, if by such a Supreme Head they were not excited to Tumults. Whether this be so or not, may be learned and confirmed too in part from those Histories.

But here it may be said, That things are much altered within these 100 Years last, for *Holland* then subsisted mostly by Agriculture, and there were then no Souldiery, Treasure, or fortified Places to be at the Earl's disposal.

But

But when he had Wars, it was with the help of his Homagers and Tenants, only Subsidies or Money being given him at his Request by the States of the Country. And moreover, the Cities of *Holland*, and Castles of the Nobility were (according to the then Method of War) so strong, that they could not be taken by the said Earls, without great Forces imployed against them; so that the States of *Holland* in their Assemblies, have boldly contended for their Rights against the Earls Encroachments. Therefore these Earls, on the other side, by reason of their great Dignity, had many Adherents that depended on them, which must needs make that Government by Earls every way unsteady, weak, and tumultuous.

To this an approver of Monarchical Government may further add, That *Holland* now wholly subsists by Traffick, and that one Supreme Head, Captain-General, or Stadtholder, would have his own Life-Guards at the *Hague*, the Place of Assembly, and likewise the Assistance of a great and well-paid Army, and of all the Preachers, and by them the love of the whole Populace; and that at his Pleasure he may dispose of all the impregnable Frontier Towns of those Provinces that have no Suffrages or Voices in the State, tho he should not increase his Strength by any foreign Alliances, or by Collusion and Flattery with the Deputies of the other Provinces of the Generality, insomuch that the States of *Holland* would not dare, no not in their Assemblies, to open their Mouths against the Interest of such a Supreme Head, or if they did, he would order his Souldiers to take them by the Collar, and might easily overpower most of the Cities of *Holland*, the

the People being unaccustomed to Arms, and moreover divided. Fortifications built and meant in comparison of the present way of Fortifying. So that one may truly say, That the *Hollanders*, by setting up one Supreme Head over themselves, may now with Ease and without Tumult, be govern'd like Sheep, by an irresistible Sovereign, against whom they durst not speak one word, when he should think fit to sheer, flea, or devour them.

Now what there is in this, and whether the *Hollanders* would be happy in such a Condition, I shall at large hereafter give you my Judgment.

Whether the *Hollanders are so stupid that they can't form a Commonwealth.*

But as to the Stupidity of the *Hollanders*, whether that be so great, as that they have not Wit enough to form a free Commonwealth; and having found that precious Jewel of Freedom, would, with *Esop's* Cock, prefer a grain of Corn before it: This is what hath not been judged so hitherto, but on the contrary. Which that it may be evident to the Reader, he may be pleas'd to observe the prudent Conduct of the States of *Holland*, at their great

The States of Holland of the Year 1650, &c.

Assembly in the Years 1650 and 1651. as also seriously to ponder and weigh the manifold Reasons and Examples produced to this end in their *Deduction* of the Year 1654. All this is yet further confirmed by that magnanimous Resolution of the 23d of *January* 1657. wherein the States of *Holland* unanimously declared, after consulting the General Assemblies, or Common Halls of the respective Cities in that Province, to hold for a Fundamental and certain Maxim, "That to place a perpetual " Head, Chieftain, or General over the Ar- " my, is not only needless, but likewise ex- " ceeding prejudicial, and that accordingly in

" this

"this Province all things shall be thus directed;
"That whenever in a time of War, and pres-
"sing Necessity, the States of *Holland*, with
"the other Provinces, shall think fit to pro-
"ceed to elect a General for the Army, or
"that upon any other Occasion a Captain-
"General should be chosen, then not to chuse
"such a Chieftain as shall have a perpetual
"Commission, but for such an Expedition,
"Campagn, or Occasion only as may happen,
"&c. And moreover, you may there see, that
these, and other vigorous Resolutions of the
like Nature, were taken with this special
Proviso, "That the said Resolution shall not
"be dispensed with, but by the unanimous
"Consent of all the Members of the said As-
"sembly.

By this you may perceive, that the Supposition of the *Hollanders* being flegmatick and dull, and of a slavish Nature, is altogether groundless; for seeing they became not free but by the death of the last Stadtholder and Captain-General, and that it was unseasonable and imprudent before that time, for them to shew their commendable Zeal for their Freedom, and their Skill in point of Government: And seeing it is evident, that a Generation of Men that are in Freedom, must be overcome, before we can pass a right Judgment thereof, and stop the mouths of Opposers, we must therefore leave it to God and Time; and if such as like Monarchical Government, and those base and slavish opposers of Liberty survive those times, they will then be able to discern which of the two Governments is founded on best Reason.

It shall not satisfy me to have said thus much in general; for seeing the States of *Holland* in
their

their Deduction, *Chap 6. Art. 29.* declare, That they will not lose their Freedom, but with their Lives; I shall therefore presume to give my Opinion of the Political Maxims of *Holland*, hoping that my Sincere Zeal and Uprightness to express the same for the Benefit of the Publick, will be so acceptable to our lawful Rulers, that tho I may have failed in some things, and by stating the true Interest of my Country, have been necessitated to reflect on Persons, who seek their Advantage to the prejudice of *Holland*, as it is now governed; the said Rulers, and true Lovers of their Native Country, will so favour this Work, and its Author, against the said malevolent Persons, that it shall never repent him to have been the first generous and bold Undertaker of so commendable a Work. But howsoever things happen, or Times oppose it, *recte fecisse merces est, & ipsa sui pretium virtus*; (i.e. to do good is a Reward of it self, and Virtue carries its own Recompence along with it) I shall then, having done my Duty as an honest Man, good Citizen, and upright Christian, that may not bury his Talent, be able to take Comfort in my sincere Endeavours: And Posterity, into whose Hands these Writings may fall, will, in spite of all the present Powers that oppose it, be able to judg impartially, and that with a sound Judgment; because by that time they will have learned, by joyful or sad Experience, whether *Holland*'s Interest can be settled upon any other Foundation or Maxims than those herein exprest; and whether these Reasons of mine will not be confirmed by the Experience of following Ages.

CHAP

CHAP. II.

That the true Interest, and Political Maxims of Holland *and* West-Friesland *may be well understood,* Holland *must not be considered so, as in Speculation it should be, but as it now stands at present.*

BEING now about to enquire into, and lay down some Maxims for *Holland*'s continual Prosperity, it seems at first View to be necessary, that we consider the Nature of the Country, forasmuch as it is in it self perpetual, and what means may be found to improve it to its best Advantage, and what good Fruits and Effects are to be expected from such Improvement. In order whereunto, we are first to consider the Soil, Rivers, Meers of *Holland*, and its Situation upon the Sea, with the Communication it may have with other Nations. And next we are further to consider, what People *Holland* ought to be inhabited with, *viz.* whether with few, or many, in order to earn their Bread; as also how the Rulers ought to deport themselves towards Foreign Princes and Governments; And lastly, by what Form of Government, and how the People ought to be governed. But because such Speculations use to build *Rempublicam Platonis, Aristotelis, Eutopiam Mori*, a Philosophical Republick in the Air, or such a one as was never yet found, the thoughts of it will afford little Benefit: Nor is this strange, considering that so many People cannot be suddenly brought to an uninhabited Country, to erect a Political State, according to

Concerning all which, Expedients may be found, whereby Holland *may be improved to the most perfect Republick.*

Wherefore such Speculations would produce little Benefit.

to the said Speculation, and keep it on foot when it is establish'd. And since in all populous Countries there is some Form of Government; therefore I say again, those Speculations are for the most part useless. For if inquiry be made into the Polity of all established Governments, we shall always find, that there are ever an incredible number of ignorant and malevolent People, Enemies to all Speculation, and Remedies, how good soever, which they conceive or really foresee will be prejudicial in any wise to themselves, and rather than admit them, they will press hard to imbroil the State more than it was before. Besides, there is an endless number of Political Maxims which have so deep a Root, that it is great folly to think any Man should be able, or indeed that it should be thought fit to root them out all at once. And consequently it would be yet a greater piece of Imprudence, if in *Holland*, *tanquam in tabula rasa*, as on a smooth, and in a very clean and good piece of Ground, we should go about to sow the best Seeds, in order to make it an Angelical or Philosophical Republick: So true is that good and antient Political Maxim, * That in Polity many bad things are indulged with less inconveniency than removed, and that we ought never in Polity (as in playing at Tenis) to set the Ball fair, but must strike it as it lies, it being also true, that on every Occurrence a good Politician is bound to shew his

---

* *Multa scire pauca exequi*, Cor. Tacit.
Multa fieri non oportet quæ facta terent.
Curatio quædam majora videmus
Vulnera, quæ melius non tetigisse fuit.

and Love to his Native Country, that by such constancy the Commonwealth may by degrees be brought to a better condition. I do therefore conceive my self oblig'd to consider *Holland* in the State as it now is, and hope that those Thoughts will produce the more and better Fruits, since those that duly consider the present State of it, will find that they agree for the most part with the Climate, Soil, Rivers, Meers, Situation, and Correspondence which such a Country ought to have with other Dominions, and especially with a free Commonwealth Government, which we have now at present in being. And I hope I shall not digress from it. By the Maxims of *Holland*'s Interest, I understand the Conservation, and Increase of the Inhabitants as they now are, consisting of Rulers and Subjects. I shall likewise diligently enquire by what means this Interest may be most conveniently attained. And tho in the first place the Interest of the Rulers ought to be considered, because distinctly and at large it always seems to occasion the Subjects Welfare and Prosperity; and a good form of Government is properly the Foundation whereon all the Prosperity of the Inhabitants is built. I shall nevertheless consider in the first place the Preservation, and Increase of the number of Subjects, not only because it is evident in all Governments, and especially in all Republics, That the Number or Paucity of Subjects is the Cause of an able or weak Government; but also because ambitious Spirits can seldom find a multitude of People living out of civil Society and Government, that will subject them-

What is understood by Holland's Interest.

Namely, and especially the Prosperity, and Increase of the Subjects.

themselves to them. And on the contrary, where many Inhabitants are, there will never want Rulers, because the weakness and wickedness of Mankind is so great, that they cannot subsist without Government, insomuch that in case of a vacancy of Rulers, every one would stand Candidates for it themselves, or each other. Above all, I find myself obliged more fully to consider and promote the welfare of the Subjects in *Holland* above that of the Rulers, because in this free Commonwealth Government, it is evident that the durable and certain Prosperity of the Rulers does generally depend on the Welfare of the Subjects, as hereafter shall be particularly shewn. And to give the unexperienced Reader some insight at first, it is convenient to premise that *Holland* was not of old one Republick, but consisted of many, which in process of time chose a Head or Governor over them by the Name of *Earl*, or *Stadtholder*. But seeing he had of old no armed Men or Soldiery of his own as Dukes had, but was to be content with his own Revenues, and to rule the Land, or rather administer Justice to each Country according to their particular Customs and Laws, they nevertheless continued so many several Republicks. And tho' in process of time they were jointly brought to a Sovereign Republic, yet is it also true that the Members of this *Dutch* Republic are of very different Natures and Manners. For *Amsterdam*, *Hoorn*, *Enchuysen*, *Medenblik*, *Edam*, *Monnikendam*, *Dort*, *Schiedam*, *Briel*, &c. lying on the Sea, or on Rivers where Ships of great burden may conveniently arrive, *Haerlem*, *Delf*, *Leyden*, *Gouda*,

Chap. 2. Holland's true Maxims.

Grave, Gorcum, Schoonhoven, Alkmaer, Purmerrynde, &c. lying within Land, are not to be come at but with Vessels that draw little Water: Besides which the Gentry who live in the plain or open Countrys of *Holland*, having great Estates, and being not under any Government, seem to have a quite particular Interest. Wherefore every intelligent Person may easily judg that a diversity of Rulers, Subjects, Countrys, and Situations, must needs cause a diversity of Interests, so that I cannot write of *Holland's* Prosperity as of a distinct Country. Nevertheless I incline, and do intend to bring it under one Title, as far as all its Cities or Lands can be comprehended in one Interest, to the best of my knowledg and skill. Which to do methodically, I shall in the First Part inquire into, and show the Maxims tending to the Welfare or Damage of *Holland* within its own confines. In the Second Part I shall propose how *Holland* must procure its own Welfare as to Foreign Princes. And in the Third Part I shall enquire, and shew by what Form of Government such a Country and Inhabitants ought to be governed according to their true Interest, seeing this is the general Foundation whereon all the Prosperity or Adversity aforesaid is founded.

And yet forasmuch as they all center, and agree in one, the Interest of Holland is made evident.

CHAP.

CHAP. III.

Of Holland's *natural Burdens and Hinderances.*

<small>Holland's Seat, &c.</small> HOLLAND lying in the Latitude of 51 to 53 degrees, North Latitude upon the Sea, having many Inland Rivers, and being besides a very low and plain Country, is thereby subject to many Inconveniences.

<small>A sharp Winter, more costly to us than to other Countries.</small> *First,* There are sharp and very long Winters, so that there is need of more Light, Firing, Clothing, and Food, than in warmer Countries. besides which, all the Cattle of our Pasture-land must be then housed, tho thereby we bestow more cost and pains, and yet reap less profit of milk-meats than in Summer, or in other adjacent Lands, where the Cattle remain longer, or perhaps all the Winter in the Field.

<small>By the Seasons.</small> *Secondly,* The Seasons are here so short, that they must be very punctually observed, to return us any Profit by our Plough'd Lands; for the Seed in this moist Country being rotted and consumed in the Earth, cannot be sowed again conveniently.

<small>By the Spring and Autumn.</small> *Thirdly,* By the Vicinity of the Sea, and Plainness of the Land, it is subject in Spring, and Autumn, not only to unwholesom Weather for the Inhabitants, but in the Spring the sharp cold Winds blast most of the blossoms of the Fruit-trees, and in and about Autumn much unripe Fruit is blown down by our usual storms of Wind.

Fourthly,

Chap. 3. Holland's Burdens.

Fourthly, It is to be considered above all, That these Lands lying for the most part lower than the Floods of the Sea, and Rivers, must withstand the terrible Storms of the Ocean, and Shoals of Ice, against which it must be defended with great expence: For the making of one Rod long of a Sea Dyke costs sometimes 600 Guilders. On the Rivers also, the Charge of maintaining the Banks is very great, and the most chargeable of all is, that notwithstanding so great an expence, the Water of our Dykes and Low-lands sometimes breaks thro, and overflows the Country; so that above all this extraordinary Charge, and Damage, they cannot drain the Country by Mills in some Years. And touching the ordinary Charges in maintaining Dykes and Sluces, &c. how great an expence this must be, we may well imagine by the yearly Charges of *Rynland*, which is about 80000 Acres or * Morgens in compass, which hath not much communication with the Sea, nor with running, but only with standing Waters; and yet as to Acredg-money and inland Charges, every Acre must pay at least two Guilders; besides, for draining out of the Rain-water by Mills to turn it out by Trenches, each Acre 30 Stivers; likewise towards Foot-paths, Highways, and maintaining the Ditches, at least 20 Stivers more. And lastly, they are liable to many Fines, and Troubles, when they chuse their *Bailiffs*, *Dyk-graves*, and *Heemraden* for Life, who are wholly independent on the Landed-men; tho they may elect their Judges yearly, or continue their *Heemraden*.

And lowness of the Country.

* *A Morgen is about two English Acres.*

Fifthly,

L. It is evident that *Holland* affords no Mines, or the least Product of Mines; so that out of the Earth there is nothing to be had but Clay and Turf, nor even that, but with the spoiling or disfiguring of the Ground.

Holland it self contending and wrestling with the Sea, Rivers, and drained Meers, can hardly make 400000 profitable Acres, or Morgens of Land, Down and Heath not included. For according to the Calculation made in the Year 1554, there were found about three hundred thousand Morgens, and some hundreds more. Likewise the States of *Holland* and *Zealand* in a Remonstrance given in to the Earl of *Leicester*, say, That these two Provinces with all their Heath, Downs, and Grounds delved out, could make in all but one hundred thousand Morgens. So that I conceive they all now make in all four hundred thousand Morgens, or Acres of Land. Seeing the Chronicle of *Zealand* (according to the Account given in by the Surveyor *Everfdyk*) testifies, that in 1643 all the Parts of *Zealand* contributed to the yearly Poundage, no more than for one hundred eighty three thousand three hundred and fifty Gemeeten, and fifty three Rods of Land: The Gemeetens of the Down-lands being reckoned after the rate of three for two. So that if two Gemeetens are reckoned against one *Holland* Acre, then all the abovementioned Gemeetens would make out no more than 91675 Morgens, and 63 Rods.

F. S. And seeing the Ground in *Holland* is for the most part every where either Sand, Moor, or Fenn, it must necessarily be ditched, and
because

because such improvement of it, by reason of the loosness of the Land, sinks down, it requires it the oftner.

This is the Condition of *Holland* in a time of perfect Peace, what will it be then when we consider, that the *Hollanders* must not only scour, or clear the Sea from Enemys, and defend their Towns and Country against all Foreign Force, but that they have also charged themselves with much more than the Union of *Utrecht* obliged them to, with the keeping of many conquered Citys, and circumjacent Provinces, which bring in no Profit to *Holland*, but are a certain Charge, being supply'd by that Province with Fortifications, Ammunition-houses, Victuals, Arms, Cannon, Pay for the Soldiers, yea, and which is a shameful thing to mention, with Guard-houses, and Money for quartering of Soldiers? *So that the Mischiefs caused by War, are intolerable.*

And how heavy the said Burdens must needs be to the *Dutch*, may be easily imagined, if it be considered, that besides the Customs and other Revenues of the Earls or States of *Holland*, in the Year 1664. by the ordinary Charge which was levied of the Inhabitants, one Year with another, was paid *For by the ordinary Taxes the Inhabitants pay to the State about 14 Millions of Guilders yearly.*

	Guilders.
To the States of *Holland*	11000000
To the Admiralty of the *Mase*	472898
To the Admiralty of *Amsterdam*	2000000
To the Admiralty of the Northern Quarter	200000
In all—	13,672898

And if it be considered that since that time, by reason of the Wars, there were new ordinary Taxes imposed, and that the extraordinary, namely, the two hundredth penny brings in 2400000, and the half Verpondinge, or Poundage, 1200000; And lastly, the Chimny money six hundred and seventy thousand *Holland* Guilders, and that all those Burdens are born by the Inhabitants, besides the many Excises, and great Sums of Money which they must pay in their Citys for their Maintenance: These things I say considered, we may well conclude, that the Inhabitants of *Holland* are exceeding heavily burdened and charged

---

CHAP. IV.

Of the Natural Product and Advantages of Holland.

TO ballance these heavy Burdens before-mentioned, the inland Waters yield nothing but Fish, Water-Fowl and their Eggs, the Downs only Conys: Four hundred thousand Acres, or Morgens of Land, nothing but Brick earth, Turf, Corn, Herbs and Roots, Fruit of Trees, Flax, Hemp, Reeds, Grass, Madder, Cattel, Sheep, Horses. But the Downs may be also said to yield Lime and Sand And how unsufficient all these Products from so small and inconsiderable a Bottom are in themselves for the subsistence of so many Inhabitants, every one may easily imagine

CHAP

CHAP. V.

That the Inhabitants of Holland *cannot be fed by its own Product.*

BUT if we should suppose that all the Land in *Holland* could be, and were sowed with the most necessary Grain, *viz.* Wheat; and that every Morgen in *Holland* produced fifteen Sacks of Wheat, yet would not four hundred thousand Acres of Land yield for two millions of People, each a pound of Bread *per* day. And possibly there are now more People imployed about the manuring of Land, than can be fed on it. So that if we should make a calculation of all the Fruits which the Earth yieldeth, with what else is necessary for the use of Man, and continually imported, it would evidently appear that the Boors, or Husbandmen and their Dependents, would fall very much short of Food, Drink, Apparel, Housing and Firing. Therefore if the *Hollanders* did not by their Industry make many Manufactures, or by their Labour and Diligence reap much profit by the Seas and Rivers, the Country, or Land of *Holland*, were not worthy to be inhabited by Men, and cultivated, no not tho the People were very few in number, and no Subsidies, Imposts, or Excises raised on them, for their common defence against a Foreign Enemy. On the other side, *Holland* being now inhabited by innumerable People, who bear incredible heavy Taxes, Imposts and Excises, and must necessarily be so inhabited, the easier to bear so great a Burden,

Whereby it appears that Holland, *whether in Peace or War, cannot feed, or sustain it self.*

den, and to defend themselves against all their neighbouring Potentates. We may safely say, that *Holland* cannot in any wise subsist of it self, but that of necessity it must fetch its Food elsewhere, and continually invite new Inhabitants from Foreign Parts. I therefore find my self obliged to search into, and more particularly demonstrate the Ways and Means by which the same may be procured.

CHAP. VI.

That Holland lies very commodiously to fetch its Provisions out of the Sea, and to procure it self by other Arts and Trades and how great a means of Subsistence the Fishery may prove of.

HOlland is very well scituated to procure its Food out of the Sea, which is a common Element; it lies not only on a Strand rich of Fish near the *Dogger-Sand*, where Haddock, Cod, and Ling in great abundance be taken and cured; but also near the Herring-Fishery, which is only to be found on the Coast of *Great-Britain*, viz. from St *John's* to St *Ives*, about *Schet-Land*, *Phayl*, and *Lochtijs*, from St *Ives*'s to the Elevation of the Cross about *Buchyse* or *Suenwot*, from the Elevation of the Cross to St *Katherines* in the deep Waters Eastward of *Yarmouth*. And this Herring Fishing, which it is now 250 Years ago since *William Beukelson* of *Biervliet* first learned to gill, salt, and pack them up in Barrels, together with the Cod-Fishery, is become

become so effectual a means of Subsistence for these Lands, and especially since so many neighbouring Nations, by reason of their Religion, are obliged upon certain Days and Weeks of the Year, wholly to refrain from eating of Flesh, that the *Hollanders* alone do fish in a time of Peace with more than a thousand Busses, from 24 to 30 Lasts burden each, and with above one hundred and seventy smaller Vessels that fish for Herrings at the Mouth of the *Texel*. So that those thousand Busses being set to Sea for a Year, wherein they make three Voyages, do cost above ten Millions of Guilders, accounting only the Buss with its Tackle, at 4550 Guilders, and the setting forth to Sea 5500 Guilders, there remaining nothing of all its Victuals and Furniture the second Year, but the bare Vessel, and that much worn and tatter'd, needing great Reparation. So that if these 1000 Busses do take yearly forty thousand Last of Herrings, counting them at least worth 200 Guilders *per* Last, they would yield in *Holland* more than eight Millions of Guilders.

And seeing that of late Men have begun to make very much use of Whale-Oil, and Whale-Fins, which are taken to the Northward not far from us, insomuch that with Southerly Winds, which are common in this Country, we can sail thither within six or 8 days. The Trade of Fishing, and Salt, may easily be fix'd and settled with us; for to fix those Fisheries, and several Manufactures, and consequently the Trade and Returns thereof depending on Navigation, and Ships let out to Freight, we ought duly to consider, that the greatest Difficulty for so innumerable a

The great number of Inhabitants is a powerful means to fix Traffick in Holland.

People

People to subsist on their own Product, proves the most powerful means to attract al foreign Wares into *Holland*, not only to store them up there, and afterwards to carry them up the Country by the *Mase, Waal, Yssel*, and the *Rhine* (making together one River) to very many Cities, Towns, and People, lying on the sides of them (the most considerable in the World for consumption of Merchandise) but also to consume the said imported Goods, or to have them manufactur'd. It being well known, that no Country under Heaven, of so small a Compass, has so many People and Artificers as we have, to which may be added, that no Country in the World is so wonderfully divided with Rivers and Canals, whereby Merchandize may be carried up and down with so little Charge.

Emanuel van Meteren says, That in the space of three days, in the Year 1601. there sailed out of *Holland*, to the Eastward, between eight and nine hundred Ships, and 1500 Busses a Herring fishing, which is easy to believe, if we may credit what the *English* Authors mention, *viz.* *Gerard Malines* in his *Lex Mercatoria*, and Sir *Walter Rawleigh*, and which *Lieuin van Aitzma*, Anno 1653 *pag.* 863. doth in some measure confirm, *viz.* That there are yearly taken and spent by the *Hollanders* more than three hundred thousand Last of Herrings, and other salt Fish: And that the Whale fishing to the Northward, takes up above twelve thousand Men, which sail out of these Countries. For since the *Greenland* Company, or (to express my self better) the Monopolizing Grant thereof was annulled, and the Whale-fishing set open in common,

that

that fishery is increased from one to ten: So that when we reckon that all these fishing Vessels are built here at home, and the Ropes, Sails, Nets, and Cask made here, and that Salt is furnish'd from hence, we may easily imagine that there must be an incredible number of People that live by this means, especially when we add, That all those People must have Meat, Drink, Clothes, and Housing; and that the Fish, when caught, is transported by the *Hollanders* in their Vessels through the whole World. And indeed if that be true, which Sir *Walter Rawleigh* (who made diligent inquiry thereinto, in the Year 1618. to inform King *James* of it) affirms, That the *Hollanders* fished on the Coast of *Great Britain* with no less than 3000 Ships, and 50000 Men, and that they employed and set to Sea, to transport and sell the Fish so taken, and to make returns thereof, nine thousand Ships more, and one hundred and fifty thousand Men besides and if we hereunto add what he saith further, *viz.* that twenty Busses do maintain eight thousand People, and that the *Hollanders* had in all no less than 20000 Ships at Sea, as also that their Fishing, Navigation, and Traffick by Sea, with its Dependencies since that time, to the Year 1667, is encreased to ⅓ more: I say, if that be so, we may then easily conclude, that the Sea is a special means of *Holland*'s subsistence, seeing *Holland* by this means alone, yields by its own Industry above three hundred thousand Lasts of salt Fish. So that if we add to this, the Whale-fin, and Whale-oil, and our *Holland* Manufactures, with that which our own Rivers afford us, it must be confessed, that no Country

Who out of Envy nevertheless overrate this means of our Subsistence.

try, in the World can make so many Ships-lading of Merchandize by their own Industry, as the Province of *Holland* alone.

CHAP. VII.

That in Europe there is no Country fitter for Traffick than Holland; and how great the Share of Subsistence Commerce is to it.

Having thus considered *Holland*'s conveniency for the Fishing Trade, and it coming into my Thoughts, that all the Traffick of it doth seem chiefly to have risen out of it, and still to depend upon it, I shall now give my Opinion wherein that Aptness or Conveniency most consists.

But first let me say, that by the word *Traffick*, I mean the buying of any thing to sell again, whether for Consumption at home, or to be sold abroad, without altering its Property, as buying in foreign Countries cheap, to sell dearer abroad, the most considerable part of which is what I understand by the word *Traffick*.

Secondly, I say, that *Holland* is very conveniently seated for that end, lying in the middle of *Europe*, accounting from St *Michael* the Archangel in *Muscovy*, and *Revel*, to *St.* And as to our lying further off from *Italy*, and the *Levant*, and more to the Eastward, it is a thing very necessary, inasmuch as most of the bulky and coarse Goods, as Pitch, Tar, Ashes, Corn, Hemp, and Timber

Chap. 7. *for the Staple of Trade.*

Timber for Ships, and other uses; as also *Pomerania* and *Prussia* Wool must be fetch'd from thence, and brought hither, because the better half of those Goods is consumed or wrought up in this Country. And because very many Wares may be sent up and down the Rivers of the *Rhine* and *Mase*, whereby it appears, that the *Holl* has sail with as many more Ships to the Eastward, as they do to the Westward.

Thirdly, The conquer'd Lands, and strong Holds of the *East-India* Company are now become very considerable, in order to secure to *Holland* the Trade of all Spices, and *Indian* Commodities, which is already pretty well fixed to it. And this improvement of Trade might be made much more considerable, if the said Conquerors would not, by virtue of their Grant or Patent, hinder all the other Inhabitants of these Lands from trading to those Conquests, and to innumerable rich Countries, where the said Conquerors, for Reasons of State may not, or for other Reasons cannot, or perhaps will not trade. Yea, tho the said free Trade of our Inhabitants (to the greater benefit of the Participants) were in some measure limited, and circumscribed to those Lands and Sea-Ports lying in their District, to which they never yet traded, I should then expect to see much more fruit of that Trade, and Monopoly together, than of their Monopoly alone. For if our *East-India* Company could find some Expedient, either as to Freight of Goods, to permit all the Inhabitants of these Lands freely to lade their Goods on board the Company's own Ships, or to import and export all manner of Goods to the

To which the Conquests of the East-India Company contribute.

the Places of their Conquests, and back to this Country, or in process of Time, by laying Imposts on the Consumption of the Inhabiting Planters, who would resort thither in great numbers by reason of a Free Trade, or by any other imaginable means tending to give it an open Trade, they would thereby reap much more Profit than the poor Participants now commonly and with much uncertainty do enjoy; and then, if afterwards the said Participants would be perfuaded to deny themselves so much of their Privilege, or authorized Monopoly, as to set open that Trade in some good measure to the Inhabitants of these *United Provinces*, it would questionless produce to our Industrious and Inquisitive Nation, so many new and unheard of Consumptions of all our Manufactures, especially of Wool, and so great a Trade, Navigation, and Commerce with that vast Land of *Africa*, and the incredibly great and rich *Asia*, which lies so convenient for Trade, that many hundred Ships would yearly make Voyages thither, and bring their Returns hither, especially from and to *Amsterdam*, and by means of which alone, we should certainly, and very easily, work all other Foreigners out of those *Indian* Seas. Whereas on the other hand, to the end we may preserve our *East-India* Trade, consisting yearly of no more than 10 or 16 Ships going and coming, we find our selves continually drawn into so many Quarrels and Contentions with those foreign Nations, with eminent Danger of losing by such Dissensions and Wars, not only our *European* Trade, but also those conquered *Indian* Countries, and consequently that Trade also for want of Planters,

Chap. 7. *for the Staple of Trade.*

Planters, and by the excessive great Expences which they must be at more and more yearly, by reason of such great numbers of Soldiers as lie in their Garrisons, and which will and must rise else with their Conquests; as (God amend it) hath but too plainly appeared by the *West-India* Company of this Country.

This Advantage which *Holland* hath for Commerce and Traffick, would be yet more improved, if the *West-India* Company, in all Places of their District, would also set that Trade open. And in case things are so constituted, that the *East* and *West-India* Trade cannot be preserved but by mighty Companies, as some indeed affirm, who understand the *India* Trade, and have the Credit of affirming what they say, with good shew of Reason, yet this however must be confess'd, that the said Companies, as now constituted, do attract and preserve to *Holland* all the Trade which depends on their vast Equipages, Ladings, and Returns. *An open Trade to the West-Indies would increase Traffick and Navigation.*

Fourthly, It is a great Advantage for the Traffick of *Holland*, that Mony may be taken up by Merchants at 3 *per Cent.* for a Year, without Pawn or Pledg, whereas in other Countries there is much more given, and yet real Estates bound for the same. So that it appears, that the *Hollanders* may buy and lay out their ready Mony a whole Season, before the Goods they purchase are in being, and manufactur'd, and sell them again on Trust (which cannot be done by any other trading Nation, considering their high Interest of Mony) and therefore is one of the greatest means whereby the *Hollanders* have gotten most of the Trade from other Nations. *The low Interest of Mony helpful hereunto.*

D   Fifthly,

Fifthly, There being many Duties and Subsidies to be paid in *Holland,* and little got by Lands, Houses, or Mony let out at Interest; and we having also no Cloisters, and but few Lands in Fief, or held by Homage, and the Women moreover being very fruitful of Children, and Men making equal dividends of their Estates among them, which can therefore be but small, and so not fit to be put out to Interest. All this, I say, is another great Cause of the advancing of our Traffick.

CHAP VIII.

That Holland, *by Fishing and Traffick, hath acquired Manufacturies and Navigation; and how great a means of Subsistence Manufactury, and Ships let out to Freight prove to them.*

THO it is evident by our Histories, that in many Cities in *Holland* great quantities of Manufactures were made, when all the *European* Traffick and Navigation was mostly driven by the *Easterlings* and *Hans-Towns,* and before Fishing, Traffick, and freighting of Ships were settled in these Provinces, and that consequently we might say with good Reason, That Fishing and Traffick, together with Ships sailing for Freight, took their rise rather from the Manufactures, than the Manufactures took their rise from them: Yet generally it is certain, that in a Country where there is Fishing and Traffick, Manufacturys and freight Ships may easily be introduced. For from

from them there must of necessity rise an opportunity of bringing Commodities to be wrought up out of foreign Parts, and the Goods so manufactur'd may be sent by the same Conveniency beyond Seas, or up the Rivers into other Countries.

Thus we see that in *Holland* for the same reason, all sorts of Manufactures of Silk, Flax, Wool, Hemp, Twyne, Ropes, Cables, and Nets, are more conveniently made, and yield better Profit than in any other Country, and the like; coarse Salt boiled, and many Ships are built by that means with outlandish Timber. For it is evident that Shipwrights work in *Holland* must not be considered as a mere Consumption, but as a very considerable Manufacture and Merchandize, seeing almost all great Ships for Strangers are built by the *Hollanders*. Besides which Manufactures, there are others of necessary Use, as well as for Pleasure or Ornament; which are of such a Nature, that most of them require Water, whether it be to work them, or for cheapness of Carriage: And when by the shallowness of the Waters there would be otherwise a defect, that want is supply'd by the constant Winds that blow upon our low and plain Land, which joining to the Sea are thereby replenished.

And as to the owning of Parts of Ships let out to freight, it appears that a Ship lying for Freight in a Country where Fishing, Manufactury, and Trading flourish, will be able to get its Lading in a very short time: And that in Countrys where they don't flourish, such Ships must sail from one Port to another, and lose much time in getting Freight: So that such as are Owners of Ships, must necessarily fix

Navigation, or Shares in Shipping, depend on Manufactures, Fisheries, and Commerce.

fix in such a Country where Shipping may soonest find their full Lading.

The Climate of Holland very proper for Manufacture.

Besides all which, *Holland* lies in so cold a Climate, that the People are not hindred from working by reason of the Heat of the Country, as elsewhere: And seeing for the most part we have but a gross Air, eat coarse Diet, and drink small Beer, the People are much fitter for constant Work; and by reason of the great Impositions, they are necessitated to use all the said means of Subsistence, *viz.* to make Manufactures by Land, to fish by Sea, to navigate Ships for Trade at home and abroad, and to let out their great and small Vessels to Freight.

A free Republican Government inclines all to get Estates.

And seeing the Inhabitants under this free Government, hope by lawful Means to acquire Estates, may sit down peaceably, and use their Wealth as they please, without dreading that any indigent or wasteful Prince, or his Courtiers and Gentry, who are generally as prodigal, necessitous, and covetous as himself, should on any pretence whatever seize on the Wealth of the Subject; our Inhabitants are therefore much inclined to subsist by the forenamed and other like ways or means, and gain Riches for their Posterity, by Frugality and good Husbandry.

CHAP.

CHAP. IX.

That the Inhabitants of Holland, *being in a State of Freedom, are by a common Interest wonderfully linked together; which is also shew'd by a rough Calculation of the Number of Inhabitants, and by what Means they subsist.*

WE are moreover well to consider, That Fishing is not the sole Cause of Traffick, nor Fishing and Traffick the Cause of Manufactury; as also that these three together do not always give occasion for the Shipping that is let out to Freight, which is meant by Navigation: But that Fishing flourishes much more in those Parts, because Traffick, Navigation and Manufactures are settled among us, whereby the Fish and Oil taken may be transported and consumed. Likewise that more than the one half of our Trading would decay, in case the Trade of Fish were destroyed, as well as all other sorts of Commodities about which People are imployed in *Holland*; besides that, by consequence the *Inland Consumption* of all Foreign Goods being more than one half diminished, the Traffick in those Parts would fall proportionably. *That the forementioned means of Subsistence, and also the Inhabitants are linked together.*

It is also certain, that of necessity all sorts of Manufactures would be lessened more than a Moiety, if not annihilated, as soon as this Country should come to be bereft of Fishing, and of Trading in those Commodities which are spent abroad. And concerning Owners of Ships let out to Freight, it is evident that they *Namely the greatest Traders in Fish, and Makers of Manufacture.*

wholly

wholly depend on the Prosperity or Success of Fishing, Manufactury, and Traffick. For seeing our Country yields almost nothing out of its own Bowels, therefore the Ships that lie for Freight, can lade nothing but what the Merchants or Traders put on board them of Fish, Manufactury, or Merchandize. And as little would Foreign Ships carry Goods to *Holland*, in case no Fishermen, Merchants, or Traders dealing in Manufactury dwelt there. And contrariwise it is certain, that our Fishers, Manufacturers and Traders, find a mighty Conveniency and Benefit in our great number of Freight-ships, which continually lie for Freight in all Parts of the World, and are ready to carry the same at an easy Rate to any place desired. So that the *English* and *Flemish* Merchants, &c. do oft-times know no better way to transport their Goods to such Foreign Parts as they design, than to carry them first to *Amsterdam*, and from thence to other places, especially when our Admiralties, according to their Duty, take care to convoy and defend our Merchant Ships, with Men of War, against all Pirates, or Sea-robbers whatsoever. It is also evident, that the Husbandmen, or Boors of *Holland*, can very well sell all the Product or Profit of their Land, Cattel, Firing, &c. to the Inhabitants that are Fishers, Manufacturers, Traders, Navigators, and those that depend on them; which is a great Advantage beyond what all other Boors have, who for the most part have their Commodities spent abroad, and consequently must bear the Charges of Freight, and the Dutys outwards and inwards, and must also allow a double

Gain

Gain to the Merchants and Buyers. So that this great number of People, that are not Husbandmen, are I think the only Cause that those Country Boors, tho heavily tax'd, are able to subsist. And seeing all the said Inhabitants have need of Meat, Drink, Clothing, Housing, and of the Gain gotten by Foreign Consumption that is needful to support it; it is evident, that all the other Inhabitants depend and live upon the foresaid Fishers, Traders and Navigators.

And how remarkable it is, that all Rulers and others, who for any Service depend on them, have a Benefit by their great Numbers, is so clear, that there needs no more be said for proof. For when there were but few Inhabitants in this Country, within less than 100 Years, the most eminent Offices of Burgomaster, and *Schepens* or Sheriffs, were even in the principal Cities so great a Burden as not to be born without much Charge; whereas it is now become profitable to be but a City Messenger, or Undertaker to freight Ships, seeing Men are thereby enabled to maintain their Families. *Our Magistrates Prosperity depend on the Success of all their Subjects.*

Furthermore, having a mind to convince the Reader, not only by my Reasoning, but by his own Experience, that the Prosperity of *Holland* is built upon the foresaid means of Subsistence, and on no other; I find my self obliged to make a Calculation of the Number of People in *Holland* that are fix'd Inhabitants, or depend upon them; and at the same time, as far as I am able, to reckon in what proportion those People are maintain'd by the means of Subsistence before-mentioned. In order to this I shall on the one hand consider, that Sir *Walter Raleigh* endeavouring to move *All which is set forth by a rough Calculation, how the People in Holland maintain themselves.*

more King ... es of England to advance the
Fishing Trade, Manufactures, and Traffick
by Sea, hath possibly exceeded in his Account
of the Profits arising from it, and augmented the number of the People that live
upon it somewhat above the Truth.

And on the other hand I shall consider what
G... ... saith, in his *Lex Mercatoria*,
... 1622 that in *Flanders* there were then
counted one hundred and forty thousand Families, which being reckoned, one with
another, at five Persons each, they would a-
mount to seven hundred thousand People. I
shall likewise consider that in *Holland* that same
Year, the States laid a Poll-Tax upon all Inhabitants, none excepted save Strangers, Prisoners, and Vagrants, and those that were on
the other side the Line; yet were there found
in all *South-Holland* no more than four hundred eighty one thousand nine hundred thirty and four. Altho the Commissioners Instructions for that end were very strict and
severe, to prevent all Fraud and Deceit.
However that we may make the better guess
whether this was a faithful Account, I shall
give you the Particulars of it as registred
in the Chamber of Accounts.

D... with its Villages,	40523
H... with its Villages,	69648
Dort with its Villages,	41744
Leyden and Ryland,	94285
Amsterdam and its Villages,	115022
Gouda and its Villages,	24662
Rotterdam with its Villages,	28339
Gorinchem with its Villages,	7585

Schie-

Ch 9. *occasions the flourishing of a People.* 41

Schiedam with its Villages,	10393
Schoonhoven with its Villages,	10703
Briel with its Villages,	20156
The *Hague*,	17430
Heusden,	1444
	481934
And supposing that *West-Friesland* might yield the fourth part of the Inhabitants of *South Holland*, it would amount to	120483
In all	602417

But because possibly none but intelligent Readers, and such as have travelled, will believe, what we see is customary in all Places, that the number of People in all Populous Countrys is excessively magnified, and that the Common Readers will think, that since many would be willing to evade the Poll-Tax, there was an extraordinary Fraud in the Number given in. I shall therefore follow the common Opinion, and conclude, that the Number of People was indeed much greater, and that these Countries are since that time much improved in the Number of Inhabitants; and accordingly I shall give a guess as by vulgar Report, that the whole Number, without excluding any Inhabitants whatsoever, may amount to two Millions and four hundred thousand People, and that they maintain themselves as followeth, *viz.*

And with what proportion they live by the said means.

By the Fisherys at Sea, and setting them out with Ships, Rigging, Cask, Salt, and other Materials, or Instruments, and the Traffick that depends thereon.   450000.

By Agriculture, Inland-fishing, Herding, Hay-making, Turf-making, and by furnishing

ing those People with all sorts of Materials as they are Boors, or Husbandmen, 200000.

By making all manner of Manufactures, Shipping, Works of Art, Mechanick or Handicraft Works, which are consumed abroad; as likewise by Trade relating to the said Manufactures, 650000.

By Navigation or sailing for Freight and Trade jointly, by which I mean carriage into Foreign Parts for selling and buying; as also carrying to and from *Holland* all such Wares and Merchandise as relate not to our Fishing and Manufactury, nor depend thereon: And lastly I include herein also all Inhabitants that are any ways serviceable to such Traders, and Ships let out to Freight, amounting in all to 250000.

By all these Inhabitants, as being Men, Women, and Children, that must be provided, and by working about what is spent in this Country, as Food, Drink, Clothing, Housing, and by making or selling Houshold Stuff, and all other things for Art, Ease, Pleasure, or Ornament, 650000.

By the labour and care of all the abovementioned Persons, being Gentry without Employment or Calling, Civil Magistrates and Officers, those that live upon their Estates or Mony, Soldiers, the Poor in Hospitals, Beggars, &c. 200000.

In all 2400000.

And tho this Calculation, whether consider'd as to the Number of the Inhabitants, or their proportionable means of Subsistence, is very rough and uncertain; yet I suppose it it to be evident, that the eighth part of the Inhabitants of *Holland* could not be supplied with Necessaries out of its own product, if their Gain otherwise did not afford them all other necessaries: So that *Homo Homini Deus in Statu Politico,* one Man being a God to another under a good Government, it is an unspeakable Blessing for this Land, that there are so many People in it, who according to the Nature of the Country are honestly maintain'd by such sutable or proportionable means, and especially that the welfare of all the Inhabitants (the idle Gentry, and Foreign Soldiers in pay excepted) from the least to the greatest, does so necessarily depend on one another; and above all it is cheifly considerable, that there are none more really interested in the Prosperity of this Country than the Rulers of this Aristocratical Government, and the Persons that live on their Estates.

'Tis the Happiness of Holland to have such as are linked together in Interest.

For Fishers, Boors, or Country People, owners of Ships let to Freight, Merchants and Manufacturers, in a general destruction of a Country, could easily transport themselves into Foreign Parts, and there set up their Fishing, Agriculture, or Husbandry, Shipping, Merchandize and Manufactures: But such as have Lands, or immovable Estates, cannot do this, and supposing they could, and should sell their Estates and remove into other Countries, yet would they there have no Calling to subsist by, much less can they expect to be made use of in the Government, or procure any Office or Advantage depending upon it.

How-

However, this excellent and laudable Harmony and Union may be violated, even to the Ruin of all the Inhabitants, none excepted but Courtiers and Soldiers, and that by one sole mistake in Government, which is the Electing one Supreme Head over all these Inhabitants, or over their Armys. For seeing such a single Person for the increase of his Grandeur, may curb and obstruct *Holland*'s Greatness and Power, by the Deputies of the lesser Provinces of the Generality, who also may in their Course check the great and flourishing Cities in their own Provincial Assemblies, by the Suffrages or Votes of the envious Gentry. And the lesser Cities, and the great Persons, Courtiers and Soldiers being all of his Party, and depending on him, must needs prey upon the industrious or working Inhabitants, and make use of all their Power for their own Interest, and to the detriment of the Commons. And to the end they may more probably effect their end and strong Citizens to join with them that they would either weaken such rich Cities, and impoverish such Inhabitants, to make them obedient without controll. Which if so, we have just cause continually, to pray, *A furore Monarcharum libera nos Domine*, God preserve us and from the Fury of a Monarch, Prince, or one Supreme Head. But what there is of reality in this, shall be handled hereafter in a Chapter apart.

CHAP.

CHAP. X.

That Question consider'd, why the heavy Taxes, occasioned by War, have not driven Fishing, Trading, Manufactury, and Shipping out of Holland?

IT is not enough to know how happy in general this Country is, in finding Imployment for so many Hands, and affording them sustenance, seeing there have been many causes which would have hindred the Success of our Fishing, Navigation and Traffick, had there been but one Country among the many that are near us, well situated for Fishing, Manufactury, Traffick, and Navigation, which during our Wars and Troubles had seen and followed their own true Interest; most of our neighbouring Nations, all that time being in a profound Peace, seemed to have less hinderance for promoting Manufactures, Traffick, employing of Ships for Freight and Fishing, than our Nation. So that to pursue the true Interest and Maxims of *Holland*, we ought particularly to know the Reason, why the great inconveniencies of Taxes and Wars that we have laboured under, have not occasioned the Fishing, Manufactury, Traffick, and Navigation, to settle and fix in other Countries; as for example in *England*, where if all be well considered they have had far greater Advantages of Situation, Harbours, a clean and bold Coast, favourable Winds, and an Opportunity of transporting many unwrought Commodities, a lasting Peace, and a greater freedom from Taxes than we have.

Why Traffick has not fix'd in other Countries.

CHAP

CHAP. XI.

Before we answer the said Question, we shall relate the antient State of Manufacturies, Fisheries, and Navigation in Europe.

THAT I may from hence derive some Light, I shall premise a brief Relation how these Affairs stood in antient times.

About 700 Years ago there were few Merchants in Europe.

It is well known, that 6 or 700 Years ago, there were no Merchants in all *Europe*, except a few in the Republicks of *Italy*, who lived on the *Mediterranean*, and traded with the *Indian* Carravans in the *Levant*; or possibly there might be found some Merchants, tho but in few Places, that drove an Inland Trade: so that each Nation was necessitated to sow, build, and weave for themselves to the Northward and Eastward, where there were then no Outland nor Inland Merchants; and there-

How great Inconveniences thence are.

fore in case of superfluity of People, they were compelled by force of Arms for want of Provision, and to prevent ill Seasons, and Hunger, to conquer more Land. And this caused the Irruptions of the *Celtæ, Cimbri, Scythians, Goths, Quades, Vandals, Hunns, Franks, Burgundians, Normans,* &c. who till about the Year 1000 after Christ's Birth, were in their greatest Strength, all which People, and in a word, all that spake *Dutch* or *German*, exchanged their Superfluitys, not for Mony,

Et. Sacro annal. de Flander.

but as it is reported, thus. Two Hens for a Goose, two Geese for a Swine, three Lambs for a Sheep, three Calves for a Cow; barrering of Corn was then also in practise, by which

which they knew how much Oats was to be given for Barley, how much Barley for Rye, and Rye for Wheat, when they wanted them; so that except for eatable Wares there was neither Barter nor Traffick

The *Flemings* lying nearest to *France* were the first that began to earn their Livings by weaving, and sold the same in that fruitful Land, where the Inhabitants were not only able to feed themselves, but also by the superfluous growth of their Country could put themselves into good Apparel; which young *Boudewyn* of *Flanders*, about the Year 960, considerably improved, by setting up yearly Fares or Markets in several Places, paying no Duty or Toll for any Goods, either exported or imported. By which means that way of Merchandize improved 300 Years successively, altho those Commodities were only consumed in *France* and *Germany*, till the many prejudicial or hurtful Laws of the *Halls*, which at first were fram'd on pretence of preventing deceit, and the debasing of Commodities, but were in truth intended to fix those Manufactures to the Cities. But at last having by force, which is ever prejudicial to Traffick, driven much of this weaving Trade out of the Cities into the Villages, the Wars between *France* and *Flanders* drove it back from the Villages to *Tienen* and *Lovain* in *Brabant*; notwithstanding which the *Brabanders* being nothing more prudent, did by the same Occasion, *viz.* the Laws of the Halls, and Imposts on Manufactury during the War against *France*, occasion many Tumults and Uproars among the Weavers, about 100 Years after in *Flanders*, where at *Gent* in the Year 1301,

The Flemings *were here the first Traders in* in Manufactures

Next them the Brabanders.

in a Tumult occasion'd by some coercive Laws and Orders about their Occupation, there were slain two Magistrates, and eleven other Inhabitants. And at *Bruges* the next Year after, for the same Cause, there were slain above 1500 in a Tumult. Likewise at *Ypres*, upon the same Occasion, there being a Mutiny, the *Viscount or chief Magistrate*, with the ten *Sworn*, being all the Magistrates of the City, were killed. And such like Accidents happened afterwards in *Flanders*, amongst others at *Louvain*, where, in a great Tumult of the Cloth-weavers with their Adherents, divers Magistrates were slain in the Council-house, and several of the Offenders fled into *England* with them first carried the Art of Drapery. But many other Cloth-weavers, with their Followers, as well *Brabanders* as *Flemings*, dispersed themselves into the Counties beyond the *Mase*, and into *Holland*; and amongst other Places, many of them fixed at *Leyden*. Meanwhile, the *German* Knights of the Cross, after the Year 1200, under pretence of reducing the Heathens to the Christian Faith, made themselves Masters not only of barren *Pomerania*, and the River *Oder*, which they suffered the converted Princes to enjoy, but of then *Prussia* and *Lysland*, and the Rivers *Wessel*, *Pregel*, and *Duina*, and consequently of all those which fall into the Sea, out of fruitful *Poland*, *Lithuania*, or *Russia*. By which Conveniency the Eastern Cities that lay nearest to the Sea, began to fetch away their bulky and * unwrought Goods, and to carry them to the *Netherlands*, *England*, *Spain*, and *France*, and likewise from thence to and fro to export and import all the Goods that

that were superfluous or wanting.

And seeing by the Wars about the Year 1360, between *Denmark* and *Sweden*, they suffered great Losses by Sea, and amongst others were plundered by the famous *Wisbuy*, sixty six of their Cities covenanted together, to scour or cleanse the Seas from such Piracies, and to secure their Goods. And thus they became and continued, by that Eastern Trade, the only Traffickers and Carriers by Sea, beating by that means all other Nations out of the Ocean, till after the Year 1400, that the Art of salting and curing of Herrings being found out in *Flanders*, the Fisheries in these *Netherlands* being added to our Manufactures, proved to be of more importance than the Trade and Navigation of the *Easterlings*, and therefore encreased more and more with the Traffick by Sea to *Bruges*, which lasted to the Year 1482, when *Flanders* had Wars with the Arch-Duke *Maximilian*, about the Guardianship of his Son and his Dominions, which lasted ten Years. Mean while *Sluys*, the Sea-Port of *Bruges*, being for the most part infested, those of *Antwerp* and *Amsterdam*, to draw the Trade to their Cities, assisted the Duke in his unbridled Tyranny, and barbarous destruction of the Country, thereby regained his Favour, and attain'd their own Ends. And seeing the *Italians* by their *Levant* Trade, had gotten some Seed of Silk-worms from *China* and *Persia*, and raised such abundance of those Worms, and Mulberry Trees, that they wove many silk Stuffs, and in process of time had dispers'd their Silks every where, and began to vent many of them at *Antwerp*: And moreover, when the

When, and how the Association of the Hans-Towns was erected.

And how the Trade fell to them of Bruges, Antwerp, and Amsterdam.

Passages

Passages to the *West* and *East-Indies* by Sea were discovered, and the *Spaniards* and *Portuguese* sold their Goods and Spices at *Antwerp*; as also that the *Netherlandish* Drapery was much of it removed into *England*, and the *English* also settling their Staple at *Antwerp*, these things produc'd many new Effects.

1. Tho *Antwerp* was, in respect of its good Foundation, and far extended Traffick, the most renowned merchandizing City that ever was in the World, sending many Ships to and again from *France*, *England*, *Spain*, *Italy*, and making many silk Manufactures, yet *Brabant* and *Flanders* were too remote, and ill situated for erecting at *Antwerp*, or near it, the Fishery of Haddock, Cod, and Herring, and for making that Trade as profitable there, as it might be in *Holland*.

2. Tho the *Easterlings* built their Eastern Houses, and set up their Staple at *Antwerp*, yet had they not the Conveniency at once of transporting their Corn so far from the Eastward, in pursuance of their new correspondence with the *Spaniards* and *Italians*, but were necessitated to have it laid up anew in *Antwerp*, to prevent its spoiling, especially when we add this Consideration, That those remote Lands had not occasion to take off whole Ships ladings of fine Wares which *Antwerp* afforded, as the *Antwerpers* could take off whole Ships ladings of Herring, and salted Fish, besides the rough and unmanufactur'd Eastern and many other Commodities, which are manufactur'd and spent in this Country.

3. The *Hollanders* Fishery of Haddock, Cod, and Herring, and the great Conveniency they have of selling them all at home, and transporting

ing them abroad, was the Reason that the *Eastern* Countries took off very much of our Herrings and Salt. The Trade to that Country, since the breaking in of the Inlet or Passage into the *Texel*, about the Year 1400, when the River *Ye* began to be navigated with great Ships, settled it self by degrees mostly at *Amsterdam*, and part of it in *England*.

CHAP. XII.

For answer to the former Question, it is here particularly shewn, that Fishing and Traffick must entirely settle in Holland, *and Manufacturys must do the like for the most part, and consequently Navigation, or sailing upon Freight.*

THIS was the state of Trade till the Year 1585, when *Antwerp* was taken by the Prince of *Parma*. For that City being thus wholly shut up from the Sea, and the King of *Spain* very imprudently neglecting to open the *Scheld*, being desirous, according to the Maxims of Monarchs, to weaken that strong City, which he thought too powerful for him, and to disperse the Traffick over his many other Cities; he bent all his Strength against the Frontiers of *Gelderland*, *England*, and *France*, whereby the Merchants of *Antwerp* were necessitated to forsake their City, and consequently to chuse *Amsterdam* to settle in, which before the Troubles was, next to *Antwerp*, the greatest Mercantile City of the *Ne-*

How the Trade fell from Antwerp to Amsterdam.

therlands.

t Lands. For when we rightly consider the innumerable Inconveniencies found in all Islands, and especially Northward, by reason of Storms, and long Winters, in the Consumption of Goods bought, and the necessary Communication with our inland Neighbours; every one may easily imagine why the *Antwerpers* sat not down in the adjacent Islands of *Zeland*, and besides, neither in *France* nor *England* was there any liberty of Religion, but a Monarchical Government in both, with high Duties on Goods imported and exported. And tho' the Protestant Merchants, by reason of the great Peace, and good situation of *England*, would have most inclined to settle there, yet were they discouraged from coming into a Country, where there were no City-Excises or Imposts on Lands, or any other Taxes equally charging all, whether Inhabitants or Strangers, but heavy Taxes and Customs laid on all Goods imported and exported, by which Foreigners and their Children and Grandchildren, according to the Laws of the Land, must pay double as much as the natural *English*, yea in the Subsidies of Parliament, which extend to perpetuity on Foreigners and their Children, they must pay double Assessment. Besides which all Strangers are excluded from their Guilds and Halls of Trade and Manufactures, so that none have the Freedom there to work, either as Journeyman, or Master-workman, save in that whereof the Inhabitants are ignorant. And all these Discouragements were also for the most part in the *Eastern* Cities; yea in *England* as well as in the *Eastern* Cities, a Foreigner, tho an Inhabitant, was not suffered

to

to sell to any other but Citizens; nor to sell Wares by Retail, or for Consumption, or to buy any sort of Goods of Strangers, or of Inhabitants that are Strangers, neither by Wholesale nor Retail. All which made them think *England* no fit place for them to settle in.

It happened also at the same time, that the King of *Spain* allowing no where a Toleration of Religion, but making continual War, and utterly neglecting the scouring and cleansing of the Seas, the Fishing, and remaining Traffick of the *Flemish* Citys, which they drove into Foreign Parts, did wholly cease; so far were they from recovering the lost Trade of *Antwerp* So that the *Flemish* Fishing also fell into *Holland*: But the Manufactures were thus divided; one third of the Dealers and Weavers of Says, Damask, and Stockings, &c. went casually into *England*, &c. because that Trade was then new to the *English*, and therefore under no Halls nor Guilds Another great part of them went to *Leyden*, and the Traders in Linen settled most at *Haerlem*. But there were still a great number of Traders in Manufactures that remained in *Flanders* and *Brabant*. For seeing those Goods were continually sent to *France* and *Germany* by Land-carriage, it was impossible for us to prevent it by our Ships of War, or any other Means imaginable.

Why all the Manufactures did not abandon Flanders and Brabant, to fix with the Traffick and Navigation of Holland.

On the other side, seeing that in *Flanders* and *Brabant*, especially in the Villages where the Manufactures are mostly made, there are but small Imposts paid, and in *Holland* the Taxes were very great, they might therefore have born the Charge of carrying those Goods by Land into some *French* Harbours,

Namely by reason of the heavy Taxes in Holland.

from

from whence they might have bin transported to any part of the World. And therefore upon good advice we thought it our Interest to permit those *Flemish* Manufactures, tho wrought by our Enemies, to be brought into our Country of *Holland*, charging them with somewhat less Duty than they must have been at by going the furthest way about. And thus did those Manufactures of Foreign Countrys, by means of Immunities from Imposts and Halls, greatly improve and flourish in those Villages, because they could be made as cheap or cheaper than ours, which from time to time were more and more charged with Dutys on the Consumption. Yea, and which is worthy of admiration, they were charged with Convoy-mony and other Taxes upon Exportation, till about the Year 1634. when by the *French* and *Dutch* Wars, and Winter-quarters, all the most flourishing Villages of *Flanders*, *Brabant*, and the Lands beyond the *Meuse* were plundered, and the richest Merchandizing Citys obstructed from sending away their Goods. So that the Citys of *Holland* were hereby filled with Inhabitants, and their Manufactures sold there; which was the greatest cause of the increase of Trade in this Country, and the subsequent Riches of the Inhabitants.

CHAP.

CHAP. XIII.

That Amsterdam *is provided with better means of Subsistence, and is a greater City of Traffick, and* Holland *a Richer Merchandizing Country, than ever was in the World.*

BUT above all *Amsterdam* hath thriven most in all sorts of Merchandizes, and means of Subsistence and Enlargement. For tho it seems not to be so well situated as many other Towns in *South* and *North-Holland,* for receiving Goods that come from Sea, and transporting others beyond Sea, as also because of the shallowness of the *Pampus,* for which Ships must lade, or unlade most of their Goods, and wait for Winds in that unsafe Road of the *Texel*, yet in this particular of the greatest consideration, *Amsterdam* lies better than any Town in *Holland,* and possibly better than any City in *Europe,* to receive the Fish Manufacture, and other Commoditys which are taken and made by others, and especially to receive from the Shipping into their Warehouses Store-goods to be spent at home. And it is well known to all Persons whether Owners of Ships sailing for Freight, or Merchants, that this is a very great Conveniency for readily equipping and full lading of Ships, and selling their Goods speedily, and at the highest price, which is ten times more considerable than a conveniency of importing or exporting Goods speedily, or than the damages suffered by the Storms,

Why Amsterdam *is become the greatest City of Traffick in Europe.*

Namely by reason of its situation for Trade.

which may happen (tho but seldom) in the *Tax*. For Men having an eye to their ordinary and certain Profit according to true information of the present opportunity of Gain from abroad, whether remote or near at hand, by Export and Import, they are ever moved more by such an Opportunity, than deterred by such Misfortunes, especially if they have kept or reserved such an Estate or Credit as to be still able to continue their Traffick. At least it is certain that Misfortunes depending on such unknown and uncertain Causes, and happening so seldom, are ever little apprehended, and easily forgotten by those that have not had any loss by that means. And if any one should doubt whether *Amsterdam* be situate as well and better than any other City of *Holland* for Traffick, and Ships let out to Fraight, let him but please to consider in how few hours (when the Wind is favourable) one may sail from *Amsterdam* to all the Towns of *Holland*, *Overyssel*, *Guelderland* and *North-Holland*, &c. seeing there is no alteration of Course or Tides needful. And in how short a time, and how cheap and easily one may travel from any of the Towns of *South-Holland*, or other adjacent Inland Cities to *Amsterdam*, every one knows. And it hath evidently appeared how much the convenient situation of *Amsterdam* was esteemed by the *Antwerp* Merchants, since the Trade of *Antwerp* fixed no where but at *Amsterdam*. And after that the *Antwerp* Trade was added to their Eastern Trade and Fishing, the *Amsterdamers* then got by their Sword the whole *East-India* Trade, at least the Monopoly of all the richest Spices, and a great
Trade

Trade to the *West-Indies*; and upon that followed the Whale-fishing. as also by the *German* Wars, they acquired the confumption of the *Italian* Silk Stuffs, which ufed to be carried by Land, and fold there. And befides, the raw Silks have given them a fair opportunity of making many Silk Stuffs, as did the Halls of *Leyden*, and an ill Maxim of not early laying out the Ground of a City, or not fuffering any out-Buildings beyond the place allowed for building, which was the only occafion that the weaving of Wool was practifed, not only in many other Provinces and Citys, but alfo throughout *Holland*, and efpecially at *Amfterdam* And at laft thereupon followed the Troubles in *England*, and our destructive tho fhort War with them, and theirs againft the King of *Spain*, as alfo the Wars of the Northern Kings among themfelves, which were fo prejudicial to us By those eight Years troubles the Inhabitants of *Holland* probably loft more than they had gain'd in 20 years before.

It is neverthelefs evident that the *Hollanders* having well-nigh beaten all Nations by Traffick out of the Great Ocean, the *Mediterranean*, *Indian*, and *Baltick Seas*, they are the great, and indeed only Carriers of Goods throughout the World; catching of Herring, Haddock, Cod and Whale, making many forts of Manufactures and Merchandize for Foreign Parts. Which is fo great a Bleffing for the Inhabitants, and efpecially for the Rulers of the Land, and those that are benefited by them, that a greater cannot be conceived. And feeing I may prefume to fay that I have clearly fhewn, in the foregoing

The Hollanders *are become the only Carriers and Navigators of the Seas, which is a great Blefling for all our Inhabitants.*

Chap-

Chapter, that *Holland*'s Welfare and Prosperity wholly depends on the flourishing of Manufactur}s, Fishery, Navigation of Ships on Freight, and Traffick, it seems that the Order of Nature obliges me to give my Thoughts in particular of all Matters whereby the *Holland* Manufacturies, Fisheries, Ships let out to Freight, and Traffick, may be improved or impaired. But seeing that would afford us endless Matter of Speculation, exceeds my Skill, and is inconsistent with my intended Brevity, I shall satisfy my self in laying down the Principal Heads thereof, and that in short.

CHAP. XIV.

That Freedom or Toleration in, and about the Service or Worship of God, is a powerful Means to preserve many Inhabitants in Holland, *and allure Foreigners to dwell amongst us.*

By L}y of Commerce many People may be drawn out of other Countrys to inhabit Holland.

IN the first place it is certain, that not only those that deal in Manufactures, Fishing, Traffick, Shipping, and those that depend on them, but also all civilized People must be supposed to pitch upon some outward Service of God as the best, and to be averse from all other Forms; and that such Persons do abhor to travel, and much more to go and dwell in a Country, where they are not permitted to serve and worship God outwardly, after such a manner as they think fit. And also that as to Freedom about the outward Service of God, during

Ch. 14. *the true Interest of* Holland.

during the Troubles, and shortly after; when the Manufacturies, Trading, and Navigation for Freight began to settle in *Holland*, the Magistrate was so tender and indulgent, that there were very few useful Inhabitants driven thence by any rigour or hardship, much less any Foreigners: So that it brings that Maxim into my mind, that * the surest way to keep any thing, is to make use of the same Means whereby it was at first acquired.

And among those Means, comes first into consideration the Freedom of all sorts of Religions differing from the Reformed. For in regard all our Neighbours (except *Great Britain,* and the *United Provinces*) and for the most part all far remote Lands, are not of the Reformed Religion; and that the Clergy under the Papacy have their own Jurisdiction: And seeing, if not all those that are called *Spiritual*, yet the Clergy at least that differ from us, have in all Countrys a settled Livelihood, which depends not on the Political Welfare of the Land We see that through humane Frailty, they do in all these Countrys think fit to teach and preach up all that can have a tendency to their own Credit, Profit, and Ease, yea, tho it be to the Ruin of the whole Country; and moreover, when the Doctrine, Counsel, and Admonition of these Men is not received by any of their Auditors, these Clergymen do then very unmercifully use to prosecute them *Odio Theologico*. Whereas nevertheless all Christian Clergymen ought to rest satisfied, according to their

Seeing the Clergy in all Neighbouring Nations generally persecute those that differ from the Publick Sentiments.

---

* Res facile iisdem artibus retinentur quibus initio partæ sunt.

Master's

Master's Doctrine, to enlighten the Minds of Men with the Truth, and to shew them the way to Eternal Life, and afterwards to endeavour to perswade, and turn such enlightned Persons in all humility and meekness into the Path that leads to Salvation. It is evident that all People, especially Christians, and more particularly their publick Teachers, ought to be far from compelling, either by spiritual or bodily Punishment, those that for want of Light and Perswasion are not inclined to go to the Publick Church, to do any outward Act, or to speak any words contrary to their Judgment. For *Potestas coercendi*, the coercive Power is given only to the Civil Magistrate; all the Power and Right which the Ecclesiasticks have, if they have any, must be derived from them, as the same is excellently and unanswerably shewn by *Lucius Antistius Constans*, in his Book *de Jure Ecclesiasticorum* lately printed.

Indeed the essential and only difference between the Civil and Ecclesiastical Power is this, That the Civil doth not teach and advise as the other doth, but commands and compels the Inhabitants to perform or omit such outward Actions, or to suffer some certain Punishment for their Disobedience; so that they have dominion over the Subject, *sive volentes, sive nolentes*, whether they will or no. Whereas on the other side, the Duty of Christian Teachers is to instruct and advise Men to all Christian Virtues, as trusting in God our Saviour, the hope of possessing a future eternal blessed Life, and the love of God and our Neighbour. Which Virtues consisting only in the inward
Thoughts

Thoughts of our Minds, cannot be put into us by any outward Violence or Compulsion, but only by the inlightning and convincing Reasons of Ministers, who to effect this, must on all occasions comply with the State and Condition of their Hearers, and be the least amongst them: And thus making themselves the least, and thereby converting most, and bringing forth most good Fruits, they shall be the first in the Kingdom of Heaven. *Whoso-* Mat. 20. 27. *ever will be chief among you, let him be your Servants.* And besides, it is well known that our Lord Christ pretended to no other Kingdom or Dominion on Earth *(his Kingdom not* John 18. 36. *being of this World)* than that every one being convinced of this his true Doctrine, and wholesom Advice, and of his holy Sufferings for us, should freely be subject to him, not with the outward Man only, to do or omit any Action, to speak or be silent, but with the inward Man *in Spirit and Truth,* to John 4. love God, himself, and his Neighbour; to trust in that God and Saviour in all the Occurrences of our Lives, and by his infinite Wisdom, Mercy and Power, to hope for a blessed and everlasting State for our Souls. So that it became not his Disciples, or Followers, and Apostles, much less our present publick Preachers, to set themselves above their Spiritual Lord and Master, to lord it over others. *The Kings of the Gentiles ex-* Luke 22. 25, *ercise Lordship over them; but ye shall not be so.* 26. The Gospel also teacheth us, that they should not lord it over the People, but ought to be their Servants, and Ministers of the Word of God. But notwithstanding all this, we see, that by these evil ambitious Maxims of the

Clergy,

Clergy, almoſt in all Countrys, the Diſſenters, or ſuch as own not the Opinion of the publick Preachers, are turned out of the Civil State and perſecuted, for they are not only excluded from all Government, Magiſtracys, Offices and Benefices (which is in ſome meaſure tolerable for the ſecluded Inhabitants, and agrees very well with the Maxims of Polity, in regard it is well known by experience in all Countrys to be neceſſary, as tending to the common Peace, that one Religion ſhould prevail and be ſupported above all others, and accordingly is by all means authorized, favoured, and protected by the State, yet not ſo, but that the exerciſe of other Religions at the ſame time be in ſome meaſure publickly tolerated, at leaſt not perſecuted) but are ſo perſecuted, that many honeſt and uſeful Inhabitants, to eſcape thoſe Fines, Baniſhments, or corporal Puniſhments, to which by adhering to the prohibited Service of God they are ſubject, abandon their own ſweet native Country, and, to obtain their Liberty, chuſe to come and ſit down in our barren and heavy-tax'd Country.

Yea, and which is more, in ſome Countrys theſe Churchmen will go ſo far, as by an Inquiſition to inquire who they are that differ from the Opinion of the authorized Preachers; and firſt by Admonition and Excommunication, bereave them of their Credit, and afterwards of their Liberty, Eſtate, or Life. And as heretofore the *Romiſh* Clergy were not ſatisfied with obſtructing the Divine Service of thoſe that diſſented from them, but laboured to bring the Inquiſition into all Places

Places; so would it be a great wonder if the Ecclesiasticks in *Holland* should not follow the same worldly course, to the ruin of the Country, if they conceiv'd it tended to the increase of their own Profit, Honour, Power and Grandeur. At least we see it in almost all Countrys, where the best and most moderate, yea even where the Reformed Clergy bear sway, that dissenting Assemblies are prohibited. And seeing that the Publick Divine Worship is so necessary for Mankind, that without it they would fall into great ignorance about the Service of God, and consequently into a very bad Life; and since Man's Life is subject to many Miseries, therefore every one is inclined in this wretched State to nourish or comfort his Soul with the hope of a better. And as Men hope very easily to obtain the same by a free and willing attention to a Doctrine they think to be built on a good Foundation, so every one may easily perceive how impossible it is to make any Man by compulsion to hope for such advantage, in that which he cannot apprehend to be well grounded, and accordingly the dissenting Party clearly discover the Vanity of all manner of Force in Matters of Religion

And hinders the conversion of the Erroneous.

Moreover, seeing all Matters of Fact, and likewise of Faith, must in some measure be proved by Testimony of good Credit, such as is irreproachable, or beyond exception; and that all that are thus persecuted, whether by Excommunication, Fines, Banishment, or corporal Punishments, reproach and hate their Persecutors, to wit, the publick Authorised Preachers, as their Enemies, it is evident that those Persecutors lose all their weight

weight to perswade People in Matters of Faith by means of their publick Authority, which otherwise would be great among the common People. And besides, we see, that all persecuted People continually exercise their Thoughts upon any thing that seems to confirm their own Judgment, and oft-times out of meer stomachfulness and animosity will not so deliberately consider their Enemies Reasons, so that the Persecuted People being now to slide from the Truth of God's Worship by such Violence and Compulsion, become hardned in their Error. By this means manifold Wars, Miserys, and removals of Habitations have been occasioned since the Reformation, and the like Actions will have the like Effects. How prejudicial such coercive Practices are, especially in such Trafficking Cities, *Luseck*, *Collen*, and *Antwerp* may instruct us, where both the Rulers and Subjects of those lately so famous Cities have since the Reformation lost most of their Wealth, and chiefly by such compulsion in Religion; many of the Inhabitants being thereby driven out of their respective Cities, and Strangers discouraged from coming to reside in them. And tho according to clear Reason, and Holy Writ, the true Glory and Fame of all Rulers consists in the multitude of their Subjects, yet do these Churchmen (forgetting their Credit their Country, and their God, which is a threefold Impiety,) continue to teach, That it is better to have a City of an Orthodox or sound Faith, ill stocked with People, than a very populous, and Godly City, but tainted in Belief. Thus it is evident that to allow

Chap. 14. *the true Interest of* Holland.

low all Men the exercise of their Religion with more freedom than in other Nations, would be a very effectual means for Holland to allure People out of other Countrys, and to fix them that are there already; provided such Freedom be not prejudicial to our Civil State and free Government. For, as on the one side those of the *Romish* Religion have their Spiritual Heads, and the K of *Spain* (heretofore Earl of *Holland*) for their Neighbour, who may help the *Romanists* in the time of Intestine Division, so on the other side it is manifest, that our own Government by length of time is enlarged, and the *Spanish Netherlands* become weak, and that notwithstanding the Renunciation of the said Superiority over *Holland* we are in Peace with them, it is also certain that by persecuting the *Romanists* we should drive most of the Strangers out of our Country, and the greatest number of the dissenting old Inhabitants, *viz.* the Gentry, Monied-men and Boors, who continue to dwell amongst us, would become so averse to the Government, that in time it would be either a means to bring this Country into the Hands of our Enemy, or else drive those People out of the Country: which Cruelty would not only be pernicious, but altogether unreasonable in the Rulers and Reformed Subjects, who always us'd to boast that they fought for their Liberty, and constantly maintain'd, that several publick Religions may be peaceably tolerated and practised in one and the same Country, That true Religion hath advantage enough when it's allowed to speak, *Errantis pœna doceri*, and that there is no greater sign of a false Religion (or at least

So that especially in Holland *toleration of Religion is needful.*

Pol. disc. of D. C. lib 4. Disc. 6. p. 320.

Likewise for the Roman Catholicks.

Because our Wars against Spain *are grounded on the like Reason and Equity.*

F

least or one to the truth of which Men dare not trust) than to persecute the Dissenters from it. So that it appears that Toleration and Freedom of Religion is not only exceeding beneficial for our Country in general, but particularly for the Reformed Religion, which may and ought to depend upon its own Evidence and Veracity.

CHAP. XV.

A second Means to keep Holland Populous, is a plenary Freedom for all People that will cohabit with us, to follow any Occupation for a Livelihood.

Freedom to be given to all Inhabitants, to set up, and live by their Trades.

NEXT to a Liberty of serving God, follows the Liberty of gaining a Livelihood without any dear-bought City-freedom, but only by virtue of a fixed Habitation to have the common right of other Inhabitants. Which is here very necessary for keeping the People we have, and inviting Strangers to come among us. For it is self-evident that Landed-men or others that are wealthy, being forced by any accident to leave their Country or Habitation, will never chuse *Holland* to dwell in, being so chargeable a Place, and where they have so little interest for their Mony. And for those who are less wealthy, it is well known, that no Man from abroad will come to dwell or continue in a Country where he shall not be permitted to get an honest Maintenance. And it may be easily considered how great an inconveniency

it

it would be in this Country, for the Inhabitants, especially Strangers, if they should have no Freedom of chusing and practising such honest means of livelihood as they think best for their Subsistence, or if, when they had chosen a Trade, and could not live by it, they might not chuse another. This then being evident, that Strangers without freedom of earning their Bread, and seeking a Livelihood, cannot live amongst us: and as it is certain, that our Manufactorys, Fisherys, Traffick and Navigation, with those that depend upon them, cannot without continual Supplys of Foreign Inhabitants be preserved here, and much less augmented or improved; it is likewise certain, that among the endless Advantages which accrue to *Holland* by Strangers, and which might accrue more, our Boors may be likewise profited. For we see that for want of Strangers in the Country, the Boors must give such great yearly and day-wages to their Servants, that they can scarcely live but with great toil themselves, and their Servants live rather in too great plenty. The same inconveniencies we are likewise sensible of in Citys amongst Tradesmen and Servants, who are here more chargeable and burdensom, and yet less serviceable than in any other Countries

It is certain, that in all Cities, tho they invite Strangers to cohabit with them, the antient Inhabitants have Advantage enough by the Government and its Dependencies. And it is evident, that the old Inhabitants, who live by their Occupations, have a great Advantage over the new Comers, by their many Relations, Customers, and Acquaintance, most of the old Manufactures, and great Inland Consumption. All which particulars yield the old Inhabitants certain Gain. But new Comers leaving their own Country upon any Accident, and besides their moveable Goods, bringing with them the knowledg of what is abounding, or wanting in their native Country, and of all sorts of Manufactures, they cannot live in *Holland* upon the Interest of their Mony, nor on their real Estates; so that they are compelled to lay out all their Skill and Estate in devising and forming of new Fisheries, Manufactures, Traffick, and Navigation, with the danger of losing all they have. For he that sits idle in *Holland*, must expect to get nothing but certain and speedy Poverty; but he that ventures may gain, and sometimes find out and meet with a good Fishery, Manufacture, Merchandice, or Traffick. And then the other Inhabitants may come in for a share in that new Occupation, which is also very needful, because the old Handicraft Works being beaten down lower and lower in price, yield less Profit. And therefore it is necessary that all Strangers that are Masters, Journey-men, Confectioners, Merchants, Traders, &c. should live peaceably amongst us, without any Disturbance, Let, or Molestation whatever, and use their own Estates and Trades as they shall judg best.

And tho this will be ever detrimental to some old Inhabitants, who would have all the Profit, and bereave others of it, and under one pretext or other exclude them from their Trade, and therefore will alledg, That a Citizen ought to have more Privilege than a Stran-

Stranger, yet all Inhabitants who have here a certain place of Abode, or defire to have it as they are then no Strangers, but Inhabitants, fo ought they to be permitted, as well as the Burgers, to earn their neceffary Food, feeing they are in greater want than their Oppofers. And it is notorious, that all People, who to the prejudice of the common Good would exclude others, that are likewife Inhabitants of this Land, from the common means of Subfiftence, or out of the refpective Cities, and for that end would have fome peculiar Favour from the Rulers beyond the reft, are very pernicious and mifchievous Inhabitants: It is alfo certain, that a State which cannot fubfift of it felf, ought not to deny that Strangers fhould live amongft them with equal Freedom with themfelves, under pretence of the Privilege and Right of Cities; nor fhould they exclude any Strangers, but endeavour continually to allure in new Inhabitants; elfe fuch a State will fall to ruin. For the great Dangers of carrying on new Defigns, of being robb'd at Sea, of felling their Goods by Factors to unknown People, on twelve Months Credit, and at the fame time running the hazard of all Revolutions by Wars and Monarchical Governments againft this State, and of Loffes among one another, are fo important (yet all to be expected) that many Inhabitants concerned in the Fifheries, Traffick, Manufactury, and confequently in Ships fet out to Freight, will give over their Trade, and depart the Country when they have been fo fortunate as to have gained any confiderable Eftate, to feek a fecurer way of living elfewhere. On the other hand, we are to consider, that there will ever be many Bankrupts and forsaken Trades, both by reason of the dangers of foreign Trade, and intolerable Domestick Taxes, which cannot be denied by any that knows that in *Amsterdam* alone there are yearly about three hundred abandoned or insufficient Estates registred in the Chamber of Accompts of that City, and therefore there are continually many Inhabitants, who finding the Gain uncertain, and the Charge great, are apt to relinquish it. So that it is ever necessary that we leave always open for People to subsist by, and a full Liberty, as aforesaid, to allure Foreigners to dwell among us. Moreover, tho it be not convenient in general for Strangers (that is for such, who, tho they dwell in *Holland*, and have continued there some considerable time, are not Natives) to partake of the Government, yet is it very necessary, in order to fix them here, that we do not exclude them our Laws.

CHAP. XVI.

That Monopolizing Companies and Guilds, and excluding of Persons from their Society, are very prejudicial to Holland.

MUCH less ought we to curb or restrain our Citizens and Natives, any more than Strangers, from their natural liberty of getting their livelihoods in their Native Country, by Erected authoriz'd Companies and Guilds. For when we consider, that all the

Trade

Trade of our common Inhabitants is circumscribed or bounded well nigh within *Europe*, and that in very many parts of the same, as *France*, *England*, *Sweden*, &c. our greatest Trade and Navigation thither is clampt by the high Duties, or by Patent Companies, like those of our *Indian* Societies; as also how small a part of the World *Europe* is, and how many Merchants dwell in *Holland*, and must dwell there to support it. We shall have no reason to wonder, if all the beneficial Traffick in these small adjacent Countries be either worn out, or in a short time be glutted with an over-trade. But we may much rather wonder, why the greatest part of the World should seem unfit for our common Inhabitants to trade in, and that they should continue to be debarred from it, to the end that some few Persons only may have the sole Benefit of it. It is certainly known that this Country cannot prosper, but by means of those that are most industrious and ingenious, and that such Patents or Grants do not produce the ablest Merchants. But on the other hand, because the Grantees, whether by Burgership, select Companies, or Guilds, think they need not fear that others who are much more Ingenious and Industrious than themselves, and are not of the Burgership, Companies, and Guilds, shall lessen their Profits, therefore the certain Gains they reap make them dull, slow, unactive, and less inquisitive. Whereas on the other side, we say that Necessity makes the old Wife trot, Hunger makes raw Beans sweet, and Poverty begets Ingenuity. And besides, it is well known, now especially when *Holland* is so heavily taxed, that other less bur-

To all those ways of Subsistence, whereby to deprive them, and lessen their number;

Who ever of their abundance become wasteful, dull and sloth-

...dered People, who have no Fisheries, Manufactures, Traffick, and freight Ships, cannot long ſubſiſt but by their Induſtry, Subtilty, Courage, and Frugality. In a word, theſe Patent-Companies and Guilds do certainly exclude many uſeful Inhabitants from that Trade and Traffick. But thoſe that poſſeſs theſe Privileges with ſufficient knowledg and fitneſs, need not fear that others that are more Induſtrious and Ingenious than themſelves, ſhall prevent them of their Profit by the exerciſe of the like Abilities and Parts, neither can it be ſo fully carried on and improved for the common benefit of the Country, by a ſmall number of People, as by many. So that in the mean time other People that we cannot exclude from that Traffick or Manufacture by means of our Grants and Guilds, have a great Opportunity of profitably improving that which ſo fooliſhly, and with ſo much churliſhneſs is prohibited to our common Inhabitants. Whereas otherwiſe, the provident and induſtrious *Hollanders* would eaſily draw to them all foreign Trade, and the making of incredibly more Manufactures than we now work on. That which is objected againſt this is, That the *Hollanders* are a People of ſuch a nature, that if the Trade were open into *Aſia*, *Africa*, and *America*, they would overſtock all thoſe Countries with Goods, and ſo deſtroy that Trade to the prejudice of *Holland*, which is ſo far from the truth, and all appearance thereof, that it is hardly worth anſwering. For firſt, ſo great and mighty a Trade by the *Hollanders*, in thoſe vaſt and trafficking Countries, would be the greateſt Bleſſing to them that could be wiſhed for upon Earth; would

would to God any of us could ever see *Holland* so happy. And next it cannot be denied, that even in this small *Europe*, the overstocking of Countries with Goods may indeed lessen the Gains of some particular Merchants; but yet after such a manner that the said overstocking with the said Goods really is, and can be no other than an effect or fruit of a present overgrown Trade of this Country, in proportion to the smallness of those Countries with which we are permitted to traffick. And Thirdly, It is evident, that the *Hollanders* by such overstocking have never yet lost any Trade in any Country or Place of *Europe*, nor can they lose it so long as that Trade remains open, because that superfluity of Goods transported is soon spent, and that same Trade is by the same or some other of our Merchants immediately reassumed and taken up, so soon as by a following scarcity in those Countries there is any appearance of making more Profit by those, or other Commodities. *And the impossibility thereof is made manifest.*

But supposing it to be true, that the *Dutch* Merchants by overstocking those trading Countries should run a risque of losing that Trade in some Parts, yet considering the smalness of those Lands, it would then be doubly necessary to prevent the same by setting open the Trade to *Asia, Africa,* and *America,* for all the Merchants of *Holland.* But on the other side, it is certain that the licensed monopolizing Companies, by the unfaithfulness, negligence, and chargeableness of their Servants, and by their vast, and consequently unmanageable Designs, who are not willing to drive any Trade longer than it yields *As also that trading Companies by Charter have ever lessen'd Trade and Navigation, and oftentimes quite ruin'd both.*

yields excessive Profit, must needs gain considerable in all their Trade, or otherwise relinquish and forsake all Countries that yield it not, which nevertheless would by our common Inhabitants be very plentifully carried on.

In this respect it is worthy observation, That the Authorised Greenland Company made heretofore little profit by their Fishing, because of the great Charge of setting out their Ships, and that the Train-oil, Blubber and Whale-fins were not well made, handled, or cured, and being brought hither and put into Warehouses, were not sold soon enough nor to the Company's best advantage. Whereas now that every one equips their Vessels at the cheapest Rate, follow their Fishing diligently, and manage all carefully, the Blubber, Train-oil and Whale-fins are imployed for some Uses in several Countrys, that they carry them with that conveniency that two there are now fifteen Ships for one which formerly fitted out of *Holland* on that account, and differently each of them could not therefore so many Whales as heretofore, and notwithstanding the new prohibition of *France* and some Countrys to import those Commodities, and that there is greater plenty of them yielded by our Fishers, yet those Commodities are sold much above the Value above what they were while there was a Company, that the common Inhabitants do exercise that Fishery Ship of to the much greater benefit of our Country than when it was (under the management of a Company) carried on but by a few trades very considerable. That for the most part all Trades and Manufactures managed by Guilds in *Holland*, do sell all
their

their Goods within this Country to other Inhabitants who live immediately by the Fisherys, Manufacturys, Freight-ships, and Traffick. So that no Members of those Guilds, under what pretext soever, can be countenanced or indulged in their Monopoly, or Charter, but by the excluding of all other Inhabitants, and consequently to the hindrance of their Countrys Prosperity. For how much soever those Members sell their Pairs or Commoditys dearer than if that Trade or Occupation was open or free, all the other better Inhabitants that gain their Subsistance immediately or by consequence by a Foreign consumption, must bear that loss. And indeed our Fishermen, Dealers in Manufactures, Owners of Freight-ships, and Traders, being so burdened with all manner of Imposts, to oppress them yet more in their necessity by these Monopolies of Guilds, and yet to believe that it redounds to the good of the Land, because it tends to the benefit of such Companies, is to me incomprehensible. These Guilds are said indeed to be a useful sort of People, but next to those we call idle Drones, they are the most unprofitable Inhabitants of the Country, because they bring in no profit from Foreign Lands for the Welfare of the Inhabitants of *Holland*. *Esop* hath well illustrated this folly by a Cat, who first lick'd off the Oil from an oiled File, and continued licking, not observing that she had by little and little lick'd her Tongue thorow which was given her to sustain her Life, and carry Nourishment into her Body, nor that she fed not on a File which did not consume, but on her own Blood before her Tongue was totally consumed.

On

On the contrary, I can see no good, nor appearance of good, which the Guilds in *Holland* do produce, but only that Foreign Masters and Journeymen Artificers, having made their Works abroad, and endeavouring to sell them to our Inhabitants, thereby to carry the Profit out of our Country into their own, are herein check'd and opposed by our Masters of Guilds or Corporations. But besides that this is more to the Prejudice than Advantage of the Country, since by consequence our Fishers, Manufacturers, Traders, and Owners of Ships let to Freight, are thereby bereft of the Freedom of buying their necessaries at the cheapest Rate they can; it is also evident that this feeding of Foreigners upon the *Hollander* would be more strenuously and profitably opposed and prevented, in case all handicraft Work, and Occupations were permitted to be made, sold and practised by all, and no other People, except such as have their setled Habitations in this Country.

CHAP. XVII.

That Fishers, Dealers in Manufactures, Merchants, and Owners of Freight-Ships as such, ought not at all to be charged by paying any Imposition to the Country, under what Pretext soever.

IF it be granted that the forementioned means of subsistence, namely, Fishing, Manufactury, Traffick, and Freight-ships, are

are so necessary in, and for *Holland*, as hath been above demonstrated; and if the *Hollanders* who have no native Commodities must yet hold Markets equally with other Nations, who may deal in their own Wares, or Manufactures made of their own Materials; then it follows, that our Rulers ought not, under any Pretence whatsoever, to charge or tax their own Inhabitants, Fishers, dealers in Manufactures, Owners of Freight-Ships, or Merchants as such. And I suppose every one will easily grant me this Conclusion in the general, because of its own perspicuity. For indeed, how fully and fixedly soever Fishing, Manufactury, Navigation, and Commerce seem to have settled themselves in *Holland*; yet it is evident, that one Stiver of profit or loss more or less, makes a Commodity which is *in æquilibrio*, and that happens very often (namely when it is hardly discerned whether the Profit be sufficient to continue the making of that Commodity) wholly to preponderate, or be at a stand, even as a pair of Scales wherein ten thousand Pounds or less is weighed, being ballanced, one of them is as easily weighed down with a Pound-weight, as if there were but a hundred Pounds in each Scale. And by consequence it is evident, that our own Fisherys, and Manufactures, with their dependencies, as also the Traffick in those Wares, whether imported or exported, ought not at all to pay for Tonnage, Convoy, or other Duties, nor any thing when brought to the Scale, unless they are sold. I know that all such Impositions, through the Ignorance of those that are unacquainted with Trade, are counted very light and insignificant.

Especially about Traffick in Holland.

cant; but those that are more intelligent and concerned therein, do know, that you may pull a large Fowl bare, by plucking away single Feathers, especially in *Holland*, where with light Gains men must make a heavy purse. The Antients have compared these inconsiderate People to Mice, who being to live on the Fruit of an Orchard, found that the Roots of the Trees relish'd well, and were of good Nourishment, so that they made bold to eat of them; whereby the Trees, for want of sufficient root, being depriv'd of their usual Nourishment, bore less Fruit: and the wisest of them told the others the reason of it, but were not believed by the Foolish and Greedy Mice that continued gnawing and devouring of the Root. And when in the following Year, besides this unfruitfulness, those Trees that had lost many of their Roots and Fibres, were either blown down by the Storms, or kill'd by the Frost, the wise Mice did thereupon once again warn their imprudent Brethren against it; who answered, That it was not their undermining and eating the Roots, but the fierce Storms and sharp Winter that was the cause of it. So that they continued feeding on the Roots, till the Trees were so diminished, that both the wise and foolish Mice must either die of hunger, or seek a better habitation.

Illustrated by Fact.

Besides this, antient History teacheth us, That *Agis* King of *Macedon* being imprudently covetous, was not content with the Health of his Subjects, and the Profit

---

Consilium stupidorum novis ad spem ædendo Argentum pro omnem rem magnis accessus.

which

which he and they receiv'd from the Imposts paid by Strangers, who came to drink his Mineral Waters, but he would needs tax the very Fountain it felf, by laying a Duty upon every meafure of Water, which was fo unacceptable to God and Nature, that the Fountain dried up, infomuch that he thereby loft not only the Health of his Subjects, but the Impoft on the Confumption, and for this fuper-Impoft on the Well, he was curfed and derided by his Subjects and Strangers.

And indeed if we confider, that all Dutys levied on Confumption muft at the long run be born by the Fishermen, Manufacturers, Traffickers, and Owners of Ships, who for the moft part employ all the People here directly or indirectly, we muft acknowledg, that they alone are above meafure burdened thereby, and difcouraged by Impofts above all others. Which will evidently appear, if you confider it in an Example or two, and inquire how much Wages is here paid for building and fetting to Sea a Ship of 200 Lafts, or rather how many Carpenters, Smiths, Ropemakers, Sailmakers, &c. muft be employed about fuch a Veffel, and how much in the mean while they muft altogether pay to the State, whether for Imposts, or for Poundage of Houferne. For I doubt not but it will charge a Ship with fome hundreds of Guilders more than if we had no Imposts, and confequently it muft be fold fo much the dearer. And if moreover we confider, that the Owners who fet to Sea fuch a Ship to feek a Freight, muft afterwards victual her with our Provifion and Drink for the Seamen, upon which our Imposts charge very much, you will the

From the Fisheries, Manufactures, and Traffick, is drawn from all parts, what the other Inhabitants pay to the Magistracy.

As the building of Shipping,

easier

easier discern it. And this would likewise appear manifestly, if we consider, that the price of weaving half a Piece of ordinary home-made broad Cloth, amounts to seventy Guilders, and that this Mony is presently spent, (for such Workmen, tho they can, will not lay up any thing) then we should see, that of this 70, more than twenty Guilders is paid for Imposts, and Poundage upon House-hire; for a half Piece of Cloth requires the Labour of twenty eight People for fourteen days, or at least so many may thereby be fed by the Heads of Families (reckoning five to a Family) and then we see that a half Piece of Cloth is thereby charged with twenty Guilders.

And Drapery do mar pg.

And tho the Fisheries and Traffick are not opprest near so much with such Imposts, yet it certainly is, and continues an intolerable Error, and thwarts the Welfare of the whole State, to burden any Dealers in Manufactures, Fishers, or Merchants, as such; for we do not take due care for the prosperity of the Country, unless by all Ways and Means we lighten their Burdens, and remove what makes them uneasy.

CHAP. XVIII.

That freedom of Religion is against all Reason obstructed in Holland.

Having hitherto spoken of four considerable ways of preserving the Prosperity of *Holland*, I think it not fit to go over any more

more tending to the same end, till I first briefly hint how *Holland* hath governed it self as to the said Expedients. And first as to freedom of Religion, it is certain that having till this time been greater in *Holland* than any where else, it hath brought in many Inhabitants, and driven out but few, yet it is also certain, that since the Year 1618, we have begun to depart from that laudable Maxim more and more. *Toleration of Religion was formerly more obstructed.*

First with the *Remonstrants*, persecuting them by Placaets, Fines, and Banishments, and driving them into other Lands: Afterwards with the *Romanists*, by disturbing them more and more in their Assemblies with severe Placaets, and more rigorous Execution, notwithstanding that by the Prosperity of our own Government, the great Increase of the Protestants, the Peace, and the K. of *Spain*'s Renunciation of any Pretence, Right, or Title, for himself, or his Heirs after him, to these *United Provinces*; The moving Reasons of our first Placaets against the *Romanists*, seemed to have been taken away. So that now, in order to enjoy their Liberty, they must pay a heavy Tax annually, to the Profit of the Bailiffs and Schouts, which seems to be imposed for them, and for no other Cause; for the Government reaps no Benefit by it. This is no less unreasonable, than detrimental to the Land: For if we cannot spare the Benefit which accrues to us by their Abode and Traffick, why should we prohibit that which is not hurtful to the State, and whereof the *Romish* Inhabitants make so great Account, and without which they cannot dwell amongst us? If we permit none but small Assemblies in Cities, *Namely by Placaets against the Remonstrants and Roman Catholicks.* *Altho the moving Reasons of the first Placaets now wholly cease.*

Cities, in the Houses of known Citizens, with such Priests as are best approved of by the Rulers, that inconvenience would have ceased, and Peace and Friendship increase more and more among the good Inhabitants, yea and so the Religion too. And moreover, our State would avoid that Vexation which grows by disturbing those prohibited Meetings and the like. And on the contrary, the State can nothing endanger by those well known Assemblies, where every one might have free Access, no matter of secrecy could be complained of, but the publick Safety would ever the better be secured. But what shall we say, not only the Religions, but also the Clergy and Men, and commonly the sweet Temper of such as have suffered under Persecutions, changed into Force and Violence, so far as they become Persecutors of others; then they forget the Evangelical Lesson, and the Law of Nature, to do nothing to others but what they would be done to themselves; and on the contrary, they remember and practise that old and detestable cursed Maxim, *as he hath done unto me, so I do to him*; and he that hath &c. And to speak all in few words, in all our Religious Affairs, it is good for every one to be so minded, that I might learn something without any Adversity, than in Prosperity without Trouble, neither &c. therefore Pride and Covetousness, and Violence &c.

CHAP.

CHAP. XIX.

That the Freedom of Fishery and Traffick in Holland is likewise in some measure unjustly restrain'd.

THE Freedom of Fishery and Traffick is greater in this Country than elsewhere, and yet heretofore there were many Placaets published concerning the Herring, and other Fisheries, which tend altogether to the benefit of foreign Fishers, who are not bound to obey them. We formerly manag'd the Whale-fishing by a monopolizing Company exclusive of all others, and how mischievous that proved to *Holland*, appears now, that that Fishing is open to all Men, whereby it is advanced from One to Ten, yea to Fifteen, as was before shewn more at large. But erecting an *East*, and a *West India* Company, was a quite different thing, for it appeared to be a necessary Evil, because our People would be trading in and about such Countries where our Enemies were too strong for particular Adventures. So that this seemed to have been necessary in all Respects, to lay the Foundation of that Trade by a powerful arm'd Society. And seeing this Country, ingaged in War against the King of *Spain*, had need of using all its Strength, it was very prudently done to erect those two Societies. But that Trade being now so well settled, we may justly make it a doubt, whether the said Companies ought any longer to continue

Sometimes a Monopoly Charter is useful to settle a Trade.

on the fame foot. Some wife Statefmen do with probable Reafons maintain, that the politic Rule of * preferving a thing beft, by the fame means whereby it was acquired, cannot agree with thefe Companies: For it is certain, that the firft moving Reafon of thofe Grants to them, which was the War with the King of *Spain*, now ceafeth, and that in cafe of any new War againft that People, they would no longer be formidable to us, but we to them. And fecondly, as it is well known that it was neceffary at firft to make fome Conquefts upon the Spice Iflands of the faid Enemy, becaufe the more Lands they conquered, the more Right and Ability they would acquire to the Trade which might happen in thofe parts. So it cannot be denied, that when thofe good and neceffary Conquefts are made, the Grounds and Maxims of the profperity of the faid Companies begin to juftle and oppugn the general Good of this Country, which is manifeftly known to confift in a continual increafe of our Manufactures, Traffick, and freight Ships: Whereas neverthelefs the true intereft of fuch Companies confifts in feeking the benefit of all the Members, even with Foreign, as well as our own Manufactures, and (to the great prejudice of all other our Inhabitants) by importing Manufactures and other mechanick Works into this Country, and vending them throughout *Europe*, and in fhort, by making the greateft Profit with the leaft Traffick and Navigation.

---

* Res facile ifdem artibus retinentur quibus initio partae funt.

vigation. As it is acknowledged, that if the *East-India* Company can gain more by importing *Japan* Garments, *Indian* Quilts and Carpets, &c. than raw Silk, or if the Company, by causing a scarcity of Nutmegs, Mace, Cloves, Cinamon, &c. could so raise the price of them, that they might gain as much by one hundred Lasts as by a thousand. We ought not then to expect that those raw Silks, and unnecessary and great Disbursments which they are at, should cause a greater Trade and Navigation than those hundred Lasts would just require, but that they would rather, to shun greater Traffick and Navigation, destroy all the Superfluity they have in the *Indies*.

And it can be as little denied of such Companies, that the more Lands they conquer, the more of their Stock they must necessarily spend for the Preservation and Defence of such Lands, and the more Dominion they have, the less are they able to mind and augment their Traffick. Whereas on the contrary, our particular Inhabitants by those manifold conquered strong Holds and Lands, would have so much the more Conveniency and Security to trade in the *Indies*. We have now, to say no more, quite lost our open Trade of *Guiney*, and that of Salt in the *West-Indies*, which were heretofore so considerable by the erecting of the *West-India* Company, and the Mischief which was done to the King of *Spain* in the *West-Indies*, is recoil'd back, and fallen upon us. So that we cannot cry up that Company, who have bound the hands of particular Men, and made War instead of Traffick, unless at least they would

So that that Monopoly ought then to have been taken away.

in the mean time suffer all our Inhabitants freely to trade in all their Conquests. On the contrary, that Company hath impoverish'd many of our good Inhabitants. Whereas by an open Trade, and consequently well settled Colonies, we should not only, with small Charge, have easily defended those vast Lands of *Brasil*, *Guiny*, *Angola*, St *Thomas*, &c. against all foreign Power, but (which is more considerable) have been able to carry on a very great Trade with our own Nation, without fear that any foreign Potentate should seize our Ships, Goods, or Debts, to which those Hollanders that trade only in *Europe* are continually exposed. And how profitable and secure that Trade would have been, may easily be apprehended, if it be well consider'd, that the said Lands yield the best sort of Commodities that are in request over all *Europe*, and are not to be had so good elsewhere, viz. Sugar, Brazil wood, Elephants-Teeth, Gold, &c. and that which those Inhabitants have need of in Return, *Holland* could for the most part have supplied them with, as Victuals, Duck, and Apparel, yea even with most Materials for building of Houses, Ships, &c whereas now we are deprived of all these Advantages. This is the ordinary Fruit and Efflorescence of Monopolies and Conquests, which for want of Colonies they must keep up at a continual great Charge. May our *East-India* Company consider this effectually, before it be too late.

CHAP.

CHAP. XX.
That Manufactures, and other Mechanick Works, are no less imprudently restrained.

BY the freedom allow'd Men to gain a Livelihood by such things as are liable to Corruption, or by Handicrafts, it's certain that we have kept an infinite number of People in the Country, and have besides drawn in many Foreigners to it: For in most Citys of *Holland* there has been sufficient Liberty given. But afterwards People withdrew from many Citys, through the mischievous Nature of some Men, who rather chuse a sudden Profit, tho to the general damage of their native Country, than that which comes in by degrees with continued Gain to the Republick. For private or peculiar Profit is the chief Foundation (tho it always goes under the Notion of a general Advantage) of all those Restrictions and Burdens imposed on the Citizens by Corporations or Guilds, which serve to no other end but to keep good People out of their Citys, and in the mean while to give the Members of such Corporations a lasting opportunity of being enrich'd by their fellow Inhabitants, and of selling their Goods and Manufactures the dearer to their Neighbours, and so of levying as it were an Impost upon them.

At least it cannot be denied, but that Halls relating to Manufactures, or any other sort of handicraft Ware, with Overseers or Inspectors appointed by common consent; or the chief Men of the Guilds to circumscribe or limit the same; or by publick Acts of State to appoint how those Wares must be made which we sell into Foreign Lands, are as ridiculous as prejudicial. For it supposeth two very impertinent things. First, That the Foreign Buyers must needs purchase of us such Manufactures and Mechanick Works as we shall please to make, be they what they will: And, secondly, that in other Countrys they must not make those sorts of Manufactures, and handicraft Wares which we prohibit. Whereas on the contrary it may be said, that the Makers of them have hit the right Mark, when they can best please the Buyer, and the Buyer can gain most by them. And it is certain that all our Manufactures and other Mechanick Works, may be made and spent not only in the Country Villages and Towns of *Holland*, but also in very many neighbouring Countrys; and that they may be there made with far less Imposts on the Consumption than with us. By which it appears that it would have been much better for *Holland* never to have laid on those Restrictions and Prohibitions.

CHAP. XXI.

That the heavy and manifold Imposts will at last destroy the Prosperity of this Country.

AS to Imposts upon imported or exported Goods, and Taxes upon Consumption, and real or immoveable Estates, I suppose

former

former Ages levied none such in time of Peace. For when the Earls of *Holland* supposed they should have occasion for an extraordinary Supply in time of War over and above their Revenues, they came in Person, and according to their Privilege desired it of the Assembly of States, who sometimes granted it for a short time, and sometimes refused it, and were ever very cautious of granting any standing Supply of Mony, as knowing their Liberty could not subsist but under such an Earl as had neither Forces nor Mony beforehand. And our Historians count it a great Offence in our Earls, that they endeavoured to make these Lands tributary. For which reason the Emperor *Charles* the Fifth desiring a Stiver to be imposed upon each Acre or Morgen of Land, could not obtain it, and his Son *Philip* not without great trouble, got an Impost for nine Years to help to defray the Charge of the War against *France*, but on this Condition, that all Sums so levied, should be received and disposed by such as the State impowered to do it. And on the same ground the States of *Flanders* and *Brabant* have to this day preserved their Liberty of granting the King such Requests, or (as it most commonly happens) of denying them. It makes nothing against what I have now said, that the Earls of *Holland* have heretofore receiv'd Customs upon Goods imported and exported, seeing according to their Privilege the Citizens of the Trading Citys of *Holland*, viz. *Dort, Haerlem, Delf, Leyden, Amsterdam*, &c. are Custom-free; so that such Dutys do only concern Strangers, and even for them they are very easy. But in the time of the Stadtholders

holders Government in the United Provinces, says Grotius, *being not to give* "their People so much Penny, we afford wards go to Rome, which being in "Brittany, he writes to his Friends here in "this manner: We have here all manner of "Taxes and Imposts, without preserving "the least shadow of our common Freedom. For the same Taxes are by the long continuance of the Wars now screw'd up so high, that the like was never seen in any Republick, much less in a Trafficking Country, so that it will be the greatest wonder in Nature for us to sustain those intolerable Burdens long, and having no Trade with our own native Commodities, to be able to traffick as other Nations do. Nevertheless I willingly acknowledge, that if we must needs raise no less than fifteen Millions of Guilders yearly in this Country, we have hit upon the most convenient course for it, *viz.* to charge the oldest Inhabitants most, as being most fixed to the Country by the Advantage of the Government, and their immoveable Estates: For Land is most liable to pay Poundage, the 40th Penny upon Sale, and the 20th Penny of Inheritances, by those of the Collateral ascending Line, as also the Tax of the 200th Penny most strictly levied. But those manifold, yea innumerable Imposts upon Consumption, concern Merchandize and Manufacture only so far as those who are main-

---

* *Cum adeo rem deessent quam darent.* Grot. Hist.

† *Cum data, aut re quidem Libertatis umbram retenti.*

tain'd

tain'd by them are Men, and muſt live by them. Beſides it is well known, not only that in Conſumptions there may be great variety, but alſo that People do manifeſtly ſpend moſt of their Income upon Pomp and Ornament, Superfluity, Wantonneſs, Pleaſure and Recreation. So that Fiſhermen, Manufacturers, Seamen and Watermen, who are moſtly poor, pay but little to this Tax; whereas the richer Inhabitants pay very much; and it cannot be denied but that they ſeem voluntarily to pay thoſe Impoſts on Conſumptions.

But in real Burdens and Taxations, the Favour and Hatred of the firſt Aſſeſſors has not only an Influence, but thoſe that are oppreſs'd by them, cannot free themſelves from them by prudential Forethought and Frugality. Moreover it is apparent, that he who increaſes his Eſtate by induſtrious and frugal living, is moſt burdened. And he that by lazineſs and prodigality diminiſheth his Eſtate will be leſs taxed. So that Virtue is unjuſtly oppreſt, and Vice favoured. Whereas on the contrary, the Impoſts on Conſumption fall heavy upon the Riotous, and indulge and incourage the Virtuous. But tho in all Events, the forementioned Sums of Mony yearly demanded for defence of the Country, be raiſed after the eaſieſt way poſſible; yet the immenſeneſs of the Sum will not ſuffer us to imagine that our People continuing to be thus burdened, ſhall always be able to ſell their Merchandize at as low, or lower Rates than other Foreigners, who are charged leſs, and work up their own Growth and Manufactures ready for the Merchant. So

Or, Poundage, and the eighth Penny.

That the Inhabitants ought as ſoon as poſſible to be eaſed.

that

that it is absolutely necessary that our Inhabitants be eased of such Burdens as soon as possibly may be

---

CHAP. XXII.

The Grounds and Reasons upon which the greatest Caution is to be us'd in laying the Tax of Convoy-mony, or Customs.

BUT the Impost on Goods Imported and Exported, and that on Shipping, is a quite different thing, for some may possibly be laid for the Benefit of the State, some without prejudice to it, and some cannot be laid without great and certain detriment to *Holland.* I shall therefore express my Sentiments particularly upon this Subject, and do premise, that so long as our Polity about Sea-affairs is built upon the same Foundation as it was in the Year 1597. that Prohibition of any Ships or Merchandize whatever, whether imported or exported, must always be of great Concernment to *Holland.* The like may be said of laying any new or higher Duty of Tonnage, or Convoy-mony for clearing the Seas; seeing we daily find that some Provinces, Admiralties, and Citys, intending to tolerate the same among themselves, do privately connive and suffer them to be smugl'd, or brought in Custom-free, in order to gain that Trade of Navigation and Commerce to themselves; and yet will be sure to be the most zealous in causing such Prohibitions, and the

the laying in of higher Convoy-mony and Taxes for clearing the Seas, to be imposed by the States-General. So that commonly the fairest dealing Provinces, Admiraltys and Citys of the *United Provinces*, and the most upright Merchants suffer by the said Placaets, while the most fraudulent and dishonest Merchants do generally so contrive 'Matters, as to get Friends at Court, by whose Favour they find Means to benefit themselves to the prejudice of honest Men

See the Grievances of the Magistrates of Zierickzee of the Year 1668. in Novemb.

In the first place it is worthy observation, that in this Affair, nothing can be more detrimental than to charge all Ships, or Goods coming in or going out with Tonnage-duty, without distinction: for tho it be pretended to be taken of the Shipping only, yet it is evident that all the Goods they carry must pay for it. And to pay for clearing the Seas, and thereby charging all Goods, according to their Value, with one *per Cent.* or the like, is still more prejudicial. To make this more evident, I shall insist the longer upon it. Seeing *Holland* of it self yields almost nothing, and the greatest part of our Traffick consists in Fisherys, Manufactures, Mechanic Works, and their Dependencies, so that we must take those Fish, and fetch the unwrought Materials for Manufactures, and all that is necessary thereunto from Foreign Parts, and likewise most of our Fish, and wrought Goods, must afterwards be transported to Foreign Parts. And seeing it is evident that the Fisheries, Manufactures, and other Mechanick Wares, may be practised and made in other Countrys, it is an inexcusable weakness to burden those necessary Means of Livelihood, and all other

Last-mony, as now laid, is very detrimental, because it charges all without distinction.

Mer

Merchandize without distinction, and thereby indanger the driving them into other Nations where they are less charged. How much this thwarts all good Maxim of Polity, I shall shew by an Example or two. It was antiently very wisely considered, how much we were concerned in the Manufactury of Woollen Cloth, and therefore a half-Inland made Cloth was charged with no more than 4 Stivers for Exportation, whereas if it had paid 1 per Cent. for clearing the Seas, it would have paid 30 Stivers. So that every one may perceive the Disparity, and into what danger we run by such Errors, of losing this Trade, and driving out of our Country a very great number of People, as washers of Wool, Pickers, Scourers, Carders, Spinners, Weavers, Dressers, Fullers, Dyers, Nappers, Pressers, &c. with the makers of the Instruments necessary to those Imployments. And lastly, it is the way to cause the Trade of unwrought Goods, thereunto subservient, and made use of likewise in the Manufactures, to withdraw very readily into other Countrys, especially if besides all this, we do in the same impolitick manner tax the unwrought Goods serving to the same end, which is against all good Polity, and the great Prudence of our Ancestors, who having well considered how much Weaving concerns us, very wisely ordered all Wool imported to be free, and all Yarn woven here to pay but 15 Stivers the 100, and but one per Cent. to be paid for clearing the Seas, the Wool for an Inland Half-cloth ten Stivers, and the Yarn for a home-made Camlet 15 Stivers the Piece; which yet by the ordinary Convoy or Customs

stoms (counting 15 Stivers for 100 Pounds) is charged but with one half Stiver the Piece; at least according to the first intent of the Confederate States, it ought to be charged with no more. So that it is an inexcusable Folly, and would be a very prejudicial Exaction to charge the Importer with more than 15 Stivers Convoy mony for 100 Pounds of *Turky*-Yarn brought into this Country to be woven. And it is no less imprudent so greatly to burden raw Silk imported, as if it were of no concern to us, which by winding, throwing, and weaving, is so profitable to this Country. From all which I suppose every one will easily perceive how prejudicial this great Difference is.

Of Raw Silk.

But in all Events, whether for paiment of Convoy-mony, Direction, or Tonnage-mony, or for clearing the Seas, it would be needful for the greater improvement of the Navigation of *Holland*, that all Foreign imported Goods should be less charged than those that come in by Land. Whereas on the contrary we see daily that very many *Levant*, *Italian*, &c. fine Wares are brought in by Land carriage. And how much it concerns our Inhabitants we may easily imagine, when we consider that the Ships built here, are set to Sea victual'd and mann'd, but the Curriers and their Wagons are Foreign, and of no concern to us. And besides, our Merchandize on board Ships is always in our Power, or at least we may convoy and defend them with our Men of War as they go and come, whereas those that go by Land-carriage are in the Lands and Power of other Princes, so that they may at all times make seizure of them.

To increase Navigation, it were needful to charge such Goods as come by Land carriage.

2. All

2. All Ships and Wares, coming out of Countries where our Inhabitants lade not at all, or at least not without paying Duties, ought in proportion to be charged here with as much Impost as our advantagious Situation, and great Consumption can bear: And where ours pay more Impost than is taken in the Country where the foreign Masters of Ships do live, we ought likewise to take as much of them here as was taken of ours. And thus having the Navigation to our selves, we may preserve the same, as also the Passage on the Rivers.

3. All wrought Goods which we can make in this Country, should be charged when imported with so much, and no more than the Traffick may bear. And all Foreign made Goods ought to be charged with more than those made at home, being sold for consumption or wearing, and also the same Goods in passing upon Rivers into other Countries, ought to be charged again so much, as they may not be carried with less Charge thro other Dominions to those Rivers. We are moreover duly to observe, that we ought not to charge any foreign Goods that are to be transported again, whether manufactured or not, so as that our Merchants should find it their Advantage to pass by our Havens, and chuse rather to carry those Goods from one Foreign Country to another, which might perhaps be effected, especially in very coarse Goods, whose Lading and Unlading cost more than ordinary. But the Wares Imported or Exported by the Rivers, we may charge much more, especially all coarse or bulky Goods, which cannot be brought hither by Land:

For

For the Rivers we have under our command. And again, by charging the Goods brought in by Rivers, our Navigation and Traffick is favoured, and the Cities that lie upward have for many Years past bereft the *Netherlandish* Vessels of their Freight on those Rivers, by their Staple Duty. Of which great Hardship we cannot complain with any Reason, while any Cities in *Holland* practise the like.

4. All imported rough Goods, which our Inhabitants are to work up, ought not at all to be charged. But rough Goods, as aforesaid, exported, we ought to charge so much as they can bear. *We ought to ease all imported unwrought Goods, whereof our Manufactures are made;*

5. Goods manufactured in this Country, and exported, ought not at all to be charged. But on the contrary, we should charge all foreign made Goods, either Imported or Exported, as much as may be, without hazarding the loss of that Traffick. *And to ease our own, and charge Outlandish Manufacture.*

As for charging foreign Goods, and manufactur'd Wares, Ships, and Masters of Ships, tho it be a matter of great Weight, yet I know not of any thing that hath been done in it. But the *English*, Anno 1660, settled their Rates of Customs and Convoy-Mony so well, according to these Maxims, to favour their Inhabitants as much as they could, and to burden all foreign Masters of Ships, and Merchants; that if we continue charged in this Country so unreasonably as at present, and there too, and the *English* on the other hand continue to be so favourably used, both here and at home, they will bereave us of much of our Trade, unless the Merchants there under that Government, be for other Occasions oppressed with many and heavy *Which Maxims the English have much better follow'd than we. See their Book of Rates of Tonnage and Poundage.*

heavy Taxes, whereunto Traffick, under Monarchs and Princes, is always wont to be much exposed.

CHAP. XXIII.

That in levying Convoy-mony, we in Holland differ in many particulars from the Means, and in many things have observed them well.

FIRST it is well worthy Observation, that the Inhabitants of *Holland* can trade in no Countrys but by carrying Goods thither, which having sold, and turned into Mony, they convert it into other Goods which they find there, or failing that, return their Money into *Holland* by Exchange. But if such foreign Lands have little or no occasion for our Goods, but afford rich Commodities, then is it evident that we cannot trade with them to any purpose, unless we carry thither Gold and Silver in Coin, or Bullion. And since by consequence every one knows that *Norway*, the *East-Country*, *Smyrna*, *Persia*, *India*, *China*, &c. do afford us infinitely more Merchandize then they take of us, we cannot trade with them but by Gold and Silver; and that moreover, these Provinces, at least that of *Holland*, cannot subsist without the said Traffick. Therefore we cannot enough wonder at the Ignorance, or ill Conduct of the States-General, who by many repeated Placaets in the Years 1606, 1610, 1611, 1612, 1613, 1621, &c. prohibited the exportation of coined or
un-

uncoined Gold and Silver. And tho it may be said, that the said Placaets being well known to be detrimental, had no long duration, yet is it certain that the Scouts, and Advocat Fiscal, did for a long time, nay and sometime still make use of them to molest and disquiet our trading Inhabitants.

But as to what concerns the Freedom and Advantages of Fishery, and the *Eastland* Trade, as also other unwrought Goods imported, they are indifferently well ordered, seeing they pay little or nothing of Duty, either on Import or Export, except that the Owners of the Herring-Busses, to secure themselves against Sea-Robbers, or Pyrats, do yearly at their own Charge, set out seven Ships of War. Which, for a Fishery of so much importance to the Country, is too heavy a Burden, or at least a very great Charge. But foreign Salt imported or exported, is not at all charged. Fish of our own taking, Herring, Wood, Ashes, Pitch, Tarr, Hemp, pay nothing inward, and but very little outward. But Corn, against all reason, pays Duty inward, some more, and some less, and likewise when exported is too much charged.

But the not changing of Fisheries, and the Eastern Trade, is reasonably well ordered.

See the Rates of the Convoy-mony.

But not the Corn-Trade.

If we consider how much must necessarily be gained in this Country, by Owners of Ships, Masters, Mariners, Corn-Porters, Hirers out of Granaries to stow the same, and Corn-shifters, before it is sent by our Merchants into other Countries. We ought in all respects to ease, and be more favourable to our Stores or Staple of Corn, Merchandize, and Fishery, and to keep the Staple of Corn within our Country; that so during bad Seasons, and the Scarcity thereof in other Nations, we may

And how much Holland is concerned in having the Staple of Corn.

have

have it always cheaper with us than in any other Countries, and besides that, we might enjoy many other publick Advantages, which out of so redundant a Treasure as is the Store and Staple of Corn, might in very many Cases and Accidents be improved by wise Magistrates. Whereas on the contrary, if by a imprudent burdening of that Commodity we lose that Staple, this indigent and populous Country would in many Cases, as bad Harvests, and cross Accidents of this World, fall into many extraordinary and unforeseen Inconveniencys. But above all it is to be lamented, that our own Manufactures are so unreasonably charged with Convoy-mony, or Customs, and much more with the Duty of clearing the Seas, but they are chiefly opprest by the Imposition laid on the Consumption: So that the Interest of the Manufactures and Mechanick Works is very ill look'd after. For tho undrest Wool pays but 1 *per Cent* of its worth at Importation, yet certain it is that it pays too little at Exportation. Flax, Silk, and Yarn are also too much charged upon Importation, and no more (against all reason) at Exportation. As to weaving, or to speak plainer, all woven Goods, it is wonderful why we should charge woven Goods, whether Imported or Exported by Sea, or Rivers, foreign as we found, do, or (in respect of their great Value) much more than foreign Commodities, yea (which is a shameful thing) the undrest *English* Cloths are at Importation not charged at all, and the *English* Traders enjoy every way more Freedom, and exemption from Taxes in *Holland*, than even our own Inhabitants.

Th

The Interest of our Husbandmen, or Boors, is also much neglected, for what solid Reason can be given, that the *Holland* Butter exported is double as much charged as that of *Friesland*? Likewise, that all foreign Butter and Cheese may be imported Duty free, but all foreign Cheese exported, is charged with no more than that of *Holland*.

As also our Husbandmen.

But especially we may wonder, that the Rulers of *Holland* could ever find it good to charge all Merchandize, without distinction, at Importation with 1 *per Cent.* and at Exportation with 2 *per Cent.* of its Value. as if it were not enough to subject the Merchant by the rated Convoy-mony, to the Charges, Pains, loss of Time, and Seizures, which must, and will lawfully oftimes happen, and sometimes also to the unjust Vexation and Trouble of many, and delays of the Custom-house Officers, Searchers, Collectors, and Fiscal, whereby many times fit Opportunities of sending away or selling of their Goods are lost so that by the said one and two *per Cent.* of the Value, all Merchandize, even those which ought by all means to be favoured, are so heavily charged, as in the foregoing Chapter is shew'd. And besides, power is given to the said Fiscal and head Customer or Collector, to seize all Goods for their own Use, paying one sixth part more than the Importer values them. Which is a mischievous thing to the Merchant; for in far more remote Countrys (for example, at *Smyrna*, or *Messina*, Grogram Yarn or Silk) Goods being bartered or bought, and not knowing whether those Goods may be damaged in the Voyage or not, and much less whether the same are so bartered

And especially the Interest of Merchants has been much neglected, by paying one and two per Cent upon Goods imported and exported.

Which appears plainest by raw Silk, and Grogram Yarn.

tered or bought in, as to yield Profit or Loss, yet are they bound blindly to rate these Goods. Whereas on the other side, the Fiscal or Collector may take or leave them at their Pleasure. Besides, this one and two *per Cent.* is for the Merchant so great a Charge, and deprives them of so much Profit, that by this alone very many Goods that come from abroad, and will not sell off here, pass by our Country, and are carried to other Ports.

The truth is, when we consider all these heavy burdens upon the Merchandize and Manufactures of *Holland*, and then on the other hand, that we can in no wise subsist long without them, I cannot sufficiently wonder at that Folly; for it is too nice and ticklish a Case to lay any restraints upon the Mouth, through which all Nourishment must pass into the Body. We ought to suspect and be jealous of all things which have any tendency, either to bereave or straiten us of Life, especially seeing we can fail but once, and those that guess at things are apt to mistake. Perhaps it may be said, that Necessity justifies all things, and that the Wars brought a fear upon us of losing both Country and Trade at once. Indeed he that is frighted by Water or Fire, will leap through the Fire, or catch hold of a naked Sword to preserve his Life: But they must be Fools when there is no such Necessity, that will suffer their Bodies to be harm'd by Sword or Fire. That late Puissant neighbouring Enemy, in respect of whom Merchandize was so heavily charged, is (God be praised for his Mercy) so weakned by making War against us, that for eighteen Years together he was necessitated to offer us a Peace that

was

was shameful for him, and glorious for us, before we would grant it him.

And these Provinces, that may be accounted to have been formerly unarmed, in respect of their present condition, as *Groeningen, Friesland, Over-yssel, Guelderland,* &c. have always been able to defend themselves against Foreign Force, were very hardly by dissension among themselves brought to stoop to that mighty Emperor *Charles* the 5th. So that now there is no shadow of Reason to believe that being provided for the most part by the Mony of *Holland* with Fortification, Cannon, Arms, and Ammunition, they are not now able in a profound Peace to defend themselves with their own Force against the Attempts of a weaker Neighbour. On the other hand it is true, that some of them being sensible of their own Power, are not concern'd for the uneasiness of the *Hollanders* by Sea, nor will they contribute a Penny to ease them, but contrary to the Terms of the Union of *Utrecht*, as if that Union were only made against the K. of *Spain*'s Attempts by Land, pretending that all Wars, and Robberys by Sea, ought and may be sufficiently maintained, prevented and defended by Convoy mony, and consequently sufficiently provided for by the Merchants of *Holland*. Whereas nevertheless the said *Holland* Merchants, besides their particular Burdens as Men and Inhabitants, bear all Impositions, whereby *Holland* is not only defended by Land against all Men, but likewise all the other United Inland Provinces: Which in truth hath continued to this day, at the charge of much more Contribution for *Holland*, and much less for the other Provinces,

And we in perfect Peace by Land.

Art. 5, 6. ces, than by virtue of the Union of *Utrecht* they are obliged to. So that it is high time for *Holland* to mind her own Advantage, and discharge her self of all needless Expences for these Provinces, and bestow them on her own defence, whereof she hath every way, and evermore occasion by Land, and especially by Sea. For if in truth that Maxim used by the other Provinces be true, That the Sea must maintain it self, and that consequently all means to clear the Seas, and to regain the Merchants loss after such Plunderings by Foreigners, and Damage sustained by Sea, must cause the Rates of Convoy-mony to be rais'd higher in proportion to that necessity, all which must be fetcht from the Merchant. If so, I say, *Holland* must necessarily decay and fall to ruin, considering that by the Constitution of the Trade at Sea, and the many Countrys about us, not only in the *Sound* and *Channel*, but also by the fundamental Government of *Tunis*, *Tripoli*, and *Algier*, they must be for ever pirated on by Sea. For by this Rule it would follow, that *Holland* should always bear its own Burdens, and those of the other Provinces too by Sea, and so in a time of Peace, as well as War, should also bear most of the Charge by Land. And that the others on their parts should wallow in Idleness and Gluttony with the Wealth of *Holland*.

CHAP.

CHAP. XXIV.

What Professions of the Inhabitants of Holland, ought to be more or less burdened with Taxes, or favoured by the Politick Magistrate.

BUT some will perhaps object against what I have affirmed, that during the time of the late Monarchical Government in these Provinces, and the remainders of it, as also when we waged an Offensive War, and seemed to leave our Navigation as a Prey to the *Dunkirkers*, *Holland* was burdened by Mony taken up at Interest, and other Taxes to the Sum of fifteen Millions yearly; therefore to rid our selves of so great a Burden under a free Government, it was necessary to levy Mony of the Inhabitants by several ways and means. And secondly it may be objected, That when easy or indifferent Levies will not raise Mony enough for securing the Country, and Navigation against any sudden Attempt, then we must find out other ways and methods which at present would be hurtful, but if continued any considerable time, would be mischievous to the State, yea ruin it. And therefore we in *Holland* have very prudentially practised all those and no other means and ways of raising Mony, but such as are now used by the State.

But tho the first Objection be true, yet we may doubt whether the second be so. Therefore I find it good to examine here what Ways or Expedients are fit to be used to procure

But if Holland *by a former misgovernment, must be burdened with a yearly paiment of 15 Millions of Guilders;*

Then no wonder if some hurtful ways of raising Mony have been used, and still be continued.

It will be fit to lay down some method in such Cases of Taxings.

cure Mony in such an Exigence, that so the Reader himself may more exactly judg whether, and when the Magistrates of *Holland* have in this particular taken care of the Welfare of the Land in general, or have been neglective of it. And having expressed the same in as few words as may be, I shall afterwards, because of the general Concernment of the thing, consider more fully, whether all Estates of the Inhabitants of this Country can be equally favoured, and in case they cannot, which of them ought more or less to be cherished and conniv'd at.

Under what beside a fit to be Subject to an Impost.

Namely, seeing all People do naturally endeavour to discharge and free themselves of Burdens, tho even by burdening of others, or when that cannot be fully obtained, then will they seek to ease themselves of that Burden by procuring Partners to bear it: Every one will then immediately judg that we should charge those of Foreign Nations that frequent *Holland*, who are no Members of our Political Body, which we call the State, with all imaginable Taxes, and by all means to ease our own Inhabitants, as being true Members of our own Body. But seeing we have shewn you before, that *Holland* cannot subsist without Commerce and Merchandise with Foreigners, we might by so doing take such Methods as would prevent them from coming into *Holland*, to our great prejudice; and therefore we ought to be very wary and cautious about it, especially considering, that an extraordinary charge upon those Strangers would not much ease us. So that consequently there is no other way, but to bear so great a Burden with as many helpers as we can procure,

procure. And it cannot be denied but we shall procure more Supporters, if we charge all Goods with some Impost that are usually worn or consumed by the People as they are Men and Women.

All Wares that are consumed at home.

And seeing those Imposts which are most freely and spontaneously paid are least offensive and irksom, we should therefore observe this order viz. first and most to charge such Goods as tend to Ease, Pleasure, and Ornament. And then such as no Man can be without, as Meat, Drink, Houling, Firing and Light, seeing Strangers hereby will pay alike with the Inhabitants, and none will be favoured or exempted.

And seeing by all these Means the said Sum of fifteen Millions cannot be levied, we should then afterwards in taxing the People, so charge them, as that all may bear their Parts equally, none excepted. But since this is not practicable, but by taxing all Peoples Estates to make Men pay alike without distinction, or by a blindfold Poll, both which means of raising Mony being so unequal, and full of hardship, do ever cause great distaste among the People. We ought therefore to proceed to the charging of some particular sort of Inhabitants, who bring in no Profit to the Country, but on the contrary live upon the other Inhabitants.

And also all Inhabitants of Holland.

And among them are first all Inhabitants, who from or on behalf of the State, or Citys, open Countrys, drainers of Water, makers of Dykes, have any benefit of Power, Honour, or Reward, more than other Inhabitants. For seeing they may refuse such Offices, Dignities and Employments, to escape those

But especially such as have any publick Imployments and Business of Profit in Holland, excluding others.

those Taxes, and that we need not give them but to such Inhabitants as are qualified for, and petition to have them; no Inhabitant therefore to evade such Taxes, will need to abandon the Country, nor have any reason to complain of a Burden which he annually loadeth himself with; and yet by this Expedient much Mony may be raised for the common good, without burdening any of the other Inhabitants the more.

Next to them should follow such Inhabitants as are Teachers, Artists, and their Instruments, for so much as they are imployed about Matters of Ease, Pleasure, Ornament, &c. that are made use of in this Country. And after these former, all Masters and Journymen of such Trades who live by our own Inhabitants only, such as Bakers, Brewers, sellers of Wine and Fish, butchers, Taylors, Shoemakers, Carpenters, Masons, Smiths, and Glasiers, &c. But in such a case it were needful, for the keeping of our Provision, and to suffer Strangers to live upon us as little as is possible, to charge all their Goods or Manufactures imported into *Holland* for Consumption so high, that our own may go better off than those that are Foreign.

Next would follow some Charge or Tax to be laid upon such Inhabitants as live upon our own Lands, such as are our Husbandmen, Grasiers, and Inland-fishers, for they will hardly forsake us because of our taxing them, seeing they may always be eased in better Times.

And since all these Means of raising Mony will burden none but such as are Inhabitants in this

this Country, and while they find their Maintenance amongst us; it is evident that all the said ways for raising of Mony will excite the Commonalty to Ingenuity, Diligence and Frugality, and then they will be easily born.

But in case all these Expedients will not raise Mony sufficient, we may then charge either ordinarily or extraordinarily all immoveable Goods, Lands and Houses, with yearly Taxes, or by Impositions upon Alienations and Inheritances of them, wherein nevertheless there be those Difficultys, that those Taxes will not be paid with any freedom, but wholly by compulsion. And that the said immoveable Goods being for that end to be valued, that Valuation cannot be made without partiality, and these Burdens will be then very unequally born. Besides, that by the accidental unfruitfulness of the Lands, and standing empty of their Houses, the Owners and Tenants of them wanting a great part of their yearly Rent on which they depend for the maintenance of their Familys, they must necessarily suffer these two unavoidable Inconveniences. But seeing all Owners of immoveable Estates who dwell out of the Land must also help to bear these Burdens, without any prejudice to the Estates of our common Inhabitants, and the Owners of Land that dwell in the Country, are so tied to *Holland* by their immoveable Estates, that they cannot but with great difficulty remove their Habitation to other Countrys: This means therefore of raising Mony, may be used without hurting the State.

Finally, In an extreme necessity of Mony, there may be impos'd a general Tax on all the move-

As also all immoveable Holland Goods.

By Taxes on the moveable and immoveable Goods jointly.

moveable and immoveable Estates of the Inhabitants, whereby they may pay the thousandth, two hundredth, and one hundredth Penny. I say, in an unusual great Necessity, because by these Taxes there would fall a greater hardship upon the common Inhabitants, and damage to the State, than could fall by any other Expedient of this nature, for Foreigners would bear nothing of this, but our Inhabitants only. And seeing the Assessors are wholly ignorant of Mens personal Estates, and what the Inhabitants do owe, or is owing to them, and if they did know the value of them, yet could they not tax them so equally as may be done in the case of immoveable Goods. We may therefore easily see, what by favour and hatred, and by ignorance of the Assessors, especially in the trading Province of *Holland*, where Riches are very transitory and uncertain, that there must be an intolerable inequality in bearing this Tax. Those that would honestly declare their Estates might lighten the Tax, but the fraudulent will unavoidably make it heavier. Besides, many Inhabitants possessing neither immoveable Estates nor Merchandize, but living here on the Interest of their Mony, to elude these heavy Burdens, may remove to some neighbouring Country, to the greater prejudice of this State than if any other of the forementioned Inhabitants should forsake us; for such People frequently drawing their Revenues from other Parts, and spending them here, they gain not by our Inhabitants, but they gain by them. Nevertheless, seeing such Persons as live on their Rents are in respect of the other Inhabitants

but

but few in number, and do not set many People at work for a Livelihood, therefore the said Tax may and can be raised without any remarkable prejudice to the State.

And it is more especially to be observed, that if by reason of all these Taxes many Inhabitants should forsake *Holland* and settle in other Countrys; yet they, or other such Persons, when the Tax after a while should be released, might easily be drawn to return to *Holland*, or others would succeed them out of our own Country, so long as our Manufactories, Fisherys, Traffick, and Freight-Ships remain and flourish amongst us: Seeing they are the four main Pillars by which the Welfare of the Commonalty is supported, and on which the Prosperity of all others depends, tho they earn not their Living immediately by them. This will not be denied, if we rightly apprehend, that many People are brought into our Country that are Strangers, or were formerly Inhabitants, Teachers, Artists, Consumptioners, Tradesmen, and such as live on their Rents, because there are many People here that live, or have lived by Manufactures, Fisherys, Traffick, and Freight-Ships, and do all of them afford Work, or a Livelihood for the other Inhabitants beforementioned. But that on the other side the Manufacturers, Merchants, Fishers, and Owners of Ships let to Freight, will not return from Foreign Lands to these Parts, or be invited hither because there are, or have been in *Holland* many Teachers, Artists, Consumptioners, Tradesmen, and Men that live on their Rents, seeing these do set to work or employ the foresaid People, and have their

We ought to be cautious of weakning the four Pillars of our State, viz. Manufactures, Fisherys, Traffick, and Freight-Ships.

greatest

greatest Profit from Foreign Parts, at least not from these last mentioned People that are Natives.

But supposing the general Necessity of levying Mony to be so great, that we could not raise enough by all the forementioned Taxes, or could not find out any Expedient to raise the same but what were prejudicial, so that to defend the Commonwealth, or preserve our Body Politick against some formidable Enemy, we should be so put to it, as to tax the abovementioned Pillars of the Land, and be pinch'd in our chiefest means of Livelihood for a short time, in hope that such urgent and pressing Necessitys will soon have an end, and that then those Taxes will be taken off, and doing thus, we may both secure our Country, and our Estates: Let us then see what Order we are to take in pursuit of this Method. And in the first place to express my self clearly, by the words *Manufacturers*, and *Fishers*, I understand all such as live by any Trade in or about Fishing, making, transporting, and selling of our *Holland* Manufacturys and Fisherys. And by the word *Traders*, I mean, all such Merchants that sell nothing by retail, but such as trade solely, whether at home or abroad, in all or any Commodities, except *Holland* Manufactures, and Fisherys, and such as depend on them. And by the word *Owners of Ships*, I understand no other Owners than such as set Ships to Sea, either for our own Service, or for other Merchants upon Freight.

And now to come to the matter in hand, we ought well to consider, that we must lay the least Tax upon that means of Subsistance

stance which most concerns us, and which we are apt soonest to lose, and being lost is not easily retrieved, and which might besides draw away with it other Trades or means of Subsistance. So that seeing in *Holland* there are six hundred and fifty thousand Inhabitants who are maintained by Manufactures, and such as depend on them, and those Manufactures are not certainly fixed to us, since we cannot furnish our selves with the unwrought Materials of them from our own Country, but from other Parts, yea the greater part of them being easily carried by Land, may be made, carried, and sold in Foreign upland Countrys. And if this should happen, our Merchants and Owners of Freight-Ships would be oblig'd to remove and betake themselves, either to them, or to the Countrys and Sea-Harbours next to them, and if we should once lose those Manufactures, and that our Merchants and Owners of Ships should go over to another Country which affords those Materials for the making of them, they would probably never return to us. Wherefore it appears that we must charge them little or nothing, and the rather, seeing our Manufactures are already charged with Imposts on the Consumption, much more than our Fisherys, Traffick, and Freight-Ships.

The Manufactures.

And seeing our Fisherys, by the propinquity of the Coasts, where Haddock, Cod, Herring, and Whale are taken, are more fixed to us, and always will be so than to most other Countrys, and that by our over-taxing them, we have neglected and disregarded them, they may possibly return to us again

The Fisherys more.

if we ease their Charge, considering our convenient Situation, whereby it appears that we ought to tax them sooner, and more than our Manufactures. Nevertheless seeing there are four hundred and fifty thousand People employed in the Fisherys, and the loss of the said Fisherys to our Merchants and Owners of Ships, would give them occasion to remove into those Countrys where the said Fisherys might be establish'd: It appears therefore that we ought not inconsiderately to charge our Fisherys too much.

But for as much as it cannot be apprehended, that while *Holland* preserves her Manufactures and Fisheries, she should lose all her Traffick in Foreign Manufactures, Fisherys, and other Merchandize, and that this Traffick does not at most maintain above one hundred and fifty thousand People in *Holland*. It therefore again appears, that we ought sooner, and more to charge those Trafficks than our Manufactures and Fisherys. Yet seeing those Trafficks being removed into other Countrys, our Owners of Ships might first send their Ships thither, and many of themselves follow after. It likewise appears, that we ought to charge that Traffick less than the Owners of Ships.

And seeing the Owners of Freight-Ships inhabiting these Provinces do receive incomparably more advantage from our Inland Manufactures, and our own Fisherys and Trade, than any Foreign Owners of Ships can do, yea, for as much as there be no Supporters of the Countrys Prosperity, but what are Servants to our Manufactures, Fisherys, and Trades. It is not therefore imaginable that we we can lose them so long as we can preserve our Manufactures, Fisherys, and Traffick; so that the said Ships may be charged sooner, and more than Manufactures, Fisherys, and Trafficks. Yet since those Ships lie for Freight in Foreign Countrys, and there raise Mony from Strangers, they may in some measure be esteemed a support of our Prosperity; and since there may possibly be fifty thousand People maintained that way, and that by their being charged too much our own Manufactures, Fisherys, and Traffick, for which we are most concerned, might in some measure come to suffer at long run. We ought not therefore to proceed inconsiderately to the charging of them. Tho we should lose our Freight-ships, yet we should not therefore lose our Manufactures, Fisherys, and Traffick; but on the contrary, by their means, and by lessening the Taxes at any time, the Freight-ships would easily be induced to return to Holland. We know that heretofore in *Flanders*, *Brabant*, and *Holland*, many Inhabitants were maintained by Manufactures, Fisherys, and Traffick, when the *Easterlings* were the only Carriers and Mariners by Sea: As also that the said Owners of Freight-ships were for the most part gradually compelled by our Manufactures, Fisherys, and Traffick, to forsake those *Easterlings*, and to settle in *Holland*. And we still find every day, not only that our Owners of Freight-ships are servicable to the Manufacturers, Fishers, and Traders of other Countrys, and to that end send their Ships from one Harbour to another, to transport their Goods at a price agreed on; but also that there are always Strangers here, who

And the Part-owning of Shipping most of all.

As appears by many Reasons.

for the sake of our Manufactures, Fisheries and Traffick, by reason of some Freedom and Priviledges they have above us, either in their own Country, or in their Voyage, do command out their Ships for Freight amongst us.

So that it being now shewn at large what Estates of our Common Inhabitants ought most or least to be charged with Imposts, in order to levy fifteen Millions of Guilders yearly, we may from the same reasons in some measure calculate upon all occasions which of the Inhabitants ought to be most or least favoured by the Magistracy, and consequently I shou'd finish this Chapter: But seeing the Welfare of the Inhabitants most certainly depends on the good Maxims of the Rulers in that matter, I shall enlarge somewhat more upon of it.

Altho Civil Rulers are very well termed Fathers, and the Subjects their Children, yet some here on is the difference, that Parents do indulge and take equal care of their Children to their utmost power, or at least ought not to favour one to the prejudice of another, and in no case to ruin one Child to provide for others, tho better Children. And that contrariwise the Publick Governours making up with the Generality one Body Politick, which we call the State, must shew more or less Favour, yea Hurt and Ruin, to some who are more or less profitable, or pernicious to the State. As for Instance, those that commit Theft and Murder &c. who are punished with Death or otherwise, for the good of the rest, and to deter them from committing the like Evils.

From

From which it follows; *First*, That all Inhabitants, none excepted, ought to be favoured more than Strangers, as much as is proper. Yet so that none be favoured, who by any Imployment can earn their living by others then fellow Subjects, to the prejudice of those by whom they procure their Bread: Because in such a case it would be foolish, that those who depend upon any thing should be favoured to the prejudice and ruin of that very thing whereon they depend. And besides, it is necessary that we always remember to favour most, and consequently preserve in *Holland* such Inhabitants, who can with more ease than others get their Livings in other Countrys, and transport themselves thither.

Namely, first the things themselves before their Dependencies.

Secondly, It follows by the said Maxims, That all Inhabitants who seek their Profit and Livelihood from other Countrys, ought more to be favoured than those who in this Country live on their Fellow-Inhabitants.

2ly The Foreign before the Inland Traders.

Thirdly, It follows from hence, That such Inhabitants, who by their Gains acquired by Foreign Countrys contribute most to the subsistence of the Inhabitants, and consequently of the State, ought most to be favoured; but with this Caution, That the Master should be more favoured than the Servant; and our Merchants who traffick in our own Manufactures, and Fisherys in Foreign Countrys, above all others who are employed about the making or taking of the same. All which being well considered, it unanswerably appears that the Politick Rulers of *Holland* ought least of all to favour Strangers with any Power or Privilege, and consequently more and more to favour the inhabiting Mechanicks, Masters,

3ly The Masters even before the Servants.

Journeymen, Teachers, Artists, Consumers of any Goods in the Land, Husbandmen, Graziers, Inland-Fishers, such as live on their Estates, Owners of Ships, Merchants, Fishermen, and finally almost all such Inhabitants who are employed about Manufactures spent in Foreign Parts.

And altho' some may object, That the said Advantages and Disadvantages cannot be procur'd or avoided, unless, as abovesaid, the High and Subordinate Government consists of so many Rulers and Magistrates, that none of them could benefit himself to the prejudice of the Community: Yet it is very well known, that any violent Change in the Welfare of the common Inhabitants of *Holland*, would at least much sooner ruin the best and most useful Subjects, than improve them. And consequently it ought to satisfy the lovers of their Country, if the Rulers and Magistrates take so much care that the subordinate Colleges of Polity, Treasury and Justice, about the Manufactures, Fisheries, Trade and owning of Ships, be so formed, that such Persons as are employed therein, be most interested in the Prosperity of Manufactures, Fisheries, Traffick, and Freight-ships, and consequently least in any other way of subsistence; because otherwise every one will to the prejudice of others, tho they ought more to be tendered as more profitable, draw the Water to his own Mill, and lay his Burden on another Man's Shoulders. So that there ought to be among the Directors that are the Superintendents, or have the oversight of Manufactures, at least, as I conceive, four for foreign Consumption, two to oversee the making

king of such Manufactures, one over the Inland-Consumption, and one over the Service depending on those Manufactures. As for Example, Among the Directors for the Woolen Cloth-Trade, there ought to be four Merchants dealing in Cloth, two Clothiers, one Draper, one Dyer or Cloth-worker, &c. Likewise among the Directors concerning our Foreign Fisherys, there ought to be in proportion at least four Merchants that trade in those Commoditys, two over the setting out of the Vessels and causing the Fish to be taken, one over the Inland-Consumption thereof, and one over the Fishing it self. And if the Rulers of these Lands, or any Citys thereof in particular, were inclined for preservation and increase of Traffick in general, to erect a Common Council with Authority to make Statutes and Laws relating thereunto; then such a Council ought to be form'd after this proportion, viz. of twenty four Merchants dealing in *Holland* Manufactures, sixteen Merchants in *Holland* Fisherys, six Merchants in other Commoditys which belong not to our Manufactures and Fisherys, and at most but two Owners of Ships, because such Owners and the Masters of Ships in that quality are for the most part Servants to the others, and depend on them, and without them are of small consideration. And if among the Judges or Commissioners set over the making of Manufactures, Fisherys, Assurances, Maritime Affairs, &c. there should be some interested Persons, it is evident, that in all such Colleges the same proportion ought to be observ'd, that in case Partiality should take place among the Judges, the Loser should at

Fishery.

Especially a College or Merchant-Court for Trade.

Else private Interest will be sought against the common Good.

I 4 least

least have this Comfort in his Misfortune, that his Loss would tend to the benefit of the Community, in advancing Manufactures, Fisheries, Traffick, and Freight-Ships; whereas otherwise the Trouble of seeing himself divested of his Livelihood, and Goods, by undue Orders, and unjust Sentences, and all to the loss and detriment of the Commonwealth, would be intolerable.

And that this may appear not to be spoken at random, let us please to remember that *Ever Thomasse Byvocrt*, of *Horne*, a Ship-master, or the Owner of the Ship called the *Eendracht*, having in the Year 1663, suffered his Vessel laden by the *Turkish* Emperor's Subjects, to be taken for a Prey by some Ships of War belonging to *Malta*, Leghorn, and *Home*, for which they paid him a very great Freight; the said Emperor of *Turky* required of *Lewis Hawards* our Resident at *Constantinople* satisfaction for the same. He by his Faintheartedness, Treachery, or Covetousness, made a promise within three Months and fifteen Days, to pay the Turks seventy eight thousand four hundred and forty five Lion Dollars for Satisfaction; and that the said Sum might the sooner be obtain'd, the said Resident commanded, and thereupon the Consul ordered, that not only all *Holland* Ships set out to Freight should be seized in all the Havens of the *Levant*, which hath some glimpse of Equity in it, but also all the Goods of the Innocent *Holland* Merchants, who were constrained to pay that Money for their Recompence. 'Tis easily imagined that this happened because the Resident and Consul knew that the Directors of the *Levant* Trade living

in

in *Holland*, were mostly concerned in the Ships let out to Freight that use the *Levant*, that it would have been very ill taken by them, and that they might have sat on the Skirts of the Resident and Consul, if their Ships had been seized for that reason. We afterwards saw the strength of this particular Interest clearer in *Holland*. For these Merchants who were unjustly forced to lay down this Mony, and being to be discharged, the said Directors, who give their Advice to the States-General in many Cases, laid down in this particular no Expedient, nor any thing like it, whereby to procure this Mony to the least loss of the Land, or charging themselves or other Owners or Masters of the *Levant* Ships; no, nor to charge themselves together with the Merchants, but on the contrary, have totally freed the said Owners and Masters of the same, and to the greater prejudice of the Country, yea, and the spoil of our Manufactures, charged one *per Cent.* upon all Goods outward and inward, not excepting *Holland* Cloth, raw Silks, and Yarn, making together two *per Cent.* So that the States following their Advice, Traffick and Manufacture will be for so much imprudently charged to perpetuity, since the said oppressive Tax will hardly ever be releas'd. And if we add hereunto, that all other Traffick of the common Inhabitants of the Provinces, that is not under the Tuition or Care of such Directors, being driven into Countries where our Consuls reside, the Masters and Owners of each Ship going or coming in, must pay to the Consul a certain Fee for his Consulage. But that the said Directors of the *Levant* Trade, for as much as they

Who have favoured these freight Ships more than the Holland Manufactures and Traffick,

Bringing the Charge of the Resident and Consuls Avenues, &c. on all our Manufactures and Traffick.

they are Owners of Ships, have caſt that burden from off their own Shoulders, and laid it upon our own Merchants, yea on our Manufactures and all manner of *Levant* Wares, without diſtinction of Clothes, Giogram Yarn, raw Silk, &c. going or coming to or from the *Levant*, to the benefit of the Reſident at *Conſtantinople*, and the Conſuls that reſide in thoſe Havens on the behalf of this State, charging them with 1½ *per Cent*. being together, going and coming, three *per Cent* which upon ſo rich a Trade makes up a Princely Revenue, and Royal Maintenance. And altho the ſaid Reſidents and Conſuls take their Reward of the *Holland Levant* Merchants, and having no other Buſineſs to diſpatch but the Concerns of their Traffick and Navigation, ought to have remembred, that they being only clothed with a Character of the State, the better to effect the ſame, and for no other end, unleſs for Order and Decency, are really and indeed but Miniſters of the *Levant* Merchants, and ſo muſt continue, ſeeing they have at the Port of *Conſtantinople* in effect not any the leaſt buſineſs of State to negotiate, as Peace, War, Alliances, Aſſiſtance, &c. between the reſpective States. Nevertheleſs this ſhadow of their Monarchical Adminiſtration, and aſſuming an Authority, and taking example by the Miniſters of Monarchs, who likewiſe reſide there. adding hereunto, that this too great Income for Citizens of a free Commonwealth, hath all along raiſed in them a Monarchical Pride, and beſides occaſions oft times other heavy Taxes, and continual Quarrels againſt the ſaid *Holland* Merchants, who are not willing nor able to endure ſo chargeable

able and oppressive a Power, which will destroy our important *Levant* Trade in a short time.

Let none object, that all that Mony is not exacted to the Rigor, nor comes into the Residents and Consuls Purse, for they enjoy most of it, and the Factors charge their Principals with it, insomuch that this considerable *Levant* Trade, and our Manufactures depending upon it, by this prejudicial Management of those chargeable Residents and Consuls, and by five *per Cent* unnecessarily charged, and without any reason to favour and clear the Owners and Masters of Ships, tho they cause more Troubles in those Parts than the Merchants themselves, and also in other respects are subject to them, and consequently have more occasion of our Residents and Consuls Advice than our Traders, and are the cause of their much greater Charge.

So that you may see by what I have said, that if the Courts of Justice relating to the Fisheries, Manufactures, Traffick, Insurances, and Maritime Affairs, are no better ordered according to the Maxims of *Holland*'s Prosperity, whereof I know none as yet: Then certainly our Manufactures, Fisheries, and Traffick in this Country, being too little favoured, and too much opprest, and that all concerned therein having any difference with their Labourers, Servants, Messengers, Letter Carriers, Ship-Masters, or Owners of Ships, they have great Reason ever to comply with them, or to fear a mischievous Verdict or Sentence, tho their Cause be Just and Good. For since we cannot bereave Judges of their human Nature, we ought in such Cases

So that we may expect the like Inconveniencies from all other ill reformed Colleges.

Cases to expect that they will take more care for themselves, or their Friends, than for the Publick Good.

And thus by degrees I am come down to matters of Justice about Traffick, whereof I purpose to speak more at large.

CHAP XXV.

The Antient State of Justice in Holland *and* West-Friesland *being related, it is likewise at the same time shewn, that the Laws and Courts of Justice ought to be framed for the most Advantage of Traffick.*

IT is well known that the *German* Emperors drove out of these Lands the *Normans*, and according to their Custom divided the Provinces among twelve or thirteen Lords their Favorites, making one of them the Earl, who, as the Emperors Stadtholder, was to govern this Country, with the Assistance of the said Nobility, without Souldiery. And in case of War, if he and these Noblemen, and common Inhabitants were not able to defend themselves against a foreign Power, he was to be assisted by the Dukes of the adjacent Mark-Lands, who was his superior, and had 12 Earls under him and at his disposal.

These Earls, with consent of the States of the Land, framed and appoint

---

egem Custos limitum eius Provincia. Adst. D.

ed all the Laws or Orders over the whole Province, and their respective Dykegraves, Bailiffs and Schouts, with their Counsellors, Homagers, Judges, and Sheriffs, made all peculiar Laws and Ordinances for the respective Waters in the Country, open Lands, Villages, and Cities, and omitted not in their Laws to express the Punishment and Fines which the Offender was to suffer or pay. And moreover, our Earl had power, with all other Earls, as being chief Judg himself, or by Bailiffs and Judges depending on him, and in his Name, to give Sentence and Judgment between the Inhabitants. It is observable, that all Criminals, who had forfeited their Lives, were to forfeit their Estates also, and that all Confiscations and Fines came to the Earls, or to the Bailiffs and Schouts, who for that end held their Offices by Farm. And to the end that those miserable Subjects might undergo Trial before the Judges that were Parties, we are to take notice, that our Earls following the ungodly Maxims of Monarchical Government in administring Justice, stood much upon the enlarging of their Power and Profit, and but very little on the welfare of the common People; for they empowered these Bailiffs and Schouts, according to their Will and Pleasure, to take cognizance of all Crimes and Offences, whether really committed or not, to favour or prosecute all the Inhabitants, without Appeal to any but the Patron, *viz.* the Earl. And tho it was very necessary for the Gentry, common People, and Citizens, the better to obtain just Sentences, to appoint upon all occasions a very great number of Judges, and to give them a Liberty, with-

Relation made of the State of Justice, as in the times of the Earls of Holland, who were Sovereign Lords.

'Tis shewn how defective and tyrannical it then was,

without respect of Persons, to vote with
Bails or otherwise privately. Or if few Judges were appointed in those Courts and Places
of Justice, with command to vote publickly,
that then at least those Bailiffs, Schouts and
Judges at certain times being complained of,
were obliged to give an account of their Actions before a very great number of them. Yet
our said Earls upon all, yea the most weighty
Occasions, would place no more but here and
there an *Asing*, or five or seven Judges in the
open Country, and about so many Sheriffs or
Aldermen in the Cities; obliging them, whether in Criminal or Civil Causes, ever to deliberate or vote openly in Presence of the
Earl, his Bailiffs or Scouts, and to give no
Account or Reason to any but himself for
what they acted.

By which Form of Justice, the Earls and
their Bailiffs and Schouts might favour or oppress all the Inhabitants, under pretext of
administring that sacred Justice to which they
were sworn. For they could give what Sentence they pleased by reason of the paucity
of Judges, which they were fain to comply
with, if they would hold their annual Employments, and escape the Resentment of
their said Lords. And when at best the said
Earls, Bailiffs, and Schouts did not concern
themselves with the matter in question, if
one of the Parties, whether Plantiff or Defendant, were favour'd or hated by the Judges,
and the other not, then in such Case, * an
upright Sentence was seldom passed.

---

* Quia Favor aut Odium in Judice plus valet quam optima Lex in Codice.

And tho since that time, by the abjuration of the Government of Earls, and especially since the death of the late Stadtholder of *Holland,* the greatest occasion of Favour or Hatred in respect of Judges and Sheriffs, and consequently the greatest occasion of unrighteous Sentences, either in greater or lesser Affairs, was taken away, yet nevertheless the Bailiffs and Schouts in regard of the common People, and especially in Criminal Affairs, hold their former Power and Respect. By which remainder of that Tyrannical Government by Earls, the Inhabitants may be very much oppressed upon this account, because the Judges and *Scheepens* being continued in their former small number may be misled, unless we should suppose them to be devested of their humane Nature, and not to be mov'd by their familiarity with, or hatred of the said Bailiffs and Schouts, or by the Bribes, and Love or Hatred of the Plaintiff or Defendant; and because no further Appeals, or Account is to be given to higher Powers at appointed Times and Places, upon the complaint of any Persons thereunto impowered, and likewise because they are not obliged to suffer any Punishment in case of Error.

What little Amendment hath been for the Publick Good since these times, about Matters relating to Justice.

But because I purpose more especially to consider our Administration of Justice, as it tends to the benefit and increase of our Fishery, Manufactures, Traffick and Freight-Ships, I shall pass over all these common Defects and Faults in other Matters of Justice, and pursue my Aim and Purpose in this only.

But my aim being chiefly at Trade, I shall shew,

Next

Next to the perfect Freedom of the People, and the more or less taxing and favouring the several Trades or Estates of the People of *Holland*, it is necessary that Justice be equally administred against all open Violence which may be afted in the Land, which seeing it would be hurtful, not only to the Merchants of our Manufactures, and Fisherys, and Traders in Foreign Commoditys, together with the Owners of Freight-Ships, but also to other Inhabitants, both Subjects and Rulers, so that no Assembly, or Body of Men whatever, without securing themselves against it, can possibly subsist; there is of antient Times an Order of Justice appointed, tho' very defective. But tho Fraud (whereby we may wrong a Man of his Due as well as by Force) ought not to be less punished, and that Merchandizing depending especially on the Probity of Men, yet by false Deceit may be perfectly ruined; it is therefore to be wondered at, that *Holland* hath been able to preserve its Traffick, as it must here be carried on with so many Laws, or by the help of Laws derived from the Maxims of the Warlike *Roman* Republick, which give the Merchants here an opportunity to gain more by Fraud than by honest Dealing. And on the other hand, here is so little care taken by good Orders and Laws to defend the honest Merchant against the Fraud and Deceit of those who bear the Name of Merchants, and to help them to recover their own; that we may well ask the Reason, Why all the bad People of Foreign Countrys come not into *Holland*, that under pretext of Merchandizing they may openly learn to cheat in the beneficial way now so much practised, and that with impunity? For, * 'tis the Rod makes the Children good. Now to establish some better Order in this, it would seem needful, that none should be suffered to drive any Traffick in *Holland*, till first he hath entered the Place of his Abode in a publick Register, which would have this effect. First, That the Parents and Kindred of the said Merchant, if they have not made a contrary Entry in the same Register within a Year, shall not be allowed by any last Will and Testament, to leave to the said Merchant a less Legacy than without a Will they might, to the prejudice of his Creditors. Moreover, it shall not be lawful for any Merchant, especially a Bankrupt, in any case to refuse any profitable Bequest or Legacy. For this he cannot be supposed to do but in order to defraud his Creditors; and for that reason he ought to be prohibited legally to alienate any Estate, save for a gainful Title, and that he hath receiv'd the Value of it beforehand. I understand hereby, that if he happen to be a Bankrupt afterwards, all his Donations, Conveyances and Portions given for Marriage, or Estates bequeathed or consigned to his Children, ought to be applied to the benefit of his Creditors. For we see here too often the Truth of this *English* Proverb, *Happy is that Son whose Father goes to the Devil.*

And as it ought to be unlawful for a Mer-

What Order might be taken to prevent it.

Which comes in here.

---

* Oderunt peccare mali (quales omnes natura sumus) formidine pœnæ.

chant to endow his Wife with a Marriage Jointure to the prejudice of his Creditors, so ought the Wife to be prohibited to covenant to have her Option of part in Profit or Loss: For there is nothing more rational than that he * who will have the Profit, must bear the Loss. Yea, the Parents, and nearest Kindred of such a Wife, ought to demean themselves in all things in respect of Inheritance, as the Relations of the Husband himself: And excluding Community of Estate, or the bringing in of engaged Estates, they ought to be entred in the publick Register.

The ordinary Register or Books of Accounts of such Merchants who are in Reputation for Honesty, and corroborated by Oath, ought in all respects to be equivalent to any Notars Acts, and nothing ought to be preferred to it except special Mortgage; seeing the Custom of the Country is such, that to prefer Orphans, Rent, or Jointure, &c to be first paid, is prejudicial to Traffick, and consequently to the whole Republick. But if at any time it be found that a Merchant hath falsified his Books or Register, and confirmed them by Perjury, he ought then in all respects to lose his Life as a false Coiner, that all Men may be terrified by so severe a Punishment, not to enrich themselves falsly and treacherously with other Mens Estates, to the prejudice of the Commonwealth.

Yea, it seems to me that Traffick, and the Accounts of a credible Merchant, is of so much concernment, seeing the Constitution of the same is such here, that it neither al-

---

* Quem commoda, eum incommoda sequuntur.

lows

lows or permits of any other Evidence. That therefore upon the said Register alone confirmed by Oath, there ought immediate Execution to be taken as for Mony due to the State. For if Traffick is with us *salus Populi*, the Country's Safety, what reason can there be of not using the like Means (*pari passu*) as the State doth?

It is also very prejudicial, that a Sale should be counted for ready Mony, when after delivery of the Goods the Mony is not immediately paid. For when the Seller gives up his Right of the Goods by trusting of the Buyer, he gives such knavish Buyers great Opportunitys of making great Bankrupts: And he who on the other side by his Imprudence is in the greatest Fault, does afterwards by his unjust Vindication or Prosecution for his Goods, take away the Estate of the other Crditors. *Vindications and Evictions.*

There ought in each City to be at least one particular Court of Justice to decide Matters between Buyer and Seller, that so such Suits may not only be speedily ended, but that the Judges apprehending the way of Trading the better, may give or administer the better Justice and sound Judgment for the Land. Whereas the Merchants now find, that their Suits caused by difference in Accounts, are almost never ended but by Agreement of the Partys when they grow weary of the Law, and that mostly to the benefit of the unrighteous Caviller, according to the Proverb, *The Cavillers are gainers*. *Present Justice by a Court-Merchant is very necessary.*

It is very unreasonable and prejudicial to the Merchant, That the Estate of one deceased should be suffered to have *Beneficium Inven-* *But the Beneficium Inventarii is detrimental, as are Inven-*

Of administring Justice Part I.

Likewise, the Right of making an Inventory of the Estate, when the common Creditors will become his Heirs, * feeing the Creditors muſt bear the loſs if the Eſtate falls ſhort of their Debts, they ought to reap the Profit when there is more. Whereas otherwiſe thoſe unmerciful greedy Heirs by that courſe of Juſtice in the firſt caſe they caſt off the Burden from their own backs, and in the ſecond caſe they carry away the Profit.

Letters of Ceſſion. And no leſs hurtful are Letters of Ceſſion, or Attermination, renouncing the Eſtate, and gaining of Time. And ſince no Perſons are proſecuted by the Publick for particular Debts, it is reaſonably to be preſumed, that the Creditors will not prejudice themſelves by taking over-rigorous Courſes with any Perſon that cannot really pay, but is willing to do it, nor to bereave them of their good Name, and drive them into Extremities. But on the contrary, a diſhoneſt Man having concealed and made over his Eſtate, will enrich himſelf, and ſeek eaſe, by delivering up his whole Eſtate upon a falſe Oath.

On the contrary, it would be profitable for the Commonwealth, if upon the leaſt Complaint of a Debtor's non payment, they ſhould forthwith make him give in Security; or in caſe of refuſal, to keep him and his Books of Account in cloſe Ward. For in caſe he ſhould then ſhew himſelf able to pay, he might ſoon be releaſed upon Security, and being unable, we ſhould be able to prevent

---

* Secundum naturam eſt commoda cujuſque rei eum ſequi, quem ſequentur incommoda.

his running away, and his giving in a false Account of his Debts, and his thievish making over and absconding his Books and Estate. In all such Events, it ought to be lawful to imprison knavish Debtors, with their Wives and adult Children, by Publick Authority, and to keep them in a publick Workhouse, to make them earn their own Bread, according to the Law of *Moses*, and the *Roman* Laws of the Twelve Tables. Yea and in case the wickedness of eminent and great Debtors be aggravated by foul and knavish Circumstances, we ought, according to the Proclamation of the Emperor *Charles* in the Year 1540 to use them as we do Thieves for Burglary, hang them on a Gallows, without suffering in any wise, as now it often happens, that such Bankrupts remain dwelling among us, and continue driving their Traffick under another's Name; according to the Proverb, * *Let him pay with his Person, that cannot pay with his Purse.*

What severe Punishments are necessary against design'd Bankrupts. Viz To deprive them of their Liberty. Exod 22.

Or take away their Lives.

But in case the Bankrupt be fled with his Books and Estate, without the Jurisdiction and reach of *Holland*, and is protected by the Civil Authority of that Place; I should think it convenient for the benefit of *Holland* to proceed thus. First, By virtue of a general Law, all such Persons ought to be prosecuted as publick betrayers of their Country, amounting to as much as † being guilty of High-Treason; the rather, seeing such a villanous Bankrupt hath no less need of help

---

* Qui non habet in ære, luat in pelle.
† Læsæ Majestatis reos.

to carry on his wicked Design, than to betray his Country. At least he cannot so have conceal'd Matters, but that the Accomptants and Cashiers, his Men-servants and Maid-servants must have some knowledg of it; and therefore they ought all of them to be apprehended, and if upon examination it were found that they had assisted in conveying away, with their sh Bankrupts, it were good to examine them upon the Rack more strictly if there were cause of suspicion of the thing, or else upon their Oaths according to the occasion. For if the Rack be of any good use, it must be in cases whereon the Prosperity of the Country depends, and where it's known there must be Aiders and Assisters in such gross Knaverys.

We might also at the same instant publickly proclaim throughout the whole Land, that whosoever hath any Estate of or ows any thing to the Person so fled, should immediately discover it, on pain of being punished as betrayers of their Country, and concealers of that Villany; and all persons should forthwith be examined upon Oath who are suspected to know any thing of it; declaring by promise, That all those who shall uprightly purge themselves should be accounted men of Probity, altho they had formerly assisted in that Wickedness; and if otherwise, they shall at all times be proceeded against and punished as perjured betrayers of their Country, when by a third Person it shall come to be known.

And all such as claim, and pretend to any thing of the Fugitive's Estate, ought also to be oblig'd immediately to lay claim to it upon great Penaltys, whereby two very great Evils would

would be prevented; for seeing * no Man becomes wicked to the highest degree all of a sudden, therefore all such who were lately possessed of the Estate of such Bankrupts, and consequently had not used or imployed it as their own, should immediately bring in the same: The rather that while the Act was fresh, they could not arrive at so exact a knowledg of their Estates and Books as they might afterwards, by the seizing and examination of the Offenders and their Associates And,

2*ly.* All those that pretend to any thing of the Bankrupts Estate, being also ignorant of what might come to be known of his Condition, and whether there were any appearance at any time of compounding with him, should be necessitated to give in their real Debts: Whereas we see now, that all such Estates are grasp'd by dishonest Persons in such a manner, that there is seldom any thing left for the honest Creditors, because People may conceal all Debts with impunity, and on the other side, may enlarge their Pretences after they see the Matter brought to an issue.

This being done, the Bankrupt ought to be summoned in on a certain prefixt Day and Hour, in which time the Creditors ought to have leave absolutely to compound with him, and to stop their Proceedings at Law. But if the Bankrupt neither appears nor agrees, he ought to be hanged *in effigie* on a Gallows, and all his Children Old and Young declared Infamous.

---

* Nemo repentè fit peßimus, aut fuit turpißimus.

By all means must very general Bankrupts would be prevented.

If all these Particulars could take effect immediately upon the fresh Act, and before People could have laid aside the shame of such a new piece of Knavery, I judg it would be of great influence to make Men honester: Whereas now they learn by degrees, That it is better to have other mens Estates than none at all; and * that we can spend another Man's Estate with much more Pleasure than our own. Having overcome all shame, Men can live easier and quieter in an infamous condition than to trouble themselves about Points of Honour, and pay so dear for them too. But seeing in all these Prosecutions the Benefit of the Creditors ought to be aimed at, since it is purely an endeavour to make the most of it for them, therefore they ought to be enabled after that time to agree with their Creditors, and to annul the Sentence, for *fiat Justitia & pereat mundus*, becomes a Judg's Mouth very well; for they not being Sovereigns, are for the sake of their Honour, Oath, and Office, bound to judg by the Laws, and not contrary to them: wherein if they fail, they are in all well ordered Republicks to be complained of, and punished. But the Proverb does not at all become wise Politicians, where *Salus Populi*, and not the Peoples Ruin, must be the supreme or highest Law.

And I have a better note of mens mine with great Bankrupts.

And seeing we ought on the one side to compare these Fugitives, and base and unworthy Cheats, to those vagrant and thievish Drones among the Bees, which by all means ought to be kept out of the Land, or to be pursued and

---

* — Qu'il n'y a c ere, que de gens a l'arriere.

de-

destroyed: so on the contrary we ought to look on all honest Merchants who through want of foresight, by the Injustice or breaking of others, by Storms, Misfortunes, Robberies at Sea, or War, have lost their own Estates, and part of others, and so cannot pay their Debts. I say, we ought to regard them as profitable Bees with compassion, declaring and promising them, that all such Persons, making their Losses appear, and not withdrawing themselves from Justice, shall reserve, and hold to their own use the tenth part of what they had to begin to trade with at first, and not be troubled at all by their former Creditors, and may remain in good Name and Fame with their Children, tho they had enjoyed great Portions or other Gifts, as being a righteous Fruit of their uprightness, and a Comfort in their Adversity. But seeing between these mischievous Thieves, and their Children, and these unfortunate Losers who are much to be lamented, there is no difference either in Punishment or Infamy, it causeth many who otherwise would be honest, through necessity to step out of the honest way, and to take ill Courses. For if Opportunity makes a Thief, Necessity does it much more.

But supposing all useful Laws were made for the Benefit of Traffick and Navigation, and the inferior Judges were well inclined to cause them to be put in execution, nevertheless as things now go in *Holland*, they may for the most part be made of none effect by appealing to a higher Court. For as our Courts of Judicature consist not of above 10 or 12 Judges, so they cannot hear and give

There ought to be given to an honest Bankrupt, a reasonable allowance.

Our Courts of Justice ought to consist of many Counsellors.

Judgment at more than one Bench, and much less have their Understandings exercised to comprehend all Differences that occur, whereby the Suits, because of the great number and trouble of them, remain depending there almost to perpetuity, and at last are all of a very uncertain issue. To redress which it were necessary, that the number of Judges should be so encreased, that for some particular Cases there may be some appointed out of that number, who according to the weightiness of the Causes may bring in and report the same in full Court, to have Sentence pronounced upon them. By these means quicker and better Justice would be administred, not only among the Commonalty, and especially the Merchants, but likewise among all other the more eminent Inhabitants, whether Secular or Ecclesiastic, who might be minded to promote Treason or Sedition, would be deterred by so considerable a Court, that is accountable to none but their lawful Sovereigns, that is, the Assembly of the States of *Holland* and *West-Friesland*, and would carefully watch against such villanous practices as abovementioned, which now, *impunitatis spe*, by the length of Suits, and slow Justice, are but too frequent.

CHAP.

CHAP XXVI.

That it would be very advantageous for the Rulers and People of Holland, *and for Traffick and Commerce, as well as Navigation, to erect Dutch Colonies in Foreign Countries.*

BUT supposing all the Expedients before-mentioned, to attract or allure Foreigners to become Inhabitants of *Holland*, were practised, and those Inhabitants made to subsist by due administration of Justice, yet would there be found in *Holland* many old and new Inhabitants, who for want of Estate and Credit, live very uneasily, and therefore would desire to remove thence. It is evident, first, as to Persons and Estates, that the Inhabitants here are not only exposed to the ordinary Misfortunes of Mankind, of not foreseeing future Events, Weakness, and Want; but besides, they make very uncertain Profit by Manufactures, Fishing, Trading, and Shipping. And on the other side, by Sickness, Wars, Piracies, Rocks, Sands, Storms and Bankrupts, or by the unfaithfulness of their own Masters of Ships, they may lose the greatest part of their Estates, while in the interim they continue charg'd with the natural burdens of *Holland*; as great House-rent, Imposts and Taxes. nor have they any reformed Cloisters to provide creditable Opportunities for discharging themselves by such Losses of maintaining their Children, or according to the Proverb,

In all Countrys there will ever be found many distressed Persons,

This the uncertain Profit, and certain Taxes born by the Inhabitants:

to

to * turn Soldier or Monk; so that by such Accidents falling into extreme Poverty, they consequently lose their Credit and Respect among Men, for to † have been rich is a double Poverty, and nothing is less regarded than a poor Man's Wisdom, in such Cases he would find himself in the most lamentable Condition that can befal a Man in this World.

As to the Changes of Government.

And 2 ly, as to Reputation. It is well known that in this Republick, the Government consists of very few Men in proportion to the number of Inhabitants, and that the said Government is not by Law annexed or restrained to any certain Family, but is open to all the Inhabitants, so that they who have been eight or ten Years Burgers, may be chosen to the Government in most Cities, and have the most eminent Employments of *Scheepen* or Burgomaster. Whence we may infer, That many that are the Ofspring of those that were heretofore made use of in the Government, and also many others, who by reason of their antient Stock, and great Skill in Polity and extraordinary Riches, through natural Self-love and Ambition, conceive themselves wronged, when other new ones of less fitness and Estate, are chosen to the Government before them, and therefore thinking themselves undervalued, seek a Change, and would be induced to transport themselves to other Countries, where their Qualifications, great Estate and Ambition might produce ve-

---

* Desperatio facit Militem aut Monachum.
† Ditem fuisse duplex paupertas.

ry good Effects Whereas on the other side, whilst they continue to dwell in these Lands, they speak ill of the Government and Rulers in particular. And it by this, or any other Accident, Tumults should be occasioned against the Rulers in particular, or the Government it self, they being Persons of Quality, might become the Leaders of the Seditious, who to obtain their end, and to have such Insurrections tend to their Advantage, would not rest till they had displaced and turned out the lawful Rulers, and put themselves in their Places, which is one of the saddest Calamities that can befal the Republick, or Cities. Seeing * Rulers, who became such by Mutiny, are always the Cause of horrible Enormities before they attain the Government, and must commit many Cruelties e'er they can fix themselves on the Bench of Magistracy. *Which Malecontented Inhabitants might occasion great Evil to the Land.*

And seeing we have already made many Conquests of Countries in *India*, and finding how hardly (and that with great Charge of Souldiers) they must be kept; and that the Politicians of old have taught us, that there is no better means, especially for a State which depends on Merchandize and Navigation, to preserve foreign Conquests, than by settling Colonies in them: We may easily conclude that the same Method would be very useful and expedient for our State.

Thirdly, It is well known, that the poorest People of all the Countries round about us, come to dwell in *Holland* in hope of earning *Especially because the poorest People come into Holland from the adjacent Lands.*

---

* Res dura, & Regni novitas me talia cogunt, &c *Virg.*

their

their living by Manufactury, Fisheries, Navigation, and other Trades, or failing that, that they shall have the benefit of Almshouses and Hospitals, where they will be better provided for than in their own Country. And altho in this manner very many poor People have been maintain'd, yet in bad times it could not last long, but thence might easily arise a general Uproar, with the plunder, and subversion of the whole State. To prevent which, and other the like Mischiefs, and to give discontented Persons and Men in straits an open way, the Republicks of *Tyre, Sidon, Carthage, Greece,* and *Rome,* &c. in antient times, having special regard to the true Interest of Republicks, which were perfectly founded on Traffick, or Conquests of Lands, did not neglect to erect many Colonies. Yea even the Kings of *Spain, Portugal,* and *England,* &c. have lately very profitably erected divers Colonies, and continue so doing in remote and uncultivated Countries, which formerly added an incredible Strength to those antient Republicks, and do still to *Spain, Portugal,* and *England,* &c. producing besides their Strength, the greatest Traffick and Navigation. So that it is a wonderful thing that *Holland* having these old and new Examples before their Eyes, and besides by its natural great Wants, and very great Sums of Mony given yearly for Charity to poor Inhabitants, and being yearly prest by so many broken Estates, and want of greater Traffick and Navigation, hath not hitherto made any free Colonies for the Inhabitants of *Holland*, tho we by our Shipping have discovered and navigated many fruitful uninhabited,

habited, and unmanured Countries, where, if Colonies were erected, they might be free, and yet subject to the Lords the States of *Holland*, as all the open Countries, and Cities that have no Votes amongst us are: And it might cause an incredible great and certain Traffick and Navigation with the Inhabitants of *Holland*.

It is well worthy Observation, that these Colonies would no less strengthen the Treasure and Power of the States in Peace and War, than they do those of *Spain*, *Portugal*, and *England*, which during the manifold intestine Dissensions and Revolutions of State have always adhered to their antient Native Country against their Enemies. And by this means also many ambitious and discontented Inhabitants of *Holland* might conveniently, *sub specie honoris*, be gratified, by having some Authority in and about the Government of the said Colonies. But some may object, that heretofore the Rulers of *Holland* in the respective Grants or Charters given to the *East* and *West-India* Companies, have given them alone the Power of navigating their Districts, with exclusion of all other Inhabitants, which extend so far, that out of them the whole World hath now no fruitful uninhabited Lands, where we might erect new Colonies; and that those Districts are so far spread, because our Rulers trusted that the said Companies could and would propagate and advance such Colonies: tho supposing those Colonies must indeed in Speculation be acknowledged singularly profitable for this State, yet nevertheless those respective Districts and Limits, bounds of the said Companies, were purposely extended so far

And yet would have, in case the East *and* West-India *Companies would make use of them,* far by the States General, and especially by the States of *Holland*, effectually to hinder the making of those Colonies, since our Nation is naturally averse to Husbandry, and utterly unfit to plant Colonies, and ever inclined to merchandizing.

To which I answer, That it's likely the first Grants or Charters, both of the *East* and *West*, and their copious Districts, were probably made upon mature deliberation, but that the Rulers perceiving afterwards how very few Countries the said Companies do traffick with, and what a vast many Countries and Sea-Ports in their Districts remain without Traffick or Navigation, they cannot be excused of too great imprudence in that they have, notwithstanding the continuance of such Districts to this day, kept their common trading Inhabitants consisting of so great numbers from those uninhabited Countries by our Companies. So that by reason of the want of trading Countries, or new Colonies in little *Essequebe*, and *Berbines*, the *Hollanders* are necessitated to overstock all Trade and Navigation, and to spoil and ruin them both, to the great prejudice of such Merchants and Owners of Ships on whom it falls, altho *Holland*, during that time of their Trades being overstock'd, had a greater Commerce, and deterred the Traders of other Countries from that Traffick which the *Hollanders* with the first appearance of Gain do, and must reassume, if they will continue to live in *Holland*, where all manner of foreign Trade since the erecting of the said Companies, was necessitated to be driven notwithstanding the uncertainty of Gain, and fear of over-trading our selves.

And

And that the said Companies neither have, nor do endeavour to make new Colonies for the benefit of the Lands, and the Inhabitants thereof, hath hitherto abundantly appeared, and we must not lightly believe that they will do otherwise for the future, which, I suppose, will also appear, if we consider, that the Directors from whom this should proceed, are advanc'd, and privately sworn to promote the benefit of the Subscribers of the respective Companies. So that if the Colonies should not tend to the benefit of the Subscribers in general, we cannot expect the Companies should promote them, yea supposing such Colonies should tend to the greatest profit of the said Subscribers in general, yet such is the common Corruption of Man, that those Plantations should not be erected unless such Directors or Governors can make their own Advantage by them.

But those Companies encline not thereto, because the Directors of them, as the rest, by reap no Profit.

And seeing all new Colonies in unmanured Countries, must for some Years together have Necessaries carried to them till such Plantations can maintain themselves out of their own Product, begin to trade and go to Sea, and then there is some small Duty imposed on the Planters and their Traffick or Navigation, whereby the Undertakers may be reimbursed: Yet the Partners having expended so much, are not assured that their Grant or Lease of Years shall be prolonged and continued to them on the same Terms. Moreover, in regard of these new Colonies, the Directors ought therefore to have less Salary, seeing by this free Trade of the Planters and Inhabitants, they may be eased of the great pains they take about their general Traffick and Equippage of Ships, which

Nor yet the Participants.

L. concerns

concerns them much in particular, for many considerableReasons, not here to be mentioned.

And as concerning our People in the *East* and *West*, they being hitherto of so loose a Life, are so wasteful, expensive, and lazy, that it may thence seem to be concluded, That the Nation of *Holland* is naturally and wholly unfit for new Colonies, yet I dare venture to say it is not so: but certain it is, that the Directors of the said Companies, their Mariners and Souldiers, and likewise their other Servants are hired on such strait-lac'd and severe terms, and they require of them such multitudes of Oaths, importing the Penalty of the loss of all their Wages and Estate, that very few Inhabitants of *Holland*, unless out of mere Necessity, or some poor ignorant slavish-minded and debauched Foreigners, will offer themselves to that hard servitude. It is also true, that all such as are in the *Indies*, especially the *East-Indies*, do find, that not only while they serve, but after they have served their time for which they are bound, they are under an intolerable compulsive Slavery; insomuch, that none can thrive there but their great Officers, who being placed over them, to exact the Oaths of the Mercenaries or Hirelings, and to put in execution the Companies Commands, and being without controul, to accuse or check them, they commonly favour one another, and afterwards coming home with great Treasures, are in fear that they will be seized and confiscated by the Directors. He that will be further convinced hereof, let him but read the following Placaet, or Proclamation, which was, and is yearly to be published at *Batavia*.

THE

THE *Governor General*, and *Council* of *India*, *to all that shall see, hear, or read these Presents, Greeting. Know Ye, That whereas the Directors of the General* Netherlandish *East-India Company settled by Patent, at the Assembly of Seventeen, for divers good Considerations, have found it useful and necessary that the Orders and Proclamations which we do yearly publish, and affix to the usual Place against the time of the Fleet's return to our Native Country, after having first explained the Points therein contained, and enlarged others, by some needful Additions contracted all into one Placaet, and so to publish it to the People, to the end that every one, whether in or out of the Companies Service, travelling to the* Netherlands, *may thereby the sooner and better understand by what Rules he is to govern himself before he leaves this Country. We therefore, in pursuance of that Order, having contracted all the foresaid Orders and Placaets (after previous Elucidation and Amplification, as aforesaid) into one, have found it requisite, now afresh to ordain and appoint, and by these Presents we do ordain and appoint, That all such Persons as intend to sail to the* Netherlands, *of what State, Quality or Condition soever they be, and purpose to have any Claim or Pretence upon the said Company, proceeding from what cause or thing soever, shall be obliged to make the same known, none excepted, or reserved, before their Departure hence, unto Us, or our Committees; that so having heard and examined the same, they may take such order about it as shall be found just and reasonable, upon pain that all those that shall have neglected or omitted the same, shall be taken and held to have had no Acti-*

By the yearly Placaet published at Batavia, it is Ordered,

That all Pretensions on the Company must be first adjusted by the Companies own Servants.

on

... and shall for ever be and ... As likewise none ... in the Netherlands unto the seventeen ... Present Chambers, shall be heard ... either from our special ... shall be granted if the ... nature as is not proper ... in this Country.

... any Defect or Error in ... have lost the same, are to ... Lords Commissio- ... take Cognizance there- ... as becometh. Likewise ... Servants or Freemen that de- ... Salary ... is due to them, are ... Lords Commissioners, ... that it may be signified ... that we may desire ... copy thereof

... or the Company's ... or Condition ... in India, or on their ... of any Accounts pro ... or Monthly Wages, either for ... as a Pawn or Pledge of ... or Debt, to acquire engage, and make ... that the Buyers and Sellers, ... and Transferees, that renounce ... all or any of them, not only lose ... Right and Title to the same, but also the ... Treasures shall be fined thrice as ... the ordering the account so bought or

... out of the Company's Ser... ... India, shall either for ... take with him any Silver or ... coined or uncoined, into his native Country,

ty or keep it by him; much less may he conceal it, by delivering it to Seamen Soldiers, or others, whether here on Shore, or upon the Voyage, or lend it out, or put it to Interest, upon forfeiture of all such Mony to the benefit of the Company, where, and with whomsoever the same shall be found. But such as have Mony to spare, may discharge themselves of it at the Chamber of Accounts, that in conformity to the Letter of Articles, they may receive Bills of Exchange for the same.

That none may carry away thence any Mony to the Netherlands, but deliver it to the Company to receive it by Exchange in Holland.

Every one is therefore hereby forewarned, That those that will make over any Mony to the Netherlands, whether he remains in India, or travels thither, shall beware of taking other Ways, or Courses, than by the said Chamber of Accounts, to the end they may as aforesaid receive it by Exchange; that is to say, by Means or Assistance of any European Nation. and that none remit Mony over to England, or elsewhere, either directly or indirectly, on what Pretence soever, under the Penalty, that such who shall be found doing the same, shall besides the loss of his Imployment and Service, and loss of the Salary which then shall be due, viz if he remains in the Company's Service, he shall further forfeit such Sum as shall be proved he paid, or privately made over to any other European Nation.

Moreover it shall not be allowed for any Person, being in the Company's Service, to depart to the Netherlands, unless he shall have at the least twelve full Months Salary due to him, and that by Original Account, unless he shall have paid the Contents thereof in ready Mony into the Chamber of Accounts here, upon Exchange. to be repaid him by the Company in the Netherlands.

That none may depart thence, unless they have twelve Months wages due to them.

Those that purpose to depart to the Netherlands, shall before such departure from hence, sell all their moveable and immoveable Estates, as Houses, Gardens, Lands, and Pedakkens, none excepted, whether they were sold publickly, or privately, and pay the Proceed thereof into the Chamber of Accounts aforesaid, to be made good in the Netherlands, upon pain that the Offender shall immediately forfeit all his Right to the said Goods to the Company's use.

Likewise those that are entrusted with the Administration and Disposal of any immoveable Estates, whereof the Proprietors are departed hence, shall be bound to sell the said Goods, and turn them into Mony before the departure of the next returning Ships, and to bring the Proceed thereof into the Chamber of Accounts, to receive the same by Exchange as aforesaid, upon pain as aforesaid.

The People that are free, and not in the Company's Service, and disposed to return to the Netherlands, whether single, or with their Families, shall before their departure from Batavia, pay for their Freight and Transportation Mony, at the General Chamber of Accounts as followeth, viz. For all Men and Women, being twelve years of Age and upwards, three hundred Guilders; and those under that Age, one hundred and fifty Guilders. And besides for their Diet, for Men that are accommodated in the Great Cabin, thirty Stivers, those in the Round House, eighteen Stivers, and those before the Mast, nine Stivers per diem. The Women that are above twelve years of Age, and eat in the Cabin, twenty Stivers; in the Round-house, twelve Stivers; and before the Mast, nine Stivers per diem: So that no Person, whether Man or Woman, being either above or under twelve years of Age, Children included, shall pay any less than nine *Stivers* a day. The said *Paiments* shall be made for the time of six *Months*, and accordingly they shall have *Receipts* thereof. But yet under this *Condition* and *Promise*, that if any such *Person* should happen to die in the *Voyage*, there shall be restored at the *East-India Chamber* in the *Netherlands*, whereunto that *Ship* goes consigned, to the right *Heir*, or *Executor*, &c. of the *Deceased*, so much of that *Sum* as shall be in proportion to the *Mony paid*, to be accounted from their departure hence to their death.

And seeing that notwithstanding our repeated *Prohibition*, not only the said free *People*, but even the *Company's Servants*, with their *Wives*, *Widows*, and others that are of their *Family*, do carry over much *Houshold-stuff*, and other bulky *Goods* for their own *Provision*, and other uses, in the *Company's Ships*, and do thereby greatly pester them. All such *Goods* therefore that are no *Merchandize* (seeing they ought in no wise to be carried with them, and that they ought to be seized by the *Company* for their use without any favour shewn, whether they be found out in the *Road*, or on the *Voyage*, or discovered in the *Netherlands*) shall be declared and mentioned by *Inventory* before their departure, and going on *Board*; that after they have been visited and valued by our *Commissioners* thereunto appointed, they may pay for *Freight* at the rate of two thousand *Guilders* for each *Last*, being estimated or rated by *Bulk* or *Weight*; which accordingly is to be paid at the *Chamber of Accounts*. Which *Inventory* being signed by our *Commissioners*, with the *Receipt* of having paid the *Freight*, and being shewed to the *Lords* our *Principals* in the *Netherlands*, such *Goods* being no *Merchandize* as abovesaid, shall be delivered unto him; but upon

That none may carry off any Merchandize, but for Freight of their Houshold-stuff, must pay 2000 Guilders per Last.

pain

152   *The erecting of Colonies*   Part I.

and that all such Goods not mentioned in the Inventory so taken with him, shall be, and remain confiscate to the said Company's Use. All this being intended and spoken of the Company's Servants, for so much as pertains to the Merchandize of six weeks, being three months Wages, which they are allowed to carry with them by the Letter of Articles which they carry along with them.

Natives not to be carried with them.   And for as much as it hath ever been prohibited to carry back into the Netherlands any Black Native Indians, whether Free, or Bond, Men or Women, as the Lords States General have likewise by their Placaat now thought fit to bring the same into their Dominions. We have hereby once again strictly prohibited, and prohibit all Persons to transport any such Native Blacks, whether Men or Women, from this Place, or to conceal them on board Ships, and that (for as much as it may concern the Servants of the Company) upon forfeiture of all the Wages which shall be due to them on their Voyage homeward; and for free Persons, upon pain of forfeiting one thousand Guilders in debts, over and above the Transportation and Diet-money of such Blacks for the Sum before mentioned, which at their arrival in the Netherlands shall by the Master of such Natives be made good to the Company in the said Netherlands; it is ordained also, that besides the former Sums, the said Blacks being willing to return to the Indies, shall pay in the Netherlands the like Sum for Transportation and Diet-money, as before is specified. Provided nevertheless, That in case any one for good Reason should desire to take with him an East-Indian Negroe, his Child or Children, and being granted, such Person shall all be bound to pay into the Chamber of Accounts his Diet-money of 30 Stivers per diem for the time of six

Months,

Chap. 26.   *beneficial to* Holland.   153

Months, allowing her for the same to have her Passage back again gratis *out of the* Netherlands.

And to the end that none may pretend ignorance of any the Premises herein mentioned, we have published this our Ordinance after the Ringing of the Bell at the publick and usual Place. We therefore charge and command the Advocate Fiscal of India, *the Baliff of this City, and all other Officers of Justice, to take care strictly to observe the same, and to proceed against all Offenders and Transgressors without favour, connivance, dissimulation, or forbearance; for we have found the same to tend to the Service of the said Company Given at the Castle of* Batavia *upon the Island of* Java Major, *the* — &c.

So that it is no wonder that so few good, and so many ignorant, lazy, prodigal and vitious People take Service of the *East-India* Company But it is doubly to be admired that any intelligent, frugal, diligent and vertuous People, especially *Hollanders*, unless driven by extreme necessity, should give up themselves to that slavish Servitude.

By this account no Colonies can be made there.

All which being true, let none think it strange, that the Scum of *Holland* and of most other Nations, having by their Service become Freemen there, and yet not permitted to drive any Trade by Sea, or with Foreign People, are very unfit, and have no inclination at all to those forced Colonies, and do always thirst after their own sweet and free Native Countrys of *Holland*. whereas notwithstanding on the contrary, the ingenious, frugal, industrious *Hollanders*, by those Virtues which are almost peculiar to them, are

The Hollanders *are naturally inclined and fit to erect new Colonies.*

more

more fit than any Nation in the World to erect Colonies and to live on them, when they have the Liberty given them to manure them for their own Livelihoods. And those that doubt hereof, let them please to observe, that the *Hollanders*, before and since these two Licensed Companys, even under Foreign Princes, have made very many new Colonies, namely in *Lyfland, Prussia, Brandenburgh, Pomerania, Denmark, Slefwick, France, England, Flanders*, &c. And moreover, have not only manured unfruitful unplanted Lands, but also undertaken the chargeable and hazardous task of draining of Fenlands. And it is observable, that in all the said places, their Butter, Cheese, Fruits and Product of the Earth, are more desired, and esteemed than those of their Neighbours. And if we farther observe, that no Countrys in the World, whether the Land be for breeding, or feeding, are so well ordered as those of our plain Lands in *Holland*, and that no other Boors or Husbandmen do travel so many Countrys as ours do; we shall be convinced, that no Nation under Heaven is so fit for setting up of new Colonies, and manuring of Ground as our People are. And if in our Nation there is also to be found (which however is unjustly and unwisely denied by the opposers of these new *Holland Colonies*) a very great aptness and inclination to Merchandising and Navigation, then we may in all respects believe, that we under our own free Government might erect very excellent Colonies when it shall please the State to begin and encourage the same on good Foundations, and to indulge them for a short time with their Favour and Defence.

Having

Having spoken thus far of the true Political Maxims to be observed concerning the Inhabitants, I shall here conclude the First Part of my Treatise.

The End of the First Part.

The True Interest, and Political Maxims of the Republic of *Holland* and *West-Friezland*.

PART II.

Of the Interest of Holland, in relation to Foreign Princes and States.

CHAP. I.

That an open and free Navigation ought carefully to be kept and defended, against all Pirates and Enemies. How this may be put in practice, and after what manner heretofore it has been done or omitted.

HAVING in the First Part of this Treatise seriously considered and represented the true Interest and Maxims of the Republic of *Holland* and *West-Friezland*, relating to their Affairs at home, I shall now enquire how the Welfare of the Inhabitants may be secur'd with reference to Foreign Powers. And tho very many Particulars

culars do here again present themselves to my Thoughts, which are of weight, and deserve mention; yet I shall lay down but few, and those the most important.

And whereas in the preceding Book I have shewn, that the far greater part of things necessary to our Manufacturers, Fishers and Traders, are imported from Foreign Parts, either upon Carts, and Rivers, or else by Sea in Ships let out to freight, and that they must again transport most of them, manufactur'd or unmanufactur'd, by the same means beyond the Seas. It necessarily follows, that the High-ways, Rivers, and Seas, must by all means be kept free and open, for the constant use and conveniency of the Inhabitants. Yet because the High-ways and Rivers in this respect are of least concernment, and so much in the Power of other Princes, that the securing and clearing the same cannot be expected from the Governors of *Holland*, I shall therefore say nothing more of them. But seeing the Seas are of so great importance to this end, that the Council of State in their Request for a Supply in the Year 1643 did represent, That the whole State of the *United Provinces* depends on the guarding and clearing of the Seas, that other things without this, would be but as a Body without a Soul, and a Land without Inhabitants, &c. And that the *Hollanders* alone do navigate the Seas more, and have more to lose on them, than all their Allys and other People of *Europe* put together. And moreover, seeing the Seas are so common for all Men to navigate, that they are always infested by Pirats and Enemys, and may be and are also cleared by

Aitzma's *Hist.* b 22. p. 463.

Bentivoglio Relat. lib. 1. cap. 7.

our Governors, and free Passage given for Ships and Fishers, and so kept and maintained; I purpose therefore to treat largely and closely of this Matter.

'Tis well known that our Fishers of Haddock, Doggers, Sailers of Busses, and *Greenland* Men, fishing at certain Times and Places, do always meet with Sea-Robbers, and Enemys Ships of War; and that they, and the *Northern* and *Eastland* Ships, yea, and our Salt and Wine-Ships, bringing bulky, cheap, and low-priz'd Goods, are not able to bear the Expence of well manning and arming their Ships to repel such Robbers and Enemys. And tho it cannot be denied, that our *Spanish*, *Italian*, and *Levant* Ships, are often freighted with such rich and profitable Goods, that they may well be so mann'd and arm'd as to defend themselves against the smaller sort of Pirats; yet the Riches which they carry, invite whole Fleets of such Men of War to lie in wait for such Ships; and this falls out the rather, and will always so happen, because the Bassas of *Tripoli*, *Tunis*, and *Algier*, must pay the *Turkish* Janisaries under them out of their own Purses; or if they failed, would certainly be strangled by the mutinous Souldiery. So that to procure that necessary pay, they always collect by force of Arms, the fifth part of the growth of the Country, and permit them to go to Sea as Free-booters, with condition to allow them the Moiety of all the Ships, and the eighth part of all the Goods they take in the same.

This being certain, it follows naturally, that the *North*, *Belt*, and *North* Sea, as also so the Channel being continually fished and navigated by vast numbers of our unarm'd and undefensible Ships, ought of necessity to be wholly freed from such Robbers and Enemies by our Governours. *Therefore we must necessarily scour the North Sea from Pirates,* And because the great *Spanish* and *Mediterranean* Seas are likewise navigated by few rich Ships of Force, it is by all means advisable to Convoy our said Merchant Ships with Ships of War to defend them from those *Turkish* Pirates; but it would by no means be convenient to free the *Mediterranean* of them, for we should thereby reap no more Profit than the *East-landers*, *English*, *Spanish*, and *Italians* do, who by that means, and other Advantages, might easily deprive us of our Traffick and freight Ships, and possibly drive us out of our whole Navigation, because the greatest *Eastern* Traffick depends on the Consumption of the *Eastern* Commodities in the *Western* Parts. *And keep the Mediterranean clean by Convoys.* all which Nations nevertheless through want of ordinary Convoy-ships, do not traffick so much in those Parts as we do, and would trade less if it were ordered that none of the Captains of our Convoy-Ships should take Mony to protect and defend any foreign Merchant Ships under their Convoy, or suffer them to sail in their Company: so that if we should leave this thorn of the *Turkish* Pirates in their Sides, they will be sufficiently distress'd both in that and all their other Trade, whilst we by those ordinary Convoy Ships of War, may wholly engross all the *European* Traffick and Navigation to *Holland*.

Having thus represented how necessary it is to keep the Seas open and free for the Inhabitants of *Holland*, and endeavouring now to find

find out the means whereby it may certainly be effected, this infallible political Maxim offers it self to my Thoughts, *viz.* When Men would procure or hinder the doing of a thing, the matter must be so ordered, that such People who are so resolved, may have sufficient Authority, Power, and Strength to effect or obstruct the same. Whence it unanswerably follows, that seeing our Inhabitants, who live by Manufactures, Fisheries, Traffick, and Shipping let to Freight, and which are or may be taken at Sea by Enemies, are certainly willing to defend themselves from such Losses, they ought therefore to have such Authority and Strength as may enable them to clear the said Seas. But because every one knows, that such abstracted Speculations, and general reasonings in well grounded Political Governments, neither may nor can be practised, let the Reader therefore please to take notice, that I use this infallible political Maxim, only to build a second upon it, namely, That such Cities and Countries whose Rulers ought to be presumed to be less or more inclined to clear the Seas, ought also to have more or less Authority and Power in the Polity, Treasure, Justice, and Militia relating to the Seas. And seeing Kings, Princes, Courtiers, and Souldiers are frequently Gainers, but never losers by Goods pirated at Sea, and reap the least Advantages by an open and free Navigation: And on the contrary, most of the Inhabitants of the free Republick of *Holland*, whether Rulers or Subjects, may suffer great Losses by robberies at Sea, and subsist by the flourishing of Manufactures, Fisheries, Trade, and Freight-ships; we may well conclude, that such Governour vernours must be presumed to be well inclined to keep the Seas clear, and consequently ought to be entrusted with all that Power and Authority which is necessary to effect it, either by themselves or their Commissioners.

And tho in pursuance of this Position it seems requisite to shew in what manner this ought to be done in every City of *Holland*, and jointly in a way suted to the States Assembly, I shall nevertheless (partly because it requires more knowledg than I am master of, and partly because I would avoid the great Labour and Odium which might ensue) only touch on the several ways by which Men formerly endeavoured in *Holland* to clear the Seas, and whether the Inhabitants by building on the said Foundations, or by departing from them, have gained more or less.

Whereas before the Year of our Lord 1300, the Cities of *Holland* were few and small, the Government, and consequently the clearing of the Seas depending chiefly on the Earl and Gentry, who were little concern'd in things of this Nature, and if they had attempted it, must have done it at their own Cost and Charges, we find little thereof in their antient Records, and therefore may safely believe, that the *Hollanders* at that time never undertook the guarding or clearing of the Seas. *This Maxim is confirmed, not only by Reason, but by Experience for before 1300, our Earls and Gentis neglected Navigation.*

But the Cities of *Holland* soon after, by the removal of the *Flemish* and *Braband* Manufactures, increasing daily both in greatness and number, and the Inhabitants by that means growing to be much concerned in the free use of the Sea, and perceiving that the Earl and Gentry neglected to defend or protect them *But after the Cities were concern'd in it, they took it to Heart, under the mad Earl (so called.)*

then from Piracy, they agreed with Duke *Albert* of *Bavaria*, as Stadtholder for *William* Earl of *Holland*, for leave to scour the Seas themselves, and to lay that Charge on the Country. And in the Year 1408, when the Seas were infested by certain *East-Friesland* Pirates, those of *Amsterdam*, and some of the Cities of *North-Holland*, with the Assistance of the *Lubeckers*, *Hamburgers*, and *Campeners*, suppressed those Robbers.

Soon after this the *Hollanders* being greatly annoyed by the *Flemish* Rovers, complained to Count *William*, yet we read not that he did any thing to prevent it, but sent them away with this Answer, Go you to Sea too, and let others complain of you. The *Hollanders* accordingly went to Sea, and did more hurt to the *Flemings* than they had suffered by them, whereupon these Sea-robberies soon ceased. We read also that about 30 Years after, in the time of *Philip* of *Burgundy*, Earl of *Holland*, the *Hollanders* lost to the Value of fifty thousand Guilders by the *Easterlings* upon the Seas, and could obtain no Satisfaction or Compensation, which caused the Cities of *Dort*, *Harlem*, *Amsterdam*, *Gouda*, *Rotterdam*, *Horne*, *Enchuysen*, *Middleburgh*, *Veer*, *Flushing*, and *Armuyden*, to set out many Ships to Sea; with which having beaten the *Easterlings* twice, and taken great Riches, they obtained of them in the Year 1441, a very advantageous Peace, and also of their Allies the *Spaniards*, *Venetians* and *Prussians*, the other *Netherland* Provinces who were also under the subjection of *Philip* of *Burgundy*, not concerning themselves in these matters. And it is also true, that the *Hollanders* and *Zelanders* in the

Year

Year 1464, endeavoured without *Philip's* Consent, to surprize the famous Pirate *Ru-* Phil. de Co-*bempre*, who infested their Coast with his munes. Robberies And it is observable that no Convoy-mony was in those times ever required of the Merchant for clearing the Seas, but the Expence was born by the Country, or by the Earls themselves, and was constantly deducted from the Subsidies granted to him; nor were there any other except the ordinary Judges to determine of matters concerning Prizes and Goods taken.

All which, except the last, remained constantly in use in the times of the Earls, who were of the House of *Austria*, for the *Eastern* Cities in the Year 1510, making War against J. F. le Petit. the King of *Denmark*, prohibited the *Hol-* Cronique. *landers*, *Zelanders*, and *Frieslanders*, to trade in those Countries, who not complying, and the *Eastlanders* thereupon taking eight *Holland* Ships, the Province of *Holland* alone fell into an open War with them, which the other *Netherland* Provinces took so little notice of, that the *Easterlings* having at several times during the War taken fifty *Holland* Ships, went to sell some of their Prizes even in *Zeland* and *Flanders*. And tho they were sued there by the Owners, and the Goods restored by the Admiralties as unlawful Prizes, yet 'tis evident that this was obtained rather on the account of Favour than Justice.

The Emperor *Charles* the 5th, in the Year Emp. Charles V. 1531. having recommended Queen *Mary* of Borre, lib. 21 *Hungary* his Sister to the Government of the p. 7. *Netherlands*, and chosen a good Council of State for her, caused these words to be inserted in their Instructions " That they should
M 2 " con-

"continue to the Cities their former Customs,
"that in time of Need, and when matters
"can suffer no delay, they may set out Ships
"of War at the Charge of the Country,
"that so they may resist all Pirates and such
"like Enemies of the Commonwealth, and
"take and make prize of them, provided
"that the Punishment be left to the Judg-
"ment of the Admiralty. Whereupon in
the Year 1532, it hapned, That the *Hollanders*, by Order of the said Emperor, as
Earl of *Holland*, put certain Ships into the
hands of his Brother-in-law *Christiernus* of
Denmark, in order to recover his Kingdom,
from which he had been expell'd. Upon this
the *Easterlings* forbidding all *Holland* Ships to
pass the *Sound*, caus'd great Poverty in *Amsterdam*, and the Northern Quarter, without
redress from the Emperor, or any other Province, till the *Lubeckers*, in the following
Year, taking a Ship of *Edam* upon the Coast
of *Zeland*, the *Amsterdammers*, to whom the
Lading belonged, complained at the Court of
Brussels, and obtained a general seizure of all
the Ships and Goods belonging to the *Lubeckers* and *Hamburgers*, that were to be found in
these *Netherlands*. For seeing, notwithstanding the Wars with *Holland*, they continually
kept their Traffick going in *Brabant* and *Flanders*, they by this seizure suffered so great a
Loss, that immediately a Peace was clap'd
up, yet with this Condition, that the *Hollanders* should not assist King *Christiernus*, nor
during the War use his Havens of *Norway*.

By all this we may easily perceive how slen-
derly the free Navigation was then defended
or secured, and things will never be better

in *Holland* whilst Courtiers have any Command there. On the other side, we may also see what singular Care the States of *Holland* took on the 26th of *August* 1547. and would always take for a free Navigation whensoever that Matter should be intrusted to them, for tho their Condition was then low, and the times peaceable, yet they fitted out eight Ships of War for the defence of our Herring Fishery, and for their paiment established that Tax which is called the *Great Impost*. And even in the time of that Tyrant King *Philip* the 2d, it is evident by the Advice of the Provincial Court to those of the Secret Council, relating to the Admiralty, " That " pursuant to the Privileges, Judgments, and " antient Customs, the Stadtholders of *Hol-* " *land* used to take cognizance of all Matters " pertaining to the Admiralty, and are sub- " ject to no other Admiral; and that the " Placaet transmitted by *Adolph* of *Burgundy* " ought not to take place, till the Stadthol- " der and States of *Holland* were first heard " concerning it; and that all the Power gi- " ven by the same Placaet ought to be attri- " buted to the Stadtholder, and that Count " *Horn* being appointed Admiral-General " of the *Netherlands* by the King of *Spain*, an- " swered thereupon in the Year 1562. That " he desired first to see the forenamed Pri- " vileges, and then would give his further " answer thereunto.

But during the Troubles which soon after followed, this Affair took quite another course. For Count *Horn* the Admiral-General being beheaded, and Prince *William* of *Orange* as Stadtholder of *Holland*, *Zealand* and *Utrecht*,

Semein's Herring Fishery.

King Philip 2d

P. William took care to scour the Seas, because he could not subsist but by the

Utrecht, being in the Year 1568. banish'd the Country, and knowing no Expedient to raise Men and Mony in order to his return, made use of his own Authority, *Anno* 1569 and as Admiral-General gave out Commissions to take all *Swedish* and other Ships that sailed without his Commission. And afterwards in *July* 1572 obtained liberty of the States of *Holland* to appoint a Lieutenant Admiral, who by the Advice and Approbation of the Maritime Towns, should make choice of the Captains of the Ships of War. And moreover obtained leave to constitute Commissioners to take cognizance of Maritime Affairs, who were to receive the 10*th* part of all the Prizes for the Commonwealth, and the 5*th* of that 10*th* part for the Admiral General.

Whereupon in *Octob.* of that same Year, the first Dutys of Customs were introduced in *Zealand*, the Government there prohibiting, upon pain of Confiscation, all transporting of Goods to and from the Enemys Countrys, unless they paid for each Species as much Duty as they could in any measure bear without the loss of their Trade. In the next Year and Month of *April*, this was imitated, and practised by those of *Holland*. And being thus begun, in order to distress the Enemy and weaken the *Antwerpers*, as well as to increase the Trade and Navigation of *Holland* and *Zealand*, it yielded in Custom the first year eight hundred and fifty thousand Guilders. And this pleased them so in that great necessity of Mony for their common and necessary Defence, that soon after they found it expedient to charge all Goods exported or imported to and from neutral places, sailing out or com-

coming into these Countrys, with Convoy-mony. And tho this tended to the extreme prejudice of the Trade and Navigation of *Holland*, yet there was no Remedy, partly because all *Holland* would otherwise have been conquered by the *Spanish* Forces, and partly because by the Pacification of *Gent, Anno* 1576 Customs or Licence-mony was to cease, whereby the *Antwerpers* were most of all burdened with Convoy-mony.

 In the mean time Pr. *William* had on *July* 11, 1575. procured a Power of the States of *Holland* during the War with *Spain*, either in the King's Name, or his own, to command or prohibit any thing as he thought good, both in Polity, Contribution or War, by Water or Land: And on the 25th of *April* 1576. by the Union of *Holland* with *Zealand*, he there obtained the like Authority On the 22d of *Sept*. in the Year 1576. the College of Admiralty of *Zealand* was erected, where one *Holland* and six *Zealand* Counsellors were to determine by the plurality of Voices all matters that might occur, yet so, that the Lieutenant Admiral of *Zealand* should be obliged to obey the said Prince or his Lieutenant Governour Count *Hohenlo* in all things. Which Orders were continued both in *Holland* and *Zealand* to the Year 1584. without any great prejudice to the Inhabitants. For tho the Prosperity of the Country, and clearing of the Seas from Enemies depended merely on the care and will of one only Person, and that there was no reason to expect they should be employed to the Advantage of the People, but so long (and no longer) than it agreed with that Person's own Benefit, and tended to the augmentation

P. Borre, B. 8. pag. 119.

Book 9. pag. 138.

B. 9. pag. 154.

cution of his Power. Yet the People of Holland and Zealand were then very fortunate, hereto, all the Netherlandish Havens revolting from the King, we being still permitted to drive our Trade with Spain, and very few Pyracies being committed: And besides, the said Prince could not attend, support, and augment his own private Interests and Grandeur against that great and formidable Power of Spain, both in conjunction with the Prosperity of those despised small Countrys, and their poor Inhabitants, which on that account he endeavoured to promote.

Notwithstanding which, after the death of the said Prince *William*, the States of *Holland* and *Zealand* thought not fit that the property of the Land, and clearing of the Seas should be wholly in the hands of one single Person. For tho they did on the first of *November Anno* 1585. make his Son *Maurice* Stadtholder of *Holland* and *Zealand*, and consequently also Admiral of the said Countrys; yet they limited him by his Commission and Instructions, commanding him to execute all Affairs relating to War and Polity with Advice and Consent of the Gentry and Council of the said Countrys, who were to assist his Excellency, and also to consent to such further Instructions as should be given him. And besides, on the first of *Feb.* 1586 they placed *Robert Dudly* Earl of *Leicester* above him, as Governour, Captain, and Admiral-General; to whom they added the Council of State, with Instructions importing among other things, Artic. 12 and 13. That,

" The Mony proceeding from Convoys
" shall be every where equally levied, and
" the

" the Charges of such Convoys first paid with
" the cost of equipping the Ships of War,
" and all that belongs to them, as they were
" design'd and originally appointed, and that
" the said Convoy-mony shall not be imploy-
" ed to any other use than for paiment of the
" said Charge, and setting out the said Ships
" of War; for which end also shall be added
" whatever Sums shall proceed from Prizes,
" and Customs, in case his Excellency shall at
" any time think fit, pursuant to the Act of
" Consent agreed on by the States General,
" in relation to the matter of Contributi-
" on.

" Nevertheless, the Citys have and shall
" continue to have the liberty (as often as
" shall be found necessary) and when the
" Matter can bear no delay, to arm themselves
" for the Sea, and set out Ships of War at the
" Cost and Charge of the Country, against
" Pirats and other Enemies of the Common-
" wealth, to withstand, take and seize them,
" provided the Cognizance and Punishment
" of such Crimes, with the Ships and Goods so
" taken, be left to the decision and disposal
" of the Admiralty, which his Excellency
" shall chuse and commissionate out of the
" Provinces that subsist by Maritime Traf- *Placet Book*
" fick *P. 532.*

Moreover the said Governour and Captain-
General declared on the 30th of *April* of the
same Year by Placaet touching the paiment
of Convoy and Custom,

" That the States General of the *United*
" *Provinces* of the *Netherlands*, to support the
" charge of setting out such Ships of War
" as are necessary for the defence and security
" of

"of the foresaid *United Provinces*, have con-
"sented, given and put into his hands, the
"produce of certain Impositions, and publick
"Revenues, which they have consented to
"be given, and received for Convoy, upon
"Goods imported into and exported out of
"these said Countrys, according to the Book
"of Rates already made or to be made
"as also the Profits and Sums which we
"may levy upon Merchandize, that under
"the Title of Licence, or safe Conduct may
"be permitted to be carried to the Havens
"and Places of the Enemies Jurisdiction.

But the Earl of *Leicester* was not so irreconcilable to *Spain* as the Prince of *Orange*, and relying on the Power of the *English* designed to defend these Countrys against *Spain*, and then to divide and share the whole 17 Provinces with the Prince of *Parma*, whom he had tempted to comply; well knowing that if the worst should happen, he could return to *England* and live upon his own Estate. So that the defects of this Order soon appeared, and the too great Authority in Maritime Affairs was entrusted to a Person who was not sufficiently concerned for the Prosperity of Holland's Navigation, and who to establish his Tyrannical Power with the *English* of his Faction about him, favoured Strangers and Foreigners, more than the Natives of *Holland*. For about two Months after, he prohibited by publick Proclamation, not only our Navigation to *Spain*, and all the Enemies Countrys, but even to carry to neutral places all Provisions and Ammunition of War, whatever is necessary for Shipping. He also strictly prohibited the sending of any kind of Merchandize out

Chap. 1. *the Seas from Pirates.* 171

of these Countrys by the *Maze, Rhine,* &c. or by Sea, on this side of *Roven* and *Bremen*; notwithstanding the States of *Holland* and *Zealand* earnestly represented to him how much this would tend to the Benefit of all adjacent Foreign Countrys, and in particular of *England*, and to the great detriment of our own Inhabitants. So that if this Earl of *Leicester* had not the next year after been necessitated to depart out of these Countrys to *England*, by the Courage and Resolution of the States of *Holland*, and there, by Command of Queen *Elizabeth*, to deliver up his Commission of Governour, Captain, and Admiral-General, these Countrys had been utterly ruined.

Prince *Maurice* had almost the same Powers conferred on him nominally, but the whole management was really in the States of the several Provinces, and Governours of the Maritim Citys during his Youth. In which time the Affairs of the Sea were so well look'd after, that in our Historys we read of very few, or no Sea-Robberys, till the Month of *June* in the Year 1595 when some *Holland* Ships of War that were lying on the Watch before *Dunkirk*, and about the *Maes*, were commanded away to *France* by the Prince (who was then at the Age of 28 years) to bring over the old Princess of *Orange*. The *Dunkirkers* taking that opportunity, took many of our Herring Busses, and Merchantmen, for the most part before our own Ports. And altho the Admiraltys, especially those of *Amstredam* and *Horn*, complained of this ill Court-Government at the *Hague* to the Committee of Council and Deputys at their General Assem-

After his departure, that care, in regard of Pr. Maurice's Minority, was devolv'd on the States and Cities concern'd therein.

P. Borre, book 32. fol. 38
In 1593, we began, for the Princes Pleasure, to neglect the Seafaring Inhabitants.

sembly, and above all others had the greatest Reason to complain of Prince *Maurice*, at whose pleasure our good People that live by Trade and Fishery, were left for a Prey; yet durst they not blame him for it, but only desired to have better Orders kept for the future. But the dread of this Prince, increasing with his Years, was already become so great, that in lieu of better Orders, his Favorites under that Pretext obtain'd an Order, whereby the Authority and Power of those *Holland Cities* that had suffered most, and must still suffer in time to come, were curb'd and broken, and on the other side, the Authority and Power of the *Generality*, and especially of the Prince, who are little or not at all affected by Losses at Sea, was greatly increased. For in the year 1597. Prince *Maurice*, the States General, and the five Admiralties agreed on an Order, which for the most part is still in being, pretending it would be an Expedient for the better management and executing the Affairs of the Admiralty and its Dependances. But because Kings and Princes, and Inland Provinces, never use to consider the Guard of the Sea, but always to neglect it, unless they fear that for want of a free Navigation they cannot subsist on the Land, the mischief of this Order was soon discovered, for by it Prince *Maurice* (being now at the Age of 30, and conceiving that these Countrys were brought into such a Condition, that they could very well subsist against the Power of *Spain*) had Power to do all things, since no Persons without his Commission could set out any Ships of War against Pirates or other Enemys, and that he could

make

make choice of all Captains and **Superior** Officers to command the Ships of the States, out of a double List laid before him, and indeed without it; and besides, might sit as Admiral General, and his Lieutenant-Admiral of *Holland* and *Zealand*, or *Friezland*, in all or any of those Admiraltys, and vote at the upper end of the Board to direct all Affairs relating to the Treasury, Justice and War, as well as the Sea.

The Prince of Orange, and the Inland Provinces, tho little or nothing concern'd, were vested with a Power in Sea Affairs.

And moreover the Inland Provinces, whom the Navigation concerned not at all, obtain'd nevertheless by that Order a right of Electing from among themselves; *viz. Guelderland* three, *Utrecht* two, and *Over-yssel* likewise two Commissioners for the Affairs of the Admiralty: And *Holland*, which alone frequents the Sea ten times more than *Zealand*, *Friesland*, and *Groningen*, must by that Rule permit in all their three Admiralties, that to their four Commissioners, three out of the other Provinces be added, *Holland* in lieu thereof only having the privilege of chusing one Commissioner to the Admiralty of *Friesland*, which Admiralty for want of ordinary Revenue doth not use to set out any Ships for clearing the Seas, even in time of the greatest general Necessity, and consequently could avail them nothing. For tho the Province of *Zealand* frequent the Sea more than *Friesland*, and therefore by its Revenue can set out Ships of War; and supposing *Holland* might send two Commissioners of Admiralty thither, yet would it not tend to the Benefit of *Holland*, seeing the States of *Zealand*, with whom Prince *Maurice* could do what he pleased, when he should in earnest advise them

them to it, cannot now be moved by the States of *Holland*, and of the other Provinces, to range themselves in that Order with *Holland*. But the *Zealanders* will continually govern all Affairs at Land and Sea by their seven Commissioners, assuming the Name of *Commissioners of the Admiralty*, when two Commissioners out of *Holland*, one for *Utrecht*, and one for *Groningen* are joined with them. So that these seven Commissioners of *Zealand*, with the additional Power of the States of *Zealand*, as also by their former separate Assembly and Deliberation, do often exclude the other Commissioners from all Matters; and thereby always so easily overvote them, that they can do no service for the common Good and for *Holland*, but when it pleaseth the *Zealanders*. And before they may serve, or take the Charge of their Offices in the respective Admiralties as Commissioners, those that are so elected must receive their Commissions of the States General, and there make Oath, as well as the Receivers General of the respective Quarters, Fiscals, Secretarys, Head-Commissioners, Collectors and Comptrollers, who nevertheless being nominated by the respective Admiralties, are chosen by the States General out of a double number. But the respective Admiralties do each in their Quarters absolutely dispose of the Offices of the Equipage-Master, and Vendu-Master, Doorkeepers, Messengers and Searchers, &c.

And moreover by these new Orders, *Comptoirs* or Offices were erected, as well in the Inland Provinces, as in the other, and on the Rivers and Inlets of the Sea, in all those Countrys that have no Vote to receive Mony for Convoy and Custom of all Goods going to and from *Holland*, and other *United Provinces* situate on the Sea, and that by Officers and License-Masters depending on the said States General, or the respective Admiralties. So that tho the Inhabitants of *Holland* paid seven parts of eight of all Customs and Convoy mony, which used to be imployed for the Service of *Holland*, or at least at the Pleasure of that Province alone, yet since that Order they are all nevertheless made subject to the Admiraltys, or to the States General, where *Holland* hath but one Vote; or to the other Provinces, where *Holland* hath no Vote. Of all which Revenues, and of extraordinary Subsidies, the Admiralties are not bound to give account to the States of the Provinces wherein they reside, but to the States General, among whom there are so many Persons unconcern'd, and besides, considering the Deficiency of those from whom they have their Commissions, in bringing in their Quota's or Shares of Mony, it must be presumed that they will always keep none of the best Accounts against themselves, and consequently are unfit to keep other Colleges so under the Bridle, and especially consisting of so few as seven Persons, they may enrich themselves with the Publick Mony, and be able to play at the Game of *hodie mihi cras tibi*.

Yet have they obtained a great Power of Direction about the Maritime Affairs of Holland.

On the other side, *Zealand* holding all its Administrative Power of Maritime Affairs within it self, sent nevertheless into all Admiralties one Commissioner, who was to continue there during Life, with the Triennial Commissioners of *Holland*, by that long continuance

tinuance or perpetuity, subtilly to encourage the *Hollanders* to assist them in managing all Maritime Affairs according to their particular Interest. Therefore that this new Order might not be too offensive to *Holland*, it was proposed by the States General, and Prince *Maurice of Orange*, that it should take place but for a Year, without any intention of prejudicing the Provinces in general, or any of the Provinces, Citys, or Members in particular, or creating to themselves any new Power, tho all Men might easily imagine, that the Power of the States General, and Prince of *Orange*, being sufficient to introduce this Order for a Year, would be also sufficient to continue the same so long as it tended to their profit.

And indeed we have found by the continuation of this Order, that the States General, or the other Provinces, together with the Admiralties that were out of *Holland*, have done very little towards the Guard of the Seas, but on the contrary have, to the Prejudice of *Holland*, and for the Benefit of their own Inhabitants, so managed their Courts and Admiralties, in order to draw the Trade to themselves, or at least the Passage of the Merchandizes of *Holland*, that they have suffered Goods coming in, or going out, to pay either none sometimes, or at other times much less Duty of Convoy and Customs, than is expressed in the Book of Rates, and yet have given Inland Passports and Discharges as if the Duty had been fully paid, that so they may by the way of *Bergen*, the *Sas of Gent*, *Sluys*, &c. and *Zealand* without further question, carry them into

Holland

Holland. Nay, we have often seen that when the States General, with the United Suffrages of our common Allys, have prohibited some certain Commoditys to be imported into, or exported out of the *United Provinces*; yet hath the Admiralty of *Zealand* by their own Authority, suffered such Goods to be Imported and Exported, to the great Benefit of their Inhabitants, and the intolerable Burden of ours. And in like manner when the States General have thought fit to distress the Common Enemy, by tolerating Privateers, or Freebooting Ships; we have then always heard Complaints of the Judicature of the Admiralty of *Zealand*, viz. that not only the Goods of Strangers in Amity with us, but even the Goods of *Holland*, under pretence of having saved the Duty, are too slightly and unjustly seized, and confiscated; partly in favour of their Privateering Inhabitants, and partly by such Vexation and Trouble, to draw the Trade from *Holland* into *Zealand*.

L. V. Aitzm. Book 16 p. 301.

A remarkable Example of the perfidiousness of the Zealand Capers. Aitzma, Book 42. p. 723.

And as to what relates to all the Colleges of the Generality, as well as the Admiralties residing in *Holland*, it is well known that the other Provinces, in order to obtain more Power and Authority to their respective Principals, tho to the prejudice of the common Freedom, and of *Holland* in particular, * do send and continue all their Commissioners for the most part during their Lives, or at least for many Years: Whereby they being strangers in *Holland*, do

Especially when the Zealanders or other strangers are permitted to be the Gecommitteerde Raeden ad vitam, or for very many Years.

---

* Libertatis enim interest ne magna Imperia diuturna sint.

often carry things against our Triennial Commissioners of *[...]*, even in the disposal of our own Affairs, conferring most of the Offices and Benefices depending on Colleges upon their Favourites, and often also upon Strangers.

[...] is found to be most of all prejudicial to *[...]* when the Fiscals, Secretarys, Receivers, chief Customers, Commissioners of the Navy and Prizes, &c. belonging to the said Colleges of the Admiralty, who serve in those Offices for the most part during Life, and besides are Strangers in *Holland*, through *[...]* natural love to themselves, their own Country, or their own College, or by an innate Envy, to the Welfare of *Holland*, use their Authority and Power to the utmost against the *Holland* Merchants, to the prejudice of our Trade, but very faintly against the Inhabitants of their own Province. Yea, tho the Advocate, Fiscal, or chief Customer be a *Hollander*, yet if his Habitation lie on the *Mase*, or in the *Northern* Quarter; by the same evil Inclination and Envy he can so plague the Merchants of the rich City of *Amsterdam*, by seizing their Goods, and so greatly favour those of the *Mase*, or the *Northern* Quarter, in the Entries of their imported and exported Goods, that they are compelled forthwith to transport their Trade, and passage of their Goods from the places where they are oppress't to those Parts or Colleges of Admiralty where they may be justly dealt with.

And tho *[...]* at the beginning of these *[...]* Orders of the Year 1597 was so happy, that our Enemys had only two Havens or the

the North Sea, *Sluys* (lying between *Ostend* and the Island *Walcheren*) and *Dunkirk*, at that time without the *Schwartien*, having so narrow and shallow a Haven, that our laden Flyboats and Busses which they took, or their very Gallys, could not lie in safety; so that both these Sea Ports could do us but little damage, when we would take care to lie before them, or pick up those petty Capers in these Narrow Seas. And tho we happen'd to lose *Ostend*, yet in recompence we took from the Enemy the City of *Sluys*, and its mischievous Gallys. Notwithstanding all this, I say, the *Dunkirkers* did us continually much greater damage after these Admiralties were erected, than ever before. So that the Merchants in the Year 1599 complained, "That "they could not at all weaken the Enemy by "so many Ships of War, and so much Convoy-"Mony paid and raised for that end. That "the Sea-Captains were chosen more for "Favour than Fitness, and that in the Ad-"miralties men were placed who under-"stood nothing of Maritime Affairs, nor "valued them, as having nothing to lose "that way.

And tho all these Accusations might have been more justly laid to the Charge of the States General, and the Prince of *Orange*, than on these new Commissioners of the Admiralty, yet neither the Merchants, nor our Fishers, durst make the least complaint of his excessive Power, nor of their own Losses; tho in the Year 1600 many of their Ships and Busses were burnt and sunk; and their 3 Convoys were by 14 *Dunkirk* Ships of War taken, or forced to fly. After which the States

The Dunkirkers began to infest the Sea.
E. Reyd *Hist.* p. 636.

Ema. Meeteren, Book 21.

States General, in lieu of better defending the trading Inhabitants of these Countrys, took upon them in the Year 1602 to prohibit them to traffick beyond the *Cape de Buona Esperança*, in any of those incredibly great and rich *Asiatick* Countrys, by granting that Commerce wholly to an *East-India* Company for the Term of one and twenty Years then next ensuing.

And as the States General in the Year 1603. seemed publickly to acknowledg the insufficiency of these new Admiraltys, partly by making the first Ordinances for the arming and manning out of all Ships sailing upon account of Merchandize or Fishing, together with the Admiraltys; and partly seeing the Inhabitants of these Countrys were by these new Ordinances unmeasurably taxed, and yet no better defended than formerly against Piracy, and Enemys at Sea, they were necessitated to give such Inhabitants as desired it, Commissions to set out Ships of War to weaken the Enemy. In which it was observed, that the said Privateers sought rather for the Enemys Merchant-ships, where they might meet with great Prize and few Blows, than their Ships of War and Pirats, where there was small Prize and many Blows to be expected. And accordingly our own Merchant-ships and Fishers were little or nothing relieved thereby, and likewise our own Privateers molested and damaged, as well the good Inhabitants of the *United Provinces*, as the Subjects of Kings, Princes, and Republicks in Amity with us, both in their Persons and Estates. Upon which the States General in the Year 1606. found it necessary to revoke

and

and call in all such Commissions, and to raise four hundred thousand Guilders by an extraordinary Subsidy, to set to Sea more Ships of War against the Enemy; which notwithstanding did not perform the designed work aimed at of scouring or clearing the Seas.

'Tis a Matter very worthy observation, that before the Year 1597. when the Sea was render'd safe and navigable by those Governors who were most concerned, there was very little damage suffered; and the great Overplus of the Convoy and Custom-Mony, was imployed in getting things necessary for the War by Land: And that since the erecting of these new Admiralties, we have not only continually suffer'd great Losses by Sea; but besides the Convoy and Custom-mony, very many extraordinary Subsidies have been levied upon the People for the Guard of the Sea.

And thus the State of these Maritime Affairs continued till the Truce was made; at which time the States supposing that all robbing at Sea would cease, greatly lessened the Dutys upon imported and exported Goods, in favour of Trade and Navigation. And on the other side, by our security and want of Ships of War, the *Moors* of *Algier, Tunis,* and *Sally*, who had been expelled from *Spain* about that time, as well as our discharged Seamen, who then served under *Simon den Danser*, Capt. *Ward, Nicholas Campane,* and others, had great Opportunities of taking our richest Ships, in and about the *Mediterranean* Sea, both during and after the Truce. And because this happen'd so very frequently, I shall not detain the Reader with the

The Hollanders *about the* Mediterranean *much plagued by Pirats.*

See the Netherlandish *Wars, by* D H. D *in* 1612. *printed at* Arnhem, p. 199.

the Relation of these Accidents, but leave him to calculate how great and prejudicial those Pirates were, since the *Algerines* in the Years 1728, and 1729, within the space of thirteen Months took 180 Sail of Ships alone the *Sallateens* alone esteemed their Loss at 12 Tuns of Gold, and the whole was computed at 300 Tuns of Gold.

And whereas during the Truce with *Spain*, our Whale-fishing increased much, it usually happened that the *English*, when they were Fishing to the Northward, drove away our Fishers, and took some of their Ships and Fish, and King *James* refused to give satisfaction, or redress, insisting that his Subjects had the sole Right of fishing in those Seas. And on the contrary, when the *Hollanders* were stronger, though first attacked, yet the *English* Ships taken by us, and brought into these Countrys, were by Order of the States General restored again to the *English*, which Disorders, and taking our Whale-fishers, continued all along the Truce, and was much increased by the King of *Denmark*, who pretending to the Right of those *Northern* Seas, did great damage to that Fishery.

So that I shall think it worth while to shew the Means which the States General, the Pr. of Orange, and the Admiraltys used to free our Inhabitants, who subsisted by the Sea, from those Mischiefs and Molestations. And first as to our Trade and Navigation in the *Mediterranean*. After *Simon Danser*, *Nicholas Campus*, and others had taken and plunder'd great numbers of our Ships, and were grown weary of Pirating, it was found convenient to save the Expences of taking and punishing them;

them, and on the contrary, to grant them Pardons, and to permit them to return to their own Country, where all the good People that had sustained Losses by them, have seen those Pirats with aking Hearts, and not without fear, that by such impunity other debauched Persons might be encouraged to the like villanous Attempts. And as to the *Turkish* Pirats, who could not be invited to come in, and leave their Piracys, it was found expedient, *Anno* 1612. to send *Haga* Ambassador to *Constantinople*, and in the Year 1622. to send *Pynaker* to *Algier* and *Tunis*. Which Ambassadors arriving with great Presents, and Fleets of Ships of War, easily obtained Capitulations and Agreements of free Commerce, upon which our Inhabitants relying too much, the Pirats fell again to their usual Trade, as soon as our Ships of War were sailed away, and we suffered more Losses from time to time, than if there never had been any Peace or Accord made. Upon this the States General endeavoured by our Ambassadors in *France*, *Spain*, and *England*, to move those Kings to suppress those Pirats with some Ships of Force. But seeing those Monarchs valued not their Subjects so much as to be at that Charge for them, and that the Freedom of the Seas from Piracy was not so much their Concern as ours, or that the *Turks* being not able, by reason of their inconsiderable Navigation, to depredate so much on their Subjects as they could on ours, and would much rather make Peace with *France* and *England*, and keep it better too than with us; the States General caused the Admiraltys successively to set to Sea Ships of War to destroy

Wissen's historical Relation.

Scheltema's Index Geographicus & profundus, in view, Suppl. Ast. Actorum 1632, p. 630.

Baudart, Hyst. p. 182. of 1612. and p. 118. of 1623.

As also our absurd Polity of rooting out the Turkish Pirats.

destroy the Pirats, in the Years 1614, 16, 17, 18, 20, 22, &c.

But taking few Pirate Ships, because most of them while our Men of War cruis'd in the *Mediterranean*, came not out of their Harbours; this answered not our ends, till finally after the Year 1650. during the free Government of *Holland*, it was observed that we could neither make any firm and durable Peace with those Pirates, nor root them out, and that if we suppress'd them at our own charge, yet our Traffick and Navigation would not, according to our aim and desire, be at all encreased, but rather diminish. Upon which the Admiralty of *Amsterdam*, and afterwards other Admiraltys, pursuing closely the true Interest of *Holland*, sent out yearly a number of Ships of War to convoy our Merchant Ships (which according to certain Rules agreed on, were to be well mann'd and arm'd) through the *Straits* of *Gibralter*, and out and home from the *Levant*. So that the *Hollanders* since that time have sustained very little loss, and have very much increased their Navigation and Trade into those Parts.

In the 2*d* place concerning the disturbing of our Whale-Fishery, 'tis plain that the States General have done nothing more, than by their Ambassadors to pray the respective Kings, that such Actions might cease in time to come. And afterwards observing such Addresses to prove ineffectual, they thought fit in the Year 1622 to grant a Patent to a *Greenland* Company, excluding all others from taking of Whale, that so the said Company by their own Power and Strength might defend

defend themselves against the Molestations and Robberys of Strangers. Which Grant continued till the Year 1643 when the *English* by reason of their Intestine Wars, and the *Danes*, either by reason of the growing Power of the *Swedes*, had more need of our Favour than formerly, or fearing our Arms, and consequently being less dreaded by our Whale-fishers, all the Inhabitants of these Countrys were permitted to fish on the said North Coast; and the said Fishing by that freedom improved so incredibly, that the States General in the 2*d* War against *England*, being not able to defend them there, prohibited them to fish, principally for the use they had of Mariners to man out our Ships of War for the defence of our Country and free Navigation

But Thirdly, of the many Robberies committed by the *Dunkirkers*, and the means used against them, it is necessary to speak more largely.

In *Flanders* upon the expiration of the Truce, the *Spaniard* had built at the enterance into *Dunkirk* upon the Arm of the Sea, the Fort of *Mardike*, and also that which is called the *Houte Wambais*, or *Wooden-doublet*, so that great Ships might at all times sail out and bring their Prizes in thither. The King of *Spain* caused likewise twelve Ships of War to be built in *Flanders*, and encouraged the *Flemings* to privateering against us by Sea. And besides this till the Year 1625. he sent such powerful Armys into the Field, that *Gulick* and *Breda* were taken from us, to the eternal shame of the States General, or to say better, of the new and violently intruded Deputies of the

After Pr. Maurice would allow of no Prolongation of the Truce, and the Scans of Mardike was built, the Dunkirkers endamag'd us greatly by Sea.

the Generality, and of *Maurice* Prince of O-*range*, who, since they would admit of no prolongation of the Truce at the desire of the *Spaniard*, or the Arch-Duke, ought not to have rejected their Offer so suddenly, but have hearkned to it, or at least feign'd to have done so, that by this means they might have excited the Kings of *France* and *England*, who were then very jealous of the Power of *Spain*, and feared that by continuation of the Truce the *Spaniard* would fall upon them, to assist us with a yearly number of Men and a Sum of Mony, in case we had reingaged in a War against *Spain*. Or lastly, Those Deputies of the Generality, and the said Prince should have made use of that delay to put our Frontiers into a better state of Defence, and to fall upon the Enemy when they would grant him no further Cessation. And no less prudence had been necessary to increase our Traffick, freedom of Navigation and Fisheries. Whereas on the other side, they prohibited all our Inhabitants to trade in *America*, and *Africa*, by erecting a *West-India* Company A⁰ 1621 under colour of distressing the Enemy more in those parts. And in the said Year they likewise prohibited our Inhabitants to sail to the *Mediterranean*, or to *Cape del Rey* in the *West Indies* for Salt, unless in Consortship, promising them Ships of War to convoy and defend them back again. But this Promise was without effect. For to free the Admiraltys of those Charges, and to favour the said Company with that Salt-trade, the States General, Prince *Maurice*, and the Admiraltys very easily found it convenient to deprive the Inhabitants of these

these Countrys of that most considerable Trade of Salt, in favour of the *West-India* Company, where it continued only to the Year 1623 when the K. of *Spain*, fearing that the said Company, by fortifying themselves, and by their own Power, would engross those Salt-pans, caused a Fort to be raised there himself. So that our Inhabitants by the Placaet of the States General, and our *West-India* Company, and by means of that Fort, were utterly deprived of that Salt Trade.

And instead of protecting and defending our Navigation from Piracy, with better Order and more Strength, they again drew in the Inhabitants to fit out Privateers, reducing the worted Duty out of the Prize Goods, to the Admiraltys and Admiral General, from 30 *per Cent.* to 18 *per Cent* viz. 12 to the State, and six for the Admiral-General. Orders were also published, that none should sail to the East Country, and *Norway*, but in Fleets of 40 or more Ships with two Convoyers, or else with Ships of defence without Convoy. Yea, the States and the Prince of *Orange* thought it convenient to continue that mischievous Grant or Charter to the *East-India* Company for 21 Years to come. So that the States General and the Admiraltys discharged themselves of scouring the Seas, as far as concern'd *Asia*, *Africa*, and *America*, and the Traffick of those parts, together with the Northern Whale-fishing, upon supposition that all those respective Companys were sufficient to drive on their Trade without Convoys from the State, and to take care of their own Affairs. But on the contrary, they found that the Trade of these Societies was carried on

See the Placaet Book.

And the select East-India Company had their Charter prolonged.

To the great detriment of all the Inhabitants of Holland &expl.

on with so great prejudice to the rest of the People, who were excluded, that if our Governours had then or should now deal in the same manner with the Trade of *Europe*, by erecting Companys exclusive of all others; for example, one Company for the Dealers in the *Mediterranean*, a 2d of the *French* and *Spanish* Merchants, a 3d for the *Eastern* and *Northern* Merchants, a 4th for the *British* and *Irish* Traders, a 5th for the Haddock, Cod, and Herring Fisherys, &c. I say, if they had done this, one 10th part of our Inhabitants would not have been able to live, and earn their Bread. So that *Holland* would soon have been ruin'd, even tho the Trade of those Companys had been carried on with so great industry, that notwithstanding any Resolutions taken by *France*, *England*, *Sweden*, and the States of *Italy*, to disturb, prohibit, and prevent Foreign Manufactures, and consequently those of *Holland* to be brought into their Countrys, yet each of those Companys in the small compass of our *Europe* had driven a greater Trade than the whole *East-India* Company now drives to the incomparably greater, mightier and richer *Asia*, both in Goods and Mony. For it cannot be denied, that the free *Eastern* Trade alone, the Herring-fishing alone, and the *French* Trade alone, produce ten times more profit to the State, and the Commonalty of *Holland*, than 12 or 16 Ships which yearly sail from *Holland* to the *East-Indies* do now yield to the State, and the Inhabitants.

And as to the Administration and care of our Admiraltys with respect to the Sea, after the expiration of the Truce, and during the Life

See Aitzma's Hist.

Life of Prince *Maurice*, a Million of Florens was raised for the Year 1623, and 600000 for 1624, by extraordinary Subsidies, with Admiralty and Convoy-mony, and product of Customs, which were again levied as in the Year 1603. With these Aids they fitted out Ships of War, ordering some to lie before the *Flemish* Havens, and others to convoy our Merchantmen to the Eastward and Westward. yet such was the management, that our Ships of War came often so late before those Havens, that the Enemies Ships were put out to Sea, before their Arrival; or else to avoid the usual Storms of Autumn, or to be revictualled, left the *Flemish* Coast so early, that commonly before, or at least in the Winter, the Enemy with many of their Ships of War, would go out sometimes by Night, or even by Daylight in sight of our Ships, and confidence of their better sailing, or of our Captains Negligence or Cowardice; and not only got ten times more Booty from our Merchant Ships, than our Capers and Ships of War could take from the Enemy, but also sometimes would take, or put to flight, our Ships that were appointed for Guards and Convoys.

And yet loaded the Commonalty of Holland more than ever with extraordinary Subsidies for scouring the Seas, as much infested as before.

See Wassenar's *Hist.*

All which Losses were not attributed to the Deputies of the Generality, and the Admiral General, who after the death of the *Heer Opdam* Lieut. Admiral of *Holland*, which hapned *Sept.* 1623. till *June* 1625 when young *William* of *Nassau* was chosen, had put all the Naval Power of *Holland* under the Command of the *Zealand* Lieut Admiral *Hautain*, nor was it imputed to the Provinces who were deficient, or backward in bringing in the Mony they had consented to give, by which means the

Ships designed for the Service were either delayed, or not fitted out at all; but the blame was wholly laid at the door of the Admiralty's disorderly Management, and Negligence. So that thereupon a Resolution was made in the Year 1624. but with little success, for Prince *Maurice* dying in *April* 1625. and Prince *Henry* being hastily chosen Captain Admiral General, and Stadtholder of *Holland*, *Zeeland*, &c. we soon saw that he concerned himself but little in husbanding the Treasure, or providing for a free and open Navigation, in which the Welfare of *Holland* consists.

And that the Reader may see what ground there was for that Assertion, which some of our Writers have delivered as a known Truth, viz. That the said Prince *Henry*, during the whole time of his Government, as much as in him lay, endeavoured to exhaust the Treasure of *Holland*, and by the burden of her Debts to break her back: It will not be amiss to represent in short from Authors of credit what was done and suffered in this matter to the Year 1632. and so forward to the time of our Peace with *Spain*, and the decease of the said Prince *Henry*. The Treasure and Power of *Spain* was, by the chargeable Sieges of *Bergen op Zoom* and *Breda*, and especially by our vigorous carrying on the War against him by our *West-India* Company, who greatly annoyed him in those parts, so broken and exhausted, that since that time he has not been able to carry on an offensive War against us, and therefore Year after Year seriously and early made offers to treat of an Accommodation of a Peace, very honourable for this State, and necessary for our Tra-

Trading Inhabitants, as well as desired by all the rest. But those Offers were as often rejected by the Deputies of the Generality at the instigation of the Prince of *Orange*, and in their room our Taxes were continually increased with Prince *Henry*'s Government, both by the Addition of Souldiery, and otherwise by his ill Husbandry, from 12 Millions 543840 Guilders, to 15 Millions 433800 Guilders, according to a Petition of the Council of State in the Year 1626, and were successively granted Year after Year, rather more than less.

Aitzma's Treaty of Peace Aitzma's Hist. p. 637. Pr. Henry obstinately continued the War beyond Holland's Ability. Aitzma p. 59.

And tho *Holland* alone bore of this Charge 58 *per* 100, and by these heavy burdens, and ill Husbandry, our Treasury from the expiration of the Truce to the Year 1632. was found to be 55 Millions in Arrear. Yet nothing at all was done for the benefit of the Inhabitants of that Province thus needlesly and purposely oppress'd beyond their Abilitys by their unnecessary offensive Field-Armies: Unless they could believe that it was very advantagious to them that *Oldensul* was taken that same Year, *Grol* in 1627. and in the Year 1628, many chargeable Fortifications were made about *Bergen op Zoom*, and *Steenbergen*: And that thereupon, in 1629, *Boisleduc* was taken for the State, and *Weesel* for the Elector of *Brandenburg*, for which our Country smarted severely, by the *Spaniards* falling in, and plundering in and about the *Veluwe*; add to this, that notwithstanding the continued high demands for Mony to carry on the War in the Year 1630. our Souldiery stirred not out of their Garisons, and that in the Year 1631. we got nothing by a chargeable Attempt upon *Flanders* but disgrace, which nevertheless was some-

So that Holland was in the Years of his Administration, 51 Millions in Arrear.

somewhat lessened by the unsuccessful Shallop-design of the *Spaniard* upon *Zealand*. And lastly, that in the Year 1632. *Ruremond, Venlo*, and *Mastricht* were taken from the Enemy, more by Count *Henry Vanden Bergh*'s means, than the conduct of the Prince of *Orange*.

<small>*Aitzma, Hist. Pag 323.*</small>

In the mean time most of the Provinces except *Holland* were so backward in consenting to contribute Mony, and the Charges were so enlarged above what was consented to be given, that the Council of State in their Petition complained yearly on behalf of their honest Creditors, who had trusted them for 3 or 4 Years, that they became so troublesom and importunate that those Counsellors were hardly safe in their own Houses; and that all things necessary for the publick Service, might be bought or made for the $\frac{1}{4}$ or $\frac{1}{3}$ part cheaper, if ready Mony were paid, and that also for want of Pay, the Captains, who had really $\frac{1}{3}$, yea $\frac{1}{2}$ less number of Souldiers in Service than were paid for, must be conniv'd at.

During all which Confusions by Land, the Maritime Affairs were carried on after the following manner. First, concerning the Treasury; the Admiraltys did in the Year 1625. petition for 600000 Guilders; for the Year 1626 800000 Guilders; for the Year 1627. 1000000 Guilders, and for the Years 1628, 1629, 1630, 1631, 1632. yearly and successively, two Millions of Guilders extraordinary Subsidies for guarding the Seas. And moreover, the States General deviated so far in the Years 1625, and 1631. from the true Grounds and Maxims of maintaining Trade and Navigation, that they did not only considerably raise the Dutys of Convoy, and Cus-

<small>*See the particular Petitionary Demands in Aitzma's Hist.*</small>

<small>*And the Extraordinary paid their Subsidies. See the particular Placaets in the Book of the States General.*</small>

toms, ordering the 4*th* part of them to be farm'd out to those that bid most, and consequently as much as in them lay made all Traffick and Navigation subject to those innumerable and unimaginable Vexations of Farmers. But besides, in the Front of their Placaet they roundly declared, That of all the Publick Revenues, the Convoy and Customs were the most tolerable and least hurtful, that are laid on Goods imported and exported; whereas the Rates then imposed, and yet in force, are known to be the most intolerable, and for the Country the most prejudicial of all the Revenues of *Holland*, as has been already shewn in our 23*d* Chapter of *Part* I

All which Convoys and Customs so augmented, produced yearly, as by example in the year 1628,

	Guilders.
To the Admiralty of *Rotterdam,*	330737
Amsterdam,	803659
The Northern Quarter,	125000
	1259396
Zealand,	329367
All Charges incident to those Colleges and their Offices deducted--	1588763

But the Admiralty of *Friesland*, bearing the yearly Charges of the College, and Watching, fell short with all its Revenue twelve thousand Guilders, which were to be made good out of the extraordinary Subsidies: and therefore they not sending Ships to Sea, those Provinces of *Friesland*, and *Groeningen*, with the Inland Provinces, became very unwilling to consent to the Subsidies, very backward

O in

in bringing them in, and always very slowly.

See the Placaet &c.

Moreover in the Year 1625. on the 24th of June, all Ships sailing to the *Mediterranean*, were by Placaet commanded to pay 16 Stivers on Last every Voyage to the benefit of the Agents in the *Levant*, which in the Year 1630 was raised to 20 Stivers, and successively, in the Years 1625, 1627, 1628, 1629, 1630, 1632 the arming and manning of Ships sailing for Merchandize or Fishing was from time to time charged upon the Inhabitants of these Countrys by Placaets.

But to look further, and enquire what hath been done with such great Subsidies and Taxes (which oppressed all the Inhabitants of *Holland*, and especially the Merchants) for the benefit of free Navigation: So soon as Prince *Henry* was made Admiral-General, he placed and appointed young *William* of *Nassau Heer van de Lek* his Lieutenant Admiral of *Holland*, who was likewise obliged to serve as Colonel in the War by Land, and went very little to Sea, till in *August* 1627. when he was kill'd by a Shot before *Grol*. And instead of defending our Merchantmen and Fishers, the Lieutenant-Admiral of *Zealand*, *Hautain* was sent with 22 Sail of Ships *Anno* 1625. to reduce our Protestant Brethren of *Rochel* under the Obedience of the King of *France*; and at the same time two Ships of War only were allow'd to secure one thousand Busses in their Fishing. Besides as to Trade, the Seas were more infested than ever: For six *Dunkirk* Ships of War meeting our Fleet which came from the Northward in *June*, *Anno* 1625. without Convoy, drove them back to

Chap. I. *the Seas from Pirates.* 195

to *Norway*; and having taken two *Eastland*, and three other Ships, came all six to an Anchor before the *Texel*, and lay there along time, as our Ships used to lie before *Dunkirk*, taking all Vessels that came in, or sailed out; which caused such a Consternation among our People, that none durst venture to Sea. And soon after the departure of these *Dunkirkers*, arrived happily eight Northern, and Eastland Merchant Ships, with one Convoy only.

Again, in the same Year 1625. after our Ships of War were withdrawn from the *Flemish* Coast, and come into Harbour, the *Dunkirk* Ships steered directly away to our Fishers, as knowing they were provided but with two Convoyers, and scattered our Busses, taking and sinking many of them; by which accident those of *Enchuysen* alone lost at the least 100, and other Places in proportion; and at least 150 Masters and Mates of those Busses were made Prisoners, and carried to *Flanders*. So that the Directors of that great Fishery observing from time to time how little the securing of their Livelihood was regarded, soon after resolved at their own charge, to set out seven great and well-armed Ships of War, and to put them all under their own Commander of the Busses, of which seven those of *Enchuysen* were to set out and pay 4, and the Buss-Owners about the *Maese* three, that they might fish in more safety under their Guard, seeing the chief Trade of the Land, *viz.* Fishing, was neglected

The Directors of the great Fishery necessitated to provide Convoys at their own charges.

And to the end the Deputies of the Generality and Prince *Henry* might not always seem

to neglect the Sea, it was resolved that they would set forth for the Year 1626 thirty well appointed Ships of War, and set a reward for the taking and destroying of any Ship of War, belonging to the Enemy, being of 100 or more Last, the Sum of Guilders —————— 30000
From 70 to 100 ——— 20000
50 to 70 ——— 15000
30 to 50 ——— 10000
20 to 30 ——— 8000
Mounted with four Guns of 20 Lasts or under, } 4000

'Twas also resolved to put the Law in execution, that commands the Men of *Dunkirk* to be thrown over-board. But those Provinces that were least concerned in securing the Seas, remaining backward in bringing in the Mony necessary for the said Equipage and Rewards, and the States General having deprived the Admiraltys of a great part of their Revenues, by prohibiting the Importation of some Goods, and yet on the other side requiring to set forth a greater Strength to Sea than ordinary, with the Profuseness of Prince *Henry* as Captain and Admiral General, there arose in all the Colleges of the Generality, and especially in the Admiraltys, an Arrear of two Millions five hundred and eight thousand and fifteen Guilders running on at Interest, besides three Millions nine hundred twenty and three thousand two hundred ninety and five Guilders in debts, which caused the Seamen, who not getting their Wages, were necessitated to sell their Debentures, at very low Rates, with many of our Mariners who were not able to live for
want

want of Pay, and therefore not willing to serve here any longer, to go over to the *Dunkirkers*, and sail with them upon Free-booting. And our Fleet under the Admiral of *Zealand*, *Jonker Philips van Dorp*, came not before the *Schuurtjen* of *Dunkirk* upon the Watch till about the Month of *July*, when most of their Men of War were gone out to Sea, and according to their old custom, had taken many of our Merchants Ships, and very many Busses which they sunk and burnt; insomuch that all that could escape, fled for safety to the *English* Harbours. And our Doggers of the *Muse* hearing that the *Dunkirk* Capers threw over-board all the Men of the Merchant Ships and Fishing-Vessels which they took, in revenge of what we had done by their Men, durst not go to Sea to follow their Occupations.

Which proved dangerous to our Fishers and Merchantmen.

And notwithstanding *Van Dorp* lay with the Fleet before *Dunkirk*, many small Frigats and Shallops sailed out for Prize; so that at last in *October* that Year, young *William* of *Nassaw* as Lieutenant-Admiral of *Holland*, was charged to keep that Post Which he performed till *December* following, but no better than *Van Dorp* had done And as to our Cruisers and other Convoyers, it is observable that we do not know that they ever took any one of the twelve new built King's Ships of *Dunkirk*, pretending they were better Sailers; which is altogether incredible, for our Ships from time to time could take Ships of less Force, and better Sailers, and throw their Men over-board. Whereas on the other side the *Dunkirkers*, as well before as since, fighting several of our Ships of War,

This infesting of the Sea proceeded from our selves.

War, forced our Captains, after Quarter promised, to surrender themselves. So that it is rather to be believed, that our Admirals and Sea Captains, fearing much more the *Dunk.* Ships of War, and their requital of throwing them over-board, rather than our terrible Justice for the neglect of their Dutys, sought not out those *Dunkirkers* but where they were not to be found. However it is true, that they did commonly, as well heretofore as afterwards, and particularly in this Year 1646. come to the Assistance of the Merchantmen and Fishers, when 'twas too late. Wherefore *John van de Sande* in his History says, That the Sea-Captains kept themselves usually on the Rivers where no Enemy came, and fled from those they met. So that the Council of State, in their petitionary demand of Supply for the following Year, declared, " That the poor People are " henceforward afraid to go to Sea to fol-" low their Callings, the throwing them " over-board making a great cry and altera-" tion among those that earn their Bread so " hardly at Sea.

And tho it be true, that the greatest part of all these Hardships of our Inhabitants was caused by the ill Government of the Deputys of the Generality, and the Prince of *Orange*, who used the Power of these Countrys to make new Conquests, not to defend Trade and Navigation, and yet as if we had bin the only Masters at Sea, and had no unarmed Ships abroad, nor the *Dunkirkers* any Ships of defence, we followed those incredibly foolish Councils, of resolving to throw over-board all *Dunkirkers* taken at Sea in Ships of War. Whereas

on

on the contrary, the *Flemings* used very prudent Maxims about this Matter, namely to throw the Men of undefensible Vessels over-board, and to give Quarter to our armed Ships of War. Nevertheless none dared to complain of this evil Government of the States General, and the Prince of *Orange*, no not even of young *William* of *Nassau*. * But the Pigs were fain to pay for the Sow's Offence, and therefore upon the ill Conduct of the Admiraltys, and especially of the College of *Roterdam*, the *Heeren Berk*, *Vander Mist*, *Segwairs*, *Verbeul*, *Nicolai*, *Vroesen*, and *Duifhuysen*, who had done no more than what was in mode during Prince *Henry*'s wasteful Administration in all the Colleges, especially that of the Generality, were nevertheless declared Infamous by Judges delegated for that end, and condemned in great Fines to allay the Discontent of the Multitude. The States General also declared, That the following Year they would set out more Ships of War in order to clear the Seas; and would make the People to believe, that a competent number of Ships should lie on the watch before *Dunkirk*, to prevent the coming out of those Ships, while another number should lie between *Dover* and *Calais*, and another at the *Schager Rif*, to watch and prevent all Sea-Robbers sailing to the *Spanish* Sea, or to the Northward. And besides all these, another number of our Ships of War should cruise in the narrow part of the North-Sea; so that the Enemy should not be able

See the Petition of the Council, 1629.

To quiet the Commonalty, some of the Admiralty were punish'd, and new Orders given out.

Aitzma of that Year, B.6.p.97.

---

* Dat veniam Corvis vexat censura Columbas.

by any means to interrupt or disturb our Navigation.

But because no better Order was settled about the Affairs of Justice, nor any thing determined about the Finances, from whence the paiment of the new appointed Rewards for taking of Enemy's Ships should proceed, nor any of our Maritime Affairs better managed than formerly; the hopes of the too credulous Commonalty soon vanished, especially when the *Dunkirkers* in the Year 1627 infested us again before our Sea-port Towns, and took as many Prizes as formerly, seizing several Busses, and two of the Busses Convoyers, whilst young *William* Admiral of *Holland* was killed before *Grol*, and *Jonke Philips van Dorp* Lieutenant Admiral of *Zealand* cruised at Sea, and none of our Ships before *Dunkirk* to keep in their Capers; who coming to lie on our Coast about the *Texel*, the *Mase*, and *Zeland*, swept away all, together with the Ship of Capt. *Bagyn*, who heretofore on many occasions had behaved himself bravely and valiantly, and from a Clothworker was by degrees preferred to the Honour of having the Command of one of our best Ships of War. But now finding himself alone in the midst of fourteen of the Enemy's Ships of War, he yielded his new and well-appointed Ship without making one shot.

The Politicians of those Times judged, " That the Trade of these Countys was never since the Truce in so ill a condition: " For *Spain* could do no good. *Portugal* was " without Trade; *France* by the King's Edicts was shut up; *England* detained all " Ships that passed the Channel, and seized

"sixty

"sixty or eighty Tuns of Gold belonging to
"the free *Netherlanders*. The Rivers of *We-*
"*ser* or *Elve, Trave, Oder,* and *Wissel,* were
"so infested and block'd up by the *Danish*
"and *Swedish* Ships of War, that little or
"no Trade could be driven with *Bremen,*
"*Hamburgh, Lubeck, Stetin,* and *Dantzick,*
"and the North Sea was render'd impra-
"cticable by the *Dunkirkers.* By which
means the Commonalty were as much dissa-
tisfied as ever, when our Ships of War came
in and had done nothing, insomuch that
those of *Flushing* fell into a Mutiny, and at
Terveer threw stones at Lieutenant Admiral
Van Dorp. So to pacify the People, they were
necessitated to fine the Pigs once again; and
some Sea-Captains were dismiss'd, and poor
Capt *Bryan* having no Friends at Court, *sum-
mo jure* lost his Head

In the Year 1628. for the greater safety of
our Navigation, three Vice-Admirals were
created in *Holland*, who nevertheless were to
be commanded by the Lieutenant-Admiral
of *Zealand.* But the *Dunkirkers,* according *So the States*
to their old custom, seized many *Straits* Ships, *of Zealand de-*
with other Merchant-men, and at two seve- *posed their Ad-*
ral times took 34 Busses, tho Lieut Admiral *miral.*
Van Dorp with a Squadron of ten Ships had *Aitzma's Hist.*
lain ten Weeks upon the Coast of *England* *B. 9. p. 730.*
without hearing of an Enemy, and our Coast
Ships and Cruisers were likewise at Sea Which
the States of *Holland* took so ill, that they dis- *Lib 8. p.527.*
missed *Philips van Dorp* at his return without
a hearing. The Council of State had also sent
a Letter in *April* of the same Year to the Provinces, complaining of the Confusions in the
"Publick Revenues, which was the cause of
"the

"the Arrears due to the Military Forces both
"by Sea and Land; and that the Revenues
"and Charges of the Country were not duly
"considered and weighed one against the
"other. That Disorders increased more
"and more, that the Credit of the Country
"was daily sinking, that the Souldiery was
"mutinous and disobedient, and that all Mi-
"litary Discipline and Justice were trodden
"under foot, &c.

These Proceedings were taken very ill by the Deputys of the Generality and the Prince, and the *Heer van Dorp* was still continued in the Land-Service. Strict enquiry was also made among the Counsellors of State, to know who they were that durst be the chief Promoters of the complaining Letter before mentioned. And all this was done to deter others from complaining against the Government of the Deputys of the Generality, and especially of the Cabinet Lords, who together with the Prince look'd after nothing more in this Confusion, than their own Profit and Grandeur.

But upon the continual Complaints of the Merchants of *Amsterdam* to their Burgomasters, of the unexpressible Damages which they sustained in their Bodys and Goods by continual Piracys, and the little care taken for their redress; the said Burgomasters, and Council, made offer to the States General and Prince of *Orange* to set to Sea ten or twelve Men of War well mann'd and furnished, to secure their Shipping, which should receive Instructions from the States General, and a Commission from the Prince; provided the Mony disbursed upon this Design might be defalked from the Contribution of that
City;

City; and that no other Person might have any Power, or be any way concerned about that Equipage and Mony but themselves. And tho formerly under the insupportable Government of the Earls of *Holland,* all the Citys of that Province used by their own Authority to do the same, yet nevertheless this good and useful Offer was rejected under the present Stadtholder's Government, as if that City would by this means obtain too great a Power at Sea. Whereas on the contrary it appeared that the Sea became more and more unnavigated, because the Country and Citys which were most concerned to keep the Sea uninfested, had no Authority put into their hands, as they had under the Government of their Earls.

And to the end that the Deputys of the Generality, and Prince of *Orange,* might shew their usual Zeal in this Affair, the Articles for the War at Sea were *Anno* 1629 inspected and made more severe. A Project also of an Insurance Company was brought in, according to which all Ships outward and inward bound, should pay for Insurance, from one to thirteen *per Cent.* in proportion to the conveniency of the Sea-Ports to or from which Ships were to sail; and the said Company was to be bound to make good all Losses sustained. After which *Peter Hein* was chosen Lieutenant Admiral of *Holland,* who for the redress of Maritime Affairs desired many new Powers relating to the Militia, Justice, and Expences on board Ships; and did not only obtain those, but also more Authority than had ever been given to any Lieutenant Admiral of *Holland.*

Aitzma's Hist. B 9 p 709.

But the Pr. of Orange, and the Deputys of the Generality manifested their wonted Zeal.

Ibid p 730.

But

But he being killed by a shot two Months after, whilst with eight Ships he was in pursuit of three *Dunkirkers*, there can be no account given of the Fruits of this new Order, save that the Charges were increased, and yet the Seas remained as much infested as before. 'Tis uneasy to me to enumerate the Losses sustained by our poor Inhabitants, which were so exceeding great, that the States of *Holland*, on the 18th of *January* 1630. remonstrated to the States General, " That the " Strength, Vigour, and Reputation of the " State by Sea was wholly decayed, and the " Navigation signally diminished. That ma" ny Mariners, for want of Care and due " Defence, were gone over to the Enemy, " and many more taken and kept in close " Imprisonment, or cruelly thrown into the " Sea. And that the said States of *Holland*, " to prevent such Mischiefs for the future, " had resolved, and now signified to the o" ther Provinces, That they would from that " time take as little care for the payment of " the Land Forces that were garison'd in the " Frontier Cities out of their Province, as " they observed was taken about the Conduct " and Affairs of the Sea.

But the States of *Holland* were under that awe and dread of the Prince of *Orange*, and the Deputys of the Generality, that they durst not deny or detain their part of the Publick Contributions to be imployed in securing the Seas, and so nothing was done but a little Dust thrown into the Eyes of the poor innocent Inhabitants of *Holland*: For the States and the Prince sent Letters with their Decrees about that Affair to the other

Provinces. But our want of paiment, and the Disorders about the Marineis, and neglecting the Guard of the Seas still continued, and increased in the Year 1631. For tho the States General had granted, that the Burgomasters and Magistrates of the Citys of *Amsterdam, Horn, Enchuysen, Edam, Medenblick, Hulingen,* &c. should chuse certain Directors, who might collect of all Ships and Goods sailing to the Eastward or *Norway*, one half *per Cent.* and returning from the same, one *per Cent.* to enable them to set out some extraordinary Convoys to secure the Trade of the said Countrys. Yet this Imposition produc'd only a part of the expected Fruit, chiefly because the Directors were in all weighty Matters of the Militia, Justice, and Prizes taken, to be wholly subject to the Prince of *Orange*, and the respective Admiraltys, depending on their Orders and Judgments. And the Deputys of the Generality continuing to advance the Prince's Grandure, and their own, more than the Welfare of *Holland*, resolved in the Name of the States General, to equip over and above the usual number, 35 Ships of War, and 10 Yachts to lie upon the *Flemish* Havens, and to cruise and keep the North-Sea clear of *Dunkirk* Robbers. And that they might with more certainty perform this (as they pretended) they brought all the said Ships under one Head, and put them under the Direction and Orders of the Prince of *Orange*, without obliging them to obey the Commands of any other. They ordered them to be paid by him, and that all Mony necessary for Wages, Rewards, and Provisions, should be brought to the *Hague in specie.* And to the

Aitzma, B.11. p. 354.

Such Shipping as sailed Northward and Eastward, had Convoys paid by themselves, but not without hard Conditions.

Ibid. p. 350.

And the Deputys of the Generality devolv'd the Authority of clearing the Seas on Pr. Henry.

the end that during the Summer-season these Ships might be kept in continual action, the respective Colleges of the Admiraltys of *Holland, Zealand* and *Friesland*, should by turns keep one of their Commissioners at *Helvoetsluys*, in order to hold a constant Correspondence with the Prince, and the Prince's Commander on the Coast, as occasion should require, touching the victualling and repairing of the said Ships; and the Commissioners of the Admiralty were not to intermeddle in the least with the disposal of the said Ships.

And this went so far, that Vice Admiral L· *Fletcher* instead of going to cruise, having convoy'd some Merchant Ships out of the Channel, tho by order of the Admiralty of *Roterdam*, was threatned to be severely punished if for the future he followed any other Orders save those of the States General and the Prince. By this means our Countrymen were oppressed, and the *Dunkirkers* so encouraged, that they ventured to take a Merchant Ship even from under the Cannon of *Flushing*, and in the North Sea two of our Ships of War; and afterwards falling in among our Doggers, took two Convoyers, besides the Doggers. So that the Insurances from *Rochel* and *Bourdeaux* rising to 8 and 10 *per Cent*, the Sea became useless to the Inhabitants of these Countrys

Bernard Lamp, having observed in his History, 'That formerly a small number of our
" Ships kept the Sea so clear against all the
" Naval Power of the King of *Spain*, that till
" the Year 1612 these Countrys had very
" few Losses, wonders that all the States
" Ships of War, being little less than an hun-
" dred Sail, either could not or would not
" keep

"keep the Seas clear of the *Dunkirkers* only, "for the King's Ships were not employed "there in those days, but some particular "Owners set out for the most part small Ships "for Booty: and adds farther, That a few "Years after that time, so many rich laden "Merchant Ships were taken by the *Dunkirk-* "ers, that the loss was valued at more than "one hundred Tuns of Gold.

So that our Historys doubt whether the State was willing to scour the Seas, for the Prince was not to be spoken of.

But if we consider how great the difference is, whether the care of scouring the Seas be entrusted to those who are much concerned in having them kept clear, and who on that account will use the best of their Endeavours, or be devolved on such as are not at all concerned in Navigation; we shall cease to wonder, when so much Power was put into the hands of such as were not interested at Sea, and were not a little suspected to fear and envy the Prosperity and Power of *Holland*, that they did not guard the Seas against a few Pirats, who for their own Profit sought their Booty where it was to be found.

In the mean time, to deceive the poor Innocent Commonalty once more, the Directors appointed to take care of the Shipping designed to the Eastward and *Norway*, were by Placaet continued, and Private Ships of War by great Rewards perswaded to take and destroy the Enemys Ships. Upon which divers good Patriots fitted out Ships for that end; and this small strength being in the hands of those who really intended to destroy the Enemys Ships, it was observed, especially of two Ships of *Flushing*, the one called the *Samson* mounted with 24 Guns, 100 Seamen, and 30 Souldiers, and the other called the *Flushing*, mounted

*But at last the Privateers being perswaded by great Rewards, it appeared how easily the narrow Seas could be scour'd.
See the Placaet book 11 of March, 1632. Aitzma p 145.*

ed with 22 Guns, 100 Seamen, and 30 Souldiers, that they took so many of the Enemies Ships, and Prisoners, that by their means a general Release was thrice made on both sides, the *Dunkirks* so discouraged and weakned, and the Seas so well cleared, that the Insurances from *Rochel* and *Bourdeaux* fell to three in the hundred.

But because these worthy Patriots, among whom *Adrian* and *Cornelis Lamsins* were the chief, for want of *Dunkirk* Privateers could fight for no more Booty, but chiefly by reason of the too slow, or refused paiments of the promised Rewards, they fitted out no more Ships, and the clearing of the Seas coming again to depend on the Deputies of the Generality, and the Prince of *Orange*, the *Dunkirkers* returned again to Sea as strong in the following Years as before, and made it equally dangerous; the Rates of Insurance rising as high as formerly. And it was very observable, that tho for the paiment of this so necessary and well deserved Reward only two hundred thousand Guilders were demanded yearly by the Council of State, yet the same Council, and the States of *Holland* and *Zealand* jointly, for the Year 1643 before Prince *Henry*'s doting old Age, could not obtain that Sum of the Generality to pay the promised Reward to the new Cruisers, whilst for the following Years, until our Peace with *Spain*, the same or greater Petitions for Mony by Land and Sea were granted to the Council of State, and consented to, and born by the *Hollanders*. So that *Holland* from the Year 1632. to the Year 1647 was necessitated to take up sixty nine Millions, making with the foremention'd fifty and one, one hundred and twenty Millions of Guilders at Interest, besides thirteen Millions that were to be paid for currant Debts, that the Prince and the Deputies of the Generality might proceed in their Offensive Wars by Land.

And as if it were not enough that the good People of these Countrys, and the State of *Holland* it self were every way opprest by Land with so many Imposts, Taxes, and immense Sums of Mony taken up at Interest, as well as by continual and unexpressibly great Losses by Sea, the Deputies of the Generality and the Prince of *Orange* likewise desired, and from time to time very subtilly, and with promises of Gratuities to the Directors of the *West-India* Company, That they would desist from their Trade which was driven for the common Benefit of the Subscribers, and which according to their Oath might not cease, and would employ that Mony for the indispensible Service of the Country, by carrying on a more vigorous War against the King of *Spain*. And by such powerful Solicitations, and artificial Promises, they were induced to make not a Merchant-like, but a Prince-like War, and to make those Royal Conquests at *Brazil*, *Angola*, St. *Thomas*, &c. for the Benefit of the States General, and of the Prince, as indeed was * at first design'd.

And then ill influence especially appear'd about the West-India Company.

See the Remonstrance and Request for continuing their Charter, 1668. p. 3, 4, &c.

By this means the greatest part of their Capital Stock was consumed and embezeled, and the honest Subscribers with other Inhabitants concerned in that Company

---

* *Tibi Roma subegerit Orbem*

P   lost

lost above one hundred and eighteen Millions of Guilders. And when the said Company afterwards were grown so weak that they could no longer keep those vast Conquests by their own Power, the Deputies of the Generality, and the successive Princes of Orange, for whose Benefit those Lands were conquered, nearly abandoning their own Interest, suffered those excellent and vast Countries to fall into and continue in the hands of the false and treacherous *Portuguese*, whereby our Inhabitants lost (besides the foresaid vast Sums) in Goods, Cattels, Houses, Debts, &c. fifty Millions of Guilders more, and were also utterly excluded from that advantageous Trade and Navigation. But to return to the Government and Conduct of Publick Affairs in our *Netherlands*, I say, that tho *Holland* was thus intolerably opprest, and torn down, yet in the Year 1633, *Rynberg* was taken, and in the Year 1634, *Breda* and *Mastricht* were besieged in vain, and our chargeable Army lay a long time in the *Langestraat*. And in the Year 1635, with a very great Army, and more charge, we did nothing in the Field, only *Tirlen* was plundered, and *Schenkenschans* lost. Likewise in the Year 1636, our Army with many Ships lay about the *Sas* of *Gent*, and afterwards in the *Langstraat* to no purpose. And in the Year 1637, *Breda* was taken with very great charges, and on the other side, *Venlo* and *Ruremond* were lost. As also in the following Year, after great Expence, we lost much Reputation before *Callo*, where the Enemy killed 2000 of our Souldiers, and took 1200 Prisoners, with all our Cannon, eighty Ships,

Ships, and much Baggage. And tho our Army that lay before *Gelder* was much stronger than the Enemy, yet we quitted the Siege, with the loss of six Demicannon, and two Standards. In the Year 1639, our Army with 15 hundred Vessels in *Flanders* effected nothing, and were again compelled to retreat from before *Gelder*, and march to *Rynberg*. The same Army did afterwards no better at *Hulst*; nor in the following Year 1640, at which time Count *Henry* of *Friesland* was there killed; and our Army tho intrench'd drew off a third time in a flying Posture from *Gelder*, without daring to encounter a much weaker Enemy, the Prince of *Orange* having then the Conduct and Command in Person, who notwithstanding many expensive and fruitless Expeditions into *Flanders*, *Brabant*, and *Gelderland*, had by his excessive Power in these Countrys gained the Name of a very Wise and Valiant General. But in *Flanders* and *Burgundy* he was derided even in their Comedies for a Coward; in one of which he was anatomiz'd, and upon search his Heart found in his Heels, the Rabble having nothing more frequently in their mouths than the following Rhyme,

J. V. Veens *Kyme.*

* *Prince* Henry *has no Courage,*
Takes neither Town nor Village.

However in the Year 1641, with excessive Expences he took *Gennep*-house after a bloody Siege of seven weeks. And in the Year 1642,

---

* Le Prince Heny est sans Courage,
Il ne prend Ville ni Village.

as also in 1643, our Army was in the Field about 6 Months without effecting any thing; but in the Year 1644, after six weeks Siege, and much blood spilt, the Sas van Gent was taken. And in 1645, in the Year 1645, after a long Campagn, and six weeks Siege, Hulst was yielded. And tho our Army lay in the Year 1646 about Antwerp, and afterwards before Venlo, yet we got nothing but Dishonour in those Attempts.

And it is observable, that all our chargeable Campagns, and Taxes for the Army, tended chiefly to increase the Power of the *French*, who in the mean time took many Cities from the *Spaniards*, but not at all to the benefit of our own People, either by Sea or Land. For tho the Province of *Holland* contributed in extraordinary Subsidies two Millions yearly for scouring of the Seas, and continued so to do to the end of the War, yet the other *United Provinces* were not so forward. And tho for some Years past, the Governments of *Spain* and *Flanders* set not out any Ships for Booty against us, but left that work to be carried on by private Capers, yet the Sea remained still infested in such a manner, that the *Dunkirkers* in the Year 1635 took all the Buss-Convoys, and many Busses, while most of our Ships of War for want of paiment lay by the Walls.

And tho the Council of State, and the States of *Holland* complained of this neglect at Sea, and pray'd that some better Order might be settled for prompt paiment of the Premiums promised to the particular Privateers, by whom we had reaped great Advantage; yet the Deputys of the Generality, or

rather

rather those of the Princes Cabinet, according to their old way, found it convenient once more to delude the well meaning People; and to appease them, *Anno* 1636 they accused and dismiss'd fourteen Sea Captains, with some further Punishment, making a new Regulation concerning the guarding of the *Flemish* Coast, and keeping the Narrow Seas uninfested by 22 Ships and ten Yachts, which were to be under the inspection of the Prince of *Orange*, and such Deputys of the Generality as he should please to chuse. These depending on the Prince's favour, and making that their Aim and Interest more than the Service of their Native Country, labouring by all means to augment the Prince's Authority, and lessen that of the States, by this means had the Name of the *Cabinet Lords* given them by the Lovers of their Countrys Freedom, and so you will find them nam'd sometimes in the following discourse. And this was really * what *Tacitus* said of *Augustus Cesar* " This Prince rais'd
" himself by degrees, grasping into his own
" hands the business of the Senate, of the
" Magistrates, and of the Laws; while no
" body dar'd to oppose him · For the stoutest
" were cut off, either by being sent to the Ar-
" my, or by Proscription. The rest of the
" Nobility, by how much the more they were
" slavish in temper, by so much the more were

Ibid. p. 344.

Polity of the Cabinet Lords was only to aggrandize the Prince, and to lessen Holland.

---

* Princeps insurgere paulatim, munia Senatus, Magistratuum, Legum in se trahere, nullo adversante · cum ferocissimi per acies, aut proscriptione cecidissent. Ceteri nobilium quanto quis servitio promptior, opibus & honoribus extollerentur ac novis ex rebus aucti, tuta & præsentia, quam vetera & periculosa mallent. *Tacit. Annal.* l. 1 c 1.

P 3 " they

"they advanced to Wealth and Honour,
"chose rather to sit down contented with
"their present State of Security, than to ven-
"ture the recovering of their antient Liber-
"ty, with running any hazard. The usual
way of all crafty and arbitrary Usurpers.

So that to enlarge the Authority of the Prince of *Orange* over the Navigation of *Holland*, and to put it effectually under his Power, eleven hundred and eight thousand eight hundred and seventy Guilders were yearly levied, and Superintendants appointed for that Service, with Purveyors or Victuallers, who were to be accountable to the Chamber of Accounts of the Generality. Also all Commanders and Captains were chosen by the said Prince, who were to be punished by a Council of War of his Nomination, and a narrow Scrutiny to be made into their Conduct. And to encourage them to do their Duties, their Wages were raised. So that according to this new Order, the respective Admiralties had nothing to transact, but to be Judges of the Prizes taken, to collect the Convoy and Custom Revenues, with which, and with two Millions of Subsidies, they were to set out Ships of War, to be Convoys to the Westward.

But it soon appeared that this new Authority, which was put into the hands of those who had nothing to lose at Sea, produced worse Effects than ever. For, before the Year 657, there was so little Care taken, that *Jacob Pieters van Dorp*, Lieutenant Admiral of *Holland*, going to Sea with this Princely Fleet very late, and his Provisions being spent in a very short time, was compelled to return home, and finding that the

Com-

Commonalty accused him, and not the Victuallers, nor the Prince of *Orange*, who really were in the Fault, and would possibly have punished him rather than the Guilty, he laid down his Commission.

In the mean time the *English* challenged the Sovereignty of the narrow Seas, alledging, That the Fishery belong'd solely to them. But then intestine Divisions, and not our Sea Forces, put a stop to that work, and their Herring-fishing, then newly begun, ceased. It is observable, that when they had taken their Herring at one and the same time and place with the *Hollanders*, and sent them to *Dantzick* in the Years 1637, and 1638, and found that the Herring taken and cured by the *Hollanders* was approved and good, and that the *English* Herring to the very last Barrel were esteemed naught; they then chang'd their Claim upon the whole Fishery, into that of having the Tenth Herring, which the diligent and frugal Inhabitants of *Holland* reputed no less than to fish for, and pay Tribute to a slothful and prodigal People, for a Passage by the Coast of *England*, which yet must have been paid, had not the free Government of the States of *Holland*, in the Year 1667, brought those Maritime Affairs into another State and Condition.

In the same Year 'twas publickly shewn, "That the Inhabitants of these Countries "could not possibly keep the Sea any long- "er after this manner, and amongst others, "they brought the Example of *Maesland- "Sluice*, whence there used every harvest Sea- "son about fifty Vessels for Haddock to go "to Sea, which number was in the last Har-

Vid. p. 621.

Selden's Mare Clausum.
Aitzma B. 16. p. 256.
Ibid. p. 277.
M. Semeins Haarlv. Vissery

And the K. of England pretended to the Dominion of the Narrow Seas.

Aitzma, Book 17. p. 622.

"vest 1636, diminished to ten, out of which
"also two were taken. That their Dog-
"ger-fishing, which was not to be parallel'd
"in *Europe*, was now become so inconsider-
"able, that it was doubted whether in the
"Year 1637, so much as one Dogger would
"go to Sea for Salt Cod, seeing since the first
"of *January* 1631, there had been taken of
"the *Maas* and *Sluice* Vessels by the *Dunkirkers*
"alone, above two hundred Ships, each of
"them, one with the other, worth above
"5000 Guilders. There having the like loss
"hapned in other Havens, of Vessels set out
"for Fishing, so that the general cry of the
"People of those Places ascended to the
"Heavens, and was sufficient to melt a Heart
"of Stone.

And seeing the Merchants who sustained the Loss, and the Wives, Children, Parents, and Relations of the imprisoned Seamen, and Fishers continually upbraided the Admiral, Vice-Admiral, and Captains of Ships, with their ill Conduct, Prince *Henry* seemed to lament their Case, more than that of the meaner Commonalty, saying, That there is no Condition more wretched than that of the Admiral, and Sea Captains, seeing that the meanest Fisher-wife having lost her Husband, exclaimed, that the Admirals and Sea-Captains did not their Duty, &c. and yet to pacify the People, who foolishly conceiv'd that the Gentlemen *Oyran*, *Hautain*, *Nassaw*, and *Dorp*, were successively the sole Cause of their past Calamitys, the Pr. of *Orange* chose two Tarpaulins (as some call them) *Martin Harpertson Tromp* and *Witte Corneliffen de Witte*, for Admiral and Vice-Admiral. But it soon appeared,

peared, that those mentioned Losses were but jointly provided against by the continual ill Management of publick Affairs at Land, and the neglect of securing the Seas. For tho the King of *Spain* and the Government of *Flanders*, had for a long time forborn to set out Ships of War to prey upon us in the narrow Seas, yet did not the Owners of Privateers at *Dunkirk* neglect to set out their Capers; but in the Year 1638, by reason of the Disorders about our Coast-Ships, and clearing of the Seas according to the old practice, they did not only go to Sea, and take many Merchant-men, but also about the end of *October* dispers'd all the Busses, which fled home very much disabled, and some without their Nets; while Admiral *Tromp* coming on Shore himself to be revictualled, accused Vice-Admiral *Berkhout*, who came in likewise, without the least Necessity, and for which he was dismissed by the new Council of War, tho unheard, and the poor suffering Commonalty were with this Punishment once again appeased in some measure, but not so the States of *Holland*, who knowing that the Prince of *Orange*, and Deputies of the Generality had now, as often before, made use of the Product of the Convoys, Customs, and Subsidies, which were only to be applied to Maritime Affairs, for carrying on the War by Land, (by which means the guarding and clearing of the Seas came to be neglected) earnestly desired that all Sums of Mony which had formerly been appropriated to the Service of the Sea, might be effectually applied that way.

And several Cities in *Holland*, together with the Province of *Utrecht*, taking notice of

Aitzma, Book 18. p. 91. and Book 19. p. 172.

When yet the losses by Sea continued, the States of Holland *complained, that the Mony collected to clear the Seas was imploy'd for Land Service.*

of the Disorder and ill Management of the Prince, and his assumed Cabinet-Council, in our Maritime Affairs, shewed their unwillingness to bring in their Portion of the 1 1088½ Guilders, which were yearly demanded by the Prince for that end, yet on account of his great Power, *Holland*, and divers other Provinces were obliged to bear the burden to the Year 1647, and our Peace with *Spain*. And tho at the beginning of the Year 1639, in a Sea-Fight about *Dunkirk*, we got the Victory, in which the *Dunkirkers* lost two Ships of War, yet did *Tromp* then with the Ships under his Command, very imprudently leave the Sea, so that the *Dunkirkers* came and brav'd us before our Harbours, where, by reason of our defective Management in refitting and victualling, they lay till mid-*June*, and took 13 of our Ships in a short time.

And whilst *Tromp* afterwards waited for the great *Spanish* Fleet, *Anno* 1639, between the two Peers of *Dover* and *Calais* and before *Dunkirk*, our Merchant men and Fishers were abandoned, thirty or forty Privateers of *Dunkirk* lying at the Mouth of our Harbours, so that none of our Merchant Ships, or Busses durst go to Sea. And upon this followed in *October* the Engagement about the *Downs*, where the *Spaniard* having lost by sinking, burning, stranding and taking, 40 Ships, most of our came home, and having left the Sea, the *Dunkirkers* came again before our Harbours, and in few days took twenty seven Prizes, of which 11 in one day. And thus by continual Disorders and Losses at Sea, the Trade of these Countries was so diminished, that the Revenues of the Admiralties, in the Year 1628,

having

having yielded about sixteen hundred thousand Guilders, those very Duties, to the 24*th* of *October* this Year, notwithstanding the new Impositions, produced to the State only twelve hundred thousand Guilders. And therefore it was thought necessary to erect a new Tax of Tonnage, which should amount to five hundred and ninety eight thousand five hundred and seventy five Guilders, and also another new Tax to clear the Seas, which might produce five hundred eighty one thousand and seventeen Guilders.

However the Deputies of *Holland*, in the Assembly of the States General, and Presence of the Prince of *Orange*, declared, " That " it was the Intention of their Princi- " pals, that the Cruisers or Privateers, by " whom the Country had been so signally " served, and who had only declined that ' Service because they were not paid their " promised Rewards, should be invited to " return to Sea, and that a certain Fund " should be appointed for their immediate " payment. But this just and useful motion was neglected.

Matters standing thus, Prince *Henry* and the Deputies of the Generality, endeavoured to persuade the States of *Holland*, and privately the Cities in an unwarrantable manner, that the Colledges and Orders of the Admiralties were not sufficient to clear the Seas from Enemies, and therefore moved the said Cities to consent, that the Equippage of Ships might be continued at *Helvoetsluce*, and for that end, that a new College of Admiralty might be erected to reside at the *Hague*, and that an Insurance Company might be esta-

Ibid. p. 230.
See the Placaet Book.

Aitzma, *p.*230.

Which the Deputies of the Generality, and P. Henry proposing to secure with many new Expedients, Aitzma, Book 19. *p.* 230.

established, as before mentioned, and settled by Patent. And moreover, that the Revenues of the Admiralties might be farmed to such as should bid most. And lastly, that all Persons being under Oath to the Generality, should be tried for their Faults and Crimes by the Council of State, or the respective Admiralties.

The States of Holland, ... Amsterdam, ... In opposition to which the States of Holland, shewed how prejudicial those Equipments, or setting out Ships to Sea, had been by means of the Superintendants and Purveyors or Victuallers at *Hevoetsluys*, and also that the Admiralties of *Zeland* and *Friesland* respectively had never consented to have any Equipments made there. That most of the Provinces, except *Holland*, in the payment of their proportion of 1108870 Guilders designed thereunto, were always slow and remiss to the whole, or else deficient in part; and that the Admiralty would and could better equip or set forth Ships to Sea than others, and that an Insurance Company would so burden and clog our Trade, that our Inhabitants would not be able to sell so cheap as our Neighbours. And that the Farmers would not have any regard to the durable Prosperity of Commerce, but to their present Profit, and so belike might value themselves upon the seizure of Goods, whereby they might so plague the Merchants, that they would rather cease trading, or leave the Country. And concerning the point of Jurisdiction to be granted to the Generality, and to the respective Admiralties, that 'tis a matter of so great Importance, that the whole Sovereignty of the Provinces wou'd necessarily be thereby transferred to them. But

But the Prince of *Orange* and the Deputies of the Generality were not well pleased with the Representation made by the States of *Holland* and *West-Friesland*, and still resolved to carry on their Design, and by their Greatness to overpower them, sending notable Addresses, however illegal, for that end, to the particular Cities, and especially to the Burgemasters and Council of *Amsterdam*, by whose good Management, and firm Opposition, as also by Prince *Henry*'s smooth and easy Maxims which hitherto he had followed, that he might be thought unlike his hated Brother, together with a fear of being reputed as Arbitrary as *Maurice* had been, this Design failed, and went no further

Aitzma, B. 19. p 176.

So that they procceded no further, the Sea in the interim being as much infested as before, tho the States of Holland represented how easily it might be kept clear.

And tho *Holland* was thus saved from sudden Ruin, yet the uneasiness and losses of the Trading and Maritime Inhabitants still continued so that the Council of State, and the States of *Holland*, once more remonstrated, that the private Capers of *Dunkirk* had done us much more Mischief than ever the King's Ships had done, and that we on our side had seen that our Cruisers fitted out by private Men, in hopes of the Reward promised for taking the Enemies Ships, had in a short time purged the Seas from Depredations, and that those Robbers were again abroad, perceiving our Capers, for want of such payment, went out no more against the *Dunkirk* Robbers, but only against Merchant Ships; and therefore the said States most instantly desired to have the Placaet renewed, whereby the said Rewards may certainly and immediately be paid. But this was not granted.

By

By means of all which Disorders it was no wonder that little less than nineteen Millions was granted according to the Petitionary Request of the Council of State for the Year, and yet nothing done. On the contrary, Lieutenant Admiral *Tromp*, on the 1st of *March* of the ensuing Year 1640, gave Advice, that the *Dunkirkers* had then 40 Sail of Ships at Sea, taking rich Prizes, and skimming the Seas by Squadrons. So that the very Convoys of this State were unsecure, and often taken; and that on our side Vice-Admiral *de Witt* was at Sea with 6 or 7 Sail only. So that the great Losses of the Merchants, which had continued so many Years, produced in the Years 1639, and 1640, in the Province of *Holland*, and chiefly at *Amsterdam*, more Bankrupts of the richest and worthiest Traders than ever had been known or heard in these Countries. And for this reason those of *Holland* proposed to the Assembly of the States-General, in Presence of the Prince of *Orange*, and concluded, That the respective Admiralties should, as formerly, set out Ships for guard of the Coast, and Cruisers; and that four Receivers should be appointed to receive the Mony required to that end, that so it might not be mixed with other Monies, or employed to pay the Debts of the Admiralties.

And in regard every one could perceive that this Order was not effectual enough to clear the Seas, 159 of the principal Merchants of *Amsterdam*, in the beginning of the Year 1641, joined with the States of *Holland*, and besought the States General, that better care might be taken to keep in the *Dunkirkers* than formerly,

formerly, adding, That in case it were not done, they would detain their Mony given for payment of 50 Companies of Souldiers, levied in the Year 1628, and clear the Seas themselves. But at that time the Prince of Orange, and the Deputies of the Generality, who were supported and encouraged by him, were still so much dreaded, that the States of *Holland* durst not undertake to intermeddle with a matter so much for the Advantage of our Trade and Fishery. Wherefore the *Dunkirkers* continued going to Sea, and not only so, but took Prizes at the Mouth of our Harbours. Particularly in *April* 1642, with 22 Frigots they seized all they met with, and among others, eighteen Ships belonging to *Zierickzee*. And on the 5th of *November* 10 *Dunkirk* Frigots were so bold, that they fell upon the whole *Russia* Fleet, and having taken of them eight Merchant Ships, and a Man of War, the other Convoy with eight *Russia* Men more, hardly escaped.

Aitzma Book 22. p. 360.

So that the Dunkirkers gain'd Ground upon us. J. V. Sand. Hist.

And altho the Deputies of the great Fishery had complained in *June* to the Deputies of the Generality of their Losses, and desired better Protection, yet we may easily perceive how little the Prince of *Orange*, and the Deputies, regarded the Loss, and Complaints of the Seamen, and trading Inhabitants, since instead of redressing matters, they had not only in the foregoing Year employed the Mony granted for that end, in setting out a Fleet of twenty Ships for the Assistance of *Portugal*, but also, tho that Fleet had effected nothing for the Benefit of these Countries, nor could do it, yet nevertheless for the same end, the Generality made a new demand

And that in lieu of redressing our Merchants and Fishers, Complaints, their Mony was diverted to assist Portugal.

mand of 600000 Guilders. So that we may justly say, that the Prince of *Orange*, with the Deputys of the Generality, and the Inland Provinces, made it their principal Business to pay their Land Army, and in case of any Deficiency, to connive at false Musters, taking all possible care so to order matters, that the Taxes for the Army might be well paid, or else *Holland* was put to find Mony or Credit for that purpose. Yet for all this, when the States of *Holland* had freely and readily levied many and great Taxes to clear the Seas, they were forced to let them fall into the hands of those who employed them to other Ends. The States of *Holland* continuing in such an awful Reverence for the Prince; and some others who laboured more to advance his Interest, and get his Favour, than to procure the Prosperity of the Country, that they durst not make use of their own Mony to clear the Sea. Only those of *Holland* and *Zealand* consulted together to scour the Seas at their own Charge, distinct from the other Provinces; but would not execute their Project for fear of offending the Prince. Yet those of *Zealand* took a vigorous Resolution to erect a *Western* Society, to set out 24 Ships of War, out of the Produce of a Duty of one *per Cent.* upon all Goods inward, and one half *per Cent.* upon all Goods outward bound, to maintain Convoys for all Ships to the *Westward*, forwards and backwards.

By all which it appears how much the Trade and Navigation of our People was at that time abandoned by the Government: For the *East* and *West-India* Companys, together with the

the *Greenland* Company, prohibited them sailing into those Seas. The great Fishery Northward and Eastward, were forc'd to pay their own Convoys. The *Straits* Ships were to defend themselves against the *Turks* by their chargeable manning and arming, according to the new Regulation. And yet they deliberated to put the Charge of Convoying Westward upon the Merchants, as if all Dutys raised for Convoys, Customs, and Subsidys, as well as all other Imposts, were paid for nothing, and ought to be wrested from the trading Inhabitants, and other People of *Holland*, to the end that Province might not increase, but decay in Power and Riches.

As if all other Taxes were paid for nothing, and all the Inhabitants that used the Sea were perfectly abandoned of the State.

But the Western Society not going on, those of *Holland* and *Zealand* jointly remonstrated so earnestly the necessity of better clearing of the Seas, and the usefulness of private Ships of War, if care were taken that the Rewards so often promised might be readily paid, that at last in the Year 1643, out of certain new Imposts a Fund was raised of 200000 Guilders to pay the Reward promised for all the Enemys Ships of War that had been taken. So that by renewing the Placaet, the Inhabitants and Magistrates of the Citys of *Holland* were encouraged to set out Ships of War for that Service.

But at last the States of Holland and Zealand procured a certain Fund for the Premium. Aitzm. p. 578.

And tho the Commonalty during this long and ill Government of Publick Affairs, were made to believe that the Sea was so wide and vast, that it could not be cleared from the *Dunkirkers*, yet by these new Cruisers which were set out by the Magistrates of *Amsterdam* and *Roterdam*, the Citys of *North-Holland,*

Sea, and some particular Persons of *Zealand*, it soon appeared, that not only the Narrow Seas, but the Ocean also could very well be freed of them. For so soon as the clearing of the Seas was effectually undertaken, and Men encouraged by the Reward, there were so many *Spanish* Men of War taken, and beaten out of the Seas, that in lieu of giving 8 or 10 per Cent. for Insurance to *Rochel* or *Bourdeaux*, it fell to two or three only.

And tho by their free and open Navigation thus procured, and the Increase of Commerce both in *Holland* and *Zealand* which followed thereupon, those Provinces were likely to grow so strong, as to be too high to crouch to the Captain and Admiral-General, yet Prince *Henry* weakned with Age, could not remedy that growing Inconveniency, as he had formerly done. Which was so well known to the States, and particularly to those of *Holland*, that in the Year 1645, the new Cruisers were encouraged to continue their care of the Seas, by more advantagious Conditions than before. Till in the end a Peace with *Spain* was concluded in the Year 1648 which put an end to the War, and *Flemish* Privateering.

But whilst the Prince of *Orange*, and his Cabinet Council, the Deputys of the Generality, transported with Ambition, and jealousy of *Holland's* Greatness and Power, helpt to break the Ballance between *France* and *Spain* to the prejudice of all *Europe*, and of us in particular, making the Crown of *France* visibly to preponderate the other, and too long favouring their Arms with so great Imprudence, that Admiral *Tromp* with his
Princely

Princely Fleet of Coast-ships, holding in the Years 1644, 1645, and 1646 successively, *Graveling, Mardike,* the *Schuurtien,* and *Dunkirk* it self block'd up by Sea, caused them to fall into the hands of the *French*. In recompence of which they burden'd our Countrymen residing in *France* with higher Dutys than any other Nation paid. Besides which they shew'd their thievish Nature, by seizing in the *Mediterranean* Seas as many as they could of our Merchant Ships, especially the Richest; and manifested their Unfaithfulness against their even too faithful Allys. So that whereas in times past we had traded in some parts of *Italy* belonging to the King of *Spain* with freedom, and without search, the *French* caused all our Ships to strike, and having by Letters or Bills of Lading found any Enemys Goods on board, they did not only confiscate them, but also all the *Holland* Goods with them. Whereby the Merchants of *Amsterdam* alone, as they have owned, lost more than ten Millions of Guilders. Which added to the Revolt of the treacherous *Portuguese* in *Brazil, Angola,* and *St Thomas,* lay so heavy upon them, that in the Years 1646, and 1647, Bankrupts were become frequent and great, our Traffick and Exchange Banks being at a stand for some time, no Man knowing whom to trust. And indeed how great those Losses must have been that were able to ruin so many rich and worthy Merchants, may appear, if we consider that the *English,* during the War of the Years 1652, and 1653, having taken in the *Channel* and *North-Sea* an incredible number of our Merchants Ships, nevertheless very few Bankrupts were seen amongst

See Aitzma on those respective Years.

At last we had Peace with Spain, but France began to prey upon us by Sea.

Which caused a vast number of Bankrupts.

amongst our Merchants, and almost none except in other parts.

With these ... depredations ceased ... of the last Captain-General, ... hereafter among the good ... peace and safety Government of ... And now for conclusion, I shall desire the Reader, if he doubt of the Truth herein treated concerning our Affairs of State and ..., Second hand, to examine the same more amply and fully by the Books of L... ... (by the confession of all ... Authentick Historian) from whence these Particulars are for the most part extracted, and to consider at the same time whether the increase of the Riches of the Inhabitants of ... in general, during the Government of these Count Lords, and successive Princes, be not very impertinently attributed to that Government, seeing that Increase, next to the Blessing of God, was caused by our good situation on the Sea, and Rivers, and, as is useful, by the * destructive Wars which lasted very long in other parts, and especially in the neighbouring Countrys. For in the time of old Prince *William*, the R... of *France* and *Flanders*, and after ...'s in the Times of the Princes *Maximilian* ... , those lasting Wars, and terrible Devastators of *Country*, and many other adjacent Countrys, supported and supplied our Citys with Manufactures, Merchants and Mechanicks, who finding here the States ... of Government not quite

---

* ... Rem. Alamans. Liv.

overthrown, have under those Remains of publick Freedom, erected many new Manufactures and Trades, and have been able to keep up the old Imployments and Traffick of Holland, especially through the Diligence, Vigilance, Valour, and Frugality, which are not only natural to the Hollanders, but by the Nature of our Country is communicated to all Foreigners that inhabit among us, according to the old Saying, * *There is a certain secret Force natural to the Country of* Holland. So that our Inhabitants by the said Qualifications for the promoting of Traffick and Navigation, having excelled all other neighbouring People, 'tis a wonder that by our beforementioned ill Government in Maritime Affairs, we were not utterly ruined.

Our thriving proceeds from the Wars of our Neighbours, our Situation and Shadow of Liberty, &c.

'Tis also to be well considered, whether the Inhabitants of *Holland* in such Cases, and indued with such Qualifications, would not have been much more happy under a Free Government by States, than under the Conduct of the three successive Princes beforementioned, and such Deputys of the Generality as continually sought to promote the Prince's Grandeur, and consequently their own, more than the Welfare of the Country.

And whether our own sad Experience hath not abundantly taught us the Truth of the Maxim proposed at the beginning of this Chapter, *viz.* That such Citys and Countrys, whose Rulers ought to be presumed to be more or less concerned to keep the Seas clear of Enemys, ought also to have more or less

---

† Occulta est Batavæ quædam vis insita terræ.

Authority and Power about Maritime Affairs, Treasure, and Militia, by which the Seas are to be kept free and open. And consequently that the Magistrates of the Cities, who are any ways concerned in the flourishing of the Manufactures, Fisheries, Traffick, Shipping, and Guard of the Seas, ought to be intrusted with them and no other Persons in the World.

CHAP. II.

Above all things War, and chiefly by Sea, is most prejudicial, and Peace very beneficial for Holland.

BUT if the scouring of the Seas against Sea-Robbers or Enemys is so necessary for Holland during Peace, then much more Peace it self. For besides that all Sea-robbing is more frequent in War, it deprives our Inhabitants at once of all their Trade to the Enemys Country, and carries it to the Inhabitants of neutral Nations, besides which, all Ships, Goods and Debts of the *Hollanders* that are in the Enemys Country are confiscated, which may give the People an incredible great Blow: For the *Hollanders* do not wait as other People till Men come to buy their Goods in their own Country, and give ready Mony for them, but they transport their Goods through the World, and keep them there in Warehouses waiting for Chapmen; and that which is most grievous, when they sell, in *Europe* they usually give a Years time for paiment. And more-

moreover, when in any Foreign Country the Growth and Manufactures of that Place are very plentiful and cheap, such Commoditys are presently bought up by our Merchants, paid with ready Mony, and kept in their Magazins there, till the Season of Exportation and Shipping presents for other Places, so that the Enemy may easily make seizure of many of our Goods, which we can by no means retaliate

Because our Debts are confiscable in an Enemys Country.

And then it also commonly happens, that our Enemys either by whole Fleets do intirely obstruct our Trade by Sea, or by Privateers may make incredible Depredations upon us. For by reason that our Fishery and Foreign Trade are so greatly dispersed, *Holland* is not able to defend them in all places, and be Masters at Sea at one and the same time; tho we had nothing else in charge but only to clear the Seas. Whereas we on the contrary can find little or no Booty at Sea, because we are the only great Traders there.

And our Navigation obstructed and disturbed.

And for War by Land, tho it be not so prejudicial to *Holland* as by Sea, yet 'tis manifestly disadvantagious to the Merchant, and greatly mischievous to all the Inhabitants in general, but especially to those that drive a Foreign Trade. And whosoever doubts of this, let him only consult the Registers of the Admiraltys of *Amsterdam*, with those of other Places, and he will see that since our Peace with *Spain* our Navigation and Commerce is increased one half. The Reader may also remember, that during the War, the Convoy and Customs together did at most amount to but 1588763 Guilders, yet when we had Peace, our Convoy-mony alone of all the Admiraltys

Aitzma, Chap. 2.

did in the Year 1654, produce 3172898 Guilders, when by calculation it was concluded that the Admiralty of Zealand had yearly 200000 Guilders of Revenue. And that is not all as yet, for the War with Spain being carried on both by Sea and Land, our Merchants were put to great troubles and straits. And 'tis a great burden to our Inhabitants to bring into the Field so great and chargeable an Army, as to gain fortified Citys from our Neighbours by long Sieges. But it is obvious ridiculous to endeavour to make Men of understanding believe that it tended to the Benefit of Holland, when an honourable Peace, or a long Truce was every year offered to us, as often to reject and refuse it, and yet Holland was forced to take up a vast Sum of Money at Interest, and then to take up another Sum to pay those Interests, and all this to carry on an offensive War to gain Conquests and Victories, which are not only useless, but must needs be very burdensom to a Country whose Frontiers, by means of the Sea and Rivers, are for the most part every where so easy to be fortified and kept, that by purely standing on its own defence, it would certainly be able to confound all Foreign Power that should attack it. Whereas on the other side it is certain, that generally all Republicks, especially those that subsist by Commerce, have been ruined by Offensive Wars and Conquests.

And that this was well known to those that sided with the Prince against those of Barnavelt's Party in this State, the President Jeannin testified on the 29th of August 1608. in a Letter to Monsieur Villeroy Secretary of State in France,

France, as follows It is certain that the States, how weak soever they are, do not lose their Courage, but rather chuse to return to War, than accept a Peace or Truce for many Years upon other Conditions than those formerly mentioned. They (I conceive he means such as by all means desired a War, and those were, as is well known, of the Prince's Party) say among themselves, If France abandons us, we must ruin, demolish, and abandon some Citys, and Parts of the remotest Provinces, which, by reason of the great charge of keeping 'em, will more weaken than strengthen us, and we must also dismantle some Places of least importance. And moreover they say, that all this being done, they shou'd have wherewith to continue in service 40000 Foot and 2500 Horse, besides the Navy, thirty years longer. And that therewith they should be strong enough so to tire the King of Spain, and after such a manner to exhaust his Treasury, that he will be necessitated to grant the Conditions which now he rejects.

Which formerly those that were of the Princes Partys, as also

And that Prince *Maurice* himself knew very well that these Countrys might be better and with less Expence defended against the Enemy with few Frontier Places than many, appears by a Letter written about 2 months after, to the said Prince by the King of *France*: in which among other Particulars is this Passage. The great Charge that the War requires you have experimented, and found that the States alone were not able to bear it, nay hardly with the help of Friends, who formerly contributed of their own to bear those Expences. And if it should happen that you by weakness, or want of Mony be necessitated to quit and leave some part of the Country to the Enemy, whereby to defend the rest the better, as the said **Lambert** (*the Prince's Envoy*) hath declared

Prince Maurice knew well enough.

clared to me on your behalf, that you are resolved to do so rather than enter into the said Treaty unless it be first express'd in plain Terms, That the Sovereignty shall ever be and remain in the States, &c.

And not to Conquer any, takes from

All which Particulars above mentioned being in those days agreed by Statesmen and experienced Souldiers, 'tis as certain that since that time by the Conduct of Prince *Henry*, very many remote Places about the *Schelt*, *Maes* and *Rhyne*, have been taken in and fortified, and that the Generality out of all the Lands and Citys situate out of the voting Provinces (for some of them are not allowed to have their Suffrages) about the Year 1664, had only one Million of Guilders annual Revenue, and yet the keeping of them cost more than 4 Millions yearly, so that those that are of the Prince's Party must in all respects acknowledg, That the States of *Holland* did in the Year 1640, very well represent the matter to Prince *Henry*, by telling him, That it deserv'd consideration, whether it were not better to make no more Conquests, or even to lose some that are already acquired, than by long Sieges, and consequently great Charge to the State, to suffer them suddenly to sink and fall in like an undermined Hill. Upon which there was nothing replied by the Prince, but only that he could not be well pleased to see the Conquests which had cost the Country so much Blood and Treasure, so little esteemed. From all which it is certain that *Holland*'s Interest is to seek after Peace, and not War.

Breaks altogether year a Million yearly, and require far more to

So that all offensive Wars are to be forborn

Aitzma F 2. p 104.

CHAP.

CHAP. III.

That Holland *hath antiently received these Maxims of Peace.*

AND that the Trading Provinces of the Netherlands have always followed these Maxims, manifestly appears in antient History. For the Sovereigns of the Country were never suffered by their own Authority to make War, or lay any Imposition for maintenance of Military Forces, nay not to do it in the meetings of the States, by plurality of Voices. For in these excessively prejudicial Affairs, they would not hazard their being over-voted. Whereof we have had very many Examples, not only in that rich Trading Province of *Flanders*, but also in *Holland*, especially with relation to *England*, with which Country the *Netherlands* could formerly deal well enough. For before the Halls and Tumults had removed the Weaving Trade thither, the *English* were Shepherds, and Wool-Merchants, and their King receiv'd few other Imposts than from Wool exported, no less depending on the *Netherlands* (the only Wool-weavers of *Europe*) than the Weavers on them.

The Maxims for Peace have antiently been well known in Holland.

And amongst others we read in the Year 1389, That Duke *Albert* of *Bavaria*, as Earl of *Holland* and *Zealand*, &c. having brought these Provinces, without the consent of *Dort* and *Zierickzee*, into a War with *England*, the *English* took many Ships with Wine coming from *Rochel*, and not only released all those that belonged to *Dort* and *Zierickzee*,

but

but came to those Places to sell their Prizes, because they had not consented to the War.

Which is demonstrated by the Intercursus Magnus.

And on this Foundation is built the great Intercourse (called *Intercursus Magnus*) between *England* and the *Netherlands*, containing expresly, *That the same Covenant is not only made between the Soveraign Lords of both sides, but between the Vassals, Cities, and Subjects also, so that those who had done the Injury, and not others, should be punished, the Peace and Covenant remaining in full force, for the Benefit of all others, who had not consented to the War, or Injury done.* So that if a Ship had sailed out without the Prince's Commission, or the Commission of any City, that City was to make good the Damage done by that Ship. And this Treaty (which is very observable) was not only signed by Plenipotentiaries, on the behalf of the King of *England*, and the Arch-Duke as Prince of these Lands, but also sealed and signed by the Burgo-masters of the Cities

That ratified by all the trafficking Cities.

of *Gent, Bruges, Ipres, Dunkirk, Newport, Antwerp, Bergen, Dort, Delft, Leyden, Amsterdam, Middleburgh, Zierickzee, Vere, Mechelen, Brussels*, and *Erill*, An. 1495. All which those on both sides affirm to have been transacted for the greater security of Amity and Trade.

For the Council of the Cities did not use to be under Oath to the Lord or Prince who usurped, and acquired the nomination of their Magistrates only by means of differences arising among the Cities, but the Cities might of antient times, without Approbation of the Earls, entertain Souldiers in their own Service. On the other side, the Earls used in times of Peace to have no Garisons, Souldiers,

ers, Magazines, or Treasure, which, with the Divisions of the Cities of *Amiens* and *St. Quintin* formerly mortgag'd, were the Cause that they fell from the House of *Burgundy* into the hands of the King of *France*, their antient Lord, in 1470. of which *Philip de Comines* thus speaks. Charles *Duke of Burgundy holding an Assembly of the States in his Country, (viz.* these *Provinces) represented to them the great Prejudice he had suffered, by having no Souldiery in pay on his Frontiers, as the King had, and that the Frontiers could have been well kept with* 500 *Men at Arms, and might have continued in Peace. He farther acquainted them with the great Dangers which hung over their Heads, and pressed hard for a Supply to maintain* 800 *Lanceers In the end, the States agreed to allow him* 120000 *Crowns annually, over and above what he received of his ordinary Revenues, not including* Burgundy *But his Subjects scrupled much to take that Burden upon them, tho to distress* France *with this body of Horse: (for* Lewis *the* 11th, *King of* France, *was the first in Europe, who in a time of Peace kept armed Forces on foot). And indeed the States of the* Netherlands *scrupled it not without Reason: For hardly had the Duke rais'd* 5 *or* 600 *of his Horse, but his desire of encreasing their number, and of invading all his Neighbours, grew to that height, that in a short time he brought them to the payment of five hundred thousand Crowns, keeping in pay great numbers of Horse, so that his Subjects were thereby greatly opprest.* Thus far *Comines*.

But at the Death of the Duke those standing Horse, in time of Peace, were disbanded till the Year 1547, when that formidable

Empe-

And it appeared also by the Earls of Holland having no standing Force, especially in Peace.

As also by Philip de Comines.

D. Charles of Burgundy the first who kept standing Forces.

Emperor, *Charles* the 5th, erected a certain number of standing Troops, consisting of 4000 Horse, commanded by Colonels and Captains, to be ready at all times, upon any Attempt, on the Frontiers, with their Horses and Arms. But *Philip* the 2d of *Spain*, being jealous of these armed Inhabitants, neglected to pay and muster them; so that these Regiments of the Militia coming to nothing, and he purposing in lieu of them, to maintain a standing Army of *Spaniards* in these Countries, was opposed in that Attempt by the States of the *Netherlands*, which was one of the principal Occasions of our Commotions and Wars that ensued.

And lastly, by the Union of Utrecht, the States have carefully the Netherlands not to end a War.

And with the Union of *Utrecht*, *Holland* neglected not altogether its Interest in this Particular: For according to the 9th Article, no plurality of Votes takes place in Affairs of a new War, Contribution, and Peace. Which Freedom the particular Members of *Holland* have constantly kept, as well as in the Assembly of the States; and not without Reason: For seeing it is contrary to the Law of Nature, for Men to give another the Power of taking away their Lives, on Condition and Promise that he will use it wholly for their Benefit; but yet that if he makes an ill use of that Power, and will take away their Lives, they may not in Self-Defence use their natural Strength against him: It follows, that all Obligations which do so powerfully oppose and prejudice the Welfare of our Country, must be null and void, so long as we are masters of our own Government.

CHAP.

CHAP. IV.

Some Cases laid down, in which it seems advisable for Holland *to engage in a War; and yet those being well weighed, it is concluded, that* Holland *nevertheless ought to seek for Peace.*

HAVING in the two last Chapters clearly shewed, what *Holland*'s Maxims ought to be, and have been of old, *viz.* Peace for her Inhabitants, to pursue the same by all convenient means, and decline War: Yet in several Cases whereby our People might be incumbred, or vexed, or in danger to be so, and when it may be presumed that our Free-State by Revolution of Time and Affairs, may run the Hazard of being ruined; it may be doubted, whether it would not be advisable for *Holland* to begin an offensive War.

I shall therefore give you my Thoughts about some of them, and do say, That we ought never to undertake a War by reason of any foreign Imposition or Toll whatsoever upon Goods; for those Remedies will always be worse for *Holland* than the Disease. And the same seems to be with much more conveniency removed, by charging their Commodities as much here, as our Wares, Merchants, and Mariners are charged in those Parts. In all such Cases we generally find, that either the high Impositions are prohibitions of themselves, or that the Traffick in those overburdened Commodities thrives as well as before: For if by those Tolls the Commodities

Enquiry made whether it be advisable,

To make no War, tho to free our selves from foreign Taxes?

modities burdened are prevented from being imported, he then that so charged them, immediately, finds thereby so great a Loss, that of his own accord he usually takes off this Imposition.

And of this we have innumerable Examples; for Histories are filled with Wars which have been in vain carried on, by reason of the laying such Tolls, as the Electors themselves have at last been glad to lessen, or take wholly away, as lately in *September* 1662, the Republick of *France* perceiving how much their Traffick by Sea was diminished, of their own Motion discharged two Tolls, the one named the 6 *per Cent.* and the other on Goods that came Westward from Sea.

On the other side, there occurs to my thoughts another great piece of Folly, *viz.* That the Merchants of *Holland*, and the State it self being founded upon Traffick, should yet make use of it for a perpetual Maxim, and continue in their present unfortified Condition, in which often for fear of a future and sharper War, they will be contriving to ballance the States of *Europe*. For when we have impregnably fortified all our Cities and Frontiers, as we ought, we may then, according to the Interest of our State say to all People, *Give Peace in our days, O Lord.* And if the worst happens, by sitting still we shall so strengthen and improve our Land, Sea-forces, and Treasure, that no Power will be easily brought to attack us, but rather some weaker State. Whereas now on the contrary, we exhaust our Treasure, and weaken our selves every way, not knowing whether we shall ever overcome these Inconveniences, which either by want

of

of Fortifications, or our obstinacy, we pull down upon our own Heads: and being weaker by our own Negligence or Wantonness, we may, after having wrestled with those Difficulties, more easily fall from one weakness into another, and so be at last overpowered.

As all skilful Physicians hold it for a good Maxim, * That one means of preserving Health, is to refrain from Health-drinking: So they always dissuade from taking Physick in time of Health, for fear of future Sickness, because thereby we frequently bring Sickness and Death upon our selves: Whereas by good Fortifications, and temporizing, we may escape, *Chi ha tempo ha vita*. And in all Cases Physick weakens the Body, and the continual use of it shortens a Man's Life. And therefore we may well make use of that wholesom Counsel, as most agreeable to our Provinces, *viz.* of using no Physician. For if *Holland* takes care to provide every thing necessary, and then stands in its own Defence, it is not to be overpowered by any Potentate on Earth. If we run to quench every Fire, for fear the War should pass over others, and kindle in our own Buildings, we shall certainly consume our selves by degrees, and by our own Actions be ruined.

In short, *Holland* taking due care of things, is so powerful as not to be conquered by any, except perhaps by *England*, if that Nation shall be willing to ruin it self. So that we may truly say, That if *Holland*, for fear of a

Holland's *Interest, since the weakness of the Spaniard, is perfectly another thing.*

---

† *Una salus sanis nullam potare salutem.*

War,

War, should begin a War, it must for fear of the Smoak leap into the Fire. And this Folly cannot be excused in any measure by that Maxim which we used here, in the beginning of our Troubles, * *War is better than uncertain Peace.* For seeing we then made War for our Freedom, or at least the shadow of it, against our own Prince, it is certain that all Peace, of what nature soever, would have disarmed the States of these Provinces, and depriv'd them of their Strength. And on the other side, the King of *Spain* remaining Prince of these Countries, and able to keep on foot some standing Forces in all his other Territories, might have made himself, at any time, absolute Lord of these Parts, without regard either to Promises, Oaths, or Seals; and then have punished all those at Will and Pleasure, who at any time had opposed him.

But now, God be praised, the States of *Holland* living in a time of Peace, are alone in possession of all the Strength of the Country, and are able to govern it better than in War, without the controul of any, according to their own Pleasures. So that the contrary is now true in *Holland*, † *War is much worse than an uncertain Peace.* And among all pernicious things, except the intolerable slavery of being govern'd by the Will of a single Person, nothing is more mischievous than a War. for if War be the very worst thing that can befal a Nation, then an uncertain Peace must be

---

* Pace dubia Bellum potius.
† Bellum pace dubia pejus, & majorum omnium pessimum.

bad, because a War is likely to ensue.

But some may further ask; seeing Peace is so necessary for *Holland*, whether out of a strong desire of a firm and lasting Peace, we ought not, when once engaged, to continue in War, till we have compell'd the Enemy to a well grounded Peace?

To this I answer, If we consider the uncertainty of this World, especially in *Europe*, and that we by Traffick and Navigation have occasion to deal with all Nations, we ought to hold for a firm and general Maxim, that an assured Peace is, in relation to *Holland*, a mere Chimera, a Dream, a Fiction, used only by those, who like Syrens or Mermaids, endeavour by their melodious singing of a pleasant and firm Peace, to delude the credulous *Hollanders*, till they split upon the Rocks.

No such thing as a certain Peace.

Therefore it is, and will remain a Truth, That next to the Freedom of the Rulers and Inhabitants at home, nothing is more necessary to us than Peace with all Men, and in such a time of Peace to make effectual provision for good Fortifications on the Frontiers of our Provinces, to keep a competent number of Men of War at Sea, to husband our Treasure at home, and as soon as possibly we may, to take off those Imposts that are most burdensom, especially that of Convoys; holding our selves assured, that without these means, whereby to procure a firm Peace, and to preserve our Country in Prosperity, as far as the wickedness of this World will admit, all other Expedients will be found prejudicial to *Holland*, and that we on the contrary, relying on these Maxims and Means, ought always to wait till others make War upon us, us, directly and indeed, because by our diligent and continual preparation, they would soon understand, that there is more to be gotten by us in a time of Peace and good Trading, than by War, and the ruin of Trade.

But because these Conclusions concerning the Prosperity of *Holland*, seem to oppose the known Rules of Polity, 1*st*, That a defensive War is a consumptive War, and 2*dly*, That no Rule can subsist, unless they put on the Skin of a Lion, as well as that of the Fox, I shall give you my Thoughts upon these two Maxims. And truly if we may say of Subjects, as the Italians,

* *One half they live by Fraud and Art,*
 By Art and Fraud they live the other part.

We may with as good Reason say of those that govern,

* *One half they live by Force and Art,*
 By Art and Force they live the other part.

But he who looks further into matters shall find, that in using these Maxims there is great distinction to be made. For tho it be true of

---

* Con arte e con ingano.
 Vive mezzo l'anno.
 Con ingano e con arte,
 Vive l'altra parte.

* Con forza e con ingauno
 Vive mezzo l'anno
 Con forza e con arte
 Vive l'altra parte.

Monarchs and Princes, who will suffer no Fortifications, that a defensive is a consumptive War, yet in Republicks which live by Traffick, and have fortified themselves well, all offensive War is prejudicial and consuming. So that such Countries can never subsist without good Fortifications in this World, where the lovers of Peace cannot always obtain their wish.

The truth is, great Monarchs are justly compar'd to the Lion, who is King of Beasts, never contented with the produce of their own Country, but living upon the Flesh of their Enemies, I wish I could not say Subjects, conquering and plundering their Neighbours, and burdening their own People with Taxes and Contributions. Yet tho they appropriate to themselves all the Advantages of the Country, they would still be deficient in Strength, if by means of the Fox's Skin they could not sometimes answer their Enemies, and even their own Subjects, and escape the Snares laid for them by others. Whereas Republicks governing with more Gentleness, Wisdom, and Moderation, have naturally a more powerful and numberless train of Inhabitants adhering to them than Monarchs, and therefore stand not in need of such Maxims, especially those that subsist by Trade, who ought in this matter to follow the commendable example of a Cat. For she never converses with strange Beasts, but either keeps at home, or accompanys those of her own Species, meddling with none, but in order to defend her own, very vigilant to provide for Food, and preserve her young ones she neither barks nor snarls at those that

Because t'ey are sin,' and do greatly oppress their Subjects.

Whereas the Rulers of a Republick are many, and govern more gently.

They must naturally be shy of a War.

that provoke or abuse her, so shy and fearful, that being pursued, she immediately takes her flight into some Hole or Place of natural Strength, where she remains quiet till the noise be over. But if it happens that she can by no means avoid the Combat, she is more fierce than a Lion, defends her self with Tooth and Nail, and better than any other Beast, making use of all her well husbanded Strength, without the least neglect or fainting in her Extremity. So that by these Arts that Species enjoy more quiet every where, live longer, are more acceptable, and in greater number than Lions, Tygers, Wolves, Foxes, Bears, or any other Beasts of Prey, which often perish by their own Strength, and are taken where they lie in wait for others.

A Cat indeed is outwardly like a Lion, yet she is, and will remain but a Cat still, and so we who are naturally Merchants, cannot be turned into Souldiers. But because the Cat of *Holland* hath a great round Head, fiery Eyes, a dreadful Beard, sharp Teeth, fierce Claws, a long Tail, and a thick hairy Coat, by means of our Merchants, our Stadtholder and Captain-General from time to time, and after him some of our Allies or Rulers, who had reaped Profit by War, have made use of those said Features, and the stout Defence which this Cat made when she was straitned and pinch'd by the *Spanish* Lion, as so many Reasons to prove that she was become a Lion, and have made her so far to believe it, against the manifest Truth, that they have prevail'd with her for fifty Years successively to fall upon other Beasts, and fight with them. But the sad Experience of what is past, the Decay of of all inward Strength, the death of the last Captain-General, and the free Government of the State, which by God's unspeakable Goodness ensued, ought certainly to take off the Scales from the Eyes of the stupid *Hollander*, and so make him see and know, that *Holland* by so doing was no Lion, but a burden-bearing Ass. For the Conquests obtained by her Labour and Blood, have not served to feed her, but to break her back, and to make our former Captain-General, and the Stadtholders so to increase in Power, that they became formidable to their Masters, the States of the respective Provinces, and especially to the States of *Holland*, and still serve to make some of the crafty Allies of our Union, and some few slavish Rulers to live voluptuously, knowing how to procure many military Employments and Profits for their Children and Friends, and are therefore continually advising *Holland* to prosecute the War.

Tho by bearing Impositions she may be compared to an Ass,

In times of our Stadtholders.

And tho *Holland*, since the last sixteen Years seems very well to have apprehended the Mischief received by the Lion's Skin, yet she seems not to have discerned the fraudulent Damage of the Foxes, which will be found well nigh as mischievous. For *Holland* hath very imprudently made use of the Fox's Skin in *Poland* and *Denmark*. Upon the whole matter, 'tis certainly best for *Holland* to strengthen her Frontiers and inland Cities so soon as may be, and when they are impregnably fortified, let her not engage her self with any but her next and oldest Allies, of the other *United Provinces*, and leave the rest of the World to take their course. And this done, let us only concern our selves with our

And therefore must by degrees leave that ill Custom.

own Affairs, according to the good Proverb, *Toe niet haas jow, &c., cock niet.* And because it seems to me that such evident Truths make the deepest Impressions, and are best apprehended by Proverbs and Fables, I shall conclude this Chapter with the following Fables.

The First Fable

The Lion, King of Beasts, having heard many Complaints of his Subjects concerning the cruel Persecution, and Murders committed by the Huntsmen, and fearing that if he should any longer bear such unrighteous Dealings, he should lose his Royal Honour and Respect among his Subjects, went in Person to fight the Huntsman, who first by his Shooting, afterwards by his Lance, and lastly with his Sword, so wounded the approaching Lion, that he was necessitated to fly, and having lost much of his strength by his Wounds, and more of his Honour and Esteem by his flight, said, with a lamentable Voice, To my sorrow I find the truth of this Proverb, * The strength of *Samson* is not sufficient for one that is resolv'd to revenge Evil with Evil. But he that can wait, and be patient, shall find his Enemy defeated to his hand. What need had I to streighten this crooked piece of Wood? It had been better for me to have left those Injuries to time, and

---

De wil het quaat over quaat wil wreeken,
Samsons kragt sal hem ontbreeken,
Maar die kan lyden en verdraagen
Sal zyn Vyanden verslaagen.

*

perhaps

perhaps some Tiger, Wolf, or Bear, having with like Imprudence sought out the Huntsman, might have been strong and fortunate enough to have killed him in the fight.

The Second Fable.

A certain strong wise Man, meeting a strong Fool, who had undertaken to force a Stiver from every Man he met, gave him a Stiver without a Blow or a Word. Whereupon some of his Acquaintance, young People, blam'd him for it, using these words: God hath given you at least as much Strength, and more Wisdom than to this lewd Fellow, whereby you would undoubtedly have had the Victory, and delivered the World from this Raskal, whereas contrarily, † you will be despised, if you do this. But the wise Man answered, They that buy their Peace do best: And besides, I know it is ill fighting with a strong Fool, but you know not the value of your own Peace, Welfare and Life, and much less the manner of the World. For tho I were not an old Merchant, but a prudent Soldier, yet I shall tell you, that he who will not bestow a Stiver to keep Peace, must have his Sword always drawn. And he that will be always fighting, tho with the benefit of ten Advantages against one Danger, must certainly lay out more than ten Stivers to buy Arms. And as where there is hewing of Wood, there

A Fable of a wise Man and a Fool.

For Peace-sake we ought to yield somewhat.

---

† Bonis nocet quisquis pepercerit malis & malum quod quis impedire potuit, nec impedit, fecisse videtur, veterem ferendo injuriam invitas novam.

will

will be Splinters flying on every side; so after a Man hath suffered the smart, he must give a good Reward to the Chirurgeon and Physician, even when the best happens. The Bucket will come broken home at last. And the best Fighters at last find their Masters; for the stoutest Hawk is sometimes soonest beaten. Next said he, time will inform you that I am not to streigthen all the crooked Wood I shall meet in this World. For I assure you it will happen to this strong Fool, as it did formerly with the foolish Frog, who finding a wise Crab swimming in the Water, threatned to kill him if he found him any more there. The good natur'd Crab thinking, as those who willingly shun a mad Ox which they might kill with a Gun, that he would also shun this Creature, gave the Frog good words, swimming immediately backward according to its custom, and giving place to him. But because stupidity causes boldness and self-conceit, the Frog concluded that he was stronger than the Crab, and so fel upon him. The Crab defended herself stoutly, and at last pinch'd the Frog immediately dead. And seeing the World is full of Fools, I tell you that this Coxcomb growing too confident by a few good Successes, will soon find another Fool who will knock him o' the Head, and rid the World of him. It is certainly much better that a Fool, and not a wise Man, should put his Life in the Ballance with this Fool. Which Prediction was soon after verified by experience, for a while after this Fool setting upon other People, found at last as foolish, cross and strong a Fellow as himself, that would rather fight than give him a Stiver,

Case of the Foolish Frog and a Crab.

who knock'd him down and kill'd him. Upon which the wife Man caused some Sayings to be engraven over him, among which were these: *The number of Fools is infinite, and to cure a Fool, requires one and a half; for without blows it cannot be done.* *And some old Proverbs.*

The Third Fable

A certain Fox conceiting himself not able to subsist, if the Wolves and Bears lived in mutual Amity, stirred up the one against the other, and afterwards fearing lest the Wolf which favoured him less, should get the better, and then finding himself without Enemy, should destroy him, resolved to strengthen the Bear privately with Food, which he had spared for himself, and to see the Fight between them, under pretence of being Mediator, but really to feed upon the Blood of the conquered; which when he tasted, he was so transported with the Relish, that rather than forbear the Blood, he let the Bear have so much of his other natural Food, that he was grown weak. But the two combating Beasts, observing this ill Design of the pretended Mediator, and his Weakness together, destroyed this blood-thirsty Fox, the one premeditately, the other by the Fortune of the War, besides, he fell unpitied. For suppose the Wolf and Bear had grown so weak by the Fox's Artifices, that they could not have hurt him; yet there were Lions, Tigers, and other Beasts of Prey, which could as certainly and easily have devoured him, because he had lost his Strength, and could no longer in any extremity run to his Hole, and thereby save and defend himself. Thus

The Fable of a Fox, Wolf and Bear.

Thus God and Nature punisheth those that abuse their Strength, and takes the Crafty in their own Subtilty. * As false Self-love is the Root of all Mischief, so Prudence and well-grounded Self-love is the only Cause of all good and virtuous Actions. Pursuant to which, as we say, *Do well, and look not back* ... is the greatest Polity *Holland* can use. And the richest Blessing which God can pour down upon a Nation, is to unite the Interests thereof to Peace, and the Welfare of Mankind. According to the good Rule, † *He that does himself right, is a Friend to all the World.*

The Fourth Fable.

A certain self-conceited Fox in a deriding manner asking a well-meaning Cat, how she could free her self from all the ill Accidents of this World, The Cat answered, That she was not offended when any thing was said of her in a deriding way.

In a word said she, I shew those that hate me the greatest kindness, by which I avoid all Enmity. For my only Art of all Arts is, to avoid harm. Upon this the Fox flouted with the Cat, saying, This is indeed a pretty Science becoming an unarmed

---

— — — — — — — Sumit certe
— — — — — — — parer unica vite. *Juv.*
— — — grande melie que d'estre homme de —
— — — — — meus est, hunc omneus scito ami—
— — — — — tea cerebrum non habes.

Round-

Roundhead, but I that am witty and crafty will lord it over others: and besides that, I live without want and care, for in an instant I can shake out a Bag full of Artifices. But while he was thus braving it out, and negligent, a Huntsman with his Dogs was come so near him, that not being able to escape, he was taken in his subtilty by the Dogs, and killed, while the Cat with her only flight, and even necessary Fortification, fled for her Life, running up a lofty Tree and so saved her self; and from thence saw the Case of the Fox pull'd over his Ears, comforting her self in the mean time with this Song,

Than much clutter with great craft.

Poca Brigata,
Vita Beata.
Casa mia casa mia
Pur Piccola che tu sia
Tu mi pari un' abadia.

This therefore is the great and necessary Art for *Holland*, notwithstanding the Maxims before objected, *viz.* to maintain Peace, and fortify our Frontiers, and never unnecessarily to meddle with parting of Princes that are in War by our Ambassadors, and Arbitrations: for by these means we shall be certainly drawn into the charge of a War, and besides, are like to gain the Reward of Parters, and bring the War or the hatred of both Parties upon our selves, besides the Consumption of our Treasure in expensive Embassys, even when the best happens. And tho the Troubles of this World cannot be avoided always either by Force or Art, yet we ought to keep out of them as much as we can with all

It is again concluded, that Peace above all things is necessary for Holland.

our

our Strength, Prudence, and Polity. And if notwithstanding all this, War should be made upon *Holland*, she will gain a double Reputation, when with the incouragement of her own Strength, long before provided, together with the Justice and Necessity of her Defence, she shall overcome the Danger. Besides, the Opposition we should be able to make, as well as the just Hatred that always attends the Aggressor, and the Consequences that might follow the Conquest of this Country, would alarm other Princes, and give them time to deliver us.

And tho' I know these Maxims will always be rejected by most of the idle Gentry, Soldiers of Fortune, and the sottish Rabble, as if we relying only on our impregnable Fortifications, and standing on our defence, should by that means lose all that Name and Reputation we have acquired, to which I shall only say that all is not Gold that glisters, and rusty Silver is more valued by Men of Understanding than glittering Copper. So whatever is profitable to a Nation, brings also a good Reputation to perpetuity. 'Tis likewise certain, that whatever reduceth *Holland* to weakness, tho it were under the most glorious Title of the World, will really cause it to lie under an everlasting Shame and Reproach. All which God grant may be rightly apprehended by the upright, and (now) really-free Magistrates of *Holland*, while this leaky Ship of the Commonwealth may yet by labour be kept above Water.

CHAP

CHAP. V.

Enquiry is made, whether, and how the Welfare of any Country may be preserved by Treatys of Peace.

BUT seeing it appears in the preceding Discourse, that Treatys of Peace importing mutual Promises of not prejudicing one another, and allowance of Trade and Commerce reciprocally, are very necessary for *Holland*, and that the like Articles are by many intermixt with Treatys of Alliance, or Covenants among Neighbours, which nevertheless, as I conceive, have for the most part been pernicious to *Holland*, and will be found so, I find my self therefore obliged to express my thoughts on this Subject, and to say, That a Treaty of Peace is a mutual Promise of doing no hurt to each other, to which likewise Nature obligeth us. But on the contrary, an Alliance or Covenant obligeth to do something, which often without such Alliance men would not do, or omit something which without such Alliance they would not omit. *To comprehend what a Treaty of Peace, or An Alliance is,*

Since then all things past are so much beyond the Power and Conduct of Man, that human Actions and Force cannot make the least alteration therein, it appears that all mens Thoughts ought to be imployed about the obtaining of something that is good, or defending themselves from future Evil, which especially takes place in our Consultations, and Transactions with other People. For even *We ought to consider, that all Actions look either at the future, or the present, as also*

in a free and generous Gift, where all Necessity or Obligation of any thing to be done for the future seems to be excluded, yet is it evident, that it is done either out of hope of gaining some bodys Friendship, or Serviceableness, or obtaining the Name of being Kind and Liberal. But above all, those Thoughts must take place for things future in mutual Covenants, seeing the Essence thereof consists therein, and hath its eye upon it, as appears by all the Examples of it. I give or promise to give, because you promise to give, I do or shall do, because you promise to do, I give or shall give, that you shall not do, I do or shall do, that you may not do, &c. And when we are on both sides subjected to one and the same Sovereign Power, those Agreements are freely entered into, and here the Difficulty is not great, tho we perform the Covenants first, because the other Party may be compelled by the Judg to perform his Engagements, tho no body would willingly be the Compeller, but every one would ride on the Forehorse. Having is better than hoping, and what he hath beforehand is the poor Mans Riches. And when the respective Covenanters are subjected to a different Supreme Power, then Distrust begins to increase, but because men know that he that is unfaithful may be punished, they are unwilling to put it to the venture.

But all the difficulty lies here, and then appears, when Sovereign Powers enter into mutual Covenants and Alliances; seeing the strongest Potentate always enjoys the Fruit of a Peace concluded, and likewise the benefit

fit covenanted; which *Ovid* * very ingeniously shew'd: So that tho there be sometimes Peace, yet 'tis always necessary for the weakest to be so watchful, as if no true Peace were ever made by such Powers, on which the weaker Party might rely. And if on the other side, in time of Peace each Party should fortify and guard his Frontiers, and by Intelligencers endeavour to inform himself of his Neighbours Designs, in order to behave himself accordingly. It is then evident that all Treatys of Peace must be presumed by all Sovereign Powers (who expect more Advantage by War than Peace, and consequently are not founded upon Peace) to serve only for a breathing-time, and to wait an opportunity of attacking their Neighbour with more Advantage, and so to overpower him.

And so long as those Opportunitys present not, the Peace lasteth among the Potentates of the World, not by virtue of Promises, Oaths or Seals which they can at all times easily infringe, without suffering any present Punishment, but by virtue of their fear, lest some future Evil should befal the Peace-breaker. So that a true and real Peace among Sovereign Princes, especially for the weaker Party, is but a Fiction or a Dream, on which he must not rely. *And when and how long those Contracts are to be kept.*

For in this wicked World (God amend it) 'tis very evident, that most Men naturally are inclined by all imaginable industry to advance their Interest, without regard to Hand, Seal, Oath, or even to Eternity it self; *Especially with Monarchs.*

---

* Pax licet interdum est. pacis fiducia nunquam.

and above all, such Inclinations and Aims are principally found in Monarchs, Princes and great Lords: for we are taught that *Sanctitas, pietas, fides, privata bona sunt, ad quæ juvant Reges eunt.*

Amicos y Sabios
Los mas son Traydores.

For having never been private Persons, nor educated or conversant with Men equal to themselves, they learn nothing of Modesty or Condescension: neither does the Authority of Judges imprint in them a Reverence to Sacred Justice. Which is quite contrary in all Republicks, where the Rulers and Magistrates being first educated as common Citizens, must daily converse with their Equals or Superiours, and learn that which is just, otherwise they would be compelled to their Duty by the Judg, or other Virtuous and Powerful Civil Rulers; which inward motions of Modesty, Discretion and Fear leave always some remains in them, when they come afterwards to be preferred to the Government and Magistracy, for * Custom is a second Nature, which is not easily altered.

But in all Events, if in Treatys of Peace, when neither of the Covenanters do any thing but only restrain each other from all Hostil Acts, there is little certainty that the Covenants will on both sides be kept; it is as certain, that in Alliances, wherein

---

* *Adeo a teneris assuescere multum est.*
Quo semel est imbuta recens servabit odorem
Testa diu.

there

there are Engagements on both sides, for Assistance of Souldiery, Arms, or Mony, that there is a greater uncertainty of obtaining what is covenanted, and that there can be no Trust reposed in the Treatys of Sovereigns; all Advantages of Alliances consisting only in this, that one Part may possibly be drawn to perform what is covenanted before the other. And when this happens in Matters by which he that performeth is really weakened, and the other strengthened, with bare hopes only of Advantages to accrue from him afterwards, he is then a Traitor to himself, because he foolishly gives Things and Realitys, for Words, Hand, and Seal, which put all together hold no proportion to preponderate and resist the Ambition and Covetousness, Lust, Rage, and Self-conceit of great Princes. *Dat pœnas laudata fides.* For because Ambition exceeds all other Affections, and Monarchs order all Externals, and especially the Publick Religion, which is strengthened, or weakned according to the prosperity of their Government, it is therefore rightly said, that the State has neither Blood nor Religion, and that Integrity is always deceived or circumvented. So that the best way is not to trust them, and then we shall not be cheated.

And when most:

Especially when they are made with Kings or Sovereigns.

Because they have a Superintendency over Religious Worship, and value it little.

All which being most certain, it is strange that any Supreme Powers should imagine that they can oblige a formidable Sovereign Prince to gratitude for Benefits received without any preceding Promises, impoverishing themselves by Liberalitys, in order to enrich and strengthen those they fear. For we ought always to presume, that Kings will ever esteem them-

themselves obliged to any thing but their own Grandeur and Pleasure, which they endeavour to obtain, without any regard to Love, Hatred or Gratitude.

Certainly, if we affirm, that it is a cursed Religion which teacheth Men to sacrifice to the Devil, that he may do them no Mischief, we may likewise say, that nothing less than the utmost Despair can reasonably induce a Government to discover its own Weakness to a dreaded Neighbour, and to make him stronger by giving him Mony to buy off a feared Evil, which ought to be resisted by the best Arms, and most vigorous Efforts; according to the *Spanish* Proverb, * To give to Kings is a Kingly, that is, a monstrous great Folly. For the holy Wood, the blunt Cross of Prayers and Remonstrances, is of small force among Men of Power, and the Mony sacrificed to the Idol of Gratitude, is yet of less value. But he who in these horrid Disorders, betakes himself for Refuge to the Iron, and sharp two-edged Cross, the Sword, makes use of the true Cross of Miracles against Sovereign Princes, and this rightly applied, is only able to cure the King's-Evil, or State-Agues.

But if Kings, whilst they follow their own inclinations and Pleasures, will suffer Favourites to govern their Kingdoms, it is then clear, that such Favourites will by all means endeavour, during their uncertain Favour, to enrich themselves; and therefore by proper Bribes to such Creatures, dangerous Resolutions may be prevented; and if a dangerous War be at any time very much feared, may be well and profitably bestowed. But

---

* *El dar cuesta ad un Reyes.*

yet this is not to be done till the utmost Extremity. For we are taught, that Courtiers may very well be resembled to hungry biting Dogs, who as they will soon observe, when their Bread is given for snarling at or biting the Giver. So Courtiers who are always wasting their Estates, and always hungry, will, in hopes of obtaining new Presents, be always most ready to threaten such generous Givers, nay and bite them too, unless such openhanded Persons take a good Resolution to arm themselves, in order to resist their Menaces and Attempts by Force, and by that means to obtain Peace. *Which the Fable of the hungry Dogs, to which Courtiers were resembled, plainly teaches us.*

And to express my self more amply in this particular, I shall say, that all Treaties and Capitulations between supreme Governors and States, arise by reason of a mutual Diffidence of one and the same Neighbour, or of several stronger Neighbours, and by a mutual desire to be able to defend themselves against one or more mighty Potentates. *The general Causes of all Contentions and Treaties, are Peace,*

Or, secondly, Through a desire of the same thing, appertaining to a third Person, and to enrich themselves by an Alliance and Conjunction with another. Or thirdly, Through Arrogance, Vain-Glory, and Ambition. *Hope and Vainglory.*

Yet it matters not much upon what Reason these Dissensions and Alliances arise, but whether the Covenanters and Allies do equally fear, or have need of one another, and whether they are equally concerned in that which they desire to obtain or defend. For we learn, that * Damage parts Friendship,

---

* Idem velle idem nolle, ea demum firma amicitia est.

and Complainers have no Friends.

In a word, all consists in this, Whether they that enter into a League, have a common Interest to avoid or obtain that which they both have in their Eye. For where that is not, all Alliances and Covenants are made for the benefit of the strongest, and to the prejudice of the weakest. So that if he cannot withstand the stronger, without entering into Capitulation with him, he will by such Capitulation be the sooner overthrown, if by virtue thereof he makes War upon a Neighbour that is stronger than he. For it is better to have many mighty Neighbours than one, according to the Fable, which says, That a Bear may easily be taken by one able Huntsman, but that his Hide or Skin cannot be divided among many before he be caught, and therefore he is suffered to live.

Whence it necessarily and irrefragably follows, that all States and Sovereigns ought not to enter into Alliances with those who are stronger, but rather with such as are inferior to themselves in Power, by which means they may make such covenant, that the weaker shall first make good his Engagement; and in all doubtful Cases, where mention is made of enjoining him to do any thing, he may interpret them to his Advantage, at least afterwards, so as to do no more than he will, according to the Italian Proverb, * *Be quick to resolve, for in time an Accident may happen that may spoil or destroy any thing.* And ac-

---
* *Il ingiar presto al mal tardo, perche puo nascer qualche accidente con Impedimento.*

cording

cording to that, * *It is good riding on the fore Horse, and being a Master, for you may always transfer, or give away as much of your Right as you will, and make your self less.*

Secondly, From hence may be inferred, That when an Inferior Power treats with one superior to him, he injures himself, if he do not contract, that the Stronger shall first perform that which he promises. And if the Alliance be grounded upon a common Interest, the Superior hath little reason to fear, that when he hath performed his Engagements, he shall be deceived by the Weaker; so that if he be not willing to do this, he gives great Cause to the Weakest not to trust him, and so not to enter into such a Treaty, which like a rotten House is like to fall upon his Head.

CHAP. VI.

Some Considerations particularly relating to Alliances between Holland *and Inferior Powers.*

HAVING premised in the foregoing Chapter, that the Interest of *Holland* consists in Peace, because our Fisheries, Trade, Navigation, and Manufactures will increase more by Peace than War, and that these are the Pillars on which our State is founded, it follows, that all Covenants and Alliances

All Alliances for Conquest detrimental to Holland.

---

† Præstat prevenire quam preveniri. Il fait bon estre Maistre, car on est tousjours valet quand on veut.

founded upon Conquest and Glory, are prejudicial to *Holland*, since by such Alliances the Peace is wilfully broken, and Wars made to the Ruin or Decay of the said Pillars of our Country.

2*ly*. It also naturally follows, that no Alliances, except such as are grounded upon mutual Fear and Defence against a much superior Power, can be profitable for *Holland*, because by this means either the Peace will be more lasting, or the War that may happen will have a better and speedier end.

3*ly*. If we consider the States of *Europe* in their present Condition, 'tis true, all Republicks being founded on Peace and Trade, have the same Interest with *Holland*, to preserve and maintain Peace on every side. But they by continual endeavours to draw our Trade, and its Dependencies to themselves, always oust our principal Design, which is the increase of Traffick. And considering also that they are of so little Power to assist *Holland* when in Distress, against a greater Force, 'tis wholly unadvisable to enter into an Alliance with any of them for common Defence. For as to the defence by Land, relating to the *United Provinces* themselves, we have found how fruitless a thing, and burdensom a load the Union or our common Defence has always been (I will not say as it was made, but as that Union was formerly managed by our Captains-General and Stadtholders) to the Province of *Holland*.

And tho during our free Commonwealth Government, all those Abuses of the said Union which have been so prejudicial to us, and arose merely from fear of offending the late

late Heads of our Republick, ought to have ceased; yet by long continuance they have so much tended to the Advantage of our separate Allies, and their Deputies of the Generality, and taken so deep a root, that our Republick of *Holland* and *West-Friesland* can hardly compass or obtain any Reformation, or any new and profitable Orders for their own particular Benefit, tho with never so much Right demanded, without being subject to the undue Oppositions and Thwartings of the said Allies of our Union, and their Deputies, with whom we are forced to be always contending. And of this I could give the Reader infinite Examples, particularly by means of *Zealand* and *Friesland*, from that faithful and excellent History of *L. V. Aitzma*, wherein the Debates about the Seclusion of the Prince of *Orange* in 1654, and about the Order made *Anno* 1663, concerning the publick Prayers for the superior and inferior Magistracy, as also for the foresaid Allies, and their Deputies in the Generality, and Council of State, are fully related.

<small>See I. V. Aitzma's *Hist.* on those respective *Years*, and especially the *Considerations of the publick Prayers, and* Holland's *Deduction concerning the Seclusion*, &c.</small>

And if we should make Alliances with the remote *German* Republicks, we should find them both chargeable and useless; for being weaker than we, they are the sooner like to be attacked, and then we by their means should be engaged in a War contrary to our own Interest.

And as for the Republicks of *Italy*, it is well known, that in our Wars by Land, they neither could, nor would give us the least Assistance, which was formerly made evident by our Alliance with *Venice*. And except in the *Mediterranean*, they can give us less help

<small>Other Republicks, whether German or Italian, *would be much less serviceable to us.*</small>

by

by Sea, being not at all interested therein. And for the Hans Republicks, it is certain that they are not only very weak and unfit to undertake a War for our sakes against those who are too strong for us; but on the contrary, they always love to see us disturbed and obstructed at Sea, that in the mean time they may trade the more: so that we can be assisted by no Republicks in a War against a stronger Power. And because by covenanting with them for mutual Assistance, and common Defence, we may very easily fall into a War, we must never enter into any other Agreement with them, save of Friendship and Traffick; and in the mean while stand upon our Guard, as if we were to be assisted by no Republicks in the whole World in our Necessity. For tho indeed those Republican Allies and Friends, are good yet Wo to us if we stand in need of them, and ten times more Wo to us if we wilfully and deliberately order matters so, as at all times, and for ever to stand in need of our Neighbours and Allies.

As for such Monarchs and Princes, who by Alliances might have some Communication with us, I conceive that their true Interest carries them, as well as their Favorites and Courtiers, to hate all manner of Republicks, especially such as are lately established, and are their Neighbours, because they are a perpetual Reproof to them, and bring the ablest and most discerning of their Subjects to dislike Monarchical Government. And therefore if we will enter into an Alliance with any of the neighbouring Kings and Princes, or are already in League with them, we must stand

much

much more on our Guard, than if we were to make an Alliance with a free Republick, or had done so. So that it is hardly advisable to enter into any Alliance with Kings and Princes. Yet seeing things may so happen, that some such Alliance might for some short time be advantageous to us; 'tis necessary to speak of such Kings and Princes distinctly. And first, the Emperor and King of *Poland* are not considerable to us, and the Crown of *Denmark* so weak and unfit for War, that as we have nothing to fear from thence, so we cannot hope to be assisted by them in our Troubles. *Sweden* and *Brandenburgh* are so deficient, that we shall never cause them to take Arms against our Enemies, unless we will furnish them with great Sums by way of Advance: and as I said before, all such Alliances are unsteady and wavering, as we have lately learned by *Brandenburgh*, and *France* by *Sweden*; who after they had received the Mony advanced, applied it purely to their own Affairs, without any regard to their Contracts. Besides, they are both of so small Power, that if they should become our Enemies, we might ruin them by prolonging the War, and always give them the Law by Sea.

Who hating Republicks, especially ours, we must always be upon our Guard.

So that they would soon perceive, that they could gain nothing by us, that their Traffick would be spoiled, the War mischievous to both sides, and consequently Peace and Friendship would be best for both. But in all Cases, having made Alliances with Republicks or Monarchs that are weaker than our selves, which by alteration of conjunctures of Time and Interests, would certainly tend to ruin the

We may more safely make Alliances with weaker, than with stronger.

the State, or our Native Country; sufficient Reasons may always be given to those weaker Allies, why, with a saving to Honour, a Nation may depart from them, and neither may nor will either ruin themselves or their Subjects by such Leagues, and thereby make good the Proverb, * An ill Oath displeaseth God. And he that deceives a Deceiver, merits a Chain in Heaven. And indeed all Alliances made and confirmed by Oath between Sovereign Powers, ought to have this tacit Condition, to continue so long as the Interest of the Nation will admit. So that if nevertheless a Prince would punctually observe such Alliances to the ruin of his Country, he is no more to be esteemed than a silly Child that knows nothing of the World, whilst he ought to govern the Land as a Guardian to his Orphans; for according to the Rule in Law, Orphans must suffer no loss. On the other side, the Ally in such a Case neither may, nor ought to perform his part, if it be against his first Oath and Duty as a Ruler and Guardian, and to the Ruin of his Subjects who are as Orphans, and therefore it must be understood, that he will not maintain it. A Regent or Guardian ought not to be ignorant of this, but if he be so, 'tis then evident that he ought to be governed himself, and be put under Wardship. Wo be to those Countries, Cities, and Orphans that must nevertheless be governed by such Rulers and Guardians!

CHAP. VII.

Some Considerations touching the Alliances which Holland *might enter into with mightier Potentates than themselves. And first with* France.

BUT touching the three great Powers of *France*, *Spain*, and *England*, is all the Difficulty, since each of them by their own Strength can always be armed, and knowing how much we are concerned for Peace, neither of them fear us, but we must fear them. And therefore it is very necessary that we behave our selves very prudently towards them, as to the point of Alliances; which to effect the better, I conceive it necessary, as formerly, particularly to consider how much Good and Evil those three Kingdoms may receive or suffer from the *Hollanders*, and likewise what Good or Evil can befal *Holland* by each of them.

As to *France*, we are to observe, that formerly that Country subsisted wholly by Tillage, and therefore could suffer little damage by a War at Sea. But since the Reign of *Henry* the *4th*, many heavy Impositions have been laid upon all imported and exported Manufactures, and the weaving of Silk, Wool, and Linen, with many other Mechanick Works, is so considerably improved there, that the *French* can supply others with more made Stuffs, and other Manufactures, than Foreigners take off. So that a War against us, would be more prejudicial to them than to us.

What Alliances with mighty Monarchs are to be kept, viz. with France.

France *did wholly subsist by Agriculture, not so now*.

But

But because this first Point is of extraordinary weight, and perhaps not so well understood by others, I find my self obliged to draw up a List of Manufactures and Commodities exported out of *France* into Foreign Parts, especially into *Holland*, according to a Scheme presented to the King of *France* by the Society of Merchants at *Paris*, when a new and very high Imposition was laid upon all foreign imported Goods, and especially Manufactures, fearing lest the like Imposition would be laid by *Holland* and *England* upon all *French* Goods. And also from an Information exhibited by the Lord Ambassador *Boreel* in 1658 to the Lords States General of the United Provinces.

1. In the first place great quantities of Velvet, Plushes, Satins, Cloth of Gold and Silver, Taffaties, and other silk Wares, made at *Lions* and *Tours*, which amount to above six Millions.

2. In silk Ribbands, Laces, Passements, Buttons, Loops, made about *Paris*, *Roan*, and those parts, to the value of two Millions.

3. Bever-Hats, Castors, Hats of Wool and Hair, which are made in and about *Paris* and *Roan*, to the value of one Million and a half.

4. Feathers, Belts, Fans, Hoods, Masks, gilt and wrought Looking-glasses, Watches, and other small Wares, to the value of above two Millions.

5. Gloves made at *Paris*, *Roan*, *Vendome*, and *Clermont*, to the value of above a Million and a half.

6. Woollen

6. Woollen Yarn spun in all parts of *Piccardy*, worth more than one Million and a half.

7. Paper of all sorts, made in *Auvergne, Poitou, Limousin, Champagne* and *Normandy*, for upwards of two Millions.

8. Pins and Needles made at *Paris* and *Normandy*, and Combs of Box, Horn, and ivory, for a Million and a half.

9. Childrens Toys, and such as *Nuremburg* Ware, or as the *French* call them, *Quincaillerie*, made in *Auvergne*, for upwards of six hundred thousand Florins.

10. Linen Sail-cloth made in *Brittany* and *Normandy*, for upwards of five Millions of Florins.

11. Houshold-goods, Beds, Matrasses, Hangings, Coverlids, Quilts, Crespines, Fringes and Molets of Silk, above five Millions of Florins.

12. Wines from *Gascony, Xaintoigne, Nantois*, and other places, for above five Millions.

13. Brandys, Vinegars, and Sider, for fifteen hundred thousand Livers.

14. Saffron, Woad, Soap, Hony, Almonds, Olives, Capers, Prunes, Prunellas, for above two Millions.

15. Salt, yearly the lading of five or 600 Ships, exported from *Rochel, Maran, Brouage*, the Islands of *Oleron* and *Rec*.

Of these Goods there are yearly transported above 30 Millions, whereof Holland *takes off the greatest part.*

And if we add to this the *French* Companys of Train and Whale-fins, of Cod and Pickled-Herrings, of Refining and fine Sugars, of all Spices and *Indian*-Wares, with prohibition to all that are not of the Company to import any into *France*; every one may

may then observe, that by a *French* War against us, the Inhabitants of *France* will be much more prejudiced than those of *Holland* in their Navigation and Traffick.

Secondly, It is apparent, That the *French* have very few of their own Ships and Mariners, so that all their Traffick is driven (some few *English* Ships and Traffick excepted) by *Holland* Ships to *Holland*, or at least unlading there. And moreover, when any Goods are to be transported from one *French* Harbour to another, they are put on board *Holland* Vessels.

Thirdly, It is clear, That the *Hollanders* do buy up most of the *French* Wines and Salt that are exported, and that Salt might be had in other Countrys, and particularly in *Portugal*, *Spain*, and *Punto del Rey*. As it is likewise true, that we can better forbear those Wines in *Holland*, than the *French* Nobility and Ecclesiasticks (to whom most of the Wines belong) can forbear our Mony. And besides, by reason of the Peace in *Germany*, in case of War with *France*, the greatest part of that Trade may be supplied with *Rhenish* Wines, and possibly continue so alienated, altho the same were not so profitable for *Holland*, as the Trade by Sea in *French* Wines would be.

Fourthly, 'Tis well known, That in *France* very many *Dutch* Cloths, Says, Linen, Herrings, Cod, and other Wares, transported thither by our Ships, were formerly spent there, which now by new Impositions is much lessened, or wholly prohibited.

Fifthly, It is evident that *France* cannot attack us by Land, nor by Sea, for want of good

good Shipping, and on account of the danger of our Coast. So that if they feize our Goods, Debts, and ships, they can do us no further mischief except by small Capers at Sea, which we may easily prevent by keeping Convoy-ships about *Ushant*, and sending some few Cruisers to pick up the Privateers that ply about the *Garonne*, and the *Loire*, and clear the North Sea of them. But the greatest harm that the *French* can do the *Hollanders*, would be in the *Mediterranean* Seas, where, by reason of our remote situation, we cannot without great expence overpower them in Shipping. But our good Orders, according to which our Ships must be armed and manned, would preserve them from many Depredations.

But in the Mediterranean.

Sixthly, It cannot on the other side be denied, that *Holland* with its great strength of Shipping, would be able to plunder all that far extended *French* Sea-Coast from the North-Sea to *Italy*, and take these weak Towns and burn them, unless they were prevented by an extraordinary Force of Soldiery by Land; there being in *France* on the Sea-side very many weak Towns and Villages, and no Ships of War that dare keep the Sea against ours. Besides which, we should destroy all their Trade to the *East* and *West-Indies*, and indeed thorow all *Europe*, which is at present of so much importance to *France*, as hath been formerly declared. And when we further consider, that in all Governments of a Single Person, the Treasure in a time of War is miserably wasted, as shall be farther demonstrated when we come to speak of *England*, we shall have reason to believe, that

*On *France*'s Sea-Coast and West-Indies may keep France in a continual Alarm.*

So that Holland is able to compel the French to a Peace.

T we

we should be able either to ruin the *French*, or compel them to a Peace.

By all which it clearly appears, that a King of *France* may not make War upon us, for fear of receiving great damage from us, or others in our behalf, nor in hope of conquering us, nor yet through vain Glory: But that on the contrary a War against us would immediately cause all *French* Traffick and Navigation to be at a stand, and endanger the loss of it for the future.

And moreover, if we observe that *Spain* in some measure, and *England* yet more, used to be formidable to *France*, it will further appear, that we never ought, by any Threatnings of *France* to make War against us, to suffer our selves to be drawn in to make an, League with *France*, which we conceive would be prejudicial to us. And much less ought we, to please *France*, to suffer our selves to be brought into any War, by which the Strength of *Spain* or *England* should be impaired by the *French*. For having once done so, we should meet with more bold and troublesom Rencounters from them, and expect at last a more severe War from that Kingdom.

CHAP.

CHAP. VIII.

Considerations concerning Holland's *entring into Alliance with* Spain.

AS to *Spain*, it is very observable, that all the Welfare of that Kingdom depends on their Trade to the *West Indies*. And that *Spain* affords only Wool, Fruit and Iron, and in lieu of this, requires so many *Holland* Manufactures and Commodities, that all the *Spanish* and *West-Indian* Wares are not sufficient to make returns for them. *[Spain subsists by its Commerce with the West-Indies. Yields Wool, articles off n ne of our Manufacture]*

So that the *Holland* Merchants, who carry Mony to most parts of the World to buy Commodities, must out of this single Country of all *Europe* carry home Mony, which they receive in paiment for their Goods, without benefit and by stealth, over that raging and boisterous Sea.

2. It is well known that *Spain* during our Wars, lost most of their Naval Forces; and that we during our Peace, have for the most part beat the *Eastern* Merchants and *English* out of that Trade. So that it is now certain, that in *Spain* all the Coast is navigated with few other than *Holland* Ships; and that their Ships and Seamen are so few, that since the Peace they have publickly begun to hire our Ships to sail to the *Indies*, whereas they were formerly so careful to exclude all Foreigners thence. *[Has Ships not Mariners]*

3. It is manifest, that the *West-Indies*, being as the Stomach in the Body to *Spain*, must be joined to the *Spanish* Head by a Sea force. *[Its Dominions much dispers'd]*

T 2 And

And that the Kingdom of *Naples* with the *Netherlands*, being like two Arms, they cannot lay out their Strength and Vigour for *Spain*, nor receive any from thence but by shipping. All which may be very easily done by our Naval Power in a time of Peace, and may as well be obstructed in a time of War.

And therefore our Naval Power can hinder their mutual Communication.

4. It is likewise certain, that *Holland* by its naval Strength, is able wonderfully to encumber and perplex this whole dispers'd Body in time of War, and accordingly put them to the charge of maintaining an incredible number of Land Forces in Garisons.

But on the other side it is likewise true,

Spain stands in fear of France.

1. That the King of *Spain* must continually maintain a great Military Strength against the mighty Kingdom of *France*, and in those great and jealous *Netherlandish* Citys, or else lose his Countrys.

Hath had pretensions upon Holland.

2. It is known, That the said King has Pretensions to *Holland*, and a very powerful adherence of the *Roman* Catholicks, tho the strength of both these since our Peace, and his laying down all Pretensions to our Country, and especially by the expiration of so many Years, and our own confirmed and improved Government, is very much diminished, and almost annihilated.

It bords upon Holland.

3. It is likewise evident that *Spain*, by *Brabant*'s bordering on *Holland*, and by means of the *Flemish* Sea-Havens, is able to disturb our Fisherys, and Traffick, in this small North Sea.

Offensive Wars hurtful to Holland.

4. It is certain, That this State of Free Government will not think it advisable, tho they should fall into a War with *Spain*, to take

take any more *Netherlandish* Cities by exceeding chargeable Sieges.

5 It is manifest that all the Frontiers of the *United Netherlands* are so well fortified, that we are not likely to lose any of them unless by their great number; and yet if they are in any wise well defended, they would hardly pay the damage to *Spain*. *We are in a good condition for a defensive War.*

Moreover, *Spain* would then have Reason to expect that we should excite *France*, according to the Interest of the Kingdom, to prevent any additional Increase of *Spain* by making War on his Frontiers, which would always in such Cases be very terrible to *Spain*.

So that by all that hath been said, it is manifest, that *Spain* may receive many great Advantages by *Holland* in time of Peace, and that a War is very prejudicial for both sides: yet so, that there is much more appearance for the King of *Spain* to gain upon us by Land, than for us upon him, unless we should reckon the plundering and burning of his Citys in *Spain*, and the losing his Gallions at Sea to ballance it. Because, as we have said before, our free Rulers having their eye upon Trade do always decline an Offensive War, and will carry on none but what is necessary and defensive only. *Whereby we may pursue our Interest against Spain.*

Whence we may also infer, that out of fear of a War we ought never, against the interest of this State in it self considered, to make Alliances with *Spain*; and much less should we suffer our selves to be led away to make the least War against any of our Neighbours who are formidable to him; since the greatest quiet of this State consists in this, That *France* be formidable to *Spain*, and *England* a Friend to us.

T 3 CHAP.

CHAP. IX

Considerations touching Holland's *entring into Alliance with* England.

AS for *England*, we are to know, that heretofore it wholly subsisted by Husbandry, and was wont to be so naked of any Naval Power, that the Hans-Towns being at War with *England*, they compelled King *Edward* in the Year 1470, to make Peace upon Terms of Advantage to them. And so long as the *English* used to transport nothing but a few Minerals, and much Wool, which they carried to *Calais* by a small number of their own Ships, and sold only to *Netherlandish* Clothiers, it would have been so prejudicial for the King to forbear his Customs of Wool (which at *Calais* there amounted to 50000 Crowns *per Annum*) and likewise to the Subject, in case he had made War upon the *Netherlands*, That we read not that these trading Provinces ever broke out into a perfect open War against *England*. For tho sometimes War hapned between the Princes of the respective Countrys, nevertheless most of the Citys concerned in Traffick and Drapery, continued in Amity. Insomuch that all the Wars of that rich and plentiful Country broke out against *France*, and consequently against *Scotland*, or else against *Wales* and *Ireland*, and sometimes against *Spain*.

But afterwards, when the compulsive Laws of the *Netherlandish* Halls, and the tumultuous rising against them which followed, together

ther with our Inland and Foreign Wars, had first driven the Cloth-weaving into our Villages, and thence into *England*, and by the Cruelty of the Duke of *Alva* the Say-weaving went also after it; the *English* by degrees fell to vend their Manufactures throughout *Europe*, became potent at Sea, and began no longer to depend on these *Netherlands*. Then by the discovery of that unexpressible rich Cod-bank of *Newfoundland*, those of *Bristol* in particular made use of that advantage; and ballasting their Ships with *English* Lead, Tin, and other Wares, when they had compleated their Fishing of Cod on the said Bank, they sailed with it to *Spain*, and throughout the *Mediterranean*, to vend their *English* Wares with their *Baccaleau*, or *Poor-John*, in all those parts, and in return carried other Goods of those Lands to *England*.

Finally, we may add the long Persecution of the Puritans in *England*, which causing the planting of many *English* Colonies in *America*, hath given *England* a very great conveniency to drive a mighty Foreign Trade with the *Indies* and the said Colonies

So that this mighty Island, united with the Kingdom of *Ireland* under the Government of one King, seems not to have need of any Carisons to repel a Foreign Enemy, is situated in the midst of *Europe*, having a clean deep Coast, furnished with good Harbours and Bays, in so narrow a Sea, that all Foreign Ships that sail to the Eastward or Westward, are necessitated even in fair Weather to shun the dangerous *French* Coast, and sail along that of *England*, and in stormy Weather to run in and preserve their Lives, Ships, and Goods,

Is become formidable to all the Princes of Europe, and why.

Gods, […] So that it is easy to [judge that the …] having acquired a con[siderable …] Power, and being independ[ent of their Neighbours] as to Trade, is [to be consider'd by all] that are concerned in [the interest of] the […]ow Seas.

[…] to the Proverb, * A Master [… is … that is at Land], and especially a [King of …], seeing he is able both by [… Fleets of Ships], and private Ships of [War, … to seize Ships] that sail by [that Course, the Westerly] Winds which blow [… often] on this side the *Tropick*, gi[ving the …] great Opportunitys to sail out [of their … Bays and] Harbours at plea[sure to … Navigation]. And if this Co[mmerce to the Eastward] and Westward [were stopt, or prevented], it would certainly [… ruin of …]

[… the formidable] Power of the Kingdom [of …, but His] Majesty the Sub was so sensible [of this … used to use] this Device, † He [… will be Master]. And according[ly, … he lived], sometimes against [France, sometimes … Spain], which was [then first … in the] *German* Empire, [… making] peace at his [own pleasure … with *Francis*] the First, and [*Charles* the Fifth], whom he durst so horribly [despise, as to repudiate] his Aunt

So that *England* now by a conjunction with S[cotland] being much increased in Strength, [as well as by] Manufactures, and a great Na-

---

* [Imperio …], Terra Dom[inus]
† C[…]

figavigation, will in all respects be formidable to all Europe, so soon as an Absolute King shall make use of that Power against his Neighbours, without the check and control of a Parliament.

But on the other side, it is also certain that England in a time of Peace has great advantages by the Hollanders, whom their passage are necessitated to frequent their Havens. And there are now in Holland many more English Commoditys, which we could very well spare, that are transported and used by us, than Holland hath Wares in England, because the Holland and other Foreign Manufactures have for the most part long since been prohibited. And since the Prohibition in England of importing any Goods, save those of the Growth and Manufacture of the Country, by Foreign Ships into England, all our Navigation to that Kingdom is at a stand. *How much England may be assisted by a Peace with Holland, or damaged by a War.*

2. It is evident, that the Rivers in England are very small, and remote from one another, so that all mutual Traffick, and transporting of Goods there, being necessarily done upon the open Sea, the English may suffer great Losses by our private Ships of War.

3. It is certain that the English Traffick by Sea being so great, and remote, may be most prejudiced in the Mediterranean Sea, and the East-Indies, by the Holland Ships, which during our free Government are much augmented, and must and will be increased more and more. *By our great Naval Power.*

4. It is clear, that considering our small and dangerous Coast, the English by Land can make no Conquest upon Holland, unless they can

can get footing by means of our intestine Divisions, nor we on them, for another reason. Besides, Kings will ever be conquering of Lands, and prudent Republicks which thrive best by Peace, will never do so, but rather erect Colonys.

5. It is therefore consequently true, That the English cannot make War upon us but by Sea. And since those Wars must be carried on purely with Mony, because Naval Power cannot subsist by plundering, and quartering in an Enemys Country, and that the King of England cannot employ his Revenue for that end, having occasion for that and more to maintain his Court, It also follows that he would have need of another standing Revenue or Fund to be enabled to carry on the said War by Sea.

6. It will be granted, That the said King having a new standing Revenue to maintain those Wars, he would never after call a Parliament to desire Subsidies from them, and consequently the Parliament will never suffer that any perpetual important Tax be established in that Kingdom, because the establishment of such a Tax would utterly devest them of so weighty a Privilege, as is the assembling of Parliaments, in which all Abuses are to be redress'd, and the Extortions, Briberies, and other Oppressions of Ministers and Courtiers prevented or punished, and Right done to the People, before they will engage by an Act of Parliament to pay those heavy Subsidies.

7. It is evident, That so long as we effectually take care of our Naval Power, and increase it as Opportunitys offer, a War with us would require so great and chargeable Fleets, that

that they could not be set to Sea, and maintained by Subsidies or Taxes only, because the Burden would be so great, so unexpected, and so uneasily born by the Inhabitants, that the King would be in continual apprehension and fear of an Insurrection of his Subjects, if he should obstinately persist to make War against us.

8. It is certain, that the Courtiers and Favourites who possess the King's Ear, may make great Profits by this War at Sea, by Prizes taken, and Subsidies granted, as long as they continue on shore to manage the same. But if they go to Sea themselves to command in the Fleet, they put themselves in as much danger of their Lives as the least Person there, by Storms, Shipwracks, Fireships, Bullets, and moreover, run the Hazard of having all their endeavours during their absence from Court misconstrued, and misrepresented to the King by other Courtiers. In a word, if those Favourites, and Courtiers, remain on shore during the War against *Holland*, they will be necessitated to see the Admiral carry away all the honour of good Successes, and they the blame of the bad; whilst instead of carefully providing all things necessary, they study to enrich themselves by the Subsidies and Prizes; and the Nation would gain little Honour or Profit by such a chargeable Naval War. And on the other side, if they go to Sea to command the Fleets, they must necessarily part from the Court, and be absent from the King, and consequently run a great Hazard, lest in the mean time some malevolent private Enemy, who hath the King's Ear, may so manage the matter, that tho they went

And a War by Sea is very unserviceable to the Courtiers.

went to Sea in the King's Forces, yet they must be called home with Disgrace.

9. It is certain that *England*, *Scotland*, and *Ireland*, having in all parts a deep and bold Coast, their Cities, Towns, and Villages in the Country being weak, or without Walls and Fortifications, they may in all places be attacked, and our Men may be landed under the Fire of our Cannon, and so plunder and burn their Places. Whereas the *English* cannot do the like in *Holland*, because our small Coast can easily be guarded and secured by our own Forces, and is so foul and shallow, that the Enemies Men of War cannot reach our Shore by reason of our Cannon; and in case they should attempt to land with their Boats, they would soon be overset by the high Surges of the Sea, or at least have their Powder spoil'd. So that what we should fall short of in our Privateering by Sea, we would ballance by our plundering on Land, and burning of Towns, and there be richly recompensed. Besides, such plundering and burning will strike a greater Terror and Consternation into the Inhabitants there, than any Losses at Sea would operate amongst us.

10. It cannot be denied, but that in all Monarchical Governments during a War, especially by Sea, vast Sums of Mony are ill laid out, and embezeld by Courtiers, Sea Officers, and Souldiers, and the Stores provided for the Navy frequently misimployed and wasted; so that in a little time the Mony raised will fall short, more especially in *England*, where the Subsidies granted by the Parliament, being always limited to a certain Sum, are indeed sufficient but not superfluous, and

Ch 9. *as to Alliances with* England.

and an *English* Court, above all others, is prodigal and uneven. Whereas on the other side, in a free Commonwealth, and in a time of War by Sea, such exact Accounts are kept, and Regulation used, that neither those that are entrusted to provide things necessary, nor those that make use of them, can either misspend or embezel the publick Mony or Provisions, and this may in a particular manner be expected from the *Hollanders*, who have always been famous for Frugality and Parsimony. And it is observable, that this Prodigality of the one Nation, and the Frugality of the other, is not only visible in the publick Treasure, but is also discerned in the private way of living, both of the *English* and *Hollanders*: so that by a War at Sea the Taxes upon the Commonalty of both sides increasing, and the Profits decreasing, *Holland*, in proportion to the Country and Purse of the Inhabitants, by well husbanding the publick Treasure, would easily hold out longer than *England*, as appeared manifestly in the Year 1667.

But all Republicks, especially Holland, *are frugal.*

All which Particulars being true, it naturally follows, that a War is for both Nations very mischievous; yet so, that *England* will be able to take many Prizes from us by Sea, and little by Land, We on the other side, few Prizes of the *English* by Sea, but great Booty by Land. But we should be sufficiently prejudiced by them, if we had not a competent number of Ships of War to match their Naval Strength, and by that means should be forced to quit the Sea to the *English*, especially if their Kings and Parliament would not lavish the strength of that Island on their Luxury and Favourites, but rather in Ships and Mariners.

A War with England *will be detrimental both to us and them.*

So

So that our only Safety is grounded upon the increase of our Naval Strength to such a Degree, that the *English* Fleets may either be over-ballanced by ours, or not able to hurt us, as likewise upon those Accidents to which a Monarchical Government is always subject, and that a War with us would be extremely pernicious to the Subjects of *England*, and likewise that *London*, by means of greater Traffick and Navigation, would be more formidable to the Kings of *England*, than any of his foreign Neighbours.

So that we ought to give the English good Words.

So that in order to avoid a War, we must in all our Differences give them good words, and gain time, in hopes that in these Monarchical Governments the Kings will either follow their Pleasures, or through excess of Luxury, and Court-robbery, waft all their Revenues, and run themselves into Debts, or die, or perhaps fall into a foreign or inteftine War.

But we are to take care, that we do not suffer our selves, for fear of a War with *England*, to be inveigled into an Alliance, jointly to carry on an offensive War against any Nation, which may be very formidable to that Country, and not so much to us. For in so doing we should make our selves considerably weaker, and *England* stronger, who having that Thorn pull'd out of their Foot, might afterwards with less fear oppress and trample upon us, while we remain deprived of that Refuge by our own Folly. The truth

Notwithstanding a War threatned.

is, since *England* is more formidable to us than any Country in the whole Universe, it were an unpardonable Fault in us, to make them yet more formidable to our selves.

And above all, we are to observe, that in order to shun or avoid a War with *England*, we must not suffer our selves to be seduced to alter the Commonwealth for a Monarchical Government, for * *The free Lion will not be bound again*, was used to be *Holland*'s Device and Sense. And it now under a free Government, we should be necessitated to make some steps that way to please the King of *England*, I would then ask how we should be able to make the least Resistance against such a Head, as would in a manner become Lord of the Country, through our Weakness and Chains, when he shall by an innate Hatred (which all Monarchs bear to Republicks) attempt to ruin our formidable Naval Strength and Trade, and deprive us of our Navigation, under colour of favouring a Prince related to him, and a Head of his own making, whilst he designs the supreme Power for himself: he would, I say, by this means make us the most miserable Nation that ever was governed by any Monarch; for such a Government would infallibly strip us of all our natural Advantages proceeding from the Seas and Rivers, and not only leave us charged with intolerable Taxes, but oppress us also with an expensive and luxurious way of Living, together with those other infinite Mischiefs which are found ever in those Governments. From whence it evidently follows, that we must defend our free Government, tho it should be by a War against *England*: For 'tis better and more commendable

Above all we ought not to please England by altering our free Government.

---

* Leo revinciri liber pernegat.

to fight for our lives, and with the utmost hazard of perishing, to cast Lots our selves like Jonas's, or else of necessity take sinking Souls in the Battel, or to murder our selves by a double Death of Soul and Body, without hopes of a Resurrection. Seeing if the worst befal us, and we be weakned by an *English* War, yet still living under a free Government, we might wait for Accidents and Alterations, and hope to have better Success at another time. Whereas on the contrary, by a more absolute Government we should for ever be deprived of our Fisheries, Manufactures, and Trade, to the Ruin of our selves and our Posterity, who might justly curse such base and cowardly Parents.

In all Events it is evident, that *England* fearing no Potentate of *Europe*, except the King of *France*, can make no Alliance with us grounded upon a common Fear, but that only, and consequently all other Alliances with that Kingdom will be prejudicial to us.

It is also evident, that we are not to make an Alliance with *England*, out of a desire of Gain at the best; when we have employed our utmost Strength in putting on the Game, we should at last most certainly differ with the *English* Lion about dividing the Prey; who taking the whole to himself, might soon after devour the wretched *Holland* Ass, or at most we should only be like Jackals, or Ferrets, to drive the Game into the *English* Net.

It were therefore in truth much better, that *Holland* in her Actions should imitate, not those two sly and unhappy Beasts, but rather the shy and wary Cat, that hunts only for her self. Since

Since then we can make no advantageous Alliances with *England*, neither for common Conquest, nor common Defence, except against *France* only, we may rationally conclude, that all Alliances with that Kingdom, unless defensive against *France*, are useless to *Holland*, even those which might proceed from fear of a War with *England:* for it is evident, that whatever advantageous Conditions that King acquires from us, we must immediately make them good; and yet expect that he will nevertheless threaten us with a War, unless we will do many harder things for him.

But a defensive Alliance with them against France may be very proper.

And indeed he that will not defend his Subjects in their Lives and Liberties, tho by troublesom and dangerous Wars, is so unworthy of Government, Liberty, and Life, that in all respects he ought to be esteemed the Off-scouring of the World, and his Posterity never to be named by succeeding Generations, without Curses and Detestation

---

CHAP. X.

Some General and Particular Inferences drawn from the foregoing Considerations, touching all our Allies.

OUT of all which foregoing Particulars, I conceive we may draw the following Corollaries.

First, That all Alliances which *Holland* might make in a time of Peace with any

Neighbouring Princes of *Europe* are wholly unserviceable to us, since in our Necessity we shall never receive Aid from them, but rather be drawn into a War. But in times of War and Trouble we should consider, according to what I formerly mentioned, whether *Holland* were able to defend it self, and continue to do against its most potent Neighbours, *France*, *Spain*, and *England*, without any Assistance from abroad. And seeing I suppose we can, it then follows, that if we are attacked by a weaker Power, we must not seek help from those great Potentates mentioned, because they would thereby become greater and mightier. And on the contrary, a good Patriot of *Holland* ought to wish, that *France* and *England* may decrease, and that *Spain* may not increase in Strength.

And if it should so fall out, that one of the three aforementioned Kingdoms should make War upon us, it is not at all needful that we therefore should seek Aid from abroad against them by Alliances, unless they of their own accord, and decently offer themselves; for otherwise we shall get nothing but a number of good Words, and if we rely on them, we shall be much hindered, as we lately found in our *English* War, when we were allied with *France*, and have learned from that inferior and ungrateful *Denmark*. But when those Alliances fall into our Laps, then, I say;

2. When *Holland* is fallen into a War with *England*, all Alliances with other Potentates are good, in order to escape, provided our Allies will perform their Engagements.

3. When *Spain* makes War with us, an offensive Alliance with *France* is good, provided

vided the French comply first with their Engagements, and if they will not, it is better to stand upon our own bottom, and to labour that we run not aground. And seeing we must run the Adventure, it is better to endeavour with full Sail to pass over the Flats, than in expectation of foreign Pilots, who all may promise to assist us with their Skill, to let our Vessel drive slowly, but certainly on the Sands, and perish.

It is always more decent and honourable for Men to shew that Courage they have, and effectually to exert their utmost Strength against an Enemy, in order to preserve their Rights, than to surrender all through Cowardice and Fear. For tho they may lose by the War, yet they sell every Advantage so dear to the Enemy, that afterwards neither he nor any other will rashly come on again. But he who for Fear, and want of Courage, gives up any part of his Estate and Right, invites and pulls down upon his own Head all that a covetous Enemy can desire, and is despised by all Men. *That in matters of Polity, relating to an Enemy, none ought to be fainthearted.*

4. All these Disturbances and Wars, whether against France (unless that Kingdom were strengthned by devouring the Spanish Netherlands, and so become our Neighbour) or against any other Potentates, may more easily be overcome without any Alliance, tho in such a Case the lesser Republicks and Potentates may, in favour of Holland, be drawn into the War by some preceding Alliance, because we having gotten what we aimed at, will ever interpret the Alliance made to our best Advantage. *Contracts with lesser States are the best.*

5. It

5. It is *cæteris paribus* more useful either for *Holland*, or other Potentates, to have Alliances with a Republick, than with a Prince or King, because such Alliances being grounded upon a common Interest, they may assure themselves that they will always be so understood by the Governors of a Commonwealth, who besides are Immortal and Perpetual. Whereas on the other side, single Persons have seldom so much understanding and knowledg, as to apprehend their own Interest, much less will they take the pains to govern by that Rule; and besides, they are very inconstant and mortal, and naturally hate all Republicks.

6. It is, and always will be dangerous for *Holland*, to make Alliances with *France*, *Spain*, or *England*, because 'tis probable that they who are more esteemed only because they are Kings, and possess larger Territories than we, will always oblige us to perform our Engagements first, and expound all ambiguous Points to their own advantage. But so long as we are in the least fear of *France*, that is, so long as *Spain* can keep the *Netherlands*, we may best enter into Alliance with that Kingdom for common defence, against those that might wrong, or make War against the one or the other. But when *France* is like to be Master of the *Netherlands*, and become our Neighbour, it is not only necessary for *Holland* to prevent that potent, and always bold and insolent Neighbour, and to take great care not to make any League, by which *France* may in any measure increase in Power; but all the Potentates and States of *Europe* ought to combine together to hinder

der the further growth of that Kingdom, which hath already overgrown all its Neighbours.

Likewise so long as we must dread *England* in the highest degree, it is perfectly useless to make the least Alliance with that Kingdom, save such as is grounded upon a common fear of a greater Power, as now *France* is, seeing all written Alliances, without common Necessity, are interpreted in favour of the greatest, as happens in all doubtful Cases: Besides that *England* will thus find more cause with appearance of Right to make War against us. For if that be found true, which mean Persons conclude, That all that are in Partnership have a Master; and that all such Partnerships begin *In the Name of God,* but use to end in that of the Devil: 'Tis much more true of Kings and Princes, who have outgrown all Justice; and consequently as true, that so long as *England* intends to have the Quiet or Disquiet of *Holland* at their own disposal, she would be the worst and most tyrannical Ally for us that were to be found in the whole World, unless the dread of a more powerful Neighbour should curb that pernicious Inclination.

Above all things we ought to make no Alliance with England save against France.

To sum up all. So long as *Holland* can stand on its own Legs, it is utterly unadvisable to make any Alliance with those who are more potent; and especially it is not good to perform any thing first, or be beforehand with those unconstant Monarchs and Princes, in hope that they will perform with us afterwards, according to the old saying, They that eat Cherrys with great Men, must pay for them themselves; and besides, suffer them

them to chuse the fairest, and expect at last to be pelted with the Stones, instead of Thanks for the Favour received.

And consequently it is certain, That all the Advantage in Articles of an Alliance consists in this, that *Holland* do always covenant that the other Allys shall first perform their Engagements. All other sort of Alliances are very prejudicial to us: For by the proper Constitution, or antient Custom of our Government, the Deputys of the Provinces upon all occasion will, where they can expect any private Benefit, suffer themselves to be moved by Foreign Ambassadors to draw in *Holland* to their Party, when they can see no detriment to accrue thereby to their particular Provinces.

And the following Proverb takes place with those especially (whose Commissioners for the Generality are not concerned for the Publick, so long as their Provinces remain unburdened) *That it is very easy to lie in the Aties with another Man's Garment, and be warm*. So also 'tis not difficult to take generous Resolutions at the cost of another, to keep Promise, to be liberal and merciful towards our Neighbours, while all other Potentates and States continue to deal openly and fairly with us. But supposing the other Provinces might be somewhat concerned therein, yet is their Interest so inconsiderable, that among their Deputys we ever find that a general Evil is weighed according to the Weigher's particular Interest and no otherwise, how heavily soever another may be oppressed thereby; especially here, because they are seldom called to account by their Superiors for their Transactions. And

And if any one doubts of the Truth of these Inferences, *viz.* That all Superior Powers, especially the Monarchs and Princes of *Europe* play with their Allys as Children do with Nine-pins, which they set up, and immediately beat down again as they please; and that he that first performs is ever the loser, and suffers shame, let him read the Historys of *Francisco Guicciardino*, and *Philip de Commines.* And if these two famous Politicians, the one an *Italian*, the other a *Netherlander*, writing of Matters in which they had the profoundest skill, and in which they were very often imploy'd, if they, I say, do not remove these Doubts, much less will it be effected by any reasoning from me.

For Potentates trifle with Oaths.

In the mean time, to conclude what hath been alledged above (*viz.* seeking our Preservation by Alliances) I shall lay before you that which the Antients have figured out by the ensuing Fable.

"A rich but weak Countryman, observing
"that his poor and strong Neighbour, con-
"trary to preceding Promises made of assist-
"ing each other, did notwithstanding steal
"his Apples, and rob'd his Orchard, told
"him of the Injustice and Perfidiousness of
"the thing, desiring that he would be satis-
"fied with what he had. To this the strong
"Boor answered, that this Sermon very well
"became a rich unarmed Man, but that he
"being hungry, could not fill his empty Belly
"with such Food. And as to his former Pro-
"mises and Engagements for mutual de-
"fence, such kind of necessity is ever excep-
"ted, and that he could not comply there-
"with. Upon this the other weak and old

The general Conclusion illustrated by a Fable of an old and rich Man, and a young Country fellow.

"Boor

"Boor having gathered a Nosegay of sweet
"Herbs and beautiful Flowers, threw them
"to the Plunderer, saying, I present you
"with these Fruits, that you may not rob
"my Orchard, which I use to sow and plant
"for the use and refreshment of Friends.
"The impudent young Fellow thinking with
"himself, that he must needs be very silly,
"who being able to take all, will be content
"with so small a matter, rob'd him more and
"more of all that came to hand; insomuch
"that the Owner became impatient, and in
"great haft gathered up some Stones, and
"threw them at the Plunderer; who being
"grievously hurt, was necessitated to leap
"down from the Tree and fly. The old
"weak Boor finding himself alone, broke
"out into these words, Formerly we used to
"say, In Words, Herbs and Stones, there
"are great Virtues: But now I really find
"the weakness of Words and Herbs, i. e.
"Alliances, and Gifts to knavish Men. For
"all Gifts and Receipts are good for the Phy-
"sician, and the true Antidote in all Poli-
"tick Distempers, is good Arms and Trea-
"sure. So that to make an end, I say, that
"no body can defend his Goods against
"wicked Men, but by Stones, that is, good
"Arms, which are the only things left us,
"whereby we can bravely defend our
"Lives and Estates

But seeing these Conclusions do affirm, that *Holland* is able to defend it self against all Foreign Power, and yet the same is not sufficiently proved, therefore I shall do it in the following Chapters more fully, with this reserve, that *Holland* notwithstanding ought

for

for its own Interest always to maintain the Union of *Utrecht*, so long as the other Provinces forsake not *Holland*, nor assault it in a hostile manner.

CHAP. XI.

That Holland *heretofore, under the Government of a single Person, was in continual Tumults and Broils. And that under a Free Government it ought, and can defend it self against all Foreign Power better than formerly.*

Because in the foregoing Chapters, which treat of *Holland*'s making or not making Alliances with its Neighbours, it could be shewn only in part and by accident, that *Holland* effectually minding its own Interest, can make a State in *Europe* independent of any other, and not to be overpowered by any Foreign Force: And that on the other side, there are many Magistrates of Opinion, or at least have been so, that *Holland* ought not only to be joined by the Union of *Utrecht*, but also by a Governor or Captain General, to all the other *United Provinces*; because if that Province should happen to be abandoned by the rest, they say, it would by no means defend it self in time of War against a powerful Enemy: To whom we may add the Courtiers, and other Flatterers of the Stadtholders Court, who have for a long time made the common Inhabitants of the *United Provinces* believe,

Advisedly to consider whether Holland *can subsist against all Potentates,*

We must not regard what flattering Courtiers have given out, but

believe, that all those Countrys united would not be able to repel the Force of *Spain* with their own Strength, and that therefore one permanent Illustrious Captain-General and Stadtholder is very necessary for us, that by his Interest and Favour we may be able to obtain Succours of *France*, *England*, or *Germany*, against *Spain*. For these Reasons, and on account of the weight of the Subject, upon which most of all that is here treated, or shall be said hereafter, depends, I find my self obliged to represent the same more at large, and that effectually.

In the first place it is evident, that there can be nothing more shameful nor prejudicial for a Sovereign Free Government, than to hold for a Maxim in the publick management of their Affairs, That in a time of War they are not able to subsist against all their Neighbours and States, whoever they be: For such Governors do thereby make the Welfare of their Native Country dependent upon those more powerful States, and content themselves of Rulers to become Subjects: Which is the most miserable condition that any Country can fall into by unsuccessful War.

And indeed if we may justly blame a sick Person, who because he thinks he is mortally sick, will therefore use no Physician; we ought much more to blame those Rulers, who by base and degenerate Maxims lay aside the use of all Wisdom, Care, and Power, to strengthen and defend their Country to the utmost Extremity: for we might excuse the Folly of a sick Person, because what he does is at his own peril. And because every one is Lord of his own, neither can it be simply said that

that he increases his Distemper by neglecting the use of Physick. But a Magistrate, who is by Nature and by his Oath to provide for the Welfare of his Subjects, and to defend them against all Force, ought to be accounted the most infamous of Men if he neglects that Duty.

If then by such ill Maxims he uses the strength of his own Country and Subjects to give advantages to another, and is not only careless of his own, but of the Welfare of his innocent People, he tempts his insolent Neighbours, and perfidious Allys, to attack and ruin his Country in that unarmed condition: Wheras if he had made such provision for the publick Defence as he ought, they would have been deterred from any attempt, and have continued peaceable and quiet. For as occasion makes the Thief, and every one will climb over into the Garden where the Wall is lowest; so likewise the Goods of unarmed People are ever common: but one Sword keeps another in the Scabbard, and two curst Dogs seldom bite one another

But to come nearer to the matter in hand, I shall premise in the general, from the Credit of undoubted History, that most of these Netherlandish Provinces, especially *Holland*, whilst for many Ages they were governed by Earls and Captains General, not only lived in continual Dissension and Division, but were in perpetual War one against the other, as well as against their Lords, and those that depended on them, unchristianly shedding one anothers Blood: And the reason of it is very evident; for tho the Interest of such Lords is often different from that of the State, and con-

Deduction, Part 2 ch.3. fol. 6. Holland I th sind of it self 700 Years together.

It had Breaches and Tumults during the Government of the Earls and Capt. Generals.

contrary to the common Good of the People, yet have they very many Persons that depend on them, and are of great Power in the Government, by which means it infallibly happens (unless such Lords could be devested of human Nature) that they will endeavour many times to advance their own particular Interests, with the assistance of their Favorites, and Dependents. Against which all good Magistrates, who value the common Happiness above all things, and esteem the Welfare of the People to be the Supreme Law, are necessitated, in discharge of their Duty, to exert themselves vigorously against such Persons, without fear of their displeasure; and by this means the Community falls into great Divisions. For on the one side, the Lord will not, and according to the Rules of the World may not bow or comply, because his Honour and Authority stands engaged. And on the other side, the honest Magistrates, relying on their Consciences as on a Wall of Brass, will not be drawn from their necessary Resolution, and if in so dangerous a Conjuncture the Lord happen to be of a violent Temper, or apt to be seduced by violent Counsels, that Country is often brought to great Extremitys.

And yet we know that notwithstanding these intestine Disorders, Suspicions and Animositys, the *Hollanders* preserved and defended themselves against all Foreign Force. And it appears by the Negotiations of the President *Jeannin*, that Prince *Maurice*, and his Partizans, in the Year 1608, was of opinion, that *Zealand* alone, parted from the other *United Provinces*, was able to defend it self against

all

all the Power of *Spain*; upon which the other Provinces declared not to agree to a Truce, but to continue the War.

This being premised in general, I come now to the matter in particular. In the first place, Antient Historys inform us, that *Holland* before the breaking in of the Inlet to the *Texel*, about the Year 1170, according to *Goederd Pantaleon*, published by *M. Vossius*, or as others say, about the Year 1400, being destitute of the *Zuyder-Sea*, lay joined to *Friesland*, *Overyssel* and *Guelderland*, or at most was parted by the *Rhine* and *Vlie*, as before the Year 1421, and before the Land near *Dort* was overflown, *Holland* on that side lay joined to *Brabant*, and consequently had many more Frontiers than now. And moreover it is evident, that these Inland Provinces had fewer Citys, and less Populous, and was therefore in respect of their Neighbours every way weaker and poorer than at present. *Holland anciently much weaker than at present.*

And yet the States of *Holland* and *West-Friesland*, from the unanimous consent of all our antient Historians, inform us in their Remonstrance to the Earl of *Leicester* in 1587 That these Lands (then Lordships speaking there of *Holland* with *West-Friesland*, and *Zealand*) *have for the most part bin victorious against all their Enemys, and have so well defended their Frontiers against their Adversaries, however powerful, that they have always had a good esteem and reputation among their Neighbours*: At least we may say with truth, that the Countrys of *Holland* and *Zealand* for the space of 800 Years have never been conquered by the Sword, or subdued either by Foreign or Intestine Wars. Which can- *Yet hath at all times defended it self well. P. Borre, Book 23 fol. 56.*

not be [afraid] [of] any other Dominions, unless of the
R[epublic] [of] Venice. Thus far the said Sta[t]es

2. It is notorious that the Provinces of *Holland* and *West-[Fries]land* never had more powerful Neighbours than the Kings of *Spain*, who
having been Earls of *Holland* and *Zealand*,
and still claiming a Right to that Dominion,
had an incredible advantage above all other
Neighbours to reduce these Countrys under
their Power, which were very much divided
by many Differences about Religion and other
Matters, and yet *Holland* and *Zealand* alone,
after they had supported a few Sieges with
resolution, so broke the formidable Power of
that wise and resolute Monarch *Philip* the
2d of *Spain*, that other Provinces afterwards
by their Example dared to resist him.

So that the other United Provinces have not
brought *Holland* and *Zealand* into a condition
of Freedom, but *Holland* and *Zealand* them.
And it is to be considered, that the other
Provinces (*Utrecht* excepted) have added nothing to strengthen and fortify the free Government of *Holland*, or to free that Province
from any Inconvenience to this day. But on
the contrary, *Holland* alone erected the Com-
monwealth-Government for the benefit of
the other Provinces, and has done so much for
the other Provinces, that every one of them
(except *Utrecht* which has always run the same
adventure with us) is now provided with well
fortified Citys, Magazines, Ammunition of
War, Provision, and Souldiers in Garison,
or to [say] better, Inhabitants, who daily receive their Pay out of *Holland*. And moreover, divers Citys and Forts in *Brabant*,
F[lander]s, *Cleve*, *East-Friesland*, *Drenth*, and
Nether-

Ch. 11. *the Government of a single Person.*

Netherland, have been conquered, fortified, and provided with Souldiers, Provisions, and Ammunition of War necessary for their defence at the expence of *Holland*.

Against this, if any will object that *Holland* in the distribution of Taxes pays no more than 58 Guilders 6 Stivers 2 ½ pence in the hundred for their share, and consequently the other *United Provinces* have in some measure helped to bear the charge of the War: We might truly answer, that *Guelderland* and *Overyssel* contributed nothing to the charge of the Army to the time of the Truce, and that to the Year 1607, we were necessitated at our own charge to compel *Groeningen* to bring in its proportion for the War by means of a Castle and Garison. And it is certain that afterwards the yearly Demand, or Request of the Council of State for Taxes to pay the Armys in the time of *Frederick Hendrick* Prince of *Orange*, was purposely raised so high, that half the Sum would very near defray that charge. So that when the said Captain General had once obliged the Province of *Holland* to give their consent to the Sum required, he used not much to trouble himself for that of the other Provinces. And we have often seen, that in the hottest of the War against *Spain*, and in the former War against *England*, together with the Eastern and Northern War, as well as in the last *English* War, they have often refused to consent to the publick Supplies, and more often have only given their Consent for form-sake, in order to induce the Province of *Holland* to consent to the Charge; and having done so, because they dared not to deny their Consents for

In comparison whereof what the other Provinces contributed was of little value.

Aitzma's Hist. lib 32. pag. 774

fear

fear of incurring the Prince's displeasure, they remained in default of paiment without being compelled to bring in their promised Proportions; because our Captain-General had rather by such Favours keep the other Provinces at his devotion, and especially their Deputys of the Generality (amongst whom were several who with good reason were called the *Cabinet Lords*) that by them he might be able perpetually to overvote the Province of *Holland*, and make them dance to his Pipe. And this is the true reason of the many Arrears of Taxes which those Provinces consented to raise, but have not brought in to this day. Tho (if we relapse not again under a new Captain-General) Expedients may be found and put in execution for recovery of them, and for prevention of the like for the future.

3. It is to be observ'd that *Holland* during all these Broils and Hardships, was under the Government of Earls and Stadtholders or Captain-Generals, who have ever sought their own private Interest to the prejudice of these Countrys, and have from time to time raised and fomented those endless intestine Divisions, in order to make a Conquest of the Estates and Rights of the Gentry and Citys of *Holland* and *Westfriesland*, so that it remains abundantly evident that all Foreign Wars have been carried on and finished only by a part, or divided Power of this Province.

4. It is likewise observable, that almost all the *United Provinces* have continually lived upon *Holland*, not only by their Deputys in some College of the Generality and other Offices of Judicature, Polity, and the Revenues; but also by great numbers of their Gentry, and

Ch. 11. *The Government of a single Person.* 305

and other Inhabitants, who by favour of the Captain-General have found means to get into the most profitable Commands in the Army, and are to be paid by the States of *Holland* and *West-Friesland*, and for that reason, even after the Peace was concluded, kept those Land-Forces long in great pay against the will of *Holland*, tho they had during the War endlessly multiplied those Offices, and Profits. And 'tis yet more remarkable, that almost all the *United Provinces* have continually prey'd upon *Holland*, by bringing in very many mere Provincial Charges to the account of the Generality, in the annual Petition of the Council of State, that under this pretext they might make *Holland* pay yearly more than 8 per Cent. of divers Sums, of which in truth *Holland* owed not one Penny.

See Catalogue of the Generalitys Officers, in Aitzma B. 41 p. 232.

Deduct. 1 put. c 9 §. 15. 2 put c. 6 §. 17, to 20

So that I shall finish all these Considerations with concluding, that the stout and powerful Lion of *Holland* had formerly strength enough to repel all his Foreign Enemys, and those of his Allies, *viz.* of the other *United Provinces*. But (God amend it) I must add, that this strong and victorious Creature, to the Year 1650, had not the foresight, or fortune to escape the Snares which were laid by his own Ministers and Servants. For our Historys tell us, that the Earls of the House of *Burgundy* and *Austria*, did by degrees more and more bridle and curb the *Holland* Lion, and it is also as evident that our former Stadtholders and Captain-Generals have very well been acquainted with the Politick Maxim of Lording it over a Country, and bringing it under subjection. That the most powerful Provinces and the strongest Citys, together with the best

Holland is cast off of all its Enemys, but that of her own Ministers.

X and

and most venerable Magistrates, were most insulted and brought into the greatest slavery.

So that every one may judg, whether the said Stadtholders, and Captain-Generals might not without difficulty lessen and depress *Holland*, with its antient and considerable Gentry, strong Citys, and venerable Magistrates, and by that means increase their own Power, since in all Colleges of the common Union or Generality they could very easily engage the most Voices, to over-vote and compel the Province of *Holland*, even in such Matters wherein plurality of Votes should have no place, neither by the right of Nature, Right of Justice, or the Common Union.

And let the Reader enquire, weigh, and consider whether the Stadtholders and Captain-Generals following the same Maxims, have not in all the Provinces, and especially in *Holland*, very often taken off the meanest and most indigent Magistrates from seeking the Countrys Welfare, and drawn them to their Party, that in conjunction with others like themselves, they may either over-vote those who are more able, and more affectionate to the lawful Government, or by force of Arms turn them out of their Magistracy, and introduce other needy Persons, and sometimes such as fly from Justice, to serve in their Places.

Besides which, our Stadtholders and Captain-Generals have left our Lion undefended against the new invented Military Arts, or to speak clearer, have left the Citys without any more than their old Fortifications,

ons, so that they are not tenable against the new invented Art of taking Towns. They have also fettered and manacled these Countrys, by means of Garisons and Citadels placed in the conquered Citys, and have so order'd matters, that most of the Governments and chief Military Offices in *Holland* have been put into the hands of Strangers, but ever of their Relations, or Creatures, and very seldom intrusted with the Gentry of *Holland*, and Lovers of their Country. *The States of Holland never so much opprest under the Earls of Burgundy or of Austria.*

So that the Power of the Captain-Generals was even in the Year 1618, grown so far above the former Power of the antient Earls; and on the other side the Power of our Nobility and Citys so much diminished, that tho many of them for very small Usurpations and Encroachments of their Earls, dared to exclude them out of their Castles and Citys, yet there was not one City of *Holland* (tho they knew that Prince *Maurice* as Captain-General came to put out of Office all Magistrates that were Lovers of their Common Freedom, and to remove them from their Benches) that durst shut their Gates, much less make head against, and drive him from their Walls. So that about the Year 1650, it might still be asked, * Whether these Countrys by their Servants of the House of *Nassau*, or their Lords of that of *Austria*, were in greater servitude. And farther, it is well known to all, that some Ministers of this unhappy Lion of *Holland* have endeavoured to break and destroy *As under the Stadtholders and Captain-Generals of the House of Orange.*

Aitzma b. 33. pag. 809.

---

* Servire Auriacis Famulis, Dominisque Philippis,
 Dic mihi conditio durior utra fuit?

all its inward Power, by causing the Union made for general Defence to be so order'd, that in reality it had the same effect in the State as a continual Hectick Fever in the Body, causing us to take up so much Mony yearly at Interest, and for paiment of yearly Interest already due, that in very few Years it would have proved as a Canker, and have consumed all its vital Strength.

Holland is better armed by the Sea and Rivers.

And on the other side it is remarkable what advantage time hath since given us, *viz.* *First*, That *Holland* is wholly surrounded with Seas, or mighty Rivers: in particular to the Eastward by the North-Sea, to the Southward by many Islands, and great Rivers, as the *Maese*, the *Rhyne* and *Issell*, in part begirting *Holland*, to the Westward, and to the Northward by the mighty Inlets of the *Texel*, and the *Vlie*, and likewise the *Zuider-Sea*, and the *Vecht* encompassing this Country in part towards the West: So that *Holland* is now in all respects inaccessible, or would be in time of War, unless to one that is Master at Sea. At least it is evident that *Holland* hath no community at all with the Frontiers or Limits of the Land, save with some few conquered Citys in *Brabant*, with a very small part of *Guelderland*, as also and especially with the Province of *Utrecht*.

And provided with great and populous Citys.

See Beativoglio, re it B.1. c. —

Secondly, It is clear, that *Holland* is now more than ever furnished with many great and populous Citys and Towns, whose Inhabitants by trading in all the Commoditys of the World, have incredibly enriched themselves, while on the other side *Brabant* and *Flanders* are become poorer and weaker. And it must be confessed, that the said Traffic sick by Sea hath improved *Holland*'s Strength of Shipping to a higher degree than ever it was formerly.

'*Thirdly*, It must be acknowledged, that *Holland* is now governed after a free Republican manner; and therefore its Inhabitants are able to pursue their own Interest with an undivided and unbroken Power, and not to be terrified or constrained in time to come by any one eminent Servant of the State with his Adherents, or by any ill practised Union or misled Allys, to be over voted, ensnared, and depressed to its own ruin.

Fourthly, It is observable, that the formidable *Burgundian* and *Austrian* Power, which formerly was so grievous to us, is now fixed in *Spain*, to govern from so great a distance those *Netherlands* that join to our Frontiers, by delegated Governours, and appointed Captain-Generals, officiating in their respective Employments for a very short time. Since therefore they with slow and limited Instructions, and tied up hands, cannot perform that Service to those extreme jealous Kings and Councils of *Spain* to the prejudice of us, we in that respect need not to fear them.

Fifthly, It is evident that the King of *Spain*, heretofore our old and most formidable Neighbour by Land, is not only weakned in his Dominions by the defection of *Portugal*; but by his manifold losses of Territorys, and Citys situate in *Brabant*, *Flanders*, *Artois*, &c. is become so inconsiderable, that to obtain a Peace of us, he in the Year 1648 found it his best course to resign up his Right to the *United Provinces*, and especially to that of

And with a free Government.

While the Burgundian and Spanish Princes remain in Spain.

And their Power is every way diminished.

Holland, with whatever he might any way pretend to; so that we are now wholly fearless from that side.

All which past Mischiefs, and present Advantages of *Holland*, being thus well weighed, methinks I might generally infer, that *Holland* is much abler now than ever 'twas formerly to defend it self against all Foreign Enemys.

But some may object, that *Holland* for fifty Years past having abandoned its own Defence, and reversed all good Maxims, has so contrived and constituted matters, that we cannot be safe unless by means of the other Provinces, and that all our great Advantages of good Situation, Populousness, and God's unspeakable Blessings upon the Diligence and Frugality of the *Hollanders*, have only served to strengthen the other Provinces and conquered Citys, so as to render them impregnable. Insomuch that they now have no more need of us, unless to draw Mony from us; and that on the other side, we have left our selves naked of all means, both of Defence and Offence.

They may also say, that at the great Assembly held in the *Hague* in the Year 1651, *Holland* granted to the Generality, and the other Provinces, the Right of giving Patents or Commissions to all the Military Officers of the respective Allies. So that it may be affirm'd, that this Province hath utterly devested themselves of all kind of Respect or Esteem from the Soldiery, who yet are paid out of our Purse, tho they are for the most part in Garisons out of the Province of *Holland*; and that we have not preserved that

natu

natural Right which we have over them. So that if we should want any Companys for the Service of our Province, we should be forced as it were to petition to have them of our said Allys.

To which may be added, that we have been burdened with so many Impositions, that it is impossible they can be long born by a Country that subsists not of its own Fund, but of Manufactures, Fishing, Trade and Shipping, whilst we are burden'd with endless incankering Sums taken up at Interest. So that we might hence conclude, that *Holland* is not indeed esteemed considerable by any of her Neighbours, or Allys by Land; and that we on the contrary must stand in fear of all our nearest Neighbours that are well armed. And he that doubts of this, let him but consider that divers Provinces during the first and second War, dared roundly to declare, That they would not bear the Charge of any War by Sea whatsoever it were. Let them likewise take notice that the Province of *Holland* to this day could never find any Means to compel the Provinces that are in Arrear of their Quota's, to bring in their multiplied Arrears, to which they gave their Consent. And therefore *Holland* in respect of all its adjacent Neighbours by Land, seems in all regards to be weaker than ever it formerly was. *Aitzma, Hist. of 1654. p. 144, 357, 358.*

And in truth, if the Province of *Holland* had not heretofore been compell'd by a Captain-General and Stadtholder, to suffer the things beforementioned, I should much wonder that we have continued so long in such an ill state of Government: For it has always *How this happened against all Rules of good Government.*

been a Custom in the World, that the Weak, to the end they might be assisted in their distress against the Strong, should enrich the Strong in a time of Peace by a yearly Payment of ......, and that the Strong having received much Money and Tribute, whether in times of Peace or War, should for all that .... them weak .... their necessity, ... with their own In............... And certainly, he is a Fool in grain, ... Water to his Neighbour's House, ... is burning. Moreover *Holland* .... more than fifty Years successively .... left disarmed, to strengthen .... Neighbours, and to make them ra............. So that in .... ought be fear lest .... and unprovided Fron............. the other great City, ... want of Fortifications, ... Arms tho they are stronger .... might be surprized, and fall into .... hands.

.... have been like .... Fence suitable to defend .... own strength, yet we .... to be circled into .... be better defended .... Arms to certain famous .... to Neighbours that boast themselves to be .... able to wrestle and fence .... and consequently to repel an Enemy, ... are visibly weaker of Body than .... So that we having for so long .... and lent out our Arms, ... of exercise and using the Sword, ..., become totally disarmed and

weak:

weak, insomuch that in case our weak Champions should come to a Battel, not only they but we also should fall by the Sword: and besides, our weak neighbouring Champions who have borrowed our Swords, are no less mischievous than any other People. And therefore we are to expect, that they not only design their own Advantage, and neglect ours, but also will conceive and esteem their own Burdens very heavy, and ours very light; for I would not say, they will use the Arms and Power they have borrowed of us to our Ruin, whenever they can effect it to their Advantage. By all which it appears, that *Holland* is now less defensible than ever.

But he that examines this general Position on both sides, must acknowledg, that as this weakness of *Holland* was caused by their own Stadtholder and Captain-General. And on the other side, *Holland* by the present free Government is enabled to make use of all its abundant inward Strength, for its own preservation, and with more ease than ever to repel all intestine and foreign Force whatsoever. Now to the end this Conclusion may the better appear, I shall in the next Chapter endeavour to shew, that *Holland* distinctly, and in regard of all her Neighbours, not comparatively, but effectually, may very well defend it self against all inward and outward Force whatsoever.

CHAP

CHAP. XII.

That Holland *during its Free Government, cannot be ruined by any Intestine Power.*

'TIS evident that no Domestick Power can subvert the Republic of *Holland*, nor destroy the Welfare of the Inhabitants, except by a general Conspiracy, Sedition, Insurrection, and Civil War of the People and Cities of *Holland* against one another, because they are so wonderfully linked together by a common Good, that those homebred Tumults and Wars are not to be supposed able to be raised, except by Inhabitants of such eminent Strength, as is able to force the Magistracy of the Country to the execution of such destructive Counsels. And seeing now in *Holland* and *West-Friesland* there is no Captain-General or Stadtholder, nor any Illustrious Person except the Prince of *Orange*, therefore we will consider, whether if the said Prince who is in no Office of the Generality, continuing in these Provinces, might be able to cause or effect such ruinous and destructive Divisions in *Holland*.

And indeed as I have a Prospect, that if he should happen to get into any Administration, he must occasion such Divisions and Breaches. Yet on the other side, I cannot see how without imployment, either from the Generality, or this Province, he could obtain so great an Interest in the Government of these Countrys, as to be able to cause a Civil War, and make himself Master of them, either

either with the old or a new Title: For he being no General, nor having any Military Dependents, and out of all Command, tho he might by seditious Preachers cause a few of the Rabble to rise against their lawful Rulers, yet this would not be like to happen at one time, and in so many places together, as to make an Alteration in the Provincial Government. And that Free Government remaining intire, the new Magistrates obtruded on the People upon this rising, would be turn'd out, and the Seditious every time signally punished. And this would also tend to the great prejudice of the Honour of the Prince of *Orange*; besides, that by this means he would lose all hopes and appearances of ever being imployed in the Country's Service; and on the other side might fear, that he and his Posterity should for ever be excluded from all Government and Service in these *United Netherlands* by a perpetual Law.

It is answered in the affirmative, but else not.

And if the Prince of *Orange* be not able to cause such Seditions and Divisions, I suppose it could less be done by any College of the Generality. For I would fain know in which of the Cities of *Holland* would the States General, or the Council of State, without a Military Head, be now able to alter the present free Government by Force or Faction? Assuredly not in any one City. And from the lesser Colleges of the Generality such Mischiefs are less to be feared.

Much less could the Deputys of the Generality, depriv'd of such a Head, be able to cause Commotions.

But perhaps some may say, that the Rulers or States of this Province, of their own accord, or seduced by Promises and Gifts, forget that warning, Fear those who are
ac-

accustomed to do ill, especially when they make Presents *, and will bring in the *Trojan* Horse. But yet the arm'd Men conceal'd in his Belly, will never be able, by the Conspiracy of some Magistrates, to destroy our Province, and to subdue and ruin our Citys by Uproars against the Rulers: but possibly they may by bringing in the horse, weaken our lawful Governors, and leave our Citys without defence, and then the horse may be drawn into the Princes Court, and into the feeble and easy Assembly of the States. As *Reason of State of the Netherlands* in general. "That they are more fiery than they should be for the preservation of their Liberties, when by once they are attempted to be taken from them, and yet never any People have been so easy almost wholly to resign them. And the Emperor *Charles the Fifth* used to say, That no People were so far from Servitude as the *Netherlanders*, and yet in the World no People so easy were here to be so easily laid on them, when they were gently treated. Besides, which Cardinal *Bentivoglio* endeavours to shew by many Reasons, That the *United Netherland Provinces* cannot long preserve their Free Government, but seeing the *Netherlands* have never before been in the quiet possession of a Free Republick, that not the *Hollanders* there can be no Example yet of their neglecting their own Election, or of corrupting them with Money for that end. For when formerly it happened to stand by unavoidable sad Accidents

---

* Three Ducats, a certain sum.

that we were necessitated to draw the *Trojan Horse* into the inward Court, we saw the Fire and Flame, snorting, neighing, and armed Men spring from his Body at pleasure, without regard either to the Benefit or Damage of the Inhabitants. So we shall always find true, in all chargeable and necessitous Countrys, governed by a few Aristocratical Rulers, and provided with but few unrewarded annual Magistrates, That a great Person obtaining there any Power in the Government or Militia, will easily draw to his Party all Rulers and Magistrates by the most considerable and profitable Offices and Benefices which he can confer; or if any dare to stand it out against him, he would keep him out of employment, or deter him from maintaining the Publick Liberty. So that every one to obtain those Advantages, or to evade those Hardships, will be tempted to give up the Freedom of his Country, and it is no wonder that we have seen such dealings so often practised in these Parts. *As this happened in part in the Netherlands*

But it is also true, that when the Princes of these Countrys were raised to such a degree, that they conceiv'd it was no longer needful for them to oblige the Rulers and Magistrates of the Gentry, and Citys, not doubting to bear them down by their great Popularity among the Inhabitants, or to suppress them by their Military Authority; it hath often appeared, that beyond expectation many good Patriots, and lovers of Liberty, especially many prudent, antient, and experienced Merchants, have then evidenced their Zeal for the defence of their Privileges, well knowing they should be forced to part with them *Viz. Because the Earls, Stadtholders, &c. were to be flattered, not contradicted.*

them under a Monarchical Government; and therefore joined with such Rulers and Magistrates as encourag'd them to maintain their Freedom, as far as they possibly could, nay even the shadow of Liberty, with their Lives and Fortunes.

[marginal note: ... Holland]

All which ought to perswade us, that the Assembly of the States of *Holland,* and the subordinate Magistrates of this present Free State, having in their own Power the bestowing of all honourable and profitable Employments, and which is more, not needing now to fear their own Military Power, and being able without scruple to command them, and by them to reduce other mutinous and seditious Inhabitants to obedience, will not now be inclined to call in, or set up a Head, which they would immediately fear no less than Idolaters do the Idols of their own making, and not only so, but they must reverence his Courtiers too, and beseech them that they would please to suffer themselves to be chosen and continued in the yearly Magistracys, and bestow some Offices and Employments on them and their Friends, changing the Liberty they now enjoy as Magistrates of a Free State, into a base and slavish dependance. Which things well considered, we ought to believe that the *Hollanders* will rather chuse to hazard their Lives and Estates for the preservation of this present free Government.

[marginal note: As the States of Holland have ... express'd ... Deduct. Part ... § ...]

But if any one should yet doubt of this, let him hear the States of *Holland* and *West-Friesland* speak in that famous *Deduction* now in print, where their Lordships have published their Sentiment in this Matter: For having

ing been accused by some of the Provinces to have done something repugnant to their dear-bought Freedom, they very roundly and plainly declared; "That they are as sensible "of those Allegations as any others; and "that they purpose, and are resolved to pre- "serve and maintain the said Freedom, as "well in respect of the State in general, as "of their Province in particular, even as "the Apple of their Eye. And that as they "were the first and chief procurers of Free- "dom both for themselves and their Allys, so "they will never suffer it to be said with "truth, that any others should out-do them "in Zeal for preserving and defending the "Common Liberty.

"§ 9 Nay, that it can hardly enter in- "to the head of any Man, according to the "Judgment of all Political Writers, who "have found Understanding, That in a Re- "publick, such great Offices of Captain-Ge- "neral, and Stadtholder, can without signal "danger of the common Freedom be confer- "red upon those, whose Ancestors were "cloth'd with the same Imployments.

"§. 10. Laying it down as unquestionable, "and well known to all those that have in "any measure been conversant with such "Authors as treat of the Rise, Constituti- "on, and Alteration of Kingdoms, States, "and Countrys, together with the Form of "their Governments, That all the Repub- "licks of the World, without exception, "which departed from such Maxims and "Customs, more particularly those who "have entrusted the whole Strength of their "Arms to a single Person during Life, with
"such

"such others as continued them too long in
"their Commands, have been by that means
"brought under subjection, and reduced to a
"Monarchical State. And after very many
"Examples produced for confirmation of
"what is alledged, their Lordships further
"add.

"§. 22. And have we not seen with our
"own Eyes, that the last deceased Captain
"General of this State endeavoured to sur-
"prize the Capital and most powerful City
"of the Land, with those very Arms which
"the States entrusted to him? And more-
"over, that he dared so unspeakably to
"wrong the States of *Holland* and *West-*
"*Friesland*, whose Persons he, as a sworn
"Minister and natural Subject, was bound to
"revere? that he seized six of the principal
"Lords, whilst they were sitting in their So-
"vereign Assembly, and carried them away
"Prisoners? And hath not God Almighty
"visibly opposed, broken and frustrated the
"secret Designs concealed under that per-
"nicious Attempt, by sending out of Hea-
"ven a thick Darkness, with a great and
"sudden storm of Rain, by which we were
"preserved?

"§. 23. And all things well considered,
"it might be questioned, according to the
"Judgment of the said Politicians, whether
"by advancing the present Prince of *Orange*
"to that Dignity, and those high Offices
"in which his Ancestors were placed, the
"Freedom of this State would not be re-
"markably endangered. For God does not
"always Miracles, neither are we to flatter
"our selves that those Countrys shall always
"escape

"escape that Destruction which has ever attended all those Nations that have taken the same course without exception.

"And lastly, the States of *Holland* and *West-Friesland* do thus express their unalterable Resolution upon the last Article. At least their Lordships will on their own behalf declare, and do hereby declare, that they are firmly resolved to strengthen the foresaid Union, *viz.* of *Utrecht*, for the Conservation of the State in general, and for maintaining the Publick Liberty, together with the Supremacy, and Rights of the respective Provinces, according to the Grounds here expressed; and at all times, and upon all occasions, will contribute their help, even to the utmost, towards the preservation and defence of their dear-bought Liberty, and the Privileges of these Countrys, which are so dear, and of such inestimable value to them, that they will not suffer themselves to be diverted from their Resolution by any Inconveniences or Extremities, nor will lay down their good Intentions but with their Lives, trusting that they shall be duly seconded herein upon all Occasions by our other Allys, for which the said States will send up their fervent Prayers to Almighty God. *Amen.*

They will not lose their free Government but with the loss of their Lives.

This done and concluded by the said States of *Holland* and *West-Friesland* in the *Hague*, the 25*th* of *July* 1654. by Command of the said States, was signed

Herbert *van Beaumont.*

To which we shall add the Perpetual Edict of the 5th of *August* 1667. containing as follows.

"The States of *Holland* and *West-Friesland*, after several Adjournments, and mature deliberation, and communication with the Knights and Gentlemen, and likewise with the Councils of the Citys, unanimously, and with the general Concurrence of all the Members, for a perpetual Edict, and everlasting Law, in order to preserve the Publick Freedom, together with the Union and Common Peace, have Enacted, as they do hereby Enact and Decree, the Points and Articles following.

"1. That the Power of Electing and Summoning in the Order of the Knighthood and Nobles, together with the Nomination and Choice of Burgomasters, Common Council, Judges, and all other Offices of the Magistracy in Citys, shall remain in the Power of the summoned Knighthood and Gentry, together with the Citys respectively, as by antient Custom, Privileges and Grants is confirmed or granted to them, or might still be confirmed or granted, with the free Exercise of the same, according to the Laws and Privileges. And that the forementioned Nomination, or Election, or any part thereof, shall not for ever be convey'd or given away.

"2. That all Offices, Charges, Services, or Benefices, which are at present in the disposal of the States of *Holland* and *West-Friesland*, shall be, and continue in them,

"with-

"without any alteration or diminution, ex-
"cepting only the Military Employments
"and Offices which may become vacant in
"the Field, and during any Expedition by
"Sea or Land, concerning which the States
"of *Holland* will by a further Order deter-
"mine, not only of the provisional Settle-
"ment, but also principally of the disposal
"thereof, so as shall be most for the Service
"and Benefit of the Land.

'3. That the States of *Holland* and *West-*
"*Friesland*, shall not only deny their Suffra-
"ges to the contrary, but also move the
"Generality with all possible efficacy, that
"it may be enacted and established with the
"unanimous Consent and Concurrence of our
"Allys, and by a Resolution of the States
"General, That whatever Person shall be
"hereafter made Captain or Admiral-Ge-
"neral, or have both the said Offices, or
"whoever shall among any other Titles have
"the chief Command over the Forces by
"Sea or Land, shall not be, or remain Stadt-
"holder of any Province, or Provinces. And *And secluding*
"forasmuch as concerns the Province of *all Stadthold-*
"*Holland* and *West-Friesland*, not only such *ers of any of*
"Person who shall be entrusted with the *from being*
"chief Command over the Forces by Sea or *Capt. General.*
"Land, but also no other Person whatever
"shall be made Stadtholder of that Province;
"but the aforesaid Office shall be, and re-
"main suppressed, mortified, and void in all
"respects And the Lords Commissioners
"of the Council, in their respective Quar-
"ters, have it recommended to them accord-
"to their Instructions, to give all necessary
"Orders, and to use such Circumspection
"and

" and Prudence, as is requisite in Affairs that
" may happen in the absence of the States
" of *Holland* and *West-Friesland*, wherein
" speedy Orders might be absolutely need-
" ful.

" 4. That for the greater stability of these
" Resolutions, and for the mutual ease and
" quiet of the Gentry and Citys, all those
" who are at present elected into the Order of
" Knighthood, or that may hereafter be e-
" lected, together with all such as may be
" hereafter chosen in the Great Council of
" the Citys, shall by their solemn Oath de-
" clare, That they will maintain the fore-
" said Points religiously and uprightly, and
" by no means suffer that there be any in-
" croachment or infraction made against the
" same, much less at any time to make, or
" cause to be made, any Proposition which
" might in any wise be repugnant thereunto.
" Likewise the Oath of the Lords that shall
" appear at the Assembly of the States of
" *Holland* and *West-Friesland*, shall be en-
" larged in the fullest and most effectual
" Form. And the Counsellor-Pensionary for
" the time being, shall also be obliged by Oath
" to preserve and maintain as much as in him
" lies, all the said Points, without ever
" making any Proposal to the contrary, or
" putting it to the question, either directly
" or indirectly, much less to form a Conclu-
" sion.

" 5. That moreover for the further stability
" of the said third Point, the same shall be ex-
" presly inserted in the Instructions to be gi-
" ven to a Captain or Admiral-General,
" and he that is so elected, shall be obliged
" by

"by Oath, not only not to seek it at any
"time directly or indirectly, much less to
"form a Design to obtain it directly or in-
"directly, but on the contrary, in case any
"other should do it beyond Expectation,
"that he shall withstand and oppose it And
"if the Dignity of Stadtholder should at any
"time be offer'd to him by any of the Pro-
"vinces, that he will refuse and decline the
"same.

And truly this solemn Declaration, and perpetual Edict of our lawful Sovereigns, which passed with the unanimous Consent of all the Members of the Assembly, who were in perfect freedom to form their own Resolutions touching the preservation of their Libertys, ought to be of greater weight with every one, and especially with us, than any other Declaration made by the States of *Holland* and *West-Friesland*, when they were under the servitude of a haughty Governour; or than the Declaration of that formidable Emperor *Charles* the 5th made to his own advantage, even tho we should add the Foreign Testimony of *Ruy Gomez de Silva*, or that of Cardinal *Bentivoglio*, since they were not capable of experiencing or feeling how intolerably those Shoes pinch'd us; much less could they be sensible how well pleased the understanding *Netherlanders* are, whether Rulers or Subjects, to find * themselves in a condition to declare with freedom their Senti-

All good Patriots admire and value this Liberty.

---

* Nunc pede libero
   Pulsanda Tellus.   *Hor.*

ments concerning the Welfare of the Nation, and living by the Laws of the Country, need to fear no Man, as before they did. But above all other Inhabitants, our Vigilant Rulers, who heretofore durst not open their Mouths for the Privileges of the Land, the Lawful Government, and Liberty of the People, without incurring the danger of being sent Prisoners to *Lovestein* Castle, may consider with themselves, that they can now freely speak their Minds for the benefit of their Country, and themselves. And let this be well weighed by every one that has but one drop of free *Netherland* Blood in his Veins.

Lastly, It is to be considered, whether the Prosperity and free Government of *Holland* would not probably be destroyed, unless they have an Illustrious Head for Life, even by the freedom which the Members of *Holland* do now actually use, in giving their Voices with the States of *Holland*, at the pleasure, and for the benefit of their respective Principals, and by cross and contrary Interests, Dissensions, and Wars of the Citys among themselves; which some great Men say, cannot be well prevented or quieted without such an Illustrious Head.

To which I answer, That indeed all Republicks, without exception, which have constituted Chief Governours for Life, vested with any considerable Power in Civil, and especially in Military Affairs, have been subject to continual Intestine Dissensions and Wars, and have fallen for the most part into Monarchical Governments. This was the fate of all the *Italian* Republicks, except some few

that

that by those Divisions and Tumults had the good fortune to expel their Tyrants, and by that means an opportunity of introducing a better Form of Government without the control of such an insolent Master. This was also the fate of all the Republicks in *Germany*, and these *Netherlands*, under their Dukes, Earls, Stadtholders, Bishops and Captain-Generals. Which is not strange, for *Divide and Reign* being the Political Maxim of such Heads, they will use all their Art and Power to raise and foment Divisions in their Territories, and fish so long in those troubled Waters, till they overcome both Partys, as all Ages can witness.

See Deduct. Part 2. ch. 3. §. 6.

2. I have considered, but cannot remember so much as one Example of a Republick without such a Head, which ever fell into any mischievous intestine Commotions that lasted long, but on the contrary, we ought to take notice, that the free Imperial Citys, or Republicks in *Germany*, never make War against one another; and that the *Cantons* of *Switzerland* being mutually bound to a common defence (even as we are by the Union of *Utrecht*) do very seldom contend among themselves, and if they do happen to take Arms, very little Blood is shed; and in a short time, without prejudice to their free Government, they are reconciled by the Mediation of the other *Cantons*: So that their Republicks have now stood near 400 years. Which can be attributed to no other cause than that the differing Parties, mutually sensible of the mischiefs they felt, were not necessitated by any such chief Head or Governor to continue a prejudicial and destructive War:

But Republicks without a Head never will;

As appears in Germany and Switzerland.

For those *Cantons* have been always careful not to elect any Commander or General during Life over the Confederated Forces of the Union. Neither have any of the said *Cantons* ever thought fit to place a perpetual Commander in Chief over their own Souldiers in the Field, but always for the Design in hand only; tho after their revolt from their Lords of the House of *Austria*, they were necessitated to support a War, as long and dangerous as that we had against those of the same Family. And for so much as concerns these *United Provinces*, let the Reader please to hear the States of *Holland* and *West-Friesland*, who after many strong and weighty Reasons add,

"that their Lordships conceive they may
"fitly conclude, that in these Lands hard-
"ly any Differences and Divisions have
"ever come, at least not of great impor-
"tance, such as have been formed on
"the account of those Heads, or by their
"Means.

3. The Citys of *Holland* by intestine Wars would on both sides suffer infinitely more loss than the *Swiss* Cantons, or any other Citys far remote from one another. For all the Inland Citys of *Holland*, nearly one excepted, do as well subsist by Trade, as those that are nearer to the Sea, and the least Sea-City would by that means be able to make the greatest Booty of the strongest. It is also known, that the least City of *Holland* may in a short time so well fortifie it self, that it could not be taken by the greater. So that our Citys lying so close together, the adjacent Lands would in case of War be immediately ruined, and all the ways by Land or Water that lead to-

wards

wards the Citys, would be so infested, that all Trading would immediately cease. Wherefore both Parties would forthwith be moved by the other disinterested Citys to chuse a more profitable Peace, in lieu of such an unprofitable and pernicious War.

Lastly, I observe, that all the Citys in *Holland* are governed by few standing Magistrates or City-Councils, but rather by annual Magistrates, and that so few Persons as serve for Magistrates so little a time, could not make so great and mischievous a War upon their Neighbouring Citys, and maintain themselves in their obstinacy, without being turn'd out of the Government by their own Inhabitants, who would not suffer such a Temper to their prejudice to continue amongst them, at least they would be kept out of the Magistracy by their Competitors. And I believe no Example can be brought of a few Aristocratical Rulers of a City, or Republick purely subsisting by Trade, who have ever long maintain'd an Offensive War, without causing at the same time their own Subjects to mutiny on that account, and to turn them out of the Government.

And accordingly I shall not only conclude, That *Holland* during its free Government shall never be more subject to any durable, destructive, intestine Dissension, much less to Intestine Wars, than the *Switzer* and *German* Republicks. But I will add, that as the perpetual and true Maxim of a Government by a single Person, is *Divide & Impera*, by raising and fomenting Divisions among the Rulers, Magistrates, and Inhabitants, to make one Party by degrees Master of the other,

Holland without a Head can never be inwardly ravish'd.

and

and then to rule both. So it is also the true and steddy Maxim of all Republicks, * to create a good Understanding and mutual Affection between the Magistrates and People, by a mild and gentle Government, because the Welfare of all Commonwealths depends upon it, and is destroyed by the contrary. Accordingly I shall finish this Chapter by saying, That we should have reason to wonder, if any wise Man ever believed that it is the Interest of free Republicks to chuse an Illustrious Head, vested with Authority for Life, in order to compose the Differences that may arise amongst them: For I think we have already proved, that no surer way can be taken to introduce perpetual Divisions into Republicks, with Foreign and Domestick Wars, and at last a Monarchical Government, than by setting up such an eminent commanding Head.

CHAP XIII.

That Holland during its free Government is ever well able to resist all Foreign P...

I Shall now endeavour to shew that the Republick of *Holland*, while an intire Free Government, can very well defend it self against any Foreign Force whatever. But first

---

* *Concordia parva crescunt, discordia maxime di-...*

I must premise and suppose, that this is a sure effect of a free Government, *viz.* That all the great Citys of *Holland* must fortify themselves, and be provided with all things necessary for their defence; as also that the States of *Holland* must out of the common Stock strengthen all the Avenues and Frontier Citys of the Provinces, which of themselves are too weak effectually to repel an Enemy. For otherwise we may well be of opinion, that *Holland* will not be able to deal with the Force of *Spain* by Land; and that it might by surprize be overrun by the Power of some other of the *United Provinces*, yea, that it might be easily plundered by its own conquered Citys. But not to cut out more Work, I shall in pursuance of that Position, look upon *Holland*, and all the other Provinces, as being without Union, League, or Alliance with its Neighbours: For as other Countrys may join in making War upon *Holland*, so *Holland* may make Leagues with Foreign Powers to make War upon others: Which Cases would cause endless Thoughts and Considerations; and therefore I will presuppose, that when *Holland* shall have Difference, or Wars with any one of its Neighbours, all the rest shall be Neuter.

Therefore to come to the Point, I say, that it seems needless for me to shew that *Holland* can very well subsist and endure all the Force of *France*, *Spain*, *England*, and other lesser remote Countrys, since I think I have done it sufficiently in the foregoing Chapters, when I treated of *Holland*'s Alliances. So it remains only to be considered, whether *Holland* be strong enough to defend it self

against

Holland, *while free, is able* Part II.
against the Power of the neighbouring *United Provinces*, and of the associated or conquered Lands and Citys?

Holland is ably — Upon which I shall premise in the general,
sufficiently — That *Holland* being so well surrounded by the
against the — Seas and Rivers, and broken by Waters, so
United Pro- — populous, so full of great, well fortified (for
vinces. — this must be supposed) and impregnable Citys lying near one another, every one of which can produce an Army, this being considered, I say no Potentate in the World could invade us with an Army: Or suppose he were entred the Country, it is clear that the said Enemy, by the continual unexpected Attacks of the adjacent Citys, and by the beating of his Convoys, or such as bring in Forage, would in a short time be necessitated, by the continual lessening of his Forces, shamefully to relinquish the Attempt and march away. All which they ought to foresee and expect, and much more of the Forces and Incursions of our neighbouring *Netherlands*, and conquered Citys.

Again, I must say, that all the said Provinces do receive incomparably more advantage by *Holland*, than *Holland* does from them, which Benefits would all cease by a War, namely, by virtue of the Union, which as it has been practised, the Rulers and Inhabitants of the other Provinces draw Profits from *Holland*, namely by Embassys Ordinary and Extraordinary, by Commissions and Deputations in the Colleges of the joint Allys; or by Offices or Benefices in and about the Government, in the Courts of Judicature, Treasurys, and Affairs of War depending on the Generality, which are paid by the joint Allys,

Allys, by which they accordingly receive above 58 *per Cent.* of all that they enjoy. To which we may add the Profits they reap by Administration, or Offices about Regulation of Trade, and Maritime Affairs, whether at home depending on the Admiraltys, or abroad by being Residents and Consuls, &c. So that it is evident enough that all Rewards must proceed from *Holland* alone, and by the Traffick of *Holland*, and its wonderful populousness and vicinity, they consume all the Manufactures and superfluous Products of the Inhabitants of the other Provinces at high Rates, and they receive out of *Holland* all that they want at easy Rates: Whereas *Holland* on the other side, in case of a War with this or that Province, would not be sensible, or suffer in its Traffick or Consumption. And besides we see, that from the Provinces of *Guelderland, Friesland, Overyssel,* &c the poor young Men and Maids that are not able to live there by their Trades and Service, subsist in *Holland* very well. So that all the Provinces are sensible, that a good and firm Peace is at least as much necessary for them as for us, to maintain the Prosperity of both. And yet it might happen, that some Provinces may be so ill advised as to be drawn aside to make War against *Holland*, and therefore I must consider, and take a view of all the *United Provinces* in particular, *viz.*

Groningen and *Friesland*, with the conquered Places of the Generality, *Bourtange, Bellingwolde, Langakkerschans,* and *Coeverden,* which they have found means to bring under their particular Power. Now seeing they appoint or chuse their Commanders there, remove

Groningen *and* Friesland *are now both by Interest of Government and Situation, separated from* Holland.

move or change their Garisons, and give Commissions to their Military Officers, whereby it appears they need nothing of ours, and that they can sufficiently defend themselves against all Foreign Force. So that if they have a Governor in Chief, which in time might induce them to take mischievous Resolutions, we might expect a destructive War to both Partys most from that Quarter, if it had not pleased God to divide us by the *Zuyder-Sea* and the Provinces of *Utrecht*, *Guelderland*, and *Over-Yssel*. So that from that side we need expect no hurt, and the rather, seeing by our strength of Navigation we may presently stop all the Commerce and Navigation of *Groningen* and *Friesland*.

Over-Yssel cannot hurt Holland, &c.

As to *Over-Yssel*, it is well known that it is divided from *Holland* by *Guelderland*, and has no communication with us but by the *Zuyder-Sea*. And moreover the strength of *Over-Yssel* is so inconsiderable, and their Land behind lys so open, that they cannot make War against us but by Sea, nor so neither, without hazarding their sudden ruin by the loss and want of all their Traffick. So that while they have a free Government, we are not to expect it. And if they duly consider

Articles of the Republick, under the &c.

the horrid Intestine and Foreign Wars and Discords, which they suffered in the times of their Bishops, and Governors of their Republicks, and likewise the violent Usurpation that they suffered afterwards under their Lords and Stadtholders, there is not the least appearance that they will ever consent to the choice of such a Head or Ruler; but if it should so happen, and they be prest by a contentious Governor to War against us, it would be be strange if such a War should be long-liv'd, for it is evident they could endamage *Holland* but little, if *Holland* would use its Force against them.

As for *Guelderland*, it is manifest it hath much more communion with *Holland* than any of the foresaid Provinces, for it joins to *Holland* about *Asperen*, and *Gorcum*, and towards *Bommelar* is divided only by the *Maese* from the Land of *Heusden* and *Altena*. Moreover it joins to the *Zuyder-Sea*, and hath under its Power the mighty Rivers of the *Yssel, Rhyne, Waal*, and *Maese*, whereby it should seem those of *Guelderland* are able to infest the Traffick of *Holland* through the *Zuyder-Sea*, and by means of the said Rivers to stop all Traffick from above. And besides, the Men of *Guelderland* were of old famous for their Soldiery, especially for Horsemen. So that it seems to lie conveniently for gaining of great Booty from *Holland* by sudden Incursions, and to make War upon us. *Guelderland may make War upon us.*

But on the other side it is as evident, that *Holland* having all the Passages into the Sea from the said Rivers under their Power, would straiten *Guelderland* more in all its Traffick, for *Holland* could carry all its fine Goods in Carts above the Confines of *Guelderland* towards the *Maese* and *Rhyne*, and there likewise receive the fine upland Goods. And considering *Harderwyk* and *Elburg* are the only Sea-Ports of *Guelderland*, which notwithstanding are without Havens, their Robberys at Sea would signify little, and besides be easily overpowered by *Holland's* great Maritime Strength. As to their Incursions by Land, whether with Horse, or Foot; it is clearly im- *But not without greater damage to it self.*

impracticable by reason of *Holland's* Populousness, and being so full of Canals, which would easily put a stop to the *Guelderlanders*.

Their bold presumption of plundering the *Hague*, and carrying away the Booty thereof in the Year 1528, does not contradict what I say. For tho the Duke of *Guelder* gave those of *Utrecht* assistance against their Bishop, and to that end sent his General, *Martin van Rossem*, with armed Men into that Town, and that on the other side, the Emperor *Charles* assisted the Bishop against *Utrecht*, yet was there no open War between *Guelderland* and *Holland*. But the Duke found it good to begin the first Hostility, or be the Aggressor, by *Martin van Rossem*, and to cause 1300 Soldiers out of that Garrison to fall suddenly into *Holland*, and having gotten a rich Booty, declared War against it. So that the *Guelderlanders* were then to be accounted to have made an unexpected treacherous Incursion upon *Holland* from that Bishoprick, when *Holland* had but few Inhabitants, and was weakned by the *Hocksche* and *Cabbeljeausche* Factions, nay was indeed indefensible by reason the Emperor *Charles* employed only the Gentry and Soldiery of *Holland* in his *Italian*, and other Foreign Wars. Besides it may be said, and not without Reason, that *Martin van Rossem* did this by the Privity of the Emperor *Charles* the Fifth Earl of *Holland*, or the connivance of *Margaret*, because the States would not at that time consent to the Mony she would have *Holland* to raise for the said Emperor, or his Governess *Margaret*, would send no Soldiery to suppress the said *Guelderlanders*, nor suffer the *Hollanders* to pursue them.

See MeerBeek *Hist. p. 8. and* Lamb Hortensius *p. 140.*

Besides,

Besides, *Martin van Rossem* did not the least prejudice to the Ministers of the Court, nor to the Officers of the Earldom

And on the contrary it is well known, that all *Guelderland*, except the City of *Zutphen*, and the District of *Nimeguen*, lies wholly open to *Holland*; so that from *Lovestein* one might plunder the whole *Bommelerwaard*, yea and cut down its Banks; and it would be the same with the *Tielerwaard*, and *Betuwe*, and that quarter of the *Veluwe* must always expect Incursions, and Plunderings by our Shipping. So that this War, which would be more prejudicial to *Guelderland* than *Holland*, would soon be ended by a firm Peace on both sides, while they continue under a free Government, and while the respective Citys of *Guelderland*, especially *Nimeguen* the chief City of that Province, do now find the Sweetness of their own Government, after having felt the weight of the late Yoke of the Stadtholders, or that of Captain-Generals, and must again suffer their legally elected Magistrates to be violently turn'd out. Therefore 'tis to be believed that they will not precipitately elect a Tyrannical Head over them.

Guelderland lies perfectly open to Holland.

As to the Province of *Utrecht*, it is well known that it lies wholly open, and jetting into *Holland*, and subsists purely by Husbandry, and in that it bounds upon the *Lek* and *Zuyder-Sea*, seems in some measure to be able to disturb the Trade of *Holland*, and for a great way to disturb the Champion Country. But he that will take notice of the great strength of *Holland*'s Shipping, may easily conceive that the *Lek*, and *Zuyder-Sea*, lying before the Province, might be made useless

The Province of Utrecht wholly indefensible.

to them by our Soldiers ravaging those Parts by their sudden Incursions and Shipping. And that *Holland* being a broken Country, by reason of its many Waters, might not only plunder their open Country much more, but also because it runs or jets so far into *Holland*, it may be absolutely seiz'd and kept by them, by which means those of *Utrecht* will be deprived of their best Champion Country.

Besides it is very observable, that all the Citys of that Province are wholly undefensible, without any appearance that they shall ever be fortified: For *Amersfort*, *Reenen*, *Wyk*, and *Montfort*, are not only unable to bear the Charge of it; and the City of *Utrecht* will not bestow their Mony to fortify Citys, which afterwards will have less dependance on them; nay possibly they might injure that undefensible City the sooner. For we ought to know that that long Square in land City being deprived of the Sea, and all great Rivers, will be ever chargeable to fortify and keep. And as if this were not enough to bridle that great City, their Bishops of old suffered Houses to be built without the Gates; whence came those four very great Suburbs upon all their considerable Avenues by which their Fortifications are made of no use. And tho every one may see that this is the usual Polity of the Heads of a Republic to weaken Citys that are too strong for their purpose; yet afterwards when Men have the good luck of having a compleat free Government, it continues remediless. And accordingly I shall conclude, that the Province of *Utrecht* being wholly undefensible, will never make War against *Holland*. And seeing it is the

And will not naysererue

It will not make either Holland nor endanger her Liberty by such a head.

Interest of *Holland* ever to seek after Peace, and that all Sparks of War so soon as they arise may be supprest during a free Government. And seeing the mighty City of *Utrecht* of old, in the time of its Episcopal Government, and in the time of the last Wars against the King of *Spain*, felt more than any Town in the *Netherlands*, the manifold Tumults and Mischiefs caused by their Bishops of the House of *Burgundy*, and other great Familys, and afterwards by the Usurpation of the Captain Generals, or Stadtholders, over their lawful Government. It is therefore most unlikely that they will easily dissolve their free Government by electing such a Ruler over them.

As for *Zealand*, it is known to consist in very fruitful populous Islands, separated by mighty Streams of the Sea from all its Neighbours, and besides it hath acquired by its Power, divers Citys and strong Places, lying on the Land of the Generalitys in *Flanders* and *Brabant*: So that the Lords of *Zealand* have the disposal of the Commands, and changing of the Garisons of *Lillo*, *Licfkenshoek*, *Axel*, *ter Neuse*, and *Biesvliet*. Insomuch that *Zealand* seems to be able to defend it self very well against all its Neighbours with its own Strength. Besides which, the two good Havens of *Walcheren*, *Flushing* and *Veer* lie very commodiously to annoy the Trade of *Holland* to the Westward with their Men of War.

If the two Vassal Citys in Zealand *depend on the first Noble, then is* Holland *not only by Situation but Interest, almost divided from* Zealand.

On the other hand it is also true, that the Inhabitants of *Middleburgh* and *Flushing* drive a great Trade by Sea; and that those of *Zierickzee* and *Veer* do subsist most by their Fishing, all which would be immediately ruined by

However it could not make War upon us but to its own ruin.

by the great Naval Power of *Holland*, which would be far more confiderable againſt them, than their Ships of War againſt us. And it is as certain, that the Traffick of *Zealand* will produce them greater and more certain Profit than any Privateering at Sea can do. Moreover, *Holland* hath by *Bommene* ſure footing on *Schouwen*, whereby they might ruin all the rich Husbandry of that Iſland. *Goes* would at leaſt have no Benefit by that War, and is not able to reſiſt the Naval Power of *Holland* in caſe they came to plunder it, or to burn their Harveſt. And on the other ſide, the *Zealand* Iſlands have not ſtrength of Shipping ſufficient to land and plunder *Holland*: Wherefore I conceive that under their Free Government, every one would be ready to cry out, in caſe of a War, *Nulla ſalus Bello*, Peace is beſt for both Partys.

But ſome may perhaps ſay, That the Prince of *Orange* might, by means of the Citys of *Fluſhing* and *Veer*, and poſſibly hereafter, by being the chief Lord, and giving his Vote firſt, in name of all the Gentry in all the Aſſemblys of the States, and in all Colleges of the Provincial Government, having the firſt and the two laſt Voices: So that having Three of the Seven, he muſt be thought ſufficient to over-rule that whole Province, and therefore the Welfare or Adverſity of the People of that Province, whether in Peace or War, will not come ſo much into conſideration as the Intereſt of ſome Court Sycophants, and of ſuch a powerful Lord, who having ſo great a Stroke in the Government of *Zealand*, would be able to carry on very miſchievous Reſolutions. I ſhall not need anſwer any thing

thing to this, save that from what has been said already it appears, that *Zealand* would not really have more, but much less Power by such a Supreme Governour, than by a free Republican Government, and that accordingly it would soon appear, *Vana sine viribus ira*, that *Zealand* could not repel the Power of *Holland*, but *Holland* could very well repel the Power of *Zealand*.

As to the conquered Lands in *Flanders*, and about the *Rhyne* and the *Maese*, it is evident that they are so far distant from *Holland*, and so divided from one another, that they cannot hurt *Holland*. But *Holland* is much concerned in the conquered Citys of *Brabant*, which are very strong. And altho *Holland* hath born most of all the Charges to subdue and fortify them, yet during the former Government of the Captain-Generals or Stadtholders, they would and could keep *Holland* so low, that this Province which bears most of the Charges of the common Union, was not allowed in any one Place of the Generality any separate Power; whereas nevertheless those Provinces that contribute so little in respect of *Holland*, as *Zealand* and *Friesland* do, have so many fortified Places belonging to the Generality, to dispose of separately, and whereof the other Allys have no Power to take cognizance. But God be praised that our Frontiers are so well fortified against *Brabant*, that they cannot be taken by the Towns of the Generality any otherwise than by Treachery. And besides we are so well divided and separated from *Brabant* by the *Maese*, *Biesbos*, and Arms of the Sea, that we need fear no Enemy that way, altho those Citys

And the conquered Citys being on the Generality Land, are less able to make War against Holland.

should rebel, yea revolt to the King of *Spain*

So that Holland is able to subsist against them all. So that by what has been said it appears, that *Holland* alone is well able to stand against all its Neighbours.

CHAP XIV.

That Holland, *tho she don't fortify her Citys, if she keep united with* Utrecht *only, is able to defend her self against all the mighty Potentates of the World.*

Holland with Utrecht, able to defend it self against the worst that can happen.

BUT now supposing the very worst that could happen, *viz.* that the Rulers of the great Citys of *Holland* neglect to put their Citys into a sufficient State of Defence, and that the States of *Holland* do not fortify the other lesser Citys of *Holland* or their Avenues.

If the other Provinces should elect one Head, and have Power to join with them against us.

And moreover I will take it for granted, that the Rulers of the respective Provinces of *Guelderland, Zealand, Friesland, Over Yssel* and *Groningen,* shall be so improvident and ill-minded, as to chuse one and the same Person to be Stadtholder, and Captain General of their Republicks, and that the Deputys of the Generality shall combine with that Ruler to make him Lord Paramount of the said Republicks. And I will also suppose that his blind Ambition shall be as great as that of *Lewis Sforza,* who to preserve the usurped Dukedom of *Milan* against the weak King of *Naples,* who pretended a Right to it, invited the Powerful King of *France* to make War against *Naples,* who as strong Auxiliaries usually do, first swal-

lowed

lowed up the Kingdom of *Naples*, and afterwards the Dukedom of *Milan*. So that I shall now suppose as certain, that such a Ruler of the other *United Provinces*, with some victorious *French* and *Swedish* Forces, or any others joining with them, may endeavour on the sudden to bring into the Heart of *Holland* a mighty Army to subdue it, and divide it among them: Supposing I say all this, yet I shall endeavour to shew, that *Holland* making due Provision beforehand, shall be able to subsist against all those Forces, as soon as the Inhabitants shall be brought to a sufficient uniform sense of the Matter, and that both Rulers and Subjects make use of their unanimous Care and Strength to repel all Foreign Hostilitys; otherwise it is certain that no Country in the World being divided and rent asunder can long subsist.

But seeing that upon such an Accident there would follow innumerable Alterations among the other Potentates of *Europe*, and those Changes I should be obliged to guess at, which would be of great difficulty, and not sutable to my purpose of making Observations upon the present State of *Holland*, I shall, that I may not miss my Aim, and to clear my self of that trouble, say briefly, That the two Provinces, *viz. Holland* and *Utrecht*, might in a little time, by making a Graft, Trench, or Channel, from the *Zuyder-Sea* into the *Lek*, order it so by Sluces, that the Country may all be overflowed at pleasure: This might be done with little Charge, and yet be so strong a Defence against any Force, that humanely speaking, it would be impossible to subdue it by any outward

Yet could we be able to repel them, and how.

outward Power. This Position is strengthned by the Judgment of *William* the elder Prince of *Orange*, who, as I have either read or heard, was ever of that Sentiment, and had Schemes of it made by the best Ingineers of that Age.

They that are skill'd in these Affairs, will find it practicable in the following manner, viz. If a Summer were spent to surround *Holland* with such a Graft or Channel, beginning at the *Zuyder-See*, between *Muyden* and *Weesderberg*, running from thence South to the *Hinderdam*, from thence to the East side of the *Vecht* through the *Overmeerse Polder* to the *Overmeer*, from thence within the East or West side of the *Vecht*, about a hundred or more Rods from the same, or close by it along to the fittest place, and in that manner following the *Vecht* to the City of *Utrecht*, and to run East about the City, and inclose it in the Line, from thence along the new *Vaart* unto *Vreeswyck*, digging throughout a Graft ten Rods wide; and the Walls, Bulworks, and proper Flankings taking up one place with another the like breadth of ten Rods. Such Walls and Grafts would certainly be invincible in so populous a Country against all the Potentates of the World. And supposing it might be taken by Approaches, yet would the whole Land be entirely open behind, that in the mean while new Intrenchments might be made. Yea moreover, supposing that were not done, what Army in the World would dare to force a Breach, where a whole Army of the Enemy should be ready on the inside to resist the Stormers, as would here be the case?

And

Ch. 14.   *to resist all Foreign Power.*   345

And if any object, that this Graft is either not practicable, or too chargeable, I shall add, that this Line would take up twelve thousand *Rhynlandish* Rods, which would require 400 Morgens or *Dutch* Acres of Land; this being valued it 700 Guilders each, it would amount to ———————————— Guilders 280000

The digging of every Rod of this Graft, with the forming of the Wall and Flanking, 100 Guilders each, which in all would cost no more than —————————— 1200000

To those concerned, and for extraordinary Charges —————— 120000

Total ———————————— 1600000

And would cost but 1600000 Guilders.

But the said Graft might likewise be digged after the following manner, which would be less chargeable, and would best sute with the unfortifiable part of the Province of *Utrecht*, namely beginning at the *Zuyder-Sea* along, or within the West side of the *Eem*, and to the Eastward of the City of *Amersford*; passing there over the *Eem*, and to the Eastward of the City of *Amersford*, to comprehend it in the Line, and thence forward South to the fittest place over *Woudenburg*, along unto the *Lek*, about and to the Eastward of *Wyk* to *Duurfteede*, for the taking of that City likewise in: which Line would be in length eleven thousand *Rhynlandish* Rods.

After another manner not above 1400000 Guilders.

The Graft and the Walls, taking them of the same breadth as before, and they taking up about three hundred and sixty Morgens at 500 Guilders each, amount unto Guilders

Guilders, —————————— 18000
 The digging of the Graft, at 100 ⎫
  Guilders the Rod, for eleven ⎬ 110000
  thousand Rods, ——————— ⎭
 For extraordinary Charges, ——— 12000
               ―――――
               140000

 If the first way be taken, then the *Lek* between *Vreeswyk* and *Hondwyk*, is to be kept with Redoubts to the length of about twelve hundred Rods. If the second way be taken the *Lek* would then be to be kept between *Wyk* to *Duurstede* and *Hondwyk*, the length of about four hundred Rods.

'Twould yet be necessary to lay out in Fortifications, 47000 Guilders, and no).   Moreover, when it were needful for securing the Land of *Gorcum*, *Viaren*, and the *Alblasserwaard* there may be digged another such like Graft and Wall from the *Lek* about *Homwyk*, to the Wall about *Lovestein*, and then over *Akkooy* along the borders of *Holland*. Which Line would be about six and thirty hundred *Rhynlandish* Rods, and by consequence there would be taken up one hundred and twenty Morgens of Land, each valued at 50
Guilders, is ————————————— 6000
 The Graft and Wall as above ——— 36000
 Extraordinary Charges ————— 5000
             ―――――
             47000

And lastly 43000 Guilders to be paid once for all.   From *Lovestein* to the City of *Heusden*, the *Maese* would be serviceable for the preservation of the Land of *Altena*, which should be provided with Redoubts the length of about 400 Rods.

 From the City of *Heusden* along and about

h.14. *to resist all Foreign Power.*

e old *Maese* to little *Waspik*, lying at the
esbos, for preservation of the Land of *Alte-*
, the making of a Graft and Wall as above,
d being about three thousand Rods, it would
quire about one hundred Morgens of Land,
ch reckoned at 500 Guilders amounts
— 50000

Digging of the Graft, and forming }
    of the Wall at 100 Guilders } 300000
    the Rod as above, is ——— }

Extraordinary Charges as above,—— 80000
─────
430000

This in all would amount to two Millions *All which* and five hundred thousand Guilders, in case *would be but one* it was begun about the *Vecht*; and if it were *sixth Part of* begun about the *Eem*, two Millions three hun- *the yearly de-* dred thousand Guilders, besides the Fortifica- *mands of the* tions which might be rais'd along the *Lek* and *Council of State* the old *Maese* *for 1629.*

And if it be observed, that the Mony which the Council of State yearly demanded in the time of Prince *Henry* of *Orange*, did ofttimes amount to more than sixteen Millions; and that the same for the Year 1629, when the *Bosch* was taken, came to twenty one Millions, and seven hundred eighty two thousand two hundred sixty eight Guilders, you will then clearly see that those Campagns, and Sieges in *And then there* that Offensive War, even when they succeed- *would be less* ed best, and we made Bonfires for joy, *to be kept by* cost the Province of *Holland* alone, omitting *Garisons than* the other *United Provinces*, 4 or 5 times more *gen, and Bre-* than such a Graft would amount unto; besides *da now require.* that the *Bosch* or *Boisleduc* with its circumjacent Forts, *Breda, Bergen op Zoom*, and *Steen-*
bergen,

tergen, with their Outworks and adjacent Forts, do make together a far greater Line, which either in Peace or War will cost abundantly more: and it is evident, that many of the honest *Hollanders* have been made to believe, that such Conquests have been very advantageous, if not necessary. So that it seems to me that such a Graft and Walls, which will last *Holland* and the Province of *Utrecht* for ever, and sufficiently free the Country from further Charge, will be found exceeding more profitable for these two Republicks, when it is effected.

Lastly, it may be objected, that it is here taken for granted, that the Province, or at least the City of *Utrecht*, ought always to join with *Holland*, whereas it may happen, that that City may join with the Enemy to ruin *Holland*. I acknowledg, *if the Sky fall we should catch store of Larks*, because all those things are possible, but it would be a great wonder if all those things should happen: At least it is not likely, that the City of *Utrecht* enjoying a free Government will ever make War against *Holland*, because the Interests of these two Republicks are perpetually link'd together, and the Province of *Utrecht* has of old been, and is at this day, the most faithful Ally to *Holland*, as lately appeared by their readily bringing in their *Quota* agreed on for carrying on the last War against *England*, as also in mortifying the Stadtholdership.

And besides that great City hath of old found the Government of a single Person so uneasy, that it hath always been of *Hoek*'s Faction, and endeavoured more than any other

ther after a free Government, being neither able nor willing to submit their Necks to the Bishops, Lords or Stadtholders Yoke. And it is observable, that for that very reason the Inhabitants have gotten the name of *Mutineers*. For those that eat Cherries in common with great Spiritual or Temporal Lords or Princes, must suffer them to chuse the fairest, and yet be pelted with the stones; or if they oppose it, they will be forthwith excommunicated for Hereticks, and punished as seditious Fellows.

Lastly, the Province is in it self very weak by its inland Situation, and continues still unfortified as well as *Holland*, by reason of the Maxims of the Lords Stadtholders and Captain-Generals. So that there is nothing more to be wish'd for by them, than their maintaining a free Government, and erecting such Fortifications. And seeing Experience and a well known Political Maxim teacheth us, *That there is no State in this World so secure, that has nothing left unsecure*, I have already given so many Reasons and Instances to prove That the Republick of *Holland* can subsist of it self against all its Neighbours, and that it is a hard matter to name any other State in the World of which the like may be said with more certainty. But if the Reader hath any doubt remaining, I shall endeavour in the next Chapter to clear it.

CHAP.

CHAP. XV.

That every great City in Holland, whether it be by Sea or by Land, is able to defend it self against all Force from without.

I Shall now endeavour to shew that each great City in *Holland* is able, no less than other Republicks consisting of one City, to stand against all the Potentates in the World. To which end this Rule of Politicians and Ingineers comes into my mind, That all great Cities that can abide a Siege of a whole Season, must be counted invincible, because, altho' all things succeed well with the Besiegers, they can in no wise compensate the Charge of the Siege; and that that Power and Expence might with much more Benefit and Certainty be applied against Citys which are not so strong nor so well fortified.

Besides which, to the taking such a City a very great Force of Men and Mony is required, which is seldom found among Monarchs because of their living so magnificently, and that the Treasurers of Kings and Princes consume all their Revenues; and we seldom find such Republicks so foolish (unless they are ridden by some Tyrant) to make such detrimental Conquests. For an incredibly great Army is necessary to surround so great a City; and while one side of it is attack'd with a great Strength, those on the other side may make such terrible Sallys, that the Enemy shall not be able to keep any Watch in the Approaches or Redoubts, so that thereby whole Armys may be ruined.

And

And lastly, tho all things succeed well with the Besiegers, it is certain that Scaling of Walls causeth great destruction among the Souldiers, because the Besieged, with the rest Military Power which they have in readiness in the Places of Arms, or about the Breaches as a Reserve, may easily beat back the Assailants. These strong Places are usually taken by Famine, and seeing the Besiegers cannot without difficulty set up Lines of Circumvallation, or enter on a City, and yet with more difficulty intrench themselves well in so great a compass of Ground, as to be able to feed themselves against a great and populous City, and to supply their own Army with all the Necessaries requisite for the famishing of the City. We therefore see for the most part, that these obstinate Besiegers do melt and consume away, and such great Armies come to nothing. And moreover the Neighbouring Potentates are commonly very jealous, because they are near to such formidable growing Conquerors, so that in time succours happen to come from whence it is not look'd for, according to the Proverb, *Late guard, much gains*, and in truth, the safety of all Men depends on these political Maxims, That no Man will trust himself to undo another. So that the contrary hereof is rather to be credited and practised in the great Citys of *Europe*, so as to make them continue in a defenceless posture.

For besides all the Reasons above-mentioned, this political Rule is established by Experience, That a great City that can hold out the Siege of a whole Season, ought to be considered to be able to subsist for ever, seeing

In which time the City may be reliev'd, or the Siege rais'd.

Which is proved by Examples.

ing at this day many Republicks, confifting of no more than one City, have maintained themfelves fome hundreds of Years againft all their Enemys, altho many amongft them are but meanly fortified, and others tho ftronger are but fmall.

And moreover among the faid Republicks, confifting but of one City, there are feveral Republicks, wherein there are neither great nor fortified Cities, and yet by their own Government, the jealoufy of their Neighbours, and other Circumftances, or humane Accidents, have ftood very long. We are indeed ftrong when we dare be our own Mafters, and when the Inhabitants begin to know the Metal or Stength of a People that will fight for their Freedom, and when the People of a Republick underftand aright the weaknefs and mutablenefs of a Monarchical War, and that the Republicks do ofttimes ruin the great Armys of Monarchs by good Fortifications and Orders, or can quietly fit down, and be Spectators of the great Defolations, and ruinous Revolutions which Monarchs do continually caufe among themfelves by their Field Battels.

Moreover, fuppofing the great Citys of *Holland* were fo improvident, as that during their free Government they fhould neglect the ftrengthning themfelves with good Fortifications, Gates, Walls, and Grafts, but took care only to furnifh themfelves fufficiently with good Arms for their Inhabitants, and to exercife them thorowly, thofe Citys might fubfift very well againft all Foreign Power, and according to the Political Maxim which teacheth us, That all populous Citys which can

can raise an Army out of their own Inhabitants, cannot be either besieged or conquered, because a dispersed Army without shelter, must needs give way to one within that is united and sheltered by a City. *Vis unita fortior disperja*, An united Force is stronger than a scatter'd one.

All that hath been said, whether of fortified or unfortified populous Citys, that provide their Inhabitants with Arms sufficient, and train them up in the use of them, is strengthned by Experience and we shall say, that lately, during that great devastation of Countrys and Citys of the great and Potent Electors and Princes of the Empire, all the free Imperial Citys have very well secur'd themselves, as *Francfort, Strasburg, Ulm, Noremberg, Breslaw, Lubeck, Hamburg, Bremen, Cologn*, &c. against the Emperor, *Spain, France*, &c. except poor innocent *Strasburg*, which tho really impregnable, yet *timore panico*, dreading the Imperial victorious Arms, took in a *Swedish* Garrison for its defence, but in truth leap'd from the Smoak into the Fire, and so lost her dear Liberty Thus have those inconsiderable, or small *Switzer*-Republicks, and Citys, viz. *Zurich, Bern, Bazil, Schaffousen, Friburgh, Lucerne, Solothurn, St Gal*, &c preserved themselves some hundreds of Years successively against *Austria, Spain, France, Savoy*, and *Burgundy*, yea, even little *Geneva* hath done the like

Thus that small City of *Ragousa* subsisted very well against the Great *Turk*; *Austria* and *Venice*, which is not above 2000 Paces in circumference, and in its greatest Prosperity could not be inhabited by more than ten
thou-

As which appears by Examples,

Of the free Imperial Citys of Germany.

The Cantons of Switzerland.

Ragousa.

thousand Souls, Men, Women, and Children. Thus ūbñfs little *Lucca*, which hath not above twenty four thousand Souls in it, yet by its Republican Government, and good Fortifications, keeps its ground against the P. and G..., and the Duke of T..., and the King of *Spain* as Duke of ...

It is not strange to see such incredible Fruits of a free Government, because for a Man to be his own Master, and consequently to feed, cloath, and defend his own Body, which he unfeignedly loves, and will provide for and defend to the utmost, is certainly an incomparable if not an infinite Advantage above Slavery, where a single Person hath the charge, takes care of or neglects other Mens Lives, Healths, and Safetys, according to his own Will and Pleasure.

And if this be true, as it certainly appears to be, we ought in my judgment to esteem that not only all our great Citys of *Holland* which are situated on Havens and great Rivers, are impregnable, yet not to be besieged or..., or close to, if once they can put themselves into a state of good defence, and convince their Inhabitants, that their own Strength is sufficient to repel all Foreign Force. But methinks it is also consequently true, that our great inland Citys, as *Harlem*, *Delft*, *Leyden*, *Alcmer*, &c. are sufficiently able to defend themselves against all Force from without, under a free Government, in case they neglect not to provide themselves with all Necessarys according to their Power.

And

And tho it may be objected that *Harlem* being formerly besieged a whole Winter by the *Spaniard*, was yet taken at last. I answer, That *Don Fredrico* who commanded there in chief, repented oft that ever he began that Siege, and he himself was for abandoning it, and would so have done, had it not been for that obstinate and impolitick Duke of *Alv's* Son, who wrote him contumelious and reflecting Letters about it, and thereby compell'd him to continue that Siege. And besides it is notorious, that some such imprudent Sieges, as that of *Alkmaer*, *Leyden*, and *Zurickzee*, did occasion the breaking of the *Spanish* Power, and the Matinys of the Souldiers at that time, as it did afterwards to Arch-Duke *Albert* when he besieged other Citys. And moreover, *Harlem* at that time had not half the Strength and number of Men as it has now; for being newly revolted from its mighty Prince the King of *Spain*, and the *Romish* Religion at once, it must necessarily, by reason of that new Government and Religion, and especially by treating the *Spanish* and *Romish* Inhabitants too hardly and reproachfully, have been at that time much divided and weakned, and not well able to handle those discontented Inhabitants. And yet with that divided Force, and then weak Walls, they were able to keep off the Army of their old Sovereign a long time. So that this Example of *Harlem* seems rather to strengthen than weaken the said Maxim, that all the great *Holland* Citys continuing in a free State, that are able to form a well-armed and disciplin'd Army out of their own Inhabitants, are impregnable. And we lie in

Vid. Strad. l.7. Where the Example of Harlem taken in 1573 by the Spaniards, &c. is fully treated.

Because our Citys have great Advantages above others, therefore is that Maxim so the stronger.

so cold a Climate, that it is impossible, unless the Enemy design to consume a whole Army, to hold out a Winter's Siege. Besides, those Cities are not above a League and a half from the Sea on low and plain Lands, which for the most part may be put under Water in the Winter, so that they have naturally and of themselves great Advantages, and besides may be fortified, and Men to defend their Fortifications are easy to be found here from their own Inhabitants, and those of neighbouring Countries. These are natural Advantages which are not to be acquired by any cost or work, but all other necessarys depend on the prudent care of the Rulers, who I confess ought ever to be imployed about that, and during their Free Government, without further loss of time, for (chi ha tempo, no aspetti tempo) He that has time, and does not improve it, shall never be wealthy. If therefore a Stadtholder or Captain-General be obtruded upon them, and they would the rather make it their business to fortify themselves, they might have cause to fear his displeasure for it.

For in the first place, the Suburbs of Citys in times of Peace having all the Privileges of Cities, and paying no Taxes, are like Wens in the Body, which attract much nourishment, and are very troublesom, and yet good for nothing; and on the other hand, the same Suburbs in time of War do not defend the City from the Enemy, but are commonly the occasion of their being lost, and so may be termed Cancers, which cannot be cut off but with the hazard of a Man's Life, a great Charge, Loss and Pain, to
which

which Extremitys People are not commonly willing to come but when 'tis too late; so that one may truly say, that that Maxim can never be sufficiently commended, That the Rulers of free Citys should prevent all Out-buildings, or Suburbs, under what Pretext soever.

And consequently the second thing to be taken care of by Rulers, is in time to inlarge their respective Citys according to the increase of their Inhabitants, or Traffick, and continually to have many void Places to set out for Buildings within their Walls, as for all publick known Uses and Accommodations, so for other unexpected Occasions, whether in Peace or War, and especially against a Siege, to secure and harbour the Country people with their Cattel, Fodder, Corn, and living, which sort of People during a Siege, can dig, and undergo Rain, Wind, Cold and Heat, and so may be singularly useful, while they have left the Land round about them naked to the Enemy, who otherwise would, by the Assistance of themselves and their Provisions, be inabled to continue the Siege longer, and to starve the City. And moreover by this Method, if a City in time of War be well fortified, many Inhabitants of the weaker neighbouring Citys may there have protection, and many of them will afterwards settle there in time of Peace, when by their Losses they have learn'd the great Advantages which in times of War, and the great Conveniences and Pleasure which in times of Peace the Inhabitants of great and strong Citys do injoy, above those small and weak ones. Rents would likewise be always kept low

And to keep want Places within the City,

Which are necessary both in War and Peace.

by reserving of Ground in Citys, to the exceeding Benefit of them in times of Peace, seeing thereby Traffick and Trades might be follow'd at a cheaper Rate, and the Inhabitants might dwell in healthful, convenient, and pleasant Houses.

The Magistrates ought to fortify their Citys well,

The 3*d* Care of Rulers ought to be to surround their Citys with good Walls and Flankings, and provide great Gates, and convenient Watch-houses; and also that each Gate have a fit place to draw up the Souldiery in And in the middle or heart of the City near the Town-hall (whence all the vigour and strength must be disperfed over the whole Body of the City) there ought to be plac'd the great Guard, and place of Assembly, with sufficient ground to draw up some thousands of Men in order to lead them out thence, where they shall be most useful, whether against Insurrections within, or Assaults from without.

And to provide all Necessarys against any Enemy,

The 4*th* Care of Rulers ought to be, to build Houses for Arms, and in time to provide them with all forts of Offensive and Defensive Weapons It is probable that every great City would require 250 Pieces of Ordnance, and Arms for ten thousand Men. Shovels, Spades, Waggons, Spars and Deals, are in such cases also necessary; as are likewise publick Buildings for Provisions, Corn, and Fewel This being once done, it might be maintain'd with very small Charge But Provisions are perishable Wares, Corn is preserv'd with great Charge, Turf may always be had in a short time out of the Country, so that in time of Peace Barns seem to be sufficient, which may be let out to the Inhabitants at a small

small Rent, who oft-times would themselves fill them with Corn, seeing the Traffick of *Holland*, and small or low Interest, added to the free hire of Garrets, might possibly cause many that live on their Rents, when the Prices of Corn are low, to lay out their Mony upon it, in hopes of profit by raising of its Price.

The 5*th* Care of Rulers ought to be, thorowly to exercise their wealthly Inhabitants in Arms, for those you have always at hand in time of need; and the rich Citizens will serve faithfully without pay to defend the Lawful Government and their dear-bought Liberty, and will stedfastly endeavour the preservation of other mens Goods from all violence, whether Domestick or Foreign. The poor Inhabitants ought in time of War to be taken into pay, tho it be but small, thereby to prevent their inclination of making Mutinies or Uproars, and they should be commanded by none but rich and trusty Citizens *And constantly to exercise the rich Citizens in Arms.*

The 6*th* and last Care of the Magistrates of Citys ought to be, to have some Mony, tho not much beforehand. And since some may wonder, considering that in the general opinion of Men, Mony is the Sinews of War, that I put it in the last Place, and besides that I presume to advise the keeping only some Mony in Cash: I shall therefore add, that the Maxim, that Mony is the Sinews of War, is never true, but where all means of Defence and Offence is provided. For every one knows, that toothless and unarm'd Gold cannot be defended but by sharp Iron: And that great and unarmed Treasures, or Chests *Lastly, to have in store some, tho not much Mony.*

of Money intice Mutineers within and all Enemys from without to plunder. At least that Maxim hath seldom any place but to make Field-Armys stand to it in Sieges, or to cause Men to keep their Station at advantageous Passes, and thereby to outstand or famish an Enemy, and when the Enemy gives way, to attaque them. But in Citys that Maxim holds not, if as they have already provided themselves with that for which Men gathered or laid up Money. And seeing in Governments where so few are Rulers, as in the Citys of *Holland*, Money is so oft measured and struk'd, and so much of it sticks to the Measure and Striker as the Rulers please, so that good Regents and Patriots must take special care, that the Money be immediately imployed about things necessary to the durable Welfare, Ease and Ornament of the City, before it be expended through alteration of the Government by indigent Rulers, and haters of the Liberty of our native Country, to obtain in building Tyrannical Castles, or by letting it drop through their Fingers into the Blew-bag.

And when Men have gotten all these necessaries, it's then time to gather a stock of Money. For in times of adversity, when things run cross, and unexpected accidents happen, Money is very necessary to procure all that was neglected or esteemed useless in time of Peace. But to great Treasures, the Citys of *Holland* should not aim at them, for these would cause great Imposts and heavy Taxes, which would make the Rulers of a rich Mercantile City consisting of a small number of People so hateful, that by such Impositions, when necessity requires not, they would be lookt on

by

by the Subject as Plunderers of the Commonalty, and run the risque of being kickt out of the Government. The People would easily think, that they had reason to believe, that if the Rulers fought only the Welfare of the Subject, and accordingly depended on their Defence, and to that end gathered of their own Inhabitants the Mony thereunto necessary, that they could then also subsist with such small Imposts as other Republicks do. And the Rulers ought to know, that many Republicks have subsisted a long time against very potent Neighbours without any Imposts; and some with very few, but none in the World by such vast ones as are levied in the Citys of *Holland*. So that it will be a Miracle from Heaven if it be long born by Citys that cannot live upon their own Fund, or Country, or unalterable Situation, but where all the Inhabitants must subsist and live upon fickle Traffick, and the uncertain consumption of Manufactures, and Fishing.

Lastly, we may add what has been said already, That the Rulers of the great *Holland* Citys ought to provide themselves with good Allys of some of the Neighbouring Citys and Lands, who are most concern'd in their safety. But when all things are so well provided, such Citys are usually helped without previous Alliances or mutual Obligations; but when unprovided, there is nothing for all their Care and Charge to be gotten but good Words under Hand and Seal, which are all but feeble things, and are construed according to the sense of the strongest, or of him that hath no need of assistance. So that such Alliances before necessity requires, need not be

Little concern needful for good Alliances,

be too anxiously sought after, especially with
the assistance of much Mony. Moreover it is well
known how firmly and well bound all the
United Provinces are by the Union of *Utrecht*,
and all the Holland Citys by the Provincial
Government.

And if the worst should happen, yet nevertheless all the great *Holland* Inland Citys,
by their Vicinity and Communication with
the North-Sea, might expect from thence in
their extremity some Succors; and if the
Besieged behaved themselves any thing well,
one or other of the Citys of *Holland* lying
at a Sea-Port, might be dispatched to help them,
we are not for losing the benefit of the Consumption or Transportation of their Commodities, which they either supply them with or
receive of them. But when all is well considered, it is most advisable for all Rulers to
provide themselves so well of all Necessaries,
as if none in the World would or were able to
help them but themselves; which is a thing
feasible enough, as hath appeared by what
hath already been laid down.

And therefore I hope by what is before alledged, it is evident, That every great City of
Holland, no less than other Republicks consisting but of one City, may very well defend
it self against the Potentates of the World.
So that it is at last made evident that this Republick, or the Gentry and Citys of *Holland*, well conjoined, may very
well be able to defend themselves against all
Foreign Powers whatsoever; which is the
thing I had undertaken to prove.

I have in the First Part observed the
interest of the Inhabitants of *Holland* in relation to
its

its Inhabitants within the Country; and in the Second Part duly confidered *Holland*'s Interest as to all Foreign Powers, I shall now end this Second Part, laying before the Reader a short View of all that has been said at once, and shew him the Inferences and Conclusions which every one ought to make from the same; *viz.* That in the first place and before all other matters, Fisherys, Manufactures, Traffick and Navigation ought to be indulged and favoured.

That Fisherys, Manufactures, Traffick, &c. ought chiefly to be indulged.

And *Secondly*, That to that end, the freedom of all Religions for all People is very necessary, *viz.* such freedom whereby all the Rulers should be of the Publick Reformed Religion, who are bound to defend and favour the same by all lawful means, yet so, that the other Religions may not be perfecuted by Placaet, but publickly tolerated or favoured, and defended against all the violence of the Rabble.

Toleration in Religion very useful to this end.

Thirdly, That neceffary Freedom be given for all Strangers to dwell in *Holland*.

Liberty for Strangers,

Fourthly, That it is neceffary that every Inhabitant of *Holland* have the liberty to follow and exercife Merchandize, their own Occupation, and Mechanick Trades, without the control of any other Inhabitants.

And all Hindrances of Trade us to deal with us

Fifthly, It is above all things neceffary, that the Rulers be prudently wary and cautious, how they lay Imposts upon Consumption, and efpecially that they be circumfpect in charging of Merchandize, or levying any Convoy-mony upon Ships or Goods imported or exported, without diftinction, as also in charging of Ships let to freight.

Freedom from Imposts, &c.

Sixthly,

The Sum and Conclusion Part II.

5 *(thly)*, That the Justice of *Holland* be accommodated or framed, not to the Benefit of the Officers of Justice, but of the Inhabitants, as also of *Mercantile Law*, more to the Interest of the Merchant.

Sixthly, Here is also shewn that which is necessary for all sorts of Governments, and especially for Republicks, which cannot subsist without continual attracting or alluring in of fresh Inhabitants, and to keep them employed about Manufactures, Fisheries, Traffick and Shipping; above all, it is absolutely necessary in *Holland*, to make new Colonys in Foreign Parts, that from time to time they may discharge their supernumerary poor, straitned, and discontented Inhabitants with Honour, Convenience and Profit, whereby also they may increase Commerce.

And forasmuch as in the Second Part we have handled *Holland*'s Just and True Maxims relating to Foreign Powers; it is in the first place clear, that the narrow Seas ought to be kept intirely free from Pirates, and that Merchants Ships in the *Spanish* and Midland Seas be continually defended, and freed by Ships of War from *Turkish* Piracys. As also that Peace should by all means be sought with all People. But yet that *Holland* must not seek its preservation from Alliances, for this is the Sheet-Anchor of the weakest Republicks and Potentates, whereas *Holland* subsists not by the Jealousy of its Neighbours, but by its own Strength. And therefore not only the other Provinces and the Generality, but especially all the Frontiers of *Holland* ought to be fortified and provided with all things necessary against any Foreign Attack or Surpri-

And above all, those great and strong Citys of *Holland* ought to be put into a posture to hold out a Year's Siege; because then they will be held impregnable, or at least stronger than many Republicks of single Inland-Citys, situated in a hilly mountanous Country, and therefore cannot be so well fortified. As for example, all the free Imperial Citys of *Germany*, the *Swiss Cantons*, *Geneva*, *Ragousa*, *Lucca*, yea even those Citys that are under Princes, as *Parma*, *Mantua*, *Modena*, which must be somewhat the weaker by reason of their own Princes, for one Sword keeps another in the Scabbard, and in this sense it is true, That two curst Dogs don't bite one another, but the good natur'd toothless ones are always bitten by the curst Curs.

But been manifested by many Examples to be so.

The End of the Second Part.

The True Interest, and Political Maxims of the Republic of *Holland* and *West-Friezland*.

PART III.

CHAP. I.

Wherein enquiry is made in what the Interest of the free Rulers of Holland, *as well as the Particulars by which the People may live happily, consists.*

HAVING hitherto shewn, that the Welfare of the Inhabitants of *Holland* is grounded upon the preservation and improvement of Fisherys, Manufactures, Traffick and Shipping, and that the same cannot be acquired nor kept but by Liberty, or to speak plainer a Toleration of all Religions, tho differing from the Reformed, and by a free Burger-right for all Strangers that will cohabit with us, with Licence to prosecute their Trades and Occupations

what

whoever without trouble or molestation from their fellow Inhabitants, in respect of any Societys, Companys, Halls, Guilds, or Corporations: And by such moderation about Convoy-monys and Tolls, that no Ships or Goods coming in, or going out, may be charged with, or eased and freed from all Taxes, otherwise than as it may be subservient to the improvement of our Fisherys, Manufactures, Traffick and Navigation. Moreover, having shewn that all the things beforementioned are not sufficient to preserve and keep up the said Fisherys, Manufactures, Traffick and Navigation, unless the Courts of Justice, and Laws be constituted and executed more than hitherto in favour of the Inhabitants, and of Traffick. And lastly that in foreign Countrys, Colonys of *Hollanders* ought to be establish'd and protected.

And in the Second Book having likewise shewn, how necessary it is that the Sea be cleared of all Free-Booters and Pirats, and that Peace be sought with all Men. And moreover, having shewed that *Holland* is to beware of entring into any prejudicial Alliances with its Neighbours and Potentates, but rather to strengthen their own Frontiers, and inland Citys, and exercise their Inhabitants well in Arms, and to keep the Sword in their own hands, against all Domestick and Foreign Power, which would be as great a strengthning and security to them, yea and more than any other Country. Therefore I judg it now useful, deliberately to examine whether a Land having such Interests, ought to be governed by a Republican or Monarchical Form of Government: For it is cer-

The Interest of Rulers. Part III.

certain that all publick Power to improve or impair the Interest of a Land, and to preserve and enlarge, or diminish and ruin a State, must be, and is in the Hands of the lawful Rulers of a Country, whether they be Monarchs, Princes, Statesmen, or the Common Burgers.

And tho I have in many places of the two first Parts of this Treatise seemed to have said enough that Holland and its Inhabitants ought to be governed by a free Republican Government, yet seeing it was done but cursorily, and as *à la volée*, and that on a Government that is well or ill constituted according to the Interest of the People, depends all their Prosperity or Adversity. It seems to me that in the Third Part of this Treatise my best Endeavours should be employed to enquire what kind of Rulers would be most profited by the Welfare of the Fisheries, Manufactures, Traffick, and Navigation, and all their Consequences, or be most injur'd by the decay or weakning of them. For seeing it is true generally speaking, that all Rulers whether high or low are alike in this, that in seeking their own Profit, they do not aim at the Benefit of the People to their own loss, but on the contrary (as no man halts of another man's sore) will out of the Common Misfortune seek their own Advantage; it is therefore evident, that of the two proposed Governments, that will be best for *Holland* in which the well or ill-being of the Rulers depends upon, or is join'd with the well or ill being of the Fishing, Manufactures, Traffick, and Navigation, and with all the necessary Consequences or Dependences of the same. And

As also that all Rulers seek their own profit more than others.

Ch. 1. *What is properly a Republic.*

And tho several kinds of Government might here come into Consideration, yet, I conceive, that of the Land of our Nativity is the fittest, and agrees best with my brief Undertaking, to guide my Thoughts upon the Government which is now there in being, and upon that which we lately had, and by many is desired again. And to that end, I conceive it needful to express what we ought to understand by the words Republick and Republican Governors, or Monarchy and Monarchical Rulers.

By the word *Republick* and *Republican Rulers*, I mean, not only such a State wherein a certain Sovereign Assembly hath the Right and Authority for coming to all Resolutions, making of Orders and Laws, or to break them, as also of requiring or prohibiting Obedience to them: But I understand thereby such a State wherein an Assembly, tho possibly without any Right, yet hath the Power to cause all their Resolutions, Orders, and Laws, to be obeyed and put in execution. And again, by the word *Monarchy* and *Monarchical Rulers*, not only such a State wherein one single Person hath all Right and Power for the taking, making, or revoking all Resolutions, Orders, and Laws, and to cause Obedience to be given to them, or to hinder the observing of them. But, I mean, thereby such a State wherein one only Person, tho without Right, yet hath the Power to cause Obedience to be given to all his Orders, Resolutions, and Laws, or to suspend or hinder all Orders, Resolutions, and Laws of the True and Lawful highest Assembly, that they be not executed, and this according to his own Pleasure.

And upon that Foundation we shall consider.

What a Republick and a Monarchy really is.

Not where the name of Freedom or Slavery is, nor yet where the Right and the Name alone is, but where the Power also thereof is present.

For

For tho it be true, that the Republican Form of Government is so acceptable to the Merchants, and all wise and vertuous Men, that many will object, that the bare name, shadow and appearance of Freedom hath been able to encourage the Traffick and Navigation of *Holland*; yet to me it seems to be no less true, that we ought to expect many more good Fruits from the thing it self, than from the appearance of it. And besides, it cannot be denied, but that the Name and the Shadow must, and shall always give way to, and vanish before the Power, Effect, and Thing it self. So that he that will narrowly enquire into the good or bad Fruits which are to be expected of such or such a kind of Government, would do very ill if he should not let his Thoughts and Observations, in this particular, run more on the Power which can operate without Right, than upon Right which without Power is insignificant, and when Violence or Force comes, must always cease.

And that this may more clearly appear, the Reader may please to consider, that by the word [Lawful Government] is meant, and must be meant, the Right of compelling Obedience to that Government; and that this is grounded upon antient Possession, or upon Laws, Customs, or Oaths, or upon all together, which are of themselves weak, unless they be back'd by Persons authorized, that are willing and ready at the Command of the lawful Rulers to punish such rebellious or perjured Subjects. Whereas on the other side, a greater or stronger adherence of People to a Governor, or some leading Men, and without the least Right, may have so great a

Power,

Power, that they shall destroy all good Orders and Customs; and such are wont to cast all the antient and virtuous lawful Rulers out of their Right and Possession.

Which adherence of the People I shall consider more at large, because thereby the Being and Power of all Government is either made or broken. I shall first consider and fix upon an unarmed State, wherein the Power of Governing used to reside in those who can force Obedience from the greater number, and especially of the meanest People. For in such a case one Man is not only a Person to be accounted as good as another, but then besides the Poor, the Ignorant, and the worst People will be always sooner ready to help to oppress lawful Rulers than the other few rich, prudent, and virtuous Inhabitants to defend them against that Violence.

Of what importance the Love of the People is,

And as to an armed State, it is held by all Men of Understanding for an infallible Maxim, That he that is Master of the Soldiery, is consequently Master of all those Places where they lie in Garrison; and he that is Master of those Places of Strength, and of the Soldiery, is likewise Master of the State, or may make himself so when he pleases. For the Soldiers have always their Officers, whose Commands they are daily accustomed to receive and obey, or else are severely punished for their Disobedience. And seeing for their Disobedience, or Crimes against the Polity of a People, they are not wont to be punished at all, or but very slackly, even when the illegal and wicked Attempts of the Captain-Generals miscarry, as also because they have nothing to lose; and lastly, seeing they have

Or, that of the Soldiery.

Interest of Public Rulers. Part III.

them also much more Advantage in Tumults and Wars, than they can hope to gain in times of Rest and Peace; therefore he that ought to be their chief Head and Master, tho' by the greatest Injustice of the World, * may suddenly set on foot all manner of undutiful Practices and Undertakings against the lawful and sacred Rulers, and fall upon them in hostile manner before they have time so to fortify their Cities, and exercise the Burgers and Boors in Arms, as to drive away the seditious Soldiery from their Gates and Walls.

And if the said Maxim, That he that is Master of the places of Strength and Soldiery, is also Master, or may make himself so, of the State, be infallibly true; then it is a more material truth, That he who, besides the command of the Soldiery, possesseth the Favour of most of the Inhabitants, or the rude Rabble, can make himself Master of the State whensoever he assembles the said Soldiery for that end. So that if any one may do this by a deputed Power, we must consider him, tho' a Servant or Minister to the State, as having in its respects the Power of the Republic in his hands; and therefore the thing it self being well considered, he is already Sovereign Monarch of that State, and is so to be understood; so that the Name and the Right of that free Republic Government will likewise soon vanish, and consequently after that, not any of the Fruits of the Free Government, or any thing vertuous to be expected. But on the contrary, as that useth to proceed

---

pessimi, pejora sequuntur.

from

from a Monarchical Government, must be supposed to happen, and therefore such a Government ought no more to be called a Republick, but a Monarchy in Practice and in Fact.

And the more, whilst the Governors of a Country, where there is such a Commander in chief, during that colour or appearance of a Free Government, must always have an Eye upon him, and in all weighty matters, Sycophant like, repair to his profound Wisdom, and take special care that they oppose it not, unless that miserable and humble Suppliant means immediately to be deposed, if not worse handled by the Rulers in Power; wherein * *Rome* may and ought to serve us for an example. For if *Rome*, which was provided with so many hundred Counsellors of State *ad vitam*, and so many hundred thousand sprightly Citizens that loved their Liberty, was not able to preserve her Freedom against the Tyranny of one such Head, it is then impossible for others to do it in the like case. *See Aitzma, how the States were fain to demean themselves. P. Henry. Which we may clearly discern by the Roman Republick.*

Especially when it is considered, that that high spirited Republick having always had several warlike General Officers, who did ever mutually envy one another, and therefore were too weak to master the Republick; yet was it fain at last to bow the Neck under them, and serve them after a slavish manner assoon as one of those principal Officers be- *Which could preserve its Freedom under several Heads of the Soltany,*

---

* Libertas inquit populi quem Regna coercent.
Libertate perit cujus servaveris umbram,
Si quicquid jubeare velis. *Lucan.*

came too strong for all the rest, or that three of them conspired together, and divided the Republick amongst them. So that a Republick, where one single Person or Head possesseth the general Favour of the Rabble and Soldiery, according to the said Maxim of State, may be accounted to have lost its universal Freedom, or shall certainly lose it.

And this infallible Maxim will of all Countrys be found truest in *Holland*, when the said Republick shall maintain a considerable Army of foreign Soldiers in constant pay, that are born and educated in Monarchical Countrys, such as *France* and *England*, &c. and put them into impregnable Cities, and Strong-holds, which surround the Republick of *Holland*, and on the other side, *Holland* consisting of Cities wholly unfortified, and governed by a very few Aristocratical Rulers, and mostly inhabited by a People so ill informed in the Grounds of their own Welfare, and in the lawful Government of the Country, that they will expect much more Prosperity under such a potent Head, than from a free Republick; and besides, will conceive, that they owe more Obedience to the Master of the Soldiers and Strong-holds, than to the said Aristocratical Rulers; in such a Condition we shall find, that where Force comes, Right yields, and that a Government cannot be safe without the possession of the Sword.

According to the known Truth and Maxim of Politicians, the Sword of War in the Hand of a Captain-General is always sharper, and

---

Interarma silent Leges. Parum tuta est sine viribus majestas.

reacheth farther than the Sword of Justice in the Hands of Political or Civil Rulers and Judges. This might be confirmed by numerous Examples which I shall not mention, because they are pertinently related in that unanswerable Deduction of the States of *Holland*, and likewise in the Political Ballance of *V. H* where it is shewn that all Republicks, which have had a Military or Political Head, have not long preserv'd their Liberty, especially when the Son of such a Head shall come to be vested in the same Office and Dignity. And now to the Matter in hand, The Reader is in the first place earnestly desired maturely to consider, whether the Author of the said Political Ballance has not abundantly shewn, that a Republican Government in all Countrys of the World, and especially in *Holland*, would be much more advantageous to the People than a Government by a single Person.

Seeing the Ministers of Government and Justice can never preserve their own against a hired Soldiery.

See the Second Part, c 1. §. 10.

Secondly, It is very well worth observation, that in Republicks the Rulers, Magistrates, and other Publick Ministers have very little Reward and Salary for their Service, who while they are in the condition of Citizens, neither may nor can enrich themselves with the Revenues of the Land, and therefore are necessitated by other ways than that of Magistracy, and publick Imployments, to maintain themselves and their Familys, as by Merchandizing, *&c.* Thus it is still, or was lately in the Republicks of *Venice, Genoua, Ragousa, Lucca, Milan, Florence,* &c. At least it is well known that in *Holland* very many Rulers and Magistrates maintain themselves by the Fisherys, Manufactures,

Fisherys, Manufactures, &c. depend upon having free Rulers.

B b

factures, Traffick and Navigation.

Or if some of the Rulers and Servants of the Republick of *Holland* do possess such Estates as to be able to live at ease on their Lands and Revenues, yet it is evident that the Reformed Religion, permitting no Cloisters or Spiritual Revenues, and the Publick Worship being performed by Ministers for a very small Reward or Salary, and by the Elders and Deacons *gratis*, there is no Relief to be had thence for distressed, impoverished Relations and Familys. So that many Rulers being sensible that according to the Proverb, Many Swine cause but thin Wash; either they themselves, or at least their Posterity in the third or fourth Generation, must in this naturally poor, tho for Merchandize well situated Country, rise again by Traffick. And hence it is that all the Rulers in *Holland* are derived of Parents that have lived by the Fisheries, Manefactures, Traffick or Navigation, and so their Children after them, and that the said Rulers do still daily to maintain their Familys find it proper to marry their Children to rich Merchants, or their Children. So that such Rulers, whether considered in themselves by their Consanguinity or Affinity, are in all respects interested in the Welfare or Illfare of the Fisheries, Manufactures, Traffick and Navigation of this Country.

This is the more credible in the Citys of *Holland*, because the Common-Council, and the Magistrates consist but of a few Persons thereto elected in such a manner, that the Government, and their particular Imployments being fixed to no particular Familys, those who by accident come to get the greatest Authority

thority or Administration, do use, out of natural Love, Ambition and Jealousy, to advance their own Friends, and to exclude the friends of the deceased Rulers and Magistrates, most of them having already had their Turn in the Government and Magistracy. So that from time to time new Familys come into the Government, and the Magistracys of Citys, which yield for the most part but little Profit, and that only during some yearly Magistracy or Commission, fall vacant so seldom, that all those new Familys cannot be provided for, much less maintained by them. Wherefore it is and will be necessary, so long as the Government is not tied or intailed to any particular Family, that many of the Relations of the Rulers in the Citys of *Holland* must live by Merchandizing.

And accordingly we must believe, that the said Rulers and Magistrates, under a Free Government, whether in their own Citys, or at the Assemblys of *Holland*, will, by their Counsels and Resolutions, indeavour to preserve and increase the same means of Subsistance for the Country in general; unless it could be proved, that the Republican Form of Government, and by its necessary Consequences (viz. Liberty of Conscience, Freedom of Burgership, and from Monopolies, laying aside all Trafficking Companys, Halls and Guilds, which defraud other Inhabitants of that way of living; likewise moderating, or taking away of Convoys and Tolls, ordering and directing Justice to the benefit of the common Inhabitants, and Merchandizing, by Colonies, by their keeping the Seas open and free from Privateers, by Peace, fortified Citys,

Whatever is necessary for the prosperity of the Country, will be profitable for the Rulers.

tys, and arming the Inhabitants) unleſs I ſay it could be proved that the Inhabitants are more endamaged by theſe, or put into a better condition by uſing Compulſion in Matters of Religion, by ſecluding from Burger Right, by Monopolys, Societys, or Companys of Merchants, by Patents, Halls and Guilds, unreaſonable high Convoy-Mony, and Tolls, corrupt Juſtice, Sea-Robberys and Wars for want of Colonys, and by weak Citys and unarmed Inhabitants. So that I find my ſelf bound to enquire a little more ſtrictly into all the parts thereof, and yet with all the brevity I can.

As to the Adminiſtration or Service of the Church, by the Preacher, Elder and Deacon in *Holland*, it muſt be confeſſed that thoſe Services there are of ſo little Profit and Credit, that the Rulers and Magiſtrates, or their Friends, are very ſeldom inclined to perform thoſe Functions. So that the freedom and toleration of the Aſſemblys of different Worſhip in *Holland*, cannot be expected (from ſuch a Supreme Head) by Rulers or Magiſtrates, becauſe the Diſſenters, under pretence of aſſembling for the Service of God, would indeavour to make Inſurrections, and thereby depoſe the Rulers to domineer over the State, and the eſtabliſh'd Religion. Againſt which it may be ſaid, that the honeſt diſſenting Inhabitants, who fare well in this Country, or poſſeſs any conſiderable Eſtates, ought not to be preſumed to fall into ſuch ſeditious Thoughts, ſo deſtructive to themſelves and the Country, ſo long as they are not imbittered by Perſecution; but on the contrary will be obliged by ſuch Liberty, eaſy and mode-

moderate Government, to shew their Gratitude to so good a Magistracy. Wherefore the rascally People, or those of mean Estates, and ambitious and seditious Inhabitants, would be deprived of all Adherents, whom otherwise under the Cloke of Religion they might the more easily gain to carry on their ill Designs.

And moreover it is well known to all prudent Men, that such Persons as seek after Sovereignty, do usually favour seditious Preachers, and zealous Devotees, that by the help of those tumultuous Spirits they may arrive at that Dignity, and yet no sooner do they acquire that Sovereign Power, but presently they are sensible how unfit those stubborn and imprudent Devotees and seditious Preachers are to be made use of in Magistracy or Government; insomuch that they then use to desert them, and in lieu of preferring and inriching them, use to punish them for their Sedition.

The Heads of the Seditious make use of the Tongues and Pens of Preachers, as the Cat's Paw.

Hereof we have lately had very remarkable Examples in *France*, when K. *Henry* IV. had so long favoured the Preachers and People of the Reformed Religion (there called *Hugenots*) as he needed them, and then abandoned and curb'd them as he saw fit: So that now among their Offspring we may see the miserable State of the *Hugenots* in that Country. And later than that we have seen the like in *England*, where *Oliver Cromwel* having craftily made use of, first of the *Presbyterians*, and then of the *Independent* Preachers, and those of their Party to favour him, and by their Multitude to gain the Protectorship, yet afterwards wholly forsook them, and often punish'd them severely. And

And that Prince *William* the Elder would have taken the same course, appears clearly by our Historys, which testify that the Reformed Preachers, who in the beginning of those Tumults were very kind to him, afterwards, when he was arrived at his highest pitch of Grandure, they hated and spake injuriously of him, because he was not kind enough to them, and gave more Liberty to those of different Perswasions in the Service of God than was pleasing to them, and things went so far, that the principal and most refined of the Reformed Preachers did in their Pulpits openly exclaim against him for an unjust, and ungodly Person: And therefore in the Year 1582, he found himself constrained to move the States of *Holland* and *Zealand* to make good and sound Laws about Church Government, declaring, that unless some good Order were taken about the same, the Reformed Religion, and the Country too, would fall to ruin. And accordingly they proceeded so far with these Spiritual Laws, that we may truly say, the only reason why they remained imperfect, was the sudden death of the said Prince. In the mean time he could very easily maintain his Power against those Ecclesiasticks, and kept it up on foot by his numerous Adherents, whom he acquired by his great Moderation as aforesaid towards the other Inhabitants that were of different Judgments and Opinions. And this aversion of the Reformed Preachers and Zealots towards Prince *William* went so far, that for that reason they greatly affected the Earl of *Leicester*, and hated his Son *Maurice* whom he left behind him, and became Stadtholder of *Holland* and *Zealand*, &c till he and the most refined of the Ministry were afterwards reconciled and united, and at last colluded together about the Political Government and Church Service in those sad unsettled Years of 1618, and 1619. Wherefore it is not to be believed that the lawful Authority of this Republick being now delivered from a single Person that aimed at the Sovereignty, will give much countenance to the most politick and chief Churchmen, or that a Toleration of Religions would easily give occasion of an Uproar here.

But if any should conceive that the Papists, who are the strongest Sect in Number, Order, and Combination (as having the Pope for their chief Head, and others their Spiritual Heads amongst them, and being generally inclined to our powerful Neighbour the King of *Spain*, who formerly was Lord of this Country) might be able, in case they had more Liberty to exercise their Religion, to subvert so mild a Government, and possess it themselves. In answer hereunto it may truly be said, That the *Roman Catholicks* in their Religion are governed in a Monarchical manner, and consequently where they are Supreme, suffer no other Sects; so that in such a case all other dissenting Inhabitants of our Land would join with the Rulers of our Republicks, whereby more than ¾ parts of the said Inhabitants would adhere to the Lawful Civil Power, to quell those seditious Persons at their first rising. *Prudent Toleration of the Romish Religion in Holland, would not be detrimental to the Civil Government.*

But in case of Compulsion there might follow a concurrence in Points of Faith among the Inhabitants; it were fit then to be considered, *But Coercion in Religion would prove more hurtful.*

dered, whether when this difference in Matters of Religion ceased, the Churchmen who have their Office during Life, and not for some few Years, by their Sermons to their Hearers, who for the most part suppose they hear nothing but God's Word out of the Ministers Mouths, and therefore believe they obey God when they obey the Ministers; and also on the other side, when they obey Political Commands and Laws, they obey Men only: I say, it ought well to be considered, whether in a short time they might not acquire a greater number of Followers or Adherents when they give themselves out for God's Ambassadors, and teach men that scriptural saying, *That we must rather obey God and his Ambassadors than Man*, and this out of a corrupt Self-love, and natural Ambition, and so find it good corruptly and impiously to instruct their Auditors, thereby to magnify themselves as it hath oft hapned, and may again happen; and whether their Adherents might not consequently make such ambitious Churchmen so powerful, as to cause the Civil Governours, who exercise the Magistracy here but for a short time, to truckle under them.

The Ecclesiasticks hereby gain too great a Party against the Civil Powers.

We have Examples of the Primitive times, that the spiritual Persons of those days, having first converted the *Roman* Emperors to Christianity, and by degrees brought under the Heathen Opposers more by that Political Power, than by a holy Life, and strong Reasons; did afterwards make use of their Sermons to aggrandize their acquired Ecclesiastical Power to the detriment of the Civil Authority, by erecting an Hierarchy, or Church-Power independent from the Political, such as is now under the Papacy:

From

From this Ambition of Churchmen the Proverb rose, * That the Clergy always fear and hate the Supreme Authority, or to vary the Phrase, It hath been an old Game; My Nunkle is ever plucking my Lords Staff out of his Hand, not only to evade being beat therewith himself, but also to beat others and make them submit to him.

This is also confirmed by *Otto Frisingensis*, tho a *Romish* Bishop, who said, That the Empire by reason of its love to Religion, impaired it self, yea was exhausted, and that it had so aggrandized the Church, that it was not only deprived of the Spiritual, but also of the Temporal Sword, which evidently belongs to the Empire, adding thereunto very ingeniously, " And altho it be above our " Power to treat hereof, so as to give Sen-" tence, yet methinks the Clergy are ve-" ry blame-worthy who endeavour to in-" jure the State, *viz.* the *German* or *Romish* " Empire, with a Sword which they have ac-" quired of the Rulers, and by the Favour of " the Emperors; unless they will herein " imitate *David*, who when he had fell'd the " *Philistine* by the Spirit of God, cut off *Goli-* " *ah*'s Head with his own Sword.

Lib. 7. Chron.

The same happen'd in the Roman and German Empire

But the truth is, if you please to enquire diligently into the Reasons of these Broils and Jealousies, between the Sovereign Rulers and Magistrates on the one side, and the Clergy on the other, we shall find, that tho the impudence and ignorance of the Rulers, and their love to the Clergy, might at first have contri-

Which might not proceed from an Ecclesiastical, but a general human frailty.

---

* Cæsares timere & odisse proprium esse Ecclesiæ.

buted

buted somewhat towards it, yet that Ignorance and Favour was not so great for a long Season after their first conversion to Christianity, as to effect it. And as to the Clergys Self-love and Ambition, we shall find that they are not Defects peculiar to the Clergy only, but common to all Mankind.

So that they that will inquire into the Causes why of late times there have been more Differences and Enmity between the Civil Rulers and the Publick Teachers of Christianity, than before under Heathenism and Judaism, must observe, that Heathenism and Judaism consisted chiefly in Sacrifices, without publick Schools and Common prayers, and much more Convocations, and that those Sacrifices, for divers things not happning daily nor weekly, but very rarely or seldom, required so little time, that among the *Heathens*, the Kings, Dictators, and Principal Field-Officers, whether all together or successively, might officiate as easily as Priests. Wherefore as no Reason can be given, why one Person vested with those two Offices, should be seditious to promote his Service in the Church, by diminishing that to the State, so we cannot see how those *Heathen* Priests, being devested of all Secular Power, could have caused Insurrections, without being immediately suppress'd by the Supreme Power.

We ought likewise strictly to observe, that the *Jewish* High Priests became such partly by birth, and that by virtue of that Office in the time of the *Jewish* free Government, they might be chosen the second, and in the time of the Kings, the first Person or President of the Supreme Court of Government and

and Justice called the *Sanhedrim*; and besides, they had all the Priests and the whole Tribe of *Levi* to follow them, whereby they had great Opportunitys to alter the Political State after their own pleasure, when they could acquire the Reputation of being gifted with the Spirit of Prophesy, and be suffered to prophesy publickly before the People. So that indeed there were also many tumults and Changes that hapned in the State when some impious Priests, and false Prophets abused the Power of the Church to make themselves great. But in regard nevertheless that the ordinary *Jewish* Worship consisted in Sacrifices, and that the high Priests were not always chosen Members of the *Sanhedrim*, or did not get the opportunity of prophesying before the People, they could not therefore put their Projects in execution to the prejudice of the Civil Power, and Advantage of the Priestly State. *Ibid p.8,c,10.*

But it is very observable on the other side, that the Christian Worship doth mostly consist in a verbal Application to God, by such as are no Civil or Armed Teachers, and in their Sermons apply themselves to a great Assembly of People. Which Administration, considering its weight, and constant preparation by Study and Employment, takes up the whole Man, and the abuse hereof may be very mischievous to the Civil Magistrate. The higher Powers have therefore appointed particular Persons to exercise the Civil and Military Offices, and others to take the Charge of the Worship of God in manner aforesaid, and to abstain from all secular Employments, so that it necessarily followed hence, *The Christian Preachers most of all, by their Sermons and Prayers.*

See the 12 first Titles of the Codex de Novell. of Justinian, and the Constitutions of the Emperor Leo,

hence, that in all those Places where such publick Teachers and their Hearers were of the same Mind or Belief, those Preachers have had a great power and influence to quiet or disquiet the Minds of the Subject.

Being always able to irritate or appease their Auditors.

So that Rulers (seeing how the Preachers influenced the People) were compelled to favour them in tumultuous times, if they would be obey'd by their Subjects, who will in such times be more moved by the Admonition of the Preachers, than by the Commands of the Civil Magistrate. For tho Rulers might easily perceive that this Increase of Ecclesiastical Power will be very prejudicial in future times to their Successors, yet they chuse to enjoy the present Benefit, to keep up their own Grandeur, and hereby many times Great, Civil or Military Officers have attempted to obtain the Supreme Power.

Especially in Countrys where the Subjects are of one Religion, and which is Monarchically governed.

So that it is not strange if Preachers, being sensible of their own Strength in Countrys where there are no Dissenters from them, have always opposed the Crown; and yet by reason of their weakness in the Government, their exclusion from Civil Imployment, and their being unarmed, they have hardly attained their Ends, but have been able continually to raise Tumults and Dissension. And tho since the Reformation, the Clergy in the *German* and *Switzer* Republics have not by their Sermons, and the Unanimity of the Inhabitants in Matters of Faith, been able hitherto to overtop or equal the Civil Power of the numerous free Rulers, great Councils, &c yet I conceive, that in case of such an unanimous Sentiment of the Inhabitants in the Citys of *Holland*, our small number of Magistrates or

City

Ch. 1. *The Interest of Public Rulers.*

City Councils could not be able to keep their yearly Magistracy without prejudice by those Preachers. For every one would clearly discern that the Party who adhere to the Clergy do far exceed the Civil Magistrates Adherents, in natural Strength, so that such Preachers would not always be kept under by mercenary Soldiers. Wherefore they and those of their Church-Councils could never have an opportunity of withdrawing themselves from under the Civil Power.

Why the same above all Republicks, should be feared in Holland.

And seeing the Preachers and their Adherents by such opportunities, are daily capable of putting their ill Designs in practice when they please, we are therefore to expect that all Preachers will not keep within their due Bounds, but that many of them in seditious Times will extend their legal and limited Employment under pretence of their Ecclesiastical Power, to the chief or Sovereign Command in the Affairs of the Church, and to an impudent boldness of expounding in the Pulpet all Political Acts or Laws, under the pretext of God's Word, and so to say whatever they have a mind to. Unless we had reason to believe, that the Reformed Preachers pretending to a Revelation and special Assistance of God's Spirit, or a special Godly Call to the Ministry, and accordingly being sufficiently qualified to that Service consisting in an extraordinary Holiness and obedient Reverence towards God, and their Lawful Magistracy, are not so subject to Ambition and Covetousness as other Clergymen are

See that excellent Book Luc. Antist. Const. de Jure Ecclesiasticorum, printed 1665.

Preachers are but Men as well as others.

But God amend it, says our Proverb, Ministers are no Saints, and therefore the same

Temptations that ensnare others, mislead them too, which hath often appeared in these Countrys formerly, and since the Reformation, by frequent Political Corrections and Banishments of Preachers from Citys for their offensive Sermons and Prayers, and every one still remembers what hapned about the same in our times at *Amsterdam*, *Utrecht*, *Delft*, *Gouda*, the *Hague*, &c. And tho' those that are good Preachers should not be oppressed for the said Defects, Weaknesses, and Ambition, yet it is necessary that Rulers so govern the State that seditious and proud Preachers shall not be able to subvert the Republick, and ruin the Prosperity of the Land.

And therefore we may presume that our wise free Rulers will ever continue to indulge and permit the Religious Assemblys of Dissenters, hereby to invite over continually more dissenting People into *Holland*, and will plant and improve the Reformed Religion, not by Compulsion but Moderation, and soft Means among their good dissenting Inhabitants; and that they will always preserve, and maintain in like manner our present publick Worship, without ever admitting of an Episcopal or any other coercive Spiritual Authority.

An open or free Burgership, with a Right for all Foreign Inhabitants to follow their Employments, being added to Liberty of Conscience in Matters religious, it will certainly cause very great and Populous Citys, and incredible many conveniences and divertisements for all the Inhabitants, so that all Civil Magistrates ought for that reason, were there no other, to endeavour it, and the more

more the better, if we obferve that in fuch *And confequent-*
lands and Citys, Offices do exceedingly mul- *ly many Offices*
tiply, and are made profitable, and that then *and Beneficus*
the Rulers would have the Power to prefer *for their*
many, if not all their Friends to make them *Friends*
to live in Credit and Eafe

Moreover, in fuch Lands and Citys there
will be found naturally among the Inhabitants
diverfities in Religion, Nations, Tongues,
and Occupations So that there would be no
occafions miniftred to the few Ariftocratical
Rulers who govern our Republick, and Citys, of dividing the People by artificial, and
often impious Defigns, in order to govern
them : for by thefe natural Divifions, and the
Diverfity of the Peoples Occupations, they *And thofe Ru-*
may as peaceably and fafely govern them, *lers will there-*
as in the open Country, for in the great *by have an eafy*
Citys of *Holland,* and other Citys filled with *Government.*
Foreign Inhabitants, as *Amfterdam, Leyden,*
Harlem, &c there have been nothing near
fo many Seditions againft the Rulers, as in o-
ther Countrys, and much lefs and worfe peo-
pled Citys, unlefs when they have been ftirred
up to Mutiny or Sedition by a Sovereign Head.
For in fuch a Cafe, I confefs that no Countrys
or Citys great or fmall, are or can be at reft,
and without Uproars of the Subjects againft
their Rulers and Magiftrates, any longer than
fuch a Head pleafeth to leave fuch Lands and
Citys in Peace

Finally, it is to be obferved, that the Ru- *And bertr*
lers of fuch populous open Countrys and Citys, *fetled againft*
are alfo much better able to defend themfelves *Foreign Power.*
againft all Foreign Power, whether by an
Army formed of their own Inhabitants, or
by ftrengthning their refpective Citys by good

Fortifications, and repelling of Enemys from their Walls. And seeing on the other side the Rulers of ⸺ will not be advantaged by Burgership that excludes all Foreigners, we may therefore believe that they will easily approve of it.

As to Societies or Companys erected by Patents, Halls and Guilds, upon Manufactures, Trades, Fisheries, Commerce, and Navigation, It is certain that the Rulers, Governours, and Masters of Guilds, having power at their pleasure, or at certain Times and Places, to call Assemblys, and by a general Interest having an united number of Dependents, Members and their Followers, whether of Mariners, Soldiers, Clothiers, and Brethren of the Guild of Workmen, &c. have ten opportunitys by Sedition to displace a few Aristocratical Rulers and put themselves into their places, as has been contrived Anciently in Citys, where heretofore such Halls and Guilds have been erected, as at *Gant*, *Bridges*, *Ipre*, *Loven*, *Amsterdam*, &c. wherein there were many Tumults proceeding from that cause.

And tho as yet there hath arisen no seditious Commotions of note from the Patent Companys, yet it is certain that they tend only to the advantage of some very few Persons, to the detriment of all other Inhabitants of the same or other dealers, and having also the Protection of the Government with one another, we may in time expect from hence the same ill consequence in our Free Government, some Commotions, unless the Civil Rulers be so prudent and happy as to appoint their Deputys in all the said Assemblys, who will not seek their own Welfare in the Govern-vernment by Faction or Combination, but by a praiseworthy desire after the Welfare of their Native Country, to seek the common Good.

So that if on the other hand we do rightly conceive that the Rulers of the *Holland* Citys by erecting of Companys, Halls and Guilds, have not the prospect of a considerable Benefit to arise thereby to themselves, we may presume to say, that hereafter they will have little inclination to bar the freedom of their Commonalty by new Grants, and consequently that the old Grants and Restrictions which hereafter shall be prolonged or continued, will be in such a plight, that they cannot, according to the Proverb, without prejudice to the Nation, be either altered or annul'd.

Concerning the Rates of Convoy-mony, or Customs upon Goods exported or imported, let them be laid on with such prudence and moderation, that they may be calculated purely for the benefit of our Manufactures, Fisherys, Traffick and Navigation. I have already shewn how much the Rulers of *Holland* are concerned in the flourishing of those Particulars. Wherefore on the other side it is evident, that during a free Government a very good Account of all Monys received ought to be given, and that the same ought to be employed for the clearing of the Seas. It is self-evident that the Rulers cannot enrich themselves with the Mony issuing thence; and therefore the said Rulers of the *Holland* Citys will not henceforth be inclin'd to charge Goods with such high and prejudicial Rates, but rather in process of time to favour the Merchants in that particular, and that the Seas be cleared by such Monys as are the publick

Free Rulers ought to set the Rates on Goods paying Convoy-mony with great caution.

Because they may not put the Mony into their own Purses.

Revenue of the Land, raised of all the Inhabitants as such, and to defend the Merchant from oppression by Sea.

Moreover, from what is said before it may be fairly inferred, that such interested free Rulers freely incline to enact good Orders and Laws, and so to frame Justice, that there may be quicker Dispatch made, and better Justice done, and that knavish Bankrupts be punished and the honest Merchants protected in their Right; for the Civil Rulers by encreasing the number of subordinate Judges and Counsellors, may be able to bestow on their best Friends more honourable and profitable Imployments, and by that means the better settle themselves in the Government and Magistracy. Whereas by the contrary, such Judges will rather be prejudiced than advantaged by Bribes, and the favour or disfavour of the Rulers, because possibly they would not give so much Mony on that score as others would.

As to Colonies, it is evident that the Rulers of Republicks do not pay out of their own Purses the Expence of erecting and protecting them from outward Violence; but it is paid out of the Publick Treasury, and in the mean while they would reap this Benefit for their indigent Relations to send them to such Colonies, when they are not able to prefer them at Home. And the like might be done with many other Inhabitants that are ambitious of Government, or publick Imployment, and these of a Colony would in no other regard be useful to the Republican Rulers. So that since those Colonys would be so generally profitable for the Land, and Inhabihabitants of *Holland*, as is heretofore described, we are then rationally to expect that they will be erected by our Rulers.

As to the clearing of the Seas against Enemys and Piccaroons, it is certain that during a free Republican Government, the Treasure requisite for building and setting forth of Ships, proceeds not out of the Rulers Purses, and that they and their Friends that trade at Sea, being as liable as other Inhabitants to lose their Goods by such Enemys, and that this may be prevented without putting them to any charge, we may likewise expect the same of them. And that the Sea may with Honour and Safety for the State be cleared by the free Rulers, cannot be denied. For tho the Admiral of a Fleet going to Sea without a sufficient Strength, should lose the said Fleet to the Enemys of the State, and thereby might excedingly mischieve our Republick, yet would it not totally bereave us of our Liberty, nor should it be dissolved by such a Treachery, but on the contrary, our Republick has ever been able to be recruited, and has oft-times been reinforced by our Land Forces, when they have been intrusted to Captain-Generals, and even when they have thought fit to use their Strength to conquer the Citys of *Holland*, and to seize their Deputys when they were assembled by Summons. And therefore since the free Rulers will not incline to carry on an Offensive War, and consequently to send a chargeable Army into the Field to take Citys from our Neighbours, it is not credible that the said Convoy-Monys paid for clearing the Seas, will be taken from the Admiraltys

And the Seas ought to be kept clean from Pirats or Enemys.

Without Prejudice to Republican Rulers.

careless to make therewith any needless and yet chargeable Conquests by Land, and in the mean while to abandon our Inhabitants, on the Coasts, to the Depredations of the Sea-Rovers.

Lastly, It is certain that the Rulers of Holland, and all their Trafficking Subjects would thrive much better in Times of Peace than in War, because then they would be reverenced and obeyed by them without any opposition. And besides, our City Magistrates cannot receive any considerable Profit by War, either by Land or Sea, but must bear some Burdens and Taxes thereby arising, as well as the other Inhabitants, and cannot be feasted on the same, as the late Heads of other States used were. It is evident the Soldiers and their Officers, who are for Monarchical Government, and an Illustrious General at their head, would not use their due and sincere endeavours to perform the Commerce and Counsels of the Republick, or those the chief Authority for the State. So that the Rulers of the Republick of *Holland*, in case of an unsuccessful War, would soon see their respect from the Subject diminished, and no wonder, as affected by the sottish illiterate Rabble, who always judg of things by the Success, and ever hate, and are ready to impeach the Aristocratical Rulers of their Republick, with whom some lavish, ambitious and debauched People, whether Rulers or Subjects, might join themselves to stir up Sedition, and under pretence of being of the Prince's or Captain-General's Faction, turn this Republick into a Monarchy, in hope of attaining the most eminent and profitable Employments under the Monarch.

And above all, the present free Governours would be liable to that hazard in case they should make use of such a Field General in their Wars by Land, whose Ancestors have had the same Trust reposed in them, for then, whether in good or bad Successes, those few Citizens that rule in *Holland* during Life, and serve in the Magistracy but a Year or two, would soon find that none amongst them would dare to tie the Bell about the Cat's Neck, to discharge such a Captain General with so many Dependents and Adherents, when they have no further need of his Service, or to punish him when he deserved it, whether by Disobedience, Correspondence with the Enemy, or any Attempt against the free Government, even tho an open Endeavour to gain the Sovereignty; so that thereby alone our Republick would be really changed into a Monarchy.

And of a Captain-General.

And moreover, suppose we should chuse a meaner Person to be our Capt. General, and give him the Command of the whole Troops of this State, and that but for a short time, yet it is evident that the Rulers of *Holland* would put themselves in great danger of being overmastered by that Captain-General, as by innumerable Examples which hapned here and in other Countrys may be perceived; unless Men could make the dull *Hollanders* to believe that God hath indued them with two miraculous Privileges above all other People in the World: The first is, that they shall never chuse any Captain-General but out of such excellent and blessed Familys, that tho they could, yet differing from all other

To be kick'd out of Imployment by a common Field-Officer.

ther Men, they would not rather chuse to be Lords than Servants, and that therefore that Ambition that is natural to all Men, even to their very Graves, should find no place in him during his whole Life. And the second is, That the *Hollanders* having at first, whether voluntarily or inadvertently, and after that on Succession or Constraint, placed over themselves a Monarch *in fact*, that then God from Heaven will snatch away such a Monarch suddenly, and by an unexpected Judgment deliver a People from Slavery, who are so unworthy of Liberty, as indeed hath sometimes happned.

But it would be cursed Divinity, which instead of forewarning us, that if we love the Danger, and will not avoid the Places where Plagues do reign, we shall find our certain ruin in those Places, and moreover instead of teaching us to be thankful to God for that great and undeserved Mercy, should continue to instigate us to seek Mercy once again, and procure him by publick and private Prayers, tending to cause us to return to *Egypt* out of that free Land of Promise, and there obstinately to pull down upon our own heads the heavy Yoke, under which our Forefathers were constrained to groan, and from which we by the Mercy and Blessing of God were wonderfully delivered.

And concerning Alliances with Foreign Princes and Potentates, it is apparent that Princes have not so much Interest in the Welfare of their Subjects as in a Republick; nor is there that Wisdom or Virtue in a Monarchy, as in a free Government; we shall here more and more than those prejudicial Ingagements

An

And as touching the Interest of the Rulers of a free Republick, or of Kings and Princes about fortifying the Frontiers and populous Citys, as also about exercising the Commonalty in Arms: I suppose it hath abundantly been shewed you in the first Chapter of this Book, that it is only to be expected of Rulers of Republicks, but not at all from Kings and Princes; so that it is needless to speak any more of it here.

And to fortify the Citys sufficiently, and provide them with Arms.

CHAP. II.

Wherein is maturely considered the Interest of the Monarchical Government in Holland as to all the foregoing Matters, by which the Commonalty may thrive or prosper.

I Come now to enquire whether Manufactures, Fishery, Traffick, or Shipping, and all the means beforementioned, that are necessary or useful for the Prosperity of the Country, would be well managed and laid to heart by Monarchical Rulers, or on the contrary neglected and ruined by them.

Monarchical Government would be very chargeable to Holland by its Court.

For the solution of this Question, we ought to consider, That so small a Country producing nothing of its own for which Foreigners bring Mony into *Holland*, and on the other side, being charged with all the natural Taxes mentioned in the third Chapter of the First Part of this Book: It would be farther charged by a Monarchical Government, whose
Family

Family Expences would yearly consume many Millions. And it is also certain that the good Inhabitants, out of whose Purses those Sums must be expected, would moreover at the same time be subject to all manner of Uneasiness, which necessarily attends a Monarchical Government, and are expressed in a Book intituled, *The True Ballance of* V. H. with many Circumstances, so that I shall be but short in relating them here.

It is acknowledged, that an intelligent Prince will by all means endeavour to bring the great Citys of *Holland* into such a state or condition, as to lord it over them without any controul, and at the best it would follow, that to weaken the Power of the old Rulers and Natives, such a Sovereign would, as much as in him lay, bring in new Upstarts or Foreigners into the Government; and would moreover continually favour the Villages and smaller Citys, to the prejudice of the great and strong ones.

And seeing neither the Rulers nor Inhabitants of the great Citys could with any patience look upon their own ruin: He will therefore fill their Garisons with Foreign Troops to force them to bear it, at least so long as those Troops are too strong for the Citizens: and since this would not give him sufficient Satisfaction, and would besides be extraordinary chargeable, he would therefore to bridle populous Citys by erecting Citadels over them.

Thus the wise and absolute *Spanish* Monarchs, *Charles* the Fifth, and *Philip* the Second, took no better course to make those great and rich Citys of *Naples* and *Milan*, *Antwerp*

Antwerp and Gent submit to their Yoke, than by forcing them with Citadels. Moreover we have seen, and may still see in our own Days, that the late King of France going *And the* yet further, and following the Maxims of the *French.* famous Cardinal *Richelieu*, he intirely dismantled and bereft of all Strength that Maritime and Frontier City of *Rochel*. And upon the same Motive *Lewis* the Fourteenth, in the Year 1667, having taken the two trading and populous Citys of *Dornick* and *Rissel*, gave command immediately to overawe and curb them with Castles.

So that it is no wonder if the City of *Amsterdam* in the Year 1571, being then about the bigness of 200 Morgens or Acres of Land, tho the Rulers thereof were no less faithful to the King than other zealous *Roman* Catholicks were, gave occasion to the said *Philip* of *Spain* to intend to build a Citadel *See Vigl. Ep.* there, because of the flourishing of their *135. ad Hop-* Eastern Trade, their Populousness, and for- *perum.* midable Greatness, or apt Situation to defend it self against all Foreign Power. But the King was moved to leave that Castle unbuilt, not so much by the *Amsterdammers* offering him two hundred thousand Guilders for the build- *Else all par-* ing of the Castle at *Flushing* which was then *ts Amster-* begun, as by reason of the sudden Troubles *dam would* which soon after ensued, with the loss of the *have been un-* *Briel* and *Flushing*, when he had no more occasi- *der the pow-* on for the *Amsterdammers* Favour. And there- *of Castles.* fore 'tis not improbable, that our last Captain General and Stadtholder, following these Maxims of Sovereignty, designed in the Year 1650 to force the City of *Amsterdam*, which was then enlarg'd to 600 Morgens

gens or Acres of Land in circumference, and inhabited by three hundred thousand Souls, by building a Castle on the *Yseladam*, and a .... on the ....

But it very seldom happens that Monarchs and Princes do rule by themselves, and not by others; there are also Children, weak-minded, and old doting Persons that bear the name of Rulers, and yet in effect must be ruled by others; and such Monarchs and Princes that are in the flower of their Age, take greatest pleasure in fulfilling their own Lusts. So that while they are Orphans, and old Men, those that are their Favorites or Guardians, whether Women, Princes, or Nobles, and sometimes Courtiers, Whores and Rogues, who minister Fewel for their Lords or Ladys Debauches and Lusts, and so gratify their Delights and Pleasures, use to rule all. And therefore it is reasonable to believe that all these Persons, whether Guardians and Favorites, or Ministers and Courtiers, that for some time govern the Land instead of their Sovereign, do not in that time wholly forget to inrich themselves and their Relations by all imaginable means, and many times by Rapine out of the Estates of the rich trading Inhabitants. All which being discoursed at large in the *Political Ballance of* V. H. I shall not hear speak of it in general, but go over it in particular, and examine how much the Manufactures, Fisherys, Traffick and Navigation of *Holland*, and its Dependences, are likely to be prejudiced or improved by a Monarchical Government.

And in the first place I conceive, that neither such Rulers as do actually govern, whether Men or Women, their Guardians, Favorites or Courtiers, Princesses or Nobles, will regard or concern themselves in the least for the Manufactures, Fisherys, Traffick or Navigation, and what depends upon them: For according to the Calculation or Number of the few Familys of the Courtiers, compared with all those of *Holland*, there are an incredible number of both honourable and profitable Imployments and Benefices belonging to the Government of the populous Countrys, and great trading Citys; and these Courtiers would make them much more beneficial for themselves than they now are, under pretence that the Monarch's Revenues would thereby be improved. Whereas indeed, when all the Revenues of the Monarch are sum'd up, the bestowing of such profitable, yea and creditable Offices which may always be made profitable, are therein included. And therefore such Guardians, Favorites and Courtiers, being able to inrich themselves and their Friends after this manner, none will be so sottish as to seek their maintenance by an uncertain Gain, and with the danger of losing all in that ever laborious and anxious way of Merchandizing. *Courtiers will drive no Trade.*

But supposing that the Sovereign, or his Guardians, Favorites, Courtiers, and their Relations should seek their gain by Manufactures, Fisherys, Traffick, and Navigation, or what depends on 'em, they would then make such Orders and Laws by their overswaying Power, or would manage it so, that it might tend to their own Benefit, tho all the other Trading Inhabitants of *Holland* should be thereby prejudic'd. *If they merchandize, it must be to the prejudice of others.*

Dd And

And besides it is certain, that the rich, and ... Clownish *Hollanders*, would not ... to gain the Love and Favour of our Monarchs, Princes, or Nobles, by Courtly Services as the indigent younger, and ingenious Sons of the *French* and *English* Gentry, or the adjacent beggarly laborious, and slavish ... of ..., who being accustomed to accost their Lords and Gentry with great ..., and many Flatteries, and to ... their own Country, are oft-times compelled by Poverty, to forsake it, and then ... introducing those genteel Foreign Recreations, and Debaucheries, as well as their ... manner of Services, they endeavour to render themselves acceptable to our Monarchs. While on the other side a Monarch or Prince of *Holland* would sooner and more expect, that such indigent Strangers (who would be indebted to him for all they ... of Estate and Office, and which without his Favour they could not hold, as being an Incroachment upon our Privileges) should be ... inclined to encrease the Authority of the Monarch, or Prince, tho to the Ruin of the Commonwealth.

All which cannot be expected from Natives who ... the Government or Magistracy of the Land, who are generally Wealthy, and as such have a Right to the said Government and Magistracy, especially when their Parents have served in the Government ... then *Holland* will be continually ruled and ... by Foreigners, who have neither by themselves nor by their Relations ever ... any measure concerned in the Prospe... or Decay of the Manufactures, Fisherys,
Traf-

Traffick and Navigation, and their Dependencies. So that those Countries would and must by all endeavours seek themselves, tho to the neglect, yea subversion of the Foundations of *Holland*'s Prosperity, and the annihilation of the Commonwealth Government, and accordingly we may conclude, that the same would certainly happen.

As for the Liberty of Religion, or Toleration, it is clear that under a Monarchical Government, it is not to be expected, for *no Bishop, no King*, is a common Maxim. As it is certainly and ever very dangerous for Kings, their Minions and Courtiers, to have Subjects, that under pretence of Right will not be subject to the Civil Government in being, but assemble to order matters of Weight by majority of Votes. So it is principally hazardous under a Monarchical Government, in Affairs which in the highest degree concern all Men, *viz.* Religion, where the Ecclesiasticks who oft-times dare undertake to demonstrate that their spiritual Authority is deriv'd, neither from the higher, nor subordinate Magistracy of the Land, would soon under pretext of such a Holy League draw in a number of discontented, ignorant, indigent, and consequently most seditious Persons. So that if they are but resolv'd to countenance their discontents against Kings, their Favorites, &c. in their Sermons and Publick Prayers, they will soon invite into them a number of considerable tho poor mutinous People, that are inclin'd to them as their Hearers, who then term them Nursing Fathers, and Men of God, and so appoint them Captains and Superior Officers

Church Government consisting of Councils, Classes and Synods, shall offend Monarchs, as with the freedom of Religion.

5. A Constitutes de Jure Ecclesiastico

of Peace would be that it is great an a-

Officers to make head against their Sovereign, his Favorites and Courtiers.

But on the other side, Kings gain a great Power in Matters of Religion, and in the affection of their Subjects, if by their own Authority they may place or depose Bishops or Superintendants that may be chosen by them in all the Chief Churches in their Diocesses, viz. their Pastors and Preachers, as will and must teach the Subject that which best agrees with the Power of the Monarch. Moreover, seeing the Bishops or Pastors are not to have their peculiar Church-Councils under a Monarch, such Kings and Princes may in case of disobedience lawfully depose them.

We take this probably the main Reason why under the Roman and Grecian Emperors an Episcopal or Monarchical Government was early introduced, which afterwards by the Papacy, and the Bishops, extended to other free Countrys Northward. And in the preceding Age we found that King *Philip* the Second of *Spain* intended to frame a greater Monarchical Power in these Provinces by Bishops of his own Election. And others also the *Legal* Protestants that love Regal Government, see no means of limiting the Kings Monarchical Power by a Presbyterian Church Council, or Republican Church-Government. So that they did not think fit in *England* now of late years to admit the same where it was set up in the late Troubles. But even in *Scotland*, where that Government stood firm since the beginning of the Reformation, even against the inclination of very many *English*, and all the

Scotish

Scotish Nation almost, to erect in lieu of a Church-Council, a Monarchical or Episcopal Church-Government. And thus likewise in *Germany* at this day, we see that the Protestant Princes have possession of the *Jura Episcopalia*, all the Power of the Bishops whom they have cast out, and none of those Princes have suffered or set up any Church-Councils, Classical or Synodical Assemblys independent of them.

And moreover we have in all Ages under the Papacy observed, that Episcopal Government is very dangerous in Republicks, so that the Bishops in many Places, especially in *Germany*, and in these *Netherlands*, where at the time when the Christian Faith was receiv'd, there was for the most part a free Popular Government, have been able by little and little, by their pretended holy Sermons to the People, to make so great a Party among them, as to get the Temporal Government of Citys and Countrys; and in other Republicks, as *Ragusa*, *Venice*, &c. there were many Laws made against such Bishops to prevent the like Usurpation. Yea among all the *Switzers*, *German*, or *Netherlandish* Republicks, that have received the Reformed Religion, there is to my knowledg not one of them that have not expelled their Bishops, and erected in their stead a Church-Council, or Republican Ecclesiastical Government, whereby the freedom of the Republick might be better preserved.

Bishops are intolerable in Republicks, and much desired in Monarchical Governments.

So that now we may conclude, that if the Monarchs of *Holland*, or their Favorites and Courtiers, should introduce Episcopal Government into the Church, we are to observe that

that the Bishops who are elected, and depofed by fuch Monarchs and Princes, muſt needs have Friends at Court, and continually make more. And if ſuch Biſhops become not the Minions of the Monarchs, and Princes of Europe, we may then well ſuppoſe that at leaſt one, will uſe all the intereſt of their Friends at Court to enlarge their own Power, Honour, and Wealth, which would chiefly conſiſt in this, That all the Subjects ſhould acknowledge and repute them for Orthodox Spiritual Fathers. And ſeeing it might very well conſiſt with the Supreme Magiſtrates Intereſt, that the Subjects who chiefly depend on him, be revered by the Inhabitants as Holy and Orthodox Perſons, the Biſhops might eaſily by this means obtain all that they deſire of the Sovereign tending to that end. And then ſuch Biſhops would never reſt, till they had procured a Law to have all Diſſenters from them in Matters of Religion, to be either brought over to their Opinion and Faction, or baniſh'd the Country, as we have had experience in former Ages under the Biſhops, and may at this day ſee in the ſame place every where. Inſomuch that under them there will never be any freedom of Religion for Diſſenters, but only for the Jews, who indeed have Liberty for theirs, which they purchaſe for Money.

Moreover, tho Kings and Princes by ſuch Chriſtian Biſhops, Superintendants, and Political Church-Councils depending on them, ſeem to be ſecured againſt the danger of Chriſtian Preachers, yet ſuch is their aptneſs to raiſe Seditions, that ofttimes by their licentious Sermons, and publick Prayers, many terrible Changes might have been occasioned *of the Princes* in that Government. As appeared in the *nicety* foregoing Age at the time of the Holy League, *chose many* for the *Romish* Religion in *France*, and in our *of Preaching* times in *Scotland* and *England* by the Holy *unto reading of* Covenant for the Reformed Religion. And *Forms, Ho-* therefore many Protestant Kings and Princes, *milys, &c.* especially those who own themselves Heads of the Church, and disown the Pope of *Rome*, did for their greater safety find it convenient to prohibit all publick Extemporary Sermons and Prayers, and in lieu thereof appointed others by their Sovereign Power to be read *verbatim*.

This the Political Martyr, *Charles* the First *This was I say* King of *England*, had in part effected by ta- *in England*, king away the Sabbath Days Afternoon's Ser- *exercised in* mons, or changing them for the reading of the *Transylvania,* Book of Common-prayer. And as I have un- *and anciently* derstood, the Protestant Prince of *Transylva-* *practised in* nia, *Ragotzki*, went yet further, and by advice of *Muscovia* four of his most Learned, Wise and Virtuous Preachers, having caused some Sermons and Prayers to be composed sutable to all Occasions, which being afterwards examined by a Synodical Assembly, and judged by Unanimous Consent very solid and edifying Sermons, and Prayers, he laid aside the Vizard, and ordered that no other Sermons, and publick Prayers should be used, but that they should have them word by word read to the People in the Churches. As of antient times also in *Vide Thuan.* *Muscovia*, where by command of the Czar *Hist. l. 5. p.* there were some old Homilies of the *Greek* *m. 325. At-* Fathers suting all Occasions translated into the *Part 1. fol. —* *Slavonian* Tongue, and upon occasion of War, Famine, or Plague, &c. appointed to be read by his Metropolitan, so that all the Preachers there were compelled to use no other Prayers or Sermons, and forced to read them *verbatim*.

Which Maxim likewise very well sutes all the Monarchs and Supreme Rulers in *Asia* and *Africa* that are addicted to *Mahometanism*, and therefore acknowledg neither Pope nor any other Head Superior to themselves. For that Religion by reason of the differing Expositors of the *Alcoran* is divided into several Sects, insomuch that the *Moors*, *Turks*, *Persians*, &c. on that behalf do very much differ, and hate and persecute one another: And that the *Mahometan* Religion being a Mixture or Collection of the Heathenish, Jewish and Christian Worship, acknowledg no Sacrifices, and in lieu thereof every Sect seems to be maintain'd by the publick Speeches or Declarations of the Priests or Teachers; yet it is certain, these Priests may do nothing in the Churches, but sing some Lessons in publick Prayers, or read the same, or the Alcoran, to the People.

On the contrary, I cannot remember that any free Republick of the Christian Religion separated from the Pope of *Rome*, and that in consequence hath acquired the Supreme Right and Power about the publick Order of Ecclesiastical Affairs, ever prohibited the ordinary publick Prayers and Sermons, or on the other side caused any set form of Prayers, or Sermons to be read *verbatim*.

As to Liberty for all Foreigners to dwell in *Holland*, and live by their Trades, and also to be taken into all Places or Employments

of

of the Government; I must acknowledg it would prove an accession of Strength to a King or supreme Head, and his Favorites and Courtiers: and therefore we ought to conceive, that under a Monarchical Government Strangers would be every where placed in the Government; as heretofore those of *Haynault*, *Burgundy*, and *Flanders*, under the Government of the Earls, and the *German*, *French* and *English* under the Captains-General, or Stadtholders of *Holland*, have had the greatest Employments in the Country. But that this tends to the benefit of Manufactury, Fishery, Commerce, and Shipping, I cannot imagine, but on the contrary, it is easier to believe, that those Strangers, whether Favourites or Courtiers, having any Employment in the Militia, Law, Civil Government, Treasury, as Captains of Foot or Horse, Colonels, Governours of Cities and Forts, Schouts, Bailiffs, &c would use all their Power to rob the richest trading Inhabitants, upon one Pretence or other, of their Wealth, and thereby enrich themselves with the Sweat and Blood of other Men For because these indigent lavish new Upstarts will have need of it every where, therefore it is certain they will seek it where it is to be had, and so they may easily borrow, or take it from unarmed People. And it is also certain, that the said Strangers will not rest till they have broken down, and destroyed both the Substance and Shadow of the States manner of Government, to the end that in time to come they might not be subjected to any Punishment for their Crimes, and destroying the Liberty of the Country, and

To the Ruin of Trade.

And the Destruction of the Government by States.

and turned out of their ill-gotten Employments.

As concerning the Freedom of all Inhabitants to set up their Trades every where in *Holland*, without Molestation from the Burgers, select Companies, and Guilds; this is not at all to be expected under a Monarchical Government. For every one knows, that at Court all Favours, Privileges, and Monopolies are to be had by Friendship, or else by Gifts and Contracts, for the King's Profit, and that of the Favourites and Courtiers. This is an epidemical Evil, and in continual Vogue in all Princes Courts, not one excepted, so that there needs no proof of it. But yet I confess that no Grants by Patents to so great Companies as our *West-India* Company have been, and our *East-India* Company still is, would be tolerable under a Monarch; so that the Grants of both, for these and many other Reasons, would be voided or nulled before the Governours or Members should arrive to be so powerful as now they are. And then those Monarchs would make Mony of those Grants again, by selling them to others to make new and weaker Companies of, and so make more Mony of the new Grants or Charters, than they could do by continuing the old ones.

Moreover, as to the charging of Convoy-monies, and Customs upon Goods with such Moderation and Prudence, that our Manufactures, Fisheries, Traffick, and Navigation, may be thereby encreased; it is apparent that this cannot be expected under a Monarchical Government. For seeing Kings with their Favourites and Courtiers, have good Reason to fear

fear, that the Prosperity of such Manufactures, Fisheries, Commerce, and Navigation, with the numerous Advantages arising thereby, will cause such mighty and flourishing Cities, as could not easily be forced by a Sovereign and his Courtiers, therefore they will endeavour to keep them as low and mean as possible. *To lessen the greatness of their Cities.*

For Monarchs and their Courtiers, in lieu of affecting the Welfare of Manufactures, Fisheries, Traffick, and Navigation, will envy the most fortunate Owners of Freight-Ships, Merchants, and Traders, because by their honest Gain and Riches they obscure the Lustre and Pomp of the Court and Gentry, and because all that they force from the Merchant and Owners of Freight Ships for Convoy-Mony and Customs, can presently be put into the King's or their own Purse, and not as by a general Imposition, equally burdening all the Inhabitants alike: So that it is not strange, if under all Monarchs it be affirmed as a good Political Maxim, That no Impositions are less hurtful than those that are laid upon Goods Imported and Exported, because they are for the most part born by Strangers, and therefore all Goods coming in, or going out, are unreasonably charged; as it appears in *Spain, Portugal, France, Sweden*, and also in these Provinces, there being still a remainder of our rigorous Government. It was the like also formerly in *England:* But since the last Troubles there have in some measure increased the Power of Parliaments, and consequently of the People, such Duties are considerably abated, and were with great Circumspection imposed on Merchandize, *Anno* 1660. *And in the mean time put the Customs into their own Coffers.*

We

We are much less to expect under a Monarchical Government, that Laws and Justice will be better framed to the Benefit of the Community, and especially of the Merchant. For (as was formerly said) besides that the rich Merchants will be pillaged and exhausted by those Rulers, or at least envied and hated by them, the Rulers, Schouts, and Bailiffs, have moreover such Friends at Court, that they publickly sell Justice, and none that are wronged dare complain of them. Yea, seeing all Laws and Judgments are made and pronounced in the King's Name, and according to his Pleasure, we cannot therefore expect under such a Government, but that all things will be carried for the benefit of the Sovereign and his Courtiers. As the Scripture teaches us, That a Prince asks not so soon what his Lust dictates, but the Judg as readily granteth it, *that they may do Evil with both Hands.* So that it is no wonder, if in all Monarchical Governments these Verses be found true, which were made by one *Owen* an *English*-man.

. . . . fuisse putavit,
Tollendum quam Leges conciliato prius.

And if any one will alledg, that this tends more to the prejudice of a Monarchy than of a Republick, let them please to consider, whether all the Monarchical Cities belonging to the *Hollanders*, as *Cutenburgh, Vyanen, Yselsten,* &c. do not so practise their Justice to the prejudice of the Merchants of *Holland,* as that they might be aptly resembled to *Algier, Tripoli, Tunis, Sally,* &c. yet with this
Dif

difference, that those Pirates being Inhabitants there, do take the Goods of the *Dutch* by force, and carry them away as good and lawful Prize. Whereas on the other side, our Inhabitants, or Strangers, having by fraud gotten some Merchants Goods into their Power, can secure them in their own Monarchical Cities, to the prejudice of the honest *Hollander*, they giving but some part of their treacherous Booty to the Servants of Justice. But in both Cases, whether by Force at Sea, or by Deceit, and such undue Countenance or Protection given to Cheats by Land, the *Holland* Merchants are equally sure to lose their Goods. And therefore we have no reason to expect an Amendment in Justice under the Government of a single Person or Monarch, to the benefit of the Trade of the Inhabitants in general.

Whereof Culenburg, Vyanen, &c. *are very sensible Examples for Holland.*

And tho Colonies would be very useful for Monarchs, thereby to ease themselves of their discontented People, which daily increase by their rigorous Government, yet is it true, that the old Monarchical Lands are thereby more depopulated, and improve not so much by foreign Traffick and Navigation as Republicks use to do. Besides, generally Kings and Princes are too indigent and unconstant, and of too short Lives, to bear those lasting Expences often required in erecting Colonies. And when such Colonies are planted, if they be not strong enough to defend themselves against any foreign Power, it is not rationally to be expected that the indigent, mutable, and mortal Prince will out of his own Purse protect such foreign Colonies by vast Expences, and continual Care for the common Good of his People, and to the Prejudice of his Courtiers so that the same, for the most part, under such a Government would fall to Ruin, and tend to the great Loss of the Inhabitants.

[marginal note: ...Portugal Spanish, and English C...]

Against which Reasons it cannot rationally be objected, that the *Portuguese*, *Spanish*, and *English* Colonies in the *Indies* have had better Progress and Success than ours, and consequently, that Republicks are neither so inclinable, nor fit for the planting and preserving of Colonies, as Monarchies are, seeing those Monarchs have born little or no Charges towards the planting and defending of their

But in answer to this, we may with truth affirm, that the Subjects of the said Monarchs are governed with more severity in their Native Country, than in the *Indies*. And moreover, the People in those Colonies enjoying ever, where a greater Freedom to plant Lands, and exercise Traffick, than in their own Country, they are excited alone by that, and not put into any better Capacity to erect or improve such Colonies, by the Act or Favour of their Prince.

It is likewise certain, that the Inhabitants of *Holland* enjoy a much softer or milder Government than they do in the *Indies*, where our privileged Companies, by their single Generals and Governours, do rule over some particular Cities and Lands with a Monarchical Severity, and oft-times despotically, not by way of Laws, and general Commands, but by separate or different Commands and Declarations and moreover, they have their Trade to themselves, with Exclusion of all

Ch. 2. *Monarchical Rulers.* 415

all the other Inhabitants. So that it appears, that this letting and incumbring of our Colonies in the *Indies*, ought not to be ascribed to the Free Government of *Holland*, but to those privileged Companies, and their Monarchical Government, as also to the Monopolys in those parts, or else to the Prince of Orange, or his Deputies of the Generality, by following whose Counsel or Command the *East-India* Company have so weakned themselves, that they have not been able to maintain that Colony they begun.

All that has been said being found true under a Monarchy, and well apprehended, I suppose none will be so foolish as to believe, that Kings, or their Favourites and Courtiers, will out of their own Purses set out Ships to clear the Seas, for the benefit of the Merchant, I say, *out of their own Purses*. For seeing all that is by Monarchs levied from the Subject, comes into their own Purse, to manage as they please, and those Sums go not into the publick Treasury, wherein no Person has a particular Interest, but must be employed only for the Service of the Country, the difference between Monarchies and Republicks is in this respect so great, that none can shew us any Monarch that ever kept the Seas clear, only for the benefit of the Merchant. On the contrary it is certain, that during our Stadtholders Government, when we possessed a shadow of Freedom, the Monys that were received of the Merchant, applicable only for clearing the Seas, were very often wrested from the Admiralties for the use of unnecessary Land Armies, and not to the Profit of *Holland* nor the Merchant, while in the

The Sea would not at all be clear'd.

Because those Princes would give no Mony out of their own Purses.

See Chap. 1. Part 2.

the interim the honest Inhabitants shamefully lost their Ships at Sea.

B—
n—
f—
l—

Lastly, It is evident, that Monarchies of themselves are more subject to Wars than Republicks, whether by Inheritances, or to secure their Relations, or to assist them in the Conquests of foreign Countries. And moreover, these Princes and Captains-General are much more inclined to War than Republicks, insomuch, that they often are the Aggressors, or pick a quarrel to make glorious Conquests, and at the same time by their Forces, which they have in readiness, they cause all their great Cities to be curb'd and made to bow to them with the greatest Humility, or to render themselves so necessary to their Republick or State, that they cannot be disbanded.

Make—
—

And as to Alliances with foreign Nations and Potentates, it is clear, that if *Holland* were governed by a single Person, or his Favorites and Courtiers, he might easily, either by Ambition, or foreign Coin, be moved to make very hurtful offensive Alliances. Since such a single Governour of *Holland* would for his great Naval Power upon all Occasions be sought to by Countries and Potentates far and near for that end.

A—
of—
—

Lastly, A King, or Prince of *Holland*, would not hasten his own Ruin, by fortifying the great Cities of *Holland*, and exercising their

---

Quod Regum, atque Imperatorum animi Virtute illa bello valeret, æquabilius atque constantius sese res humanæ haberent, neque aliud alio ferri, mutari cerneres. Sallust.

Inha

Inhabitants in Arms, to repel other Forces as well as his own: whereof, I suppose, I have spoken sufficiently. But in case any Man should yet doubt of this, I shall affirm, that formerly our Earls have demolished many of the Castles and Strong-holds of the Gentry, even when the Strength of *Holland* consisted in them. And further, to break the Strength of the Gentry, in whom only (conjointly with the Earls) the lawful Government of this Republick first consisted, they have from time to time, and especially since the Year 1200, built several Cities in *Holland*, and given freedom to the Inhabitants of certain Places and Towns of the adjacent open Countrys, or even to Foreigners, who would come and dwell in those Cities, and have freed them when they had dwelt therein a Year and a Day, from the Vassalage they were under to their Lords, or even to our own Gentry; and likewise freed such Inhabitants from all Taxes due to the Earls, and from the Jurisdiction of Bailiffs with their Assistants, and other Persons, and from the Domination of others. And those Earls did, especially in those days, indulge the said Cities, by giving them Privileges, *viz.* that their Schouts, and Schepens should be free of those Cities, and that they should make their own Laws and Statutes for all their Freemen, according to which the said Inhabitants (by their Fellow-Citizens, Schouts, and Schepens, with those who were before chosen by the Earl according to his Pleasure, or out of a great number of Men nominated to him by the People) were to have Justice done them.

Which our Earls have taught us, by razing the Castles of the Gentry.

And by raising Cities, whereby the Inhabitants might be able to curb the Gentry.

And

And tho those Burgers did moreover continue Masters of their own Mony, Provision, and Arms, and by virtue of that natural Equity did, with the Inhabitants, chuse by plurality of Voices, some of the Freemen their own Counsellors and Burgo-masters, to order and govern the Government, Treasure, and Militia of their own City; yet the Inhabitants of the Cities might not, tho at their own Charge, set up Gates and Walls to preserve their Cities, but with the special Favour and Privilege of the Earls, which was obtained commonly against their own true Interest, by giving Mony to those lavish and indigent Earls, whose Design was not to strengthen those Cities, as the Castles of the Gentry had been, but to bring the old powerful Gentry to their Bow, by the number of those inconsiderable Freemen.

And hence proceeded the Difference between walled and unwalled Cities in *Holland*, as also that the Earls of *Holland* being afterwards jealous of their walled Cities, by reason of their increasing Power, thro this Freedom, did totally burn and destroy *Vroonen*, *Gasson*, *Lisse*, &c. and pull'd down the Gates of *Utrecht*, *Delft*, *Yselsteyn*, *Alkmaer*, &c. with special Command to the Citizens never to set them up again. And this is that which *Pontus Heuters*, a Friend of those Earls and Princes, did acknowledg of our Earl *Charles* of *Burgundy*, namely, * That he as Earl of *Flanders* had firmly resolved to

---

* Decreverat ex urbe Gandavo oppidulum facere. *Pont. Heut. lib. 3. p. 75.*

make

make of that great and potent City of *Gent*, a very weak and small Town, that it might not oppose its Earl any more. Wherefore I again conclude, that *Holland* by such a Monarchical Government, according to the true Interest of such a Head, will not be more strengthned, but rather weakned, and bereft of its Strength.

CHAP. III.

Wherein is examined, whether the Reasons alledged in the two preceding Chapters, receive any Confirmation from Experience.

HAVING thus laid before you the true Interest of the Republican and Monarchical Governments, relating to Manufactures, Fisheries, Traffick, and Shipping, and their Dependencies; it is necessary that we relate Historically what hath hapned as to those Maxims of our State, both in Republican and Monarchical Governments, that so the Reader may see, whether our former Reasonings can be confirmed by Experience. In order to this, it is very necessary to observe, that to the best of my Knowledg, Merchandizing, and the general Staple of Traffick, and publick Exchange-Banks were never found, or continued long under a Monarchical or Princely Government. So that Manufactures, Fisheries, Traffick, and Navigation have thriven very little in those Monarchical Lands of *Ame-*

History teacheth that Traffick hath been in America, Asia, and Africa.

rica, Asia, and Africa, and that the great and strong Citys of those Lands have been enlarged by the Residence of great Monarchs Courts, and consequently by the exhausting, plundering, and sacking of all adjacent Countrys, whether of Enemys, or their own Subjects. Which we may perceive by the Citys of Cusco, Quito, and Mexico, &c. in America;

So Asia, Africa, Morocco, &c. China.

as also in the Asiatick great Citys of Japan, China, Persia, India; and lastly, by Morocco, Fez, Jerusalem, Ninive, Cairo, and other great Citys on the Coasts of Europe, or in Asia and Africa.

A Traffick in all free Republicks.

Moreover History tells us, that the Flower of the Traffick of these mighty Countrys is no where found but in Republicks, as Sydon, Tyre, Carthage, Bantam, Amboyna, &c. and that Traffick hath exceedingly flourished in those Lands, only so long as they enjoyed their free Government. But because these three first Places are known to be the first and most antient Trafficking Citys of the World, I shall therefore speak particularly of Sydon and Tyre, supposing it will not displease the Reader to touch on them, seeing those Matters are not much known abroad, and yet are very useful to confirm what we have advanced.

Sydon being a City in Syria, upon a Coast abounding with Fish, and good Havens, tho without Rivers, built by Sydon a Grandson of

Gen. 10.

Cham, who was Son to Noah, was in the earliest times that we have any notice of, a Mercantile or Trafficking City, which according to the Jewish computation of Time was in the Year 2000 after the Creation of the World;

Josh. 11.

and in the time of Joshua was so improved, that

that it was termed, *The great City of* Sydon. And it appears that 220 Years after, *viz.* in *Simpson's* Time, it was a very plentiful, strong, and well-fortified City, whose Inhabitants lived in profound Peace and Safety in a free Republick, having no King or Sovereign Head over them, which might have weakned them. And about 210 Years after *Simpson*, the *Sydonians* were much commended by *Homer* for great Artists. [Judg. 18.]

And that *Sydon* afterwards in the time of the Prophet *Isaiah*, and *Ezekiel* (who lived the first about 180 Years after *Homer*, and the last about 225 Years after *Isaiah*) was very famous for her Traffick, we may see in their Prophecys. Now this City of *Sydon* having flourished above 1500 Years, and raised many Colonys, it was about the Year 3590 after the Creation, besieged by *Artaxerxes Ochus* King of *Persia*, with a mighty Land Army, 300 Gallys, and 500 Ships of Burden by Sea, till they were betrayed by the Chief Head of the Republick *Tennis*, as also by their General *Mentor*. So that the *Sydonians* seeing no way to escape, and bearing a deadly hatred to a general Slavery or Monarchy, they set their own City on fire, wherein 40000 of their Inhabitants perished; and the King of *Persia* sold the Rubbish of this incredibly rich City for many Talents. And yet we read in *Q. Curtius*, that *Sydon* about 25 Years after became very considerable again; whenas the Head of the Republick, *Strato*, having first joined with *Darius* King of *Persia*, was afterwards compelled by the People to yield up the Place to *Alexander the Great*, who in the room of *Strato* set up an incon- [Isa. 23. Ezek 16. 27, 28.]

As first of all at Sydon, when it was a free Government.

Diod. Sic. l. 16.

But under its Heads of the Republick it suffered much, Just. lib. 11.

inconsiderable Person, called *Abdalonimus*, giving him Power of Life and Death over the Citizens.

But in regard *Alexander* soon after died, and his Monarchy was so rent and divided under his several Chief Commanders, that most of all the Republicks by him conquered, recovered their Freedom, we may therefore suppose the *Sydonians* did the same: For *Strabo*, who lived about 340 Years after, says, That *Sydon* was in all respects comparable to *Tyre* in Greatness, skill in Navigation, and many other Sciences and Arts relating to Traffick. And in regard he writes at large of these two Citys at once, it may be understood of the *Sydonians*, who are by him spoken of in common, tho with more regard to those of *Tyre*, viz. That they were not only left to their Freedom in the time of the old Kings of *Persia*, and had their own Government, but that under the *Romans*, by giving a small Sum of Mony, they preserv'd their Liberty.

During the Reign of the *Roman* Emperors there was little mention of *Sydon*, nor yet in the time of the *Saracens* afterwards, or of the Christian Kings of *Syria*, save that that City was taken, sometimes by one, and sometimes by another, til at last with their Hereditary Prince, formerly tributary to the *Saracens*, and the *Mamalukes* of *Cairo*, they were upon the same Conditions brought under the Monarchy of the *Turks*, about the Year of Christ 1517.

And tho since its old flourishing State, viz. about the Year 600 after Christ's Birth, the Silk-worms in those Parts, and afterwards

wards the *Turkish* Yarn came to be known; so that now much Silk is found there, and in the adjacent Places of *Begbasar* and *Angori*, much of the Yarn of Goats-hair is spun, and therefore they are able to set up a much more considerable Traffick and Navigation, by means of the Manufacturys and Fisherys: yet on the other side it is certain that *Sydon* now yields no Manufactures of their own, nor Ships, nor Trafflick, because the Inhabitants under the present Monarchical Government could not peaceably possess their Wealth, and follow their Trades, insomuch that most of their Traffick in raw Silk is now driven by Strangers, who have their own Consuls, and are always ready to depart from thence, when by the Government they find themselves too much oppressed· And it is said, that there are continually at least 200 *French* Factors that reside there, to manage that important Silk Trade.

Tyre lying within sixteen *English* miles of *Sydon*, was first built upon the Continent; from whence the Inhabitants fled to an Island lying within a quarter of a mile of it, to withdraw themselves from the Attempts of the *Israelites* who were then possessing the Land of *Canaan* under the Conduct of *Joshua*, where they built *Tyre*, who by taking of the purple Fish which were mostly in those Seas, and thereupon dealing in the dying of Purple, making of Garments after the manner of *Tyre*, and Trafficking or using Navigation, became so famous during their free Government, as you may see in the Holy Scriptures, where *Tyre* is said to be a Crown of Glory, or Pearl of Citys, and her Merchants Princes,

At Tyrus *Traffick and Navigation flourished, so long as it kept its free Government.*

Josh. 19.

Princes, and her Traders the nobleſt of thoſe Lands. That City and the Traffick thereof, is likewiſe mentioned by *Ezekiel*, of whoſe ruin he likewiſe propheſied, which happened after it had flouriſhed 680 Years, about 3360 Years after the Creation, at which time the King of *Babylon*, *Nebucadneſo*, after thirteen Years Siege, took the ſaid City, and deſtroyed it.

We read alſo, that about this time the Men of *Tyre* had in their Republick two Officers called *Sufferes*, or yearly Burgomaſters and Rulers, who ſerved in the chief Magiſtracy. And that this Republick ſoon after got its Head above Water again, for about the Year of the World 3615, and when about 255 Years were expired, *viz*. in the time of *Alexander the Great*, it was according to *Q. Curtius*, and *Diodorus Siculus*, the greateſt and moſt renowned City of all *Syria*, and ſo conſiderable in reſpect of its Navigation, that the People and Council of *Tyre* had the Courage to repulſe that victorious Commander from their City, which in no leſs than ſeven months Siege, and incredible Oppoſition, was at laſt overpowered and burnt, and almoſt all the Inhabitants were either deſtroyed or ſold. Nevertheleſs the Men of *Tyre*, in a ſhort time after the death of *Alexander the Great*, by means of their old free Government, Diligence, and Frugality, arrived to their former Power and Riches. We likewiſe read in *Strabo*, that this City of *Tyre*, during their Republican Government, and in the proceſs of 350 Years after, arrived at its antient Luſtre and Riches, by means of Traffick and Navigation. And

And tho the Emperor *Septimus Severus* about 170 Years after sacked the City of *Tyrus*, and demolished it, yet *Ulpianus* about thirty Years after this tells us, namely about 220 Years after Christ, "That *Tyre*, his na- "tive City, was an Ally of the *Roman* Em- "pire, and was very considerable and migh- "ty for War. And that they of *Tyre* had "obtained of the Emperor *Alexander Seve-* "*rus*, the Right of the free Citizens of *Ita-* "*ly*, and according as a free State had pow- "er of chusing and making their own Laws "and Magistrates. And to this day *Tyre* hath been exposed to all the same Accidents by Monarchical Governments, which those Lands were subject to in the following Times of the *Saracens*, *Christians*, and *Turks*, which we before mentioned of *Sydon*: So that *Tyre* is now inhabited by almost none but Strangers and Merchants, who for some small time reside there, among whom are many *Frenchmen* that deal in Silk.

<small>Dig. lib. 50. Tit. 15. l. 1.</small>

<small>After that it lost all its Traffick.</small>

And thus we see these two Republicks lost their Traffick and Navigation, not by Wars or Earthquakes, by which they were more than once overthrown and ruined; but by the loss of their free Government, whereas otherwise they as often resettled themselves. And in what condition those two Citys are at this time, we may be inform'd by the Travels of that worthy *English* Writer *Sandys*, who says, "That the *Emer*, or Heredi- "tary Prince of *Sydon* and *Tyre*, was sprung "from the old *French* that went thither with "the Christian King *Godfrey de Bouillon* to "conquer the Holy Land; who besides seve- "ral Taxes and Imposts he exacted of his
"Subjects,

<small>Q. Curt. l. 4. Strabo l. 16.</small>

<small>As is seen by Sandys his voyage, p. 209, to 214.</small>

"Subjects, takes the fifth part of their Re-
"venue. And tho he takes for Custom but
three *per Cent.* of Foreign Merchants for their
imported and exported Goods, yet we may
easily observe how little Traffick and Navigation can prosper there, seeing, as Mr. *Sandys*
says, " The said Christian tributary Prince,
" named *Faradyn*, keeps continually in his
" Service forty thousand Soldiers, and late-
" ly, viz. in 1611, caused false *Holland* Li-
" on Dollers to be coined, and made them
" pass current in Receits and Paiments as if
" they had been of good Alloy, and that it
" is usual with him to seize the Goods of
" Merchants that die there, yea even the
" Goods of Foreign Factors, so that the
" right Owners or Inheritors cannot get
" them out of his hands, unless they agree
" to pay him half the value. And besides,
" those Citys are wholly unfortified, having
" only a Castle for the Prince to keep his
" Court in. It is not therefore to be won-
dred at what *Sandys* says, " That these two
" Citys are so ruined, that they scarce retain
" a Shadow of their antient Grandeur and
" Renown, therefore they deserve to have
" no more said of them.

I should leave off here, but that I foresee it
will be objected, That *Sydon* had certainly
one Supreme visible Head of their Republick. And besides, the Kings of *Tyrus* are
by Sacred and Profane History represented as
very famous; from whence we may conclude,
That such a Government very well consists
with the flourishing of Trade and Navigation.
I answer, That the said Historys do clearly
inform us, that the said Sovereign Princes
of

of *Sydon*, namely *Tennis*, *Mentor* and *Strato*, were in their respective times the Ruin of *Tyrus*. And as to the King whom *Diodorus Siculus*, and *Arrianus* report in their Historys to have been in *Tyrus* when *Alexander the Great* besieged that City, the Learned affirm, that 'tis a mistake, and must be understood of *Sydon*, and its last Government.

_{Notæ Var. in Q. Curt. & Just.}

And that we may clearly expound what the Holy Scripture speaks of the Kings of *Tyre*, without contradicting what I affirm of their being a free State, I shall translate a Passage out of the 16th Book of that authentick Writer *Strabo*, and the rather, since I conceive that the State of these two Republics are there well express'd, " Next to *Sydon*, *Tyre*, says

_{Strabo lib. 16. Geogr.}

" he, is the greatest and oldest City of *Phœ-*
" *nicia*, may be compared with it for Large-
" ness, Beauty and Antiquity, and is famous
" in many Historys. And tho Poets extol
" *Sydon* more, yea and so far, that *Homer*
" makes no mention of *Tyre* at all; yet is
" *Tyre* by its Colonys extending as far as
" *Africa* and *Spain*, without the Straits of
" *Gibraltar*, become more famous. So that
" these Citys, both now as well as of antient
" Times, are so eminent for Gallantry, Lu-
" strie, and Antiquity, that at this day it is
" questioned which of them ought to be ac-
" counted the chief City of *Phœnicia*. *Sydon*
" lies on a Sea-Haven, on the Continent;
" but *Tyre* is an Island, and is almost as well
" inhabited as *Aradus*, it is joined to the
" Continent by a Bank or Causey made by
" *Alexander* when he besieged this City. It
" has two Havens, one of which was called
" the inclosed Haven, the other named the

" *Egyp-*

"*Egyptus*, or open Haven. It is said, that
"the Houses here have more Storys than
"those at *Rome*, and therefore that City
"was sometimes well nigh destroyed by
"Earthquakes, as it was by *Alexander*. But
"it overcame all those Disasters, and restored
"it self by means of its Navigation, where-
"in, as also for its Purple Dye, those of
"*Phœnicia* exceeded all other Nations. The
"Purple of *Tyre* is accounted the best, and
"that Fishery lies very near them, as do
"all the other Necessarys for Dying, and tho
"the great number of Dyers made the City
"unsafe to other Inhabitants, yet they were
"thereby enriched. They did not only un-
"der their Kings preserve their own free
"State, and Power of making what Laws
"they pleased, but also among the *Romans*,
"who for a small Tribute established their
"Council. *Hercules* is extravagantly ho-
"noured by them. How powerful they
"were at Sea, appears by their numerous
"and large Colonys. So much of *Tyrus*.

"The *Sydonians* are famous for their ma-
"nifold and excellent Arts, whereof *Homer*
"also speaketh, they are moreover renown-
"ed for their Philosophy, Astronomy and
"Arithmetick, having begun it upon Obser-
"vations and Sailing by Night. For those
"two Arts are proper for Traffick and Na-
"vigation. It's said the *Egyptians* found out
"the measuring of Land, which is needful
"to set Limits and Bounds to every Man's
"Ground, when the overflowing *Nile* de-
"stroys the Land-marks. It is believed,
"that this Art came to the *Greeks* from the
"*Egyptians*, as the *Greeks* learned Astrono-
"my

"my and Arithmetick from the *Phœnicians*;
"and all the other parts of Philosophy may
"be fetch'd out of those two Citys. Yea if
"we may believe *Possidonius*, that antient
"Learned Piece *(de Atomis)* concerning the
"indivisible Parts of all Bodys, was written by
"*Moschus* a *Sydonian*, who lived before the
"*Trojan* War. But I shall let these old things
"pass, and say, that in our time *Boethius*, with
"whom we practised *Aristotle*'s Philosophy,
"and his Brother *Diodotus*, both excellent
"Philosophers, were *Sydonians*. *Antipater*
"was of *Tyrus*, as also *Apollonius*, a little
"before our time, who made a Catalogue or
"List of all the Philosophers, and of the
"Books of *Zeno*, and of all them that fol-
"lowed his Philosophy. Thus far *Strabo*.

I shall now turn to the other Republicks of *Asia*, amongst which those small Islands of *Banda*, and *Amboyna* are very remarkable, because they were formerly governed in an Aristocratical manner by the most considerable Inhabitants of those respective Islands; which during that Government drove so great a Trade in their Spices, of Cloves, Mace, Nutmegs, and the Return and Dependencies of them, that tho the third part of the Spices were not carried by Shipping to *Calicut*, that great Staple or Storehouse of *India*; and being sold, were carried to *Bassora*, and from thence to *Cairo*, with Caravans, and lastly from thence transported to *Europe* by Shipping: nevertheless the Sultans of *Syria* and *Egypt*, thro whose Lands the same were brought hither, as also the Cloves of the *Molucca* Islands, were wont to receive yearly above eighty thousand Ducats for Custom:

Grot.Hist.l.15. The Inhabitants of Banda and Amboyna great Merchants during their Republic Government. Maffei Hist. Ind. Grot.l.11.

so that the si'd Islands flourished then in Riches.

But in 1512, when the *Portuguese* first navigated those Seas, and afterwards fought with the People of *Banda*, the Inhabitants were so terrified by these new People, and their unheard of Military Art, that conceiving themselves unable to withstand that formidable outlandish Power, they rashly agreed to elect out of their own People the most considerable Persons for their better defence, and thereby immediately lost much of their Freedom, and afterward they were, partly by the jealousy they had of each other, *viz.* of the free Inhabitants against their respective Heads, and of such Superiors among themselves, and being in part likewise overcome by the *Portuguese*, they were at length forced to submit to that Foreign Yoke.

And lastly, there was some Freedom still remaining in those Islands, when the *Netherlanders* that were Enemys to the *Portuguese* began to frequent them, and these People of *Banda* who greatly affect their Liberty, look'd upon the *Dutch* as Angels sent from Heaven to defend them, and to deliver the other Islands from the Slavery of the *Portuguese*. For which end the Natives entered into Alliances with us for common Defence, covenanting, that we might not only build Houses and Warehouses, and dwell there to trade in their Spices, but expresly agreeing that they of *Banda* and *Amboyna* should sell their Spices to no other People. Whence proceeded all that usually happens when weak States or Potentates call in too powerful Assistants, *viz.* That not only the *Portu-*

Grot. Hist.

guese

...also lost their Power over these Islands, but the Natives lost their free Government and Trade, and are now under the Dominion of the *Dutch East-India* Company. It is also very observable, That the Spices of those Islands, when brought into *Europe* by way of *Portugal*, produced yearly to the King above two hundred thousand Ducats. But the said Islands being ruin'd by the Forces of the *Portuguese*, and those of the *Dutch East-India* Company, and the said Company destroying their Spices which produced too great a quantity for them to vent, their Plenty by degrees decay'd, and their Commerce is now mightily diminished, as we may understand by the Historys of *India*, and from those that have been lately there

And are now under a miserable Subjection. Grot. l. 15.

Hitherto I have at large insisted upon the causes of the Ruin of Traffick, and Navigation, in the Republicks before mentioned, because they were not common But seeing the Cases of the following Republicks, together with their Navigation and Commerce, are sufficiently known by most men, I shall use no more words about them than may serve to the purpose we aim at. It is well known that the City of *Carthage* was built by a Colony from *Tyrus*, about the Year of the World 2940; and that it was governed by its own free popular Government, under two *Suffetes*, or yearly Burgomasters, and Judges, who jointly for that time were supreme Magistrates, and had a Council consisting of some hundreds of Persons, without any Supreme Head, and about 800 Years successively was very famous for Navigation and Commerce, and became incredibly Wealthy and Populous

The City of Carthage kept its Navigation and Trade so long as it enjoy'd its free Government.

So

So that after the said Republick and City by manifold Wars, and especially by its last against the *Romans*, had lost an infinite number of Burgers in several unfortunate Battels, and was near its ruin, yet by what *Strabo* credibly testifieth, there were remaining in *Carthage* at least seven hundred thousand Inhabitants, who also at the same time in a very short space, built and made an extraordinary number of Ships, and Arms. And besides, it is well known, that the *Carthaginians*, having in great plenty, were by their too powerful Nobility involv'd in many Wars, to make Conquests, by which at last they were so overborn by the *Romans*, who were more warlike than they, that *Carthage* was wholly destroyed, and tho it were afterwards rebuilt, and again ruined, yet being devested of its free Government by the *Romans*, and the succeeding Monarchs, it was never afterwards famous for Merchandize or Navigation. Those that desire to know more of *Carthage*, let them read *Justin*, *Diodorus*, *Polibius*, *Livy*, *Strabo*, and especially *Appianus Alexandrinus*.

Afterwards, Commerce and Navigation did incredibly flourish in the *Grecian* Republicks and Islands; amongst which *Athens* and *Rhodes* were very considerable. And it deserves our notice, that all that Country, when under the *Romans* as their Allys, did still retain a great part of their Government, together with their Commerce and Navigation but lost all after they were brought to submit to the succeeding Monarchs.

After this, Commerce, Navigation and Manufactures, settled and continued in the

Italian Republicks, so long as they enjoyed their Liberty. But we may easily perceive, that *Florence* and *Milan*, tho they became the Courts of Monarchs or Stadtholders, did much decrease in their Commerce during the Monarchical Government. It is also known that *Pisa* under a free Government was famous for a Foreign Trade, but now since its subjection has lost all its Commerce, and so in truth have all the old great *Italian* Citys since the loss of their free Government, so that they are fallen almost to nothing, unless where the Princes or Stadtholders by their Train, and the Consumption of their Courts or Families, have in some measure prevented the same. Whereas those two ill-situated Towns, *Venice* and *Genua*, by their free Government, notwithstanding the loss and removal of the *Indian* Trade, have preserved their Greatness and Traffick, as much as possible, and little *Lucca* keeps her Trade still.

viz. Milan, Florence, Pisa, &c. have lost their Liberty and Traffick.

Genua, Lucca, and Venice, retain their Liberty and Trade.

It's known that afterwards by the Conversion of *Prussia* and *Lusland*, much Foreign Traffick and Navigation settled in the *Hans* Republicks, and that all those that were not able to hold and preserve their Freedom in former Ages, lost all their Traffick, so that *Stralsond*, *Riga*, *Stettin*, *Konungsberg*, and other Citys which are under a Monarchical Government, or have lost their Liberty, can expect no more Trade than what necessarily depends on their own Situation. Whereas on the contrary, *Lubeck* and *Hamburgh*, with a free Government, have had a greater Trade and Navigation than their Situation necessarily required. As we see it still in *Germany*,

And the Hanse Towns.

F f that

that *Bremen, Embden, Munster*, &c. being continually put to wrestle or contend with their Prince or Head, are much obstructed in their Trade, and that the Traffick there could not keep its footing in any Monarchical inland Citys, but only in the free Imperial Towns, as *Nuremburg, Ausburg, Franckfort*, &c.

In the *Netherland* Provinces it is manifest by the Manufactures, Fisherys, and Foreign Traffick, that Commerce thrives best in free Governments. For when the Earls or Dukes were so weak and ill-armed, that they were forced to submit to those Citys that flourished in Traffick, and could not oppose the true Interest of the Merchants, Merchandize flourished. But when the Earls or Dukes became so powerful as to make War against the great trading Citys, Cloth-Trade, Fishery and Traffick, were by little and little driven out of the Land. This about the Year 1300, and after, the Citys of *Gent, Bruges*, and *Ipres* lost much of their Trade in Manufactures, and about the Year 1490, the City of *Bruges* lost most of her Trade by Sea, when the Arch-Duke *Maximilian* brought that Town into subjection. And lastly, all the other *Flemish* Sea-Ports lost their Fishery, when they were forced to submit to the King of *Spain*; and yet during our Wars, they would rather turn all their Force to invade us by Land, than bestow their Mony to clear the Seas for their own Inhabitants, by which they could have done *Holland* and *Zealand* much more Mischief.

The strength of *Brabant* also, particularly in *Brussels, Tirlemont*, and *Louvain*, lost much of their Trade in Manufactures about the Years 1300 and

and 1400; and in the following Age under the House of *Burgundy*, when those Dukes were so powerful as to force those Towns. Thus we saw in the following Age, that the Duke of *Anjou* being an Illustrious Prince, and a great Warrior, was no sooner become Duke of *Brabant*, than the mighty Mercantile City of *Antwerp* ran a great Hazard by the *French* Fury of losing all its Traffick. And lastly, it actually lost all its Traffick by Sea about the Year 1585, when *Philip* II. took the City by the Prince of *Parma*, and built a Castle with a *Spanish* Garison there, without ever endeavouring to restore to the Merchants their Trade, by opening the *Scheld*.

Thus were most of the antient Citys of *Holland* opprest, so long as they had their particular Lords, who used to curb the Citys, and open Country, by Forts and Castles, but would not suffer them to be walled and fortified for the Security of the Inhabitants; as appears by *Haerlem*, *Delft*, *Leyden*, *Amsterdam*, *Goude*, *Gorcum*, &c. But those Citys afterwards enjoying more Freedom under their indigent unarmed Earls, when they made use of them to overpower the antient *Holland* Gentry and Nobility, who likewise oppressed their small Citys; they did about the Year 1300 begin to gain the *Flemish* and *Brabant* Manufacturys, which forsook their places of abode; and they lost most of them again about the Year 1450, or soon after, when our Earls or Dukes of *Burgundy* were able by their Forces to subdue all those Citys. And tho during the last Troubles, and Compulsion in Matters of Religion, many *Flemish* and *Brabant* Clothiers and Merchants retired

Likewise in Holland Manufactures throve whilst the Earls were weak.

As did the Fishery and Traffick during the Government by Stadtholders.

and settled in *Holland* about the Year 1586, yet were they presently in great danger of being driven out again by the zealous, and seemingly pious Activity of our Captain-General, otherwise called the Government of the Earl of *Leicester*, who by the Interest of the Clergy with his Courtiers, and *English* Soldiery, endeavoured to make himself Lord of the Country. And for that end having reviled the States, and the Merchants for Libertines, and despicable Interlopers, issued very prejudicial Placaets against Traffick and Navigation, and lastly, design'd by surprizal to have taken and seized the three greatest trading Citys, viz. *Amsterdam*, *Leyden*, and *Enchuysen*.

So that if it is Governour and Captain General had not perceived that our Soldiery were incensed against the *English* Forces under him, and that the Government of the Land was by this means able to oppose him, by setting up another Military Head, whether it were Count *Hohenlo* or Count *Maurice* of *Nassau*, and again, if this Earl of *Leicester* had not been a Subject to Queen *Elizabeth* of *England*, whose favour he again needed to make himself Sovereign here, and besides, if afterwards he had not found himself constrained to leave these Lands by command of the said Queen, he had certainly by this his Monarchical Government, driven away our Manufactures, Fisheries, Traffick, and Navigation.

The same were afterwards in great Danger, under the succeeding Captain-Generals (when we might have had a Peace) by the continual High Convoy-monies, and the no less formidable Piracies of the *Dunkirkers* upon our Merchant-men and Fishers, and also by the needless and intolerable Imposts raised in the Year 1618, but especially in the Year 1650, at which time the Citys were brought under by our own hired Military forces, as is yet fresh in Memory.

CHAP. IV.

Reasons why the Inhabitants of Holland *were no more damnified under the Government of the Captains-General or Stadtholders.*

BUT some may object, That all these Reasons and Examples cannot weigh down a contrary Example taken from our selves, *viz.* That *Holland* having a Governour for Life, or a continued Captain-General, carrying on a constant War both by Sea Land, with a great Army in pay, obtained the Trade which removed from *Antwerp*, and keeps it still. That during the said Form of Government *Holland* hath advanced it self in all sorts of Commerce, Manufactures, Fisheries, and Navigation, incomparably above all other adjacent Countries, and especially above *Flanders* and *Brabant*, where the Trade of Manufactures and Traffick had some time before mightily flourished. so that the said Form of Government seems to consist very well with the Interest of the Country. Tho this Objection is perhaps sufficiently refuted in the foregoing Chapters, yet it will not be amiss

Object. *Has not* Holland *prospered under the Conduct of Captains General?*

First. It is to be noted in general, that at the time when *Antwerp* lost its Traffick, as also afterwards, there were in all the adjacent Countries much greater obstructions to Trade then in *Holland*, &c. among all the Monarchs and Princes, whose lavish Government preys upon all Burgers and Peasants, and lays upon the Merchant the intolerable Burdens formerly mentioned, without toleration of Religion, save only in *Poland*. And that in all the Republicks on the *Eastern* Sea, and Land-Cities, all Strangers were, by the Monopolies of the Burgership, and Guilds, excluded from Traffick, from being Owners of Ships, and medling in Manufactures, and besides they tolerated but one Religion. So that at the beginning of the Troubles especially, there being no such apparent Monarchical Government in *Holland*, but the shadow of Liberty, the Prince of *Orange* and his Favourites, to encrease his Party, and make them adhere more close to him, continually boasted that he had no other intent but to defend the common Freedom, and to increase it in these Countrys. And indeed there being at that time in *Holland* freedom of Religion, Burgership, and Guilds, with small Charge of Convoy and Customs applicable to the clearing of the Seas, which were then very little infested, it is no wonder that Traffick and Navigation settled here.

For it is evident, that all the forementioned Vexations, &c. that violent Oppression of the lawful Government, and all those Taxes with which the common Inhabitants are now burden'd, were introduced gradually, and

from

from Year to Year encreased, so that they were heaviest in the Year 1650, in a profound Peace, and likely to continue so for ever, when the Captain-General openly set himself against his lawful Sovereign, and not only impiously trampled upon his Masters that payed him his Wages, but also upon the sacred Rights of the People, and their Representatives, six of whom from the Cities of *Dort, Haerlem, Delft, Horne,* and *Medemblick,* legally appearing at the Assembly of the States of *Holland* and *West-Friesland,* his Sovereign, he dared to imprison, only for having the Courage to refuse to keep on foot some Taxes for maintenance of the Soldiery, which said Representatives he released not till they had renounced all Government in *Holland:* so that every one might see what a terrible thing a Tyrannical Monarch, Prince during Life, or Stadtholder was in *Holland,* and how little appearance there was, that the Inhabitants of the Country should ever be eased of their Taxes.

See the Deduction, Part 2. Chap. 1. §. 22.

Secondly, As to the Captains General, or Stadtholders in particular, I say, seeing these Lands under our first Captain-General, Prince *William* of *Orange,* who was a prudent Lord, were oblig'd to make War against their own puissant Prince, who was irreconcilable to the Captain-General, he was in no Condition of saving either his own Life or Estate, but by promoting the Prosperity of these small Countries as far as he was able, in order to keep his footing in them. For in case the said General had in those days not been careful to gain the good Will and Affection of the Rulers and Inhabitants, by providing for their u-

We ought to consider when the Captains General, or Stadtholders have done good or harm.

And first as to Pr. William, who placed his Safety in some measure in Holland's Prosperity.

niversal

versal Welfare and Preservation, he had certainly run the risk, which might have ensued upon the People's making their Peace with their Sovereign, which how advantageous soever the Terms might have been for the Captain-General, yet it would necessarily have drawn on his Ruin sooner or later.

Our Second Captain-General, the Earl of *Leicester*, proved so detrimental to us during his two Years Government, that if he had not stood in awe of the States of *Holland* and *Zealand*, who were still obeyed by Prince *William*'s Lieutenant, the Count of *Hohenlo*, and had he not been afraid of the Army, most of whom were *English*, and dreaded Q. *Elizabeth* of *England*, he would certainly, by continuing such Maxims, have driven away our Trade and Republican Government, and ruin'd the whole Country.

As to our third Captain-General, Prince *Maurice*, 'tis confess'd, that in the 18th year of his Age, when he became Stadtholder of *Holland* and *Zealand*, by the Conduct chiefly of *Barnevelt*, Grand Pensioner, and because in his Youth he followed that Gentleman's grave Advice, and obey'd his Masters the States, he did them great Service, and help'd to conquer many of the Enemies Cities in a little time, and with small Expence: But it is no less true, that the said Prince, especially after the Year 1600, being 32 Years of Age, and following no longer the Command of the States, nor the Counsel of the said *Barnevelt* of honourable Memory, but his own Maxims, or those of Count *William*, he was hardly able, with much greater Expence, to keep what he had gotten

At

At least, as soon as the said Prince conceiv'd that the Countrys under him could subsist against the King of *Spain*, he not only neglected, but opposed and withstood the Welfare of the Country, thinking thereby to increase his own. Thus did he set himself so violently against the Truce with *Spain*, that in the Year 1608 he wrote to the particular Cities and Members of the Government of *Holland*, and to *Henry* the 4th of *France*, contrary to the Laws and Order of the Government, to perswade them and him against the Treaty for a Truce; yea, and threatned to continue the War against the King of *Spain*, tho he should have no Assistance but that of *Zealand* only. Nor could the said Truce be concluded till Arch-Duke *Albert* had first promised to pay him or his Heirs the Sum of three hundred thousand Guilders, to take him off from his unrighteous Designs, or from his unjust Pretensions, as the Ambassador *Jeanin* wrote to *Henry* IV. and that the States of these *United Provinces* had moreover engaged to continue him, during the Suspension of Arms, as they did formerly in the War, in all his military Offices, and other Advantages which he receiv'd by the occasion of the War, and likewise in all his Annual ordinary and extraordinary Salaries or Entertainments; and moreover presented him with a yearly Hereditary Revenue of twenty five thousand Guilders, which at twenty Years Purchase would be five hundred thousand Guilders (See the Negotiations of *Jeanin*, who as Ambassador of *France*, was Mediator in that Treaty of Truce) And which is more, the said Captain-General prosecuting severely

But grown older, and following bad Counsel, did afterwards much harm.

See Negotiat. de Jeanin.

by several Persons under pretext of establishing the true Religion, the most zealous lovers of *Holland*'s Welfare were forcibly turn'd out of the Government, imprisoned, and slaughtered, and many Inhabitants driven out of the Country.

In the time of the 4th Captain-General or Stadtholder, the Reader is desired maturely to consider, whether for twenty Years together the clearing of the Seas, in as much as it concerned the Fisheries, Manufactures, Traffick and Navigation of *Holland*, was not designedly neglected, and therefore whilst the *Dunkirkers* were very strong, and did us much damage by Sea, those Monies were withdrawn from the Admiralties of *Holland*, which were necessarily designed for scouring the Seas, and levied for that end on Goods imported and exported. And moreover, we have seen those manifold Imposts raised, all the Forces of the Land made use of, and also incredible Sums of Money taken up at Interest, to make Conquests as advantageous for the Captain-General, as ever they were hurtful and chargeable for *Holland*. And how little the Captain General, or he who, in respect of his great Age and Unfitness, had then the Administration, and really ruled in his stead, was inclined to this present Peace with *Spain*, appears by this, that in the Year 1646, the 25th of *August*, Monsieur *Knuit* made a Report to the Prince, and assured him, That he had covenanted at *Munster* for his own or his Lady's particular Satisfaction, to have the value of upwards of five Millions of Guilders. Which if true, we may perceive that in the said private Treaty of Peace by the Prince of *Orange*, his Pretentensions that were annihilated at the Charge of the King of *Spain*, served only for a Cloke to his frivolous Actions, that under pretext of a Treaty he might gain the Lordships of *Montfort*, *Sevenbergen* and *Turnhout*, with the Castle called *Bant* of *Schoenvroek*, as likewise a yearly Increase of Revenue of more Lordships, to a very considerable Sum.

Making clandestine Covenants of several Lordships for himself,

And how much the exchanging of some meaner Lordships belonging to the Prince of *Orange*, has tended by a fair Pretext to gain the mighty strong City and Marquisate of *Bergen op Zoom*, may be guessed, if it be observed that the Countess of *Hohensolern*, being unwilling to quit her Right to the Marquisate, and he in the mean while dying, the Executors of the succeeding, and now reigning Prince of *Orange*, in *October* 1651, adjusted with the King of *Spain* upon that Point, *viz.* that the Prince of *Orange* should continue in possession of all those Lordships which by exchange were covenanted to him, and moreover should receive in Mony the Sum of two hundred thousand Guilders, and 5 Months after the signing of the Covenant, three hundred thousand Guilders more: And lastly, besides these five hundred thousand Guilders, a yearly Rent of eighty thousand Guilders for twenty Years to come. So that it seems by this covenanted Exchange of some Lordships against the Marquisate of *Bergen* alone, the said Prince should receive the Value of twenty one hundred thousand Guilders.

And therefore it is evident, that the King of *Spain* has been oblig'd to do much to move the Prince in particular to agree to this present Peace; which for many Years has been

Of the King of Spain's.

been so frequently offered to *Holland* by the King, and was so necessary for us: As those continual and extraordinary Robberys of the *Dunkirkers*, and the taking of our Fishermen in great numbers, and our exhausted and indebted Treasury do at this day testify. But if nevertheless it should be objected, that it is lawful and commendable for any Man, and consequently for the Prince of *Orange*, to obstruct a Peace which would be disadvantageous to himself, and afterwards during the Treaty of *Munster*, privately to covenant with the Enemy of this State for his particular Profit, to obtain as much as possibly he could; I desire it may be observed, that the States of *Holland* and *Westfriezland* will give quite another construction of this affair, viz.

"That when Monsieur *Knuyt*, Plenipotentiary of this State, at the Treaty of *Munster*, by command and instruction of the Prince of *Orange*, of Laudable Memory, without the knowledg of the State, managed and concluded the forementioned Treaty, he was nevertheless bound up to the Instructions agreed on for him, and the other Plenipotentiarys of this State upon the 28th of *October* 1645, viz. That no secret Instruction, without the previous knowledg of the States of the respective Provinces, should either be given, or sent to the Ambassadors Extraordinary, and Plenipotentiarys. And in case either of the Provinces, or any other Person, should beyond expectation attempt or endeavour such a thing, They the Ambassadors Extraordinary, and Plenipotentiarys, shall not receive, but forthwith reject it, and "give

"give immediate notice thereof to the States
"General. And that the said Monsieur
"Knuyt in pursuance of the 91st Article of
"the forementioned Instructions, had so-
"lemnly sworn thereunto. Whereunto the
said States of *Holland* and *West-Friesland*
in the 9th Chapter do add.

"§. 8. That the States and the respective
"Provinces, were certainly well informed,
"what great care and vigilancy hath been
"us'd on behalf of the State, that in all Places,
"none excepted, comprehended in the
"Treaty of Peace to be made with the King
"of *Spain*, it should be covenanted, That
"the Sovereign and ofel in Matters of Reli-
"gion should remain in the States, and by
"what serious and express Orders the fore-
"said Intention of the State was recommend-
"ed to the said Ambassadors Extraordinary,
"and Plenipotentiarys, and consequently
"to Monsieur *Knuyt*. Nevertheless the
"States, and the respective Provinces do
"find in the foresaid Treaty of the 8th of
"*January* 1647, That the said Monsieur
"*Knuyt* in the Name of his said Highness,
"did express, grant and agree, That in all
"Places which by the said Treaty were con-
"ceded and granted, either to his said High-
"ness, or to his said Lady the Princess of
"*Orange*, the *Roman* Catholick Religion
"should be maintained, as the same was at
"the time of concluding of the foresaid
"Treaty, and also the Spiritual Persons
"should be maintain'd in their Estates,
"Functions, free Exercises, and Immuni-
"ties.

For the magnifying of himself to the detriment of the United Netherlands, especially of Holland, it was carry'd on and effected.

"§ 9.

"§ 9. So that in regard of the City of Se- (which goes only over and above the other Places in the foresaid Treaty mentioned) the said City being within the Province of Holland, and lying under the Sovereign command of those States, there was granted much more to the King of *Spain*, than was made over by the Act of Seclusion to the said Lord Protector.

"§ 10. It is unquestionable that the most valuable Effect of the Sovereignty consists in the free disposal of Matters of Religion, which by the said Treaty, as far as it is therein specified, is quitted, and yielded up to the King of *Spain*.

"§ 11. Besides, the aforesaid Resignation is made by, and on behalf of them who have no disposal thereof at all. So that the foresaid Contractors did as much as in them lay clandestinely, to deprive the States of so sensible a share of their Sovereignty.

"§ 13. That tho the States being afterwards inform'd of the Contents of the said particular Treaty, did expresly declare, that they would not be subject to the said intolerable Stipulation, in respect of the practice of the said Religion in *Sevenbergen*; yet they afterwards fell into many Inconveniences by that means.

And lastly, the said States of *Holland* and West-Friesland do say:

"§ 15. That so notable a part of their Sovereignty and Right as the free disposal of Matters of Religion within their Dominions without their knowledg, by him who had not the least Power or Qualification

" to grant it, was without any apparent
" Cause yielded to the King of *Spain*.

So that it doth unanswerably appear, that our Captain General and Stadtholder, his Secret Treaty was concluded for his private Benefit, and to the prejudice of *Holland* and the Peace thereof.

Yea, after the last Captain-General had in a full Peace seized and imprisoned six Deputys of *Holland* assembled upon Summons at the *Hague*, because according to their Duty they had dared to refuse the payment of some Companys of Soldiers, and to resolve to disband them as far as concerned the Province of *Holland*, he miscarried in the Design of seizing our Principal City by surprize. So that if he had not died about three weeks after, we should in a few Years have seen that *Holland*, and *Amsterdam* first of all, would have lost all their Traffick, by contending against their own Governour and Captain-General, or would have been compelled to submit to his Yoke; as formerly *Flanders*, *Bruges*, *Brabant* and *Antwerp* were bereft of their Traffick by the Quarrels between them and the Arch-Duke *Maximilian*, and King *Philip*

'Tis well known that the ruin of Holland was design'd by our last Stadtholder.

For tho our said Captain-General's attempt on *Amsterdam* succeeded not, yet all the flourishing Citys of *Holland* that were unarm'd, and much more those many Citys which had Garisons mostly of Foreign Soldiery at his command, would have been forced eternally to have submitted to his Monarchical Yoke, if his unexpected Death had not delivered them from that Slavery.

He

Deduct
1654. P.
&c. 2 § 13,
&c.

He that doubts of this, let him hear the States of *Holland* and *West-Friesland*, as speaking of this Matter to them Also. "But especially let the said Provinces please to remember what happened in the Year 1650. within our own Bed. Did not in the same Year the Rulers of the City of *Amsterdam*, to prevent greater Evils, grant by Capitulation to his Highness Prince *William*, of immortal Memory, Father of the present Prince of *Orange*, That the *Huick Hoefts*, and *Cornelis Bikkers* should quit their Offices of Burgemasters, and Counsellors, and become private Men, and never be readmitted into the Government? And were not the Citys of *Dort*, *Haerlem*,

Pred. and examp. y. in Holland

Delf, *Horn*, and *Medenblick*, because of some honest Regents, or Magistrates in their Citys, compelled afterwards to do the like? Altho God Almighty so ordered Matters by his Providence, that some few days after the same Persons were restored to their former Dignitys. Those were the true Tokens of an usurped Power, and so much the more intolerable, because he to whom such Conditions were granted, was by the Nature and Virtue of his Commission, and likewise by his Oath therewith taken, only a Subject of that Body, whose Members he thus endeavoured to bring under subjection. It was then indeed the true time for unfeigned Patriots, and true lovers of Liberty to appear upon the Stage, and with Heart and Hand to make head against such Usurpation. But what Zeal did the foresaid Provinces then exert? Were not they the Men, who on *June* 5. of the
"fore-

"foresaid Year 1650, granted that Autho-
"rity to be lawful, at least so far, that un-
"der pretext thereof the said Prince of
"*Orange* undertook those Actions? And
"were not they also the Men who after-
"wards, when those Actions were in part
"executed, did by special Resolution or
"Letters Missive declare, that they judged
"the Resolution aforesaid of the 5th of *June*
"1650 to be applicable thereunto And
"who in pursuance thereof expresly avowed,
"approved, and commended the foresaid
"Actions; yea even thanked his Highness
"for it, and besought him (tho 'tis scarcely
"to be believed) to persevere in such a lau-
"dible Zeal?

All which being true, and the Rulers of the other Provinces, who ought to have offered their helping hand to *Holland* against these violent Oppressions, having on the contrary either of necessity or willingly flattered the Prince in this, and sought to bring our Province to a greater Thraldom No rational Man could have expected but that Traffick and Navigation, &c. would have had its overthrow here, as in other Monarchical Countrys, and that consequently all the Inhabitants of *Holland* in a few Years would necessarily have sunk into unexpressible Misery.

And had the Thanks of the other Provinces for it.

G g   CHAP.

CHAP. V.

The Reason why the General Liberty in Holland could cause no more benefit, since the Death of the Prince of Orange, then the Stadtholder of Holland and Captain General during Life.

BUT it may be objected, That God hath given us Peace with Spain, and snatch'd away our Captain-General and Stadtholder, without leaving one of Age enough to be his Successor, which seem to be the two most desirable things that the Inhabitants of Holland could wish for, seeing they are thereby become a People totally Free, subject to none of what Quality soever, but only to Reason, and to the Laws of their own Country, that can only be governed by the Interest of their own Province and Cities. And yet for all this we can see no alteration, but only in this, that the Lives, Estates, and Reputation of the Inhabitants do not depend upon one Man's Will, and that the Cities cannot by their Soldiery suddenly be surpriz'd. So that the Rulers, and Ministers of the Republick of Holland, West-Friesland, as well as those of the particular Cities, are now, in as much as concerns every Man's Person and Transactions, liable only to the Laws and Constitution of the Republick, and the Cities thereof; and being absolutely their own Masters, they need fear no more by ruling well to offend a State's Head, and consequently to lose their Authority, Life, and Estate for so doing,

In answer to this I must acknowledg, that he much wish'd for Accident aforesaid hath not hitherto produced such wholesom Fruits as might rationally have been expected, especially since hitherto there hath been no ease given to the People from such heavy Taxes and Impositions. But when the reason of it is rightly scann'd, we shall find the Cause is not to be imputed to the present free Rulers, but to the former Usurpation of the Stadtholders, Governors, and Captains General, together with the remaining Disorders that had their rise from thence. Yea, it is to be admired, that Matters in the present Conjuncture are already brought to so good a condition. For when the known and evident Causes of what is before expressed are looked into and enumerated, every one may soon perceive these four good Effects.

Why there was no easing of the Imposts.

In the *first* place, That at the time of the death of the last Stadtholder and Captain General, the Province of *Holland* being of so small a Compass, and so poor in Treasure as is before expressed, was left charged with so dreadful a capital Debt upon Interest, and such an excessive number of daily incident Debts, that it will not be believed by other Nations, nor possibly by our Successors in *Holland*, that so small a Province could subsist under such great and heavy Taxes; and that the Inhabitants thereof could bear, not only the Annual Interests of such an immense Sum, but so many Taxes besides for the defence of themselves and their Allys: It being remonstrated by the States of that Province to Prince *William*, a little before his Death, and also afterwards for Justification of their Pro-

ceedings,

...ceedings, Anno 1650. That the Province of *H...* was then charged with Mony taken up at Interest, amounting to the Sum of one hundred and forty Millions of Guilders, besides other Debts amounting to thirteen Millions.

...ly, That the good Inhabitants of the ...d Province driving their Trade to the *Le...* ...bout the same time, and especially in the Years 1650, and 1651, were by the *French* ... extremely en... ...that a part only of ... as much as the Merchants ... by Publick Command ...ght in, amounted to above one hundred ... of Gold, or ten Millions of Guilders.

...ly, That this State in the Year 1652, fell into and continued in open War with the E... and 1654, which occasioned a ...decay of Trade, and many great Losses to the Traders of the said Province.

...ly, The Eastern Wars soon after happened between the Kings of Sweden and *Denmark*, ...this State became engaged in it as Auxiliaries. All which must be acknowledged by ...one for Reasons of what I said before, but the right Grounds and true Causes are ...inquired into but by very few, and therefore are look'd upon by many as the Effects of the present Government. I have therefore thought it necessary to shew, to the best of my knowledge, how those things came ...

As for Secondly the one hundred and forty Millions of Guilders, with the other ...charged Debts aforementioned; it is
well

well known, and easy to be comprehended, but that Debt was forcibly occasioned by the Captain-General and his Flatterers, the said immense Sums being wasted to promote his Ambition and Glory, by having great Armys in the Field and undertaking great Sieges to take such Citys, as at this day tend to the heavy burdening of *Holland*. And that which is most to be bewailed was, That the Frontier Citys were intrusted to the sole command of the Captain-General, who placed therein Governors and Garisons, so that they served only for so many Citadels to hold poor *Holland* in Fetters. And we have often with grief been forced to see, that whilst so many Millions were sacrificed by Land to the Ambition of the Captain-General, the necessary Defence of Navigation and Commerce, must depend upon the Revenue of the Convoys and Customs, which are received only of the Merchant, and sometimes a part of the said Mony too was diverted to carry on the War by Land.

I know very well, that this way of management was not afterwards discommended, because many of our Inhabitants had the good Fortune not to be damnified by Losses at Sea, and the ill Conduct of the *West India* Company, whereof mention is made in the first Chapter of the Second Part of this Book; so that they fared at least as well or better than at present, and found there was then Mony to be got. Besides, those manifold destructive Wars which hapned in most of the neighbouring as well as remote Countrys, inclin'd many rich Fugitives to settle in *Holland*. But I wish those poor People would have

Our former Capt Generals, with their Defendants, th Cause of our decay'd Trations.

For the Sums justly paid in part for the Conquest of Citys.

And this but to keep Holland in slavery.

Which is illustrated by a Similitude, how much the Country under this free Government fares better than under the Stadtholders.

have a little foresight, they would then consider that it went with the Affairs of the Commonwealth, as I once remember it hapned in a certain Family that was blessed with a fair Estate. The Parents being dead, the Children were put under the Care of a lavish Guardian, who giving no Account, spent the Estate head over heels, and when there was no more Money in Cash, immediately took up a good sum upon Interest, at the Charge of the poor Orphans, so that not only the foresaid Children, but all the Children and Servants of the Neighbourhood liv'd most bravely, and had and did every thing that their Hearts could wish for. But it afterwards hapned, that the wasteful Guardian died, and the said Children fell under the care and tuition of the Chamber of Orphans, who kept a continual eye over them, and plac'd them under the daily care of an honest, diligent and sober Man, who regulated the House after a quite different manner, without any waste. So that whereas in the time of the foresaid Guardian, there was yearly more spent than the Revenue amounted to, and every time Mony taken up at Interest, the Revenue did afterwards considerably exceed the Expence, and the Surplus was laid out to pay off a part of the Debt which the former Guardian had contracted.

But then the Children murmured, saying, That their Condition was much impaired, that they had a pleasant Life under the former Guardian, and so did the Neighbours Children and Servants, they said they could enjoy themselves with delight in that Family under the former Guardian, but that it was

was now become a barren Place. But those poor Orphan little thought, that in case the former Management had lasted longer, it would have proved fatal to them in their riper Years. And we poor simple *Hollanders*, who may with reason be called Orphans, how long shall we remain in our Childhood and Minority, not observing that the Plenty we then were sensible of, proceeded from the ill Husbandry of a prodigal Guardian or Steward, which hath run us in Debt as aforesaid? At least we ought to conceive, that we must still be taxed and fleec'd to pay off the Interests of that great Sum, which Taxes alone under our present Governors, would defray the whole Charge of the Government. So that all that we must now pay for our Subsistance and Defence, and which lies so heavy upon us, must be look'd upon as the bitter Fruits of that Tree of Wantonness which that lavish Guardian hath planted among us, and which we silly Children danc'd about with so much delight, and our Neighbours Children of *Guelderland, Utrecht, Over-Yssel,* and others, to whom Plenty was no Burden, and our hired Soldiers, with whole Regiments of *French, English, Scots,* and *Walloons,* who lived in our Family, were very well pleased with that kind of Life, and it makes their Hearts to rejoice when they talk of reviving those Times. It is good cutting large Thongs out of another Man's Hide. But that we *Hollanders* should be so stupid as not to perceive that the present Government is our Safety, and that the former would infallibly have procured our Ruin, is indeed not to be comprehended.

As to the Second Cause, viz. the Depredations committed in the *Mediterranean* Seas, and thereabouts. It is first apparent, that seeing all the Wealth of *Holland*, as well the said borrowed Capital Sum, as that which is squeezed out of the Sweat and Blood of the good Inhabitants of the said Province, was sacrificed to the Ambition of the Captain-General, and by his Neglect of a vigorous Defence by Sea, there was a fair and open Field given to all Nations greedy of Prey, to set out Men of War against our rich Laden Ships. Who knows not that the greatest inticement to Evil is the hopes of Impunity? He that will always be a Sheep, must expect to be eaten of the Wolf at last. To which is to be added, that under pretext of a Peace concluded with *Spain*, as if there were no more People in the World, and as if all coveting of one anothers Goods would have thereby ceased, the Captain General by his Creatures, and Flatterers, had so subtly contrived Matters, that several of our Ships of War were sold, and thereby we were left naked of our necessary Defence by Sea. Our honest and most provident Rulers could the less oppose it, because there was another Mischief impending over them by the Captain-General, *viz.* That as soon as he (who then spent his time chiefly in Hunting, Hawking, Tennis playing, Dancing, Comedies, and other more infamous Debaucherys) should begin to apply himself to Affairs of State, he would imploy the remaining Naval Power of the Land against the Government of *England* for the advancing the Interests of his own Family, but certainly to the

oppres-

oppression of all the Inhabitants of *Holland*, especially of the Trading part.

Upon which it also followed, that some of our Ships which were thus sold, became the Chief of the foresaid *Corsairs* against us: Which brings to my remembrance, that which was publickly spoken in the Year 1651, and probably very true, *viz.* That the aforesaid Depredations, and others were to be made by Shipping that were to sail out of the *Sorlings* (or Islands of *Scilly*) and elsewhere by our Captain-General's appointment, and that some of the Earwigs of that young Prince had perswaded him, that robbing at Sea was the surest, yea the only expedient to bring the *Amsterdammers*, with whom he had been for some time before his death at great variance, to his Lure or Devotion: It being accounted a sure Maxim among such great Persons to weaken and ruin all great and strong Citys which may oppose their designs; yea, and when private Methods are wanting, to make use of open Violence for that end: as all Historys and Examples, both Antient and Modern, do clearly testify. And that Consideration alone ought to be sufficient for us *Hollanders* (whose Welfare entirely consists in flourishing, mercantile, and populous Citys) to take a firm resolution, never to put our selves under a perpetual Chief Head, by what Name or Title soever, and to persist therein immutably. *That the Pirats might bring Holland, and especially Amsterdam, to be divided and weakned.*

To the 3*d* Cause, *viz.* the War against *England*; I may well say, and that truly, that we have suffered that for the sake of the House of *Orange*. For those of the Parliament of *England* having cut off the Head of their own *The War with England was brought upon us for the sake of the House of Orange.*

own good King, and being therefore exceedingly hated by all the Monarchs in the World, and likely, in all human appearance to be called to account and punished for it by Neighbouring Princes, lest such a Crime remaining unrevenged, their own Subjects might be thereby excited to act the same thing against them. They therefore found themselves under a necessity to seek the Friendship of this State; and for that end, soon after the death of the Prince of *Orange*, they sent a considerable Embassy hither, without shewing the like Honour to any other Potentate or State in the World.

I shall not use much trouble in shewing that they offered to settle a Friendship between both Nations; it shall be sufficient to observe, That the said *English* Commissioners earnestly sollicited the States General to renew that most important Treaty of late course made between both Nations, *&c.* consider it as Treaty of amity, and have before amply proved it, That it is wholly unadvisable for this State to enter into any other League with *England*, yet by renewing the said Treaty, we should not only have settled a Friendship, but also at the same time have established our Commerce and Fishery, as to which the Articles of the said Treaty (especially in regard of the Fishery) are expressed in the most desirable terms. Yet those that accounted themselves bound as Slaves to the House of *Orange*, did not only oppose the concluding of the foresaid desirable Treaty, but also sent away those Ambassadors with a manner of reproach and dishonour. *And*, by opposing them in the publick Deliberations of the State against the progress

progress of the said Treaty, especially by framing delays, alledging that we first ought to see the issue of the Designs of the present King of *Great Britain* (then declared King in *Scotland*) and on the other side exciting the Rabble against the Persons of the said Ambassadors to such a degree, that the States of *Holland* perceiving the aversion, and daily threats that were uttered against their Persons, were necessitated, for preventing of greater Mischief, to appoint a *Corps de Guarde* to be erected before their House, to secure them from the like mischief which befel Dr. *Dorislaus*, Envoy from the said Parliament, at the Swan Inn in the *Hague*. *Which the States of Holland were willing, but not able to prevent.*

What aversion such Proceedings might have caused in the said Ambassadors, is easy to be apprehended, as it also followed, who having observed after they had stayed here a considerable time, that the Zeal of the honest and upright Governours, especially in the Province of *Holland* and *Zealand*, was not able to ballance the Faction of *Orange*, they returned in great discontent to *England*; one of them, viz. Mr. St. *John* (upon taking his leave) told the States Commissioners: *On which those Ambassadors parted discontented.* "My Lords, you have your eye upon "the Issue of the Affairs of the King of *Scot-* "*land*, and therefore have despised the "Friendship we have profered you; I will "assure you, that many in the Parliament were "of Opinion, that we ought not to have "come hither, or to have sent any Ambassa- "dor till we had first overcome our difficultys, "and seen an Ambassador from you. I now "see my Fault, and perceive very well that "those Members of Parliament judged right; *One of whom predicted, that we should repent to have rejected the Friendship of England.*

"you

"you will in a little time see our Affairs
"against the King of S—— and dispatched, and
"then you will by your Ambassadors come
"and desire what we now so cordially come
"to proffer. But ——e your selves, you will
"t—— re——ent you have rejected our Kindness.
Would to God that Experience had not verified the foresaid Discourse to our great Loss. For the King of S——'s Affairs being determined by a Battel, and a War with this State following upon it, the Wounds and Losses occasioned by that War effectually brought to pass the Repentance aforesaid, but —————————————. It's in vain to shut the Well's Mouth, when the Calf is drowned.

This is the true Reason of that lamentable War, to which may be added the intolerable Fervour of that Nation, their continual jealousy of our flourishing Traffick, and the innate hatred of Cromwel against the Prince of Orange, as a Sister's Son of that King, whom of all the World he had most reason to dread. So that every one may easily imagine what pains and care it hath cost our honest Rulers to regain a Peace with that Nation.

Lastly, As to the Fourth Point, viz. that of the E———— War. It is certain in case this State had had the good Fortune to have framed its Constitutions according to its true Interest, without having in their Breasts the same Evil which had occasioned the War with England, the growing Flames in all probability might easily have been quenched at the beginning, at least in all Events the War between Sweden and Denmark had certainly been prevented;

ed, but it is to be lamented, that all the Deliberations that hapned in the Government were travers'd and thwarted by the fluctuating and changeable Humour and Interest of the Elector of *Brandenburg*, only becauſe that Prince was related to the Houſe of *Orange* by Marriage, and acted a conſiderable, but a very ſtrange part in that Tragedy.

The D. of Brandenburg, and thoſe that were ſlaviſhly inclin'd to the Prince, wheedl'd Holland into it.

For at the beginning, when the King of *Sweden* was preparing his Attempt againſt *Poland*, the Duke of *Brandenburg* oppoſed it with a more than ordinary Animoſity; and accordingly ſeeking to ſtrengthen himſelf by Friends and Alliances, thoſe that were inclined to the Houſe of *Orange* here, were able to effect ſo much, that the States obliged themſelves firmly by a Treaty of the 27th of *July* 1655, to defend the ſaid Elector againſt the foreſaid King of *Sweden*, having after a few days deliberation undertook the Guaranty of the Electoral *Pruſſia*, a Point, which ever till then (tho it was uncertain whether there would have been any Attack to be feared about it in a long time) was looked upon to be of ſo great Weight and Importance, that for that Reaſon only, the Alliance profered by the ſaid Elector for divers years together with ſuch a Clauſe of Guaranty, never took effect. The States by this means being viſibly left out of the Neutrality, could be no effectual Mediators to end the War between *Poland* and *Sweden*, which by their Interpoſition and Direction had ever been formerly accommodated.

Firſt cauſing us to enter into an Alliance with the D of Brandenburg.

But it ſoon appeared that we were not a little miſtaken; for after the ſaid Duke began to enjoy the effect of the foreſaid Treaty, eſpe-

Who having rec iv'd a good Sum of it, got out of that Alliance, and took part with the Swede.

especially after he had received a good Sum of the promised Subsidies, he suddenly and without the privity of this State, joined with the King of Sweden, cast off the Oath of Vassalage he had sworn to the King of Poland, expresly renounced the foresaid Alliance with us, and soon after, joining his Forces with those of the King of Sweden, gave the Polish Army Battel near Warsaw.

It is true, this Action being in it self odious, and extremely contrary to the Genius of our Nation, raised in them so very great an aversion to this Elector, that the best affected to the House of Orange were for a long time ashamed openly to patronize the Interests of his Electoral Highness, by which it happened that the Faithful Rulers, taking to heart the true Interest of this State beyond all others, their wholesom Advices took place afterwards so much the better.

And accordingly with great Prudence, and upon right Maxims for a Country subsisting by Trade, that Treaty was carried on with Sweden on the 11th of September 1656, at Elbing in Prussia, between the Ambassadors of this State, and Commissioners of the King of Sweden, whereby it was firmly agreed, that seeing the Swedes had for some Years raised the Customs excessively high over their whole Country, and especially had charged the inhabitants of these Netherlands to pay more than their own Subjects, Therefore for redress thereof the Customs and other Taxes under the Power of the Swede, as well without as within the Kingdom, should be brought to the same Rate they were at about the Year 1640.

In the Second place, that in case of the raising of Customs, and new Taxes, the Inhabitants of these *United Provinces* shall be no higher or more charged than the *Swedes* themselves: So that as to that Point, there shall be kept a perfect Equality in all things between both Nations. *And no higher than the Swede himself pays.*

Thirdly, That the Inhabitants of these *Netherlands* in all places under the *Swedes* Command, as well in regard of Customs, as to all other Advantages, none excepted, shall be treated as well as any other Nation shall be treated by the *Swede*. *And as long as any Strangers pay, including all other Lands where we are concern'd.*

Fourthly, That all those on whose Preservation and Peace this State, and the Commerce of its Inhabitants, is especially concerned, as among others principally the King of *Denmark* and his Kingdoms, the Elector of *Brandenburg* and his Dominions, as also the City of *Dantzick*, and all Places belonging to them, be comprehended in the foresaid Treaty, with an express Covenant, that neither the King of *Sweden*, nor his Subjects and Inhabitants, directly nor indirectly, shall give them any molestation, or hindrance in their Traffick, much less make War against them. *Whereby much harm would have been prevented.*

Would to God, that these Affairs so well commenced had been pursued to perfection! Then should the King of *Denmark* at this day have been Master of the Province of *Schonen*, and other Countries which were taken from him, and the good Inhabitants of *Holland* have been in possession of many Millions, which in the last War were consumed on behalf of the Publick, and lost by private Persons at Sea.

But

But altho a Treaty concluded by those that are imployed and duly authorized, ought to be ratified by those who give such full Powers under their Hands and Seals, yet after the conclusion of the said Treaty, there was such a Fluctuation of humours that it could not be ratified here. I cannot with truth affirm that the Province of *Holland* was altogether blameless in this Matter, but what Authority was made use of underhand, the Sequel plainly discovered. For when the good King of *Denmark* being privatly excited to it, had put on his like Armour, and drawn the King of *Sweden* that way, then did the Elector of *Brandenburg* effectually shew what that Occasion was worth to him: for as soon as the King of *Swed.* had turned his Back upon *Fridland Prussia* he made no more scruple again to break the Covenant of Vassalage he had made with *Sweden*, than he formerly made conscience of solemnly renouncing the Alliance he had made with this State, and accordingly by that opportunity entred into a new Treaty with the King of *Poland*, and covenanted to have the Sovereignty of the Ducal *Prussia*, which he formerly held of that King in Fee, with other Advantages that are not necessary here to enumerate.

But since by not ratifying the Treaty of *Elbing*, we helpd the King of *Denmark* to put on his Armour to so little purpose, and procured those notable Advantages to the Elector of *Brandenburg*, the Kingdom of *Denmark* (God amend it) hath cost us dear enough. But that which most troubled us, was, that the said Elector again arming himself against the *Swede* and this State, being

in

in manner beforementioned drawn into the War between *Sweden* and *Denmark*, the Interest of *Brandenburg* was so powerful, that it was impossible for us afterwards either to get out of that War, or to put an end to it, till not only *Brandenburg*, but *Poland*, and the whole House of *Austria*, to whom the Elector of *Brandenburg* had obliged himself to make no Peace without them, had first concluded their Treaty, and had obtained their ends by the Arms of this State. So that for the Interest of *Brandenburg* we were just at the Point of falling into a War with *France*, *England* and *Sweden* all at once, and consequently of fixing our selves to the Party of *Austria* and *Spain*, which would have tended to our utmost Ruin. From which being at last delivered by the sage Direction and Management of the Faithful Rulers of *Holland*, tho not without their signal and personal danger, we have great cause to be highly thankful to God for it.

Who to please Brandenburg have been in the utmost danger.

CHAP. VI.

What good Fruits the beginnings of a Free Government have already produced, from the Death of the last Stadtholder and Captain-General, to the Year 1662.

AND now that I may more fully shew, that notwithstanding the sad Effects of the Relicks of the former Stadtholders, Governors and Captain-Generals; yet that our Affairs since the Death of the last, are by the

Notwithstanding the foresaid remainders of the Stadtholders Government it is evident,

H h   pru-

prudent Management and Zeal of our Faithful Rulers, brought very far on towards the Welfare of these Provinces. And first, as an eminent token of it, it is worthy observation, That not only a vigorous opposition is made against that ruinous Course of taking up excessive Sums continually upon Interest, but that in the Year 1655, by the Zeal of our good Rulers, an Expedient was found to discharge the said Province of the one hundred and forty Millions of Guilders, viz. by reducing the yearly Interest of the said Sum from the 20th to the 25th Penny, or from 5 to 4 per Cent. and employing the yearly Advance of it towards discharging those Sums. Which Advance increasing yearly, that formidable Sum of 140 Millions will in Twenty one Years (whereof a sixth part is now expired) under God's Blessing be totally discharged.

But that which is most to be gloried in is, That tho the greatest part of the Regents of that Province have lent a considerable part of their Estates to Holland and West-Friesland, nevertheless the consideration of their own Profit did not hinder them from cutting off a fifth part of their Revenue for the necessary Service of the Publick, and among others to so many thousand Merchants, Artizans, and others, who have no Estate in the hands of the Government at Interest: So is it also to be greatly lamented, that there are still Inhabitants of Holland, who either cannot or will not be sensible of the Benefit and Necessity of so doing. They ought in truth to consider that this Country is an Orphan, and that the Rulers being Guardians, they cannot with a good Conscience suffer Mony to run at so high

an

Ch 6. *Free Government in* Holland.

an Interest at the Charge of that Orphan, when the Credit of the said Orphan is so great, that he can take up Mony sufficient at 4 *per Cent.* and it would above all be inexcusable in the Guardians to keep their own Mony still at the Orphan's Charge, and require 5 *per Cent* for the same, when others, and perhaps the elder Brothers and Sisters of the Orphan, are ready to lend him their Mony at 4 *per Cent.* *And understand not that this Country's Guardians must give no higher Interest for the Orphans use, than for their own.*

But above all they ought to consider, that the Revenue of *Holland* in it self was of little or no value; and if it be now otherwise, it doth purely and merely depend on the Blessing of God upon its Commerce and Traffick; and that if any considerable diversion or diminution of it should happen, 'twere impossible to raise the seven Millions from it, which before the foresaid Reduction were yearly demanded by Petition for paiment of the foresaid one hundred and forty Millions, which by continuation of such an Oeconomy as was kept in the time of the Stadtholders and Captains-General, would in time have been so much increased, that at length it would have exceeded all the Revenue and Product of their Trade: And the neat Revenue of *Holland* being by this means brought to less than nothing, and its Credit thereby necessarily at a stand, the said Province must have sunk and come to nothing of a sudden. *Especially when the Revenue of Holland by those high Interests would have been swallow'd up.*

I can compare those People to nothing better than to a certain crack'd-brain'd Son of an industrious Husbandman, who seeing his Father once and again take a great Quantity of Corn out of his Barn, and carry it to his Land and scatter it upon the Earth, his crazy *How great the Fruits of this discharge of the Debts are, is set forth by a Similitude.*

Understanding began greatly to murmur, saying, That they had wont to take the Corn out of the Barn only by the handful, to bake Bread and Cakes, whereof he, his Brothers and Sisters were daily to eat, but by this way of taking so much together it would shrink and come to nothing; and that his Father ought not to have denied them their former Liberty. But that silly Fellow understood not that the Corn scattered upon the Land was in no wise wasted or destroyed, but sowed in the Earth in order to a great Increase the Year following, and that his Father had taken sufficient care to leave so much in the Barn as would bring the Year about without want. whereas if they had taken Corn out of that Barn from time to time for Bread and Cakes, without sowing any, it might indeed for some time have caused a merry Life, but the Event would have been sudden Misery and Famine. Even so those weak People perceive not that that which seems to be withheld from them or their Neighbours by the aforesaid Reduction, is by no means squandred away, but laid up as good Seed, to produce more Fruit from Year to Year, that it may, by the Blessing of God, be truly said to be only our Surplusage; and in case that be neglected, according to the fancy of such foolish Persons as aforesaid, and the Extremity be taken, we may for a time live in jollity, but at length the Burden of it would have ruin'd us all.

And further, to discover the difference between the present frugal and the former lavish Government, we may remember that in our time there was another Reduction made of Rents

Rents and Interests from 16 to 20, and from 6¼ to 5 *per Cent*. But the benefit of it presently dropt through our Fingers, even to the raising of more Horse and Foot, that were employed contrary to the desire of most of the honest Rulers of *Holland*, and to the great detriment of that Province sacrificed to the Ambition of the Captain-General; so that the foresaid Reduction may be truly said, not to have serv'd to the easing of the Country, but to a new and heavy taxing of the Commonalty.

Which under the Stadtholders was converted, to the levying of many needless Soldiers.

And had we then been so fortunate, that the good Rulers at that time had been able to have made use of the Advance of the foresaid Reduction (as they do now) for discharge of the capital Sum, and reducing the yearly Charge (with the Interest upon Interest) without running our selves again into new Negotiations to the prejudice of *Holland*. we should in lieu of being so vastly in Debt as at present, have been free and on even ground. And if therewith we can discharge our selves of seven Millions of yearly Imposts, and all Taxes on Consumption, which lie so heavy upon the Commonalty, and do so remarkably hinder the increase of our Trade and Commerce, and withal a good part of the Poundage upon Lands and Houses, and of the Customs and Convoys, and yet after that have a better and clearer Revenue than we have at present, besides the Benefit we should enjoy of having all Handycrafts-men, Manufacturers and Traders who would resort to us from other Countrys, under the Advantages of having the foresaid Taxes discharged: If this were, I say, so ordered, this State

Yet out of its profit, had it bin managed, Holland would now have been out of Debt.

And have subsisted without any Imposts on Consumption.

State would (humanely speaking) have been already, or at least in a few Years be the most Considerable, Puissant, and most Formidable Republick of the whole World.

And sure should certainly have possess'd and tasted that Prosperity, in case the former Government had had the freedom of making the best use of the Interest of *Holland*, so in all probability, we may yet injoy and be sensible of it in our own Persons, or at least our Children after us, if we do not shamefully suffer that Golden Liberty which is put into our hands by Heaven, to be pluck'd from us, and don't with the Sow return to the Mire. This certainly no generous *Hollander* can rightly consider, without being inflamed with an ardent Zeal to hazard his Estate and Life for the preservation of the present Government, and maintaining our true Liberty, and thereby to leave our Children at leastwise that Happiness and Success which we, in case our Predecessors could have effected that which in our Times (as aforesaid) is so commendably settled should now effectually enjoy.

Let none imagine that during the War with the King of *Spain*, it would have been impracticable to imploy the Advance of the foresaid Reduction to discharging part of the Moneys taken up at Interest, and to continue it till the whole were paid off, and the Country out of debt, seeing the contrary hath effectually appeared, that during the forementioned *English* War, where in proportion of time there was more than twice as much extraordinarily raised and paid by the Province of *Holland* as, since the foresaid first Reduction, ever hapned in the War with *Spain*;

Spain; yet the last Reduction from five to four in the Hundred, by the Care and Vigilance of the present Rulers, hath continued by the yearly Advance thereof, without any intermission or diversion, and is imployed for the discharge of the capital Debt.

In the next place we may observe, as a singular Effect of the present free Government, that by their Prudence and good Direction a good part of the supernumerary and useless Land-forces, and especially of the Foreign Soldiery, is reduced and discharged, to the ease of the Province of *Holland* in particular, of the Sum of near five hundred thousand Guilders *per Annum.* Concerning which it is specially to be noted, that the foresaid Reduction and Discharge was effected by the good Conduct of *Holland*, with the universal Satisfaction and Approbation of all the other Provinces. Whence therefore (by comparing it with what passed in the Year 1650) may be inferred, that the present time is much better than that, when our own Captain-General thrust his Sword into our Bowels, for no other Reason, but because the upright and faithful Rulers, according to Justice and Duty, did only disband and reduce some part of the said Forces for ease of the Country, and as preparatory to the necessary disburdening of the poor Commonalty.

The third fruit of this free Government is, A great part of the superfluous Soldiery, &c. is disbanded, whereby Holland saves yearly 500000 Guilders.

It is also at present firmly resolved for our Good, that the benefit of the said Reduction, as also that of Rents and Interests, shall be imployed for discharging that intolerable Burden which the Ambition of our Captain General laid upon our backs.

The Profit of which is converted to the discharge of Debts.

By this means the above levied capital Sums will be sooner paid by six Years than otherwise they could. So that now in that respect consequently a full fifth part of the time requisite for the paiment of the whole is expired, besides, that a part of the aforesaid one hundred and forty Millions, which were many Years since negotiated upon Rents for Life, and likewise a grow less every day, will infallibly expire in a few Years. So that we do visibly approach the Land of Promise, and if by reason of our unthankfulness, and murmuring against the Almighty, and against our Allies, he does not cast us back into the *Egyptian* Slavery, the remainder of the Journy through the Wilderness will foon be at an end.

Fourthly, Let us obferve, as another singular Effect of the present Free Government, That tho it was formerly judged and maintained by many, that it would be impossible, without Stadtholders or Governors of the Provinces, to compose and reconcile the Differences and Disputes of Province against Province, Quarters against Quarters, Citys against Citys, and Rulers in Citys with one another, which will infallibly arise from time to time; and that by this means the State for want of such Stadtholders and Governors, will ere long fall into great Dissensions and Civil Wars, and in time come to ruin, yet Experience hath taught us that on the contrary, the many and great Disputes and Differences that have broken out, and were mostly caused by the instigation of those that long after Slavery, have since the Death of the last Prince of *Orange* been laid down and appeased peafed with much better Order and Effect than formerly. Yea, and which is wonderful, almost all the foresaid Differences and Disputes were so well allayed, by the Authority and good Conduct of the lawful Government, that at one and the same time the differing Partys have found their satisfaction and contentment in laying them aside.

Whereas, on the other hand, we have formerly seen, that the Stadtholder irritated and stirred up such Differences, at least cherish'd them, when it was for his Interest and Advantage, and at last made the Partys who had most right, submit to the Sword, because he knew best how to arrive at his Ends by those who least regarded Right, and consequently made little Conscience, so they could please him in obstructing Justice, and the Welfare of the Land, it being the Maxim of all Great Persons, *Divide & impera*, for in troubled Waters they have best fishing.

Whereas on the other hand the Stadtholders caus'd many Differences, and generally wrong'd the Injur'd Partys.

If ever any Governour or Stadtholder, and his Adherents, had had such cause of Offence as was given to the Province of *Holland*, Anno 1650. and in case the same Stadtholder and his Adherents had had the same Power to revenge themselves as the States of *Holland* had after the death of the last Prince of *Orange*; who can doubt but their desire of Revenge would have made the whole State to tremble, and that much Christian Blood would have been sacrificed to their Passion? But seeing the common Good is more regarded and pursued by the Rulers of a free Republick, than the satisfying of any violent Passion; and that by executing that Revenge, or

All which appears by Examples, viz. by the Amnesty of 1651.

or rather just Punishment, it would have sustain'd a signal Damage, the said Crime was wisely and prudently buried by a general Amnesty or Pardon, and so that great Breach, made on purpose to keep the whole State a long time in a troublesom Alarm, was presently repair'd.

The most considerable Dissension and Rent which in the memory of Man hath hapned in these United Provinces, was that of the Province of Over-Yssel into two considerable Partys about the beginning of the Year 1654; which was of such a Nature, that both the differing Partys behaved themselves as States, and as the Lawful Sovereign Powers of that Province, insomuch that they made War against one another in that Quality, and after such a manner, that the City of Hasseld was, after a formal Siege taken by one of the Partys. In this Dissension (according to the forementioned Maxim of great Men) the Stadtholder of Friesland had concerned himself, and was received by one of the Partys for Stadtholder, Governour, and Captain-General of Over-Yssel, by which the Dissension was brought to that Extremity, and lasted between three and four Years.

But at last those Lords observing, that their Disputes were infinitely multiplied, so that the Wound was almost incurable, they submitted at the Mediation of the Pensioner of Holland, to refer all their Differences to the decision and determination of two Persons appointed by the States of the same Province, who were the *Heer van Po'sbroek* Burgomaster of the City of *Amsterdam*, and the said Pensioner, who reconciled the contending Partys of

Ch. 6. *Free Government in* Holland,

of the said Province in most of their differing Points in an amicable manner, and afterwards all the necessary Regulations, Orders, Instructions and Affidavits as to Affairs of the Government of the said Province, being set down in Writing, a solemn Sentence and Decision was made and pronounced upon the 20th of *August* 1657, of all the said Differences, in the Name of the States of *Holland* and *West-Friesland*, and all confirmed under the Great Seal of the said States, inserting therein the foresaid Regulations, Orders, Instructions, and Oaths, for preventing the like Inconveniences for the future; and all with that Prudence and Moderation, that both Partys receiv'd intire Satisfaction. Hereupon the divided Government was immediately consolidated and heal'd up, and the Quiet and Peace of the said Province restored, and so continues to this very day. *And afterward amicably ended.*

In the Province of *Groningen* and *Ommelanden*, there arose likewise a notable Dissension at the beginning of 1655, and again at the end of 1656; insomuch that the Body of the foresaid *Ommelanden*, and half of the Province being divided, all Government and Administration of Justice was at a stand. Upon this Occasion it manifestly appeared whether such Dissensions could be best composed and quieted by Stadtholders, or by the Authority and Conduct of other Rulers. The States General having gotten information of those Differences at two several times, did immediately desire the Stadtholder of that Province to be present in Person, and allay the Difference if possible. But Experience taught us, that it was but like Oil cast into the Fire: *What hapned in Groningen is worthy observation.* *Where the Stadtholder, not able to allay the Differences, desir'd the States to do it by their Deputys.*

So

So that the Stadtholder was necessitated to return answer to the States General, that he found it impracticable, and desired the States would depute some of their Number for that End. Which having performed, those Deputys composed and allayed the said Differences, to the satisfaction and contentment of both Partys, and the Government of the Country was settled and confirmed, in the Name, and under the Seal of the States General, with consent of the said Country.

It would be too tedious to mention Circumstances, how prudently and happily, by the wise Direction of the States of *Holland* or those Authorized by them, all the Commotions that hapned in the Citys of the same Province, and all Differences, as well between the said Citys against one another, as between the Rulers of one and the same City, were every time extinguished and allay'd. Yea even old Disputes, that from the time of the last Troubles had been carried on with much heat between some Members, and which under the Stadtholders could never be allayed, were by the States of *Holland* amicably decided to the satisfaction of the Partys concerned. Which Examples in respect of the Commotions that have heretofore, and now lately hapned at *Dort*, *Enchuysen*, and *Medenblick*, as likewise the appeasing of the Differences between the Governours of *Gorcum* and *Schoonhoven*, about the chusing of their Magistrates, and of those of *Rotterdam*, and the *Briel*, about the Pilotage of the *Maese*, and the Passage into *Goeree*, as also the old Disputes about the Investiture of the Colleges of the Generality, between the Members of

West-

West-Friesland and the North Quarter, which were depending beyond the memory of Man, are very notable Instances.

Here might also be shewn, that the beginnings of all the said Commotions and Dissensions were first designed or contrived by the last deceased Stadtholder; and others were excited and fomented by his Creatures that he left behind him: So that all that are Lovers of Peace and Quiet, and would rather have all Discords compos'd by wise and mild Conduct, than carried on and increas'd by Passion, or decided by the Sword, have need carefully to beware of electing a Stadtholder or new Baitmaker.

Where the beginnings of Mischiefs were contriv'd by our last Stadtholder.

But the greatest and most valuable Benefit of the present Free Government, is, that now, according to the true Interest of Holland, all the Revenues of the Land, both Ordinary and Extraordinary, that remain over and above the Paiments of the Principal and Interest of the publick Debts, are applied for the increasing and strengthening our Naval Power, whereas it was heretofore wasted upon unprofitable, nay and ofttimes pernicious Sieges and other Expeditions, according to the Vain Glory of the Captain-General. It is particularly observable, that at present the ordinary Naval Power of this State is above three or four times more formidable than ever it was during the War with the King of Spain. And as after the conclusion of the Peace with the said King, during the Life of the Prince of Orange, the first Design was (as I formerly mentioned) to sell the most considerable of our Ships; so after his Death, one of the first Cares of the States was, to put the Colleges

The first considerable Fruit of this Free Government is, that the Powers of Holland are dispos'd to strengthen our Naval Forces.

...ses of the Admiralty, in a Posture of acting Offensive at Sea. The States having (which is almost incredible) during the chargeable War against England, from 1652 to 1654, built in the space of two Years, sixty new Capital Ships of War, of such Dimensions and Force as were never before used in the Service of this State. And thus they have proceeded with the like provident care to build other Ships, to buy Cannon, to erect vast Magazines and Store-houses for securing and preserving Naval Stores, and making of publick Rope-ways, and the like, and for providing all things necessary for the equipping and setting of Ships to Sea, and generally have done all that's fit for the strengthning of our Naval Power, which hath been continued diligently, from time to time.

This is known to be the only means whereby, under the Blessing of God, this State may progressively increase in Fishing, Commerce, and Navigation, and draw an incredible concourse of People out of all Countrys, as we daily experience to our great joy. For who can be ignorant, that the awful regard to our foresaid Naval Power alone hath, next under God, been the cause of putting a stop to the aforementioned intolerable Piracys of the *French* in the *Mediterranean* Seas, by which the Government is brought into a Posture to be able, yea and did resolve to attack, take and destroy, not only common Pirates, but even the King's Ships of War which were made use of for that end? So that two of the King of *France*'s Ships being taken by Vice-Admiral *de Ruyter* in the *Mediterranean* 1657, his Majesty who had caused all our

Ships

Ships and Effects throoout his Dominions to be seized, was thereby readily brought to free us from that Inconveniency.

Without the influence of this Naval Power, it would in all humane Probability have been impossible to deliver our selves with any reputation out of the *Eastern* War formerly mentioned, without being expos'd to many more Difficultys. In short, by this means the Commerce and Navigation of these Provinces have, notwithstanding the heavy burdens forementioned, been kept in a tolerable good Posture and Condition, and do now considerably improve.

And the Eastern Affairs dispatched.

And our Traffick and Navigation considerably encreased.

So that the Folly or Malice of some People is intolerable, who dare complain of our present State of Affairs, and esteem the former Times better than the present. If those stupid or ill meaning People cannot or will not be at the pains to consider the noble Effects of the present Free Government, yet they should at least suffer themselves to be convinced by the evident Prosperity of the Citys of *Holland*. What could they answer if they were asked, Whether it be not a manifest Token of Prosperity, that the most considerable and greatest Mercantile City of the Province, viz. *Amsterdam*, hath been enlarged two parts in three; and that none can observe, that either the Houses or Inheritances are thereby lessened in Value, yea that it is so augmented in Buildings of Houses, that the Imposts on the Bulky Goods of that City only in the last Farm, yielded above thirty thousand Guilders more than in the former, and yet the said Impost was in the foregoing Years considerably improved? We may affirm the same

The stupidity of those who complain of our Affairs, is inexcusable.

Seeing the Prosperity of the Country appears by other Symptoms.

same of *Leyden* and *Dort*, and other Citys in proportion. And that the Riches, and Plenty, of many cannot be kept within the Walls of their Houses, but that over and above their Costly and Stately Buildings, they are visible in their Coaches, Horses, and other Tokens of Plenty in every Part. There are but very few in the Citys of the foresaid Provinces, that do not yearly increase their Capital. Yea, if the foresaid Complainers and Murmurers look but into their own Books, I assure my self that most of them (unless they are profuse, negligent and debauched) shall find their Stock, one Year with another, considerably increased.

CHAP. VII.

The third and last Part of this Book concludes with this, That all good Inhabitants ought to defend the Free Government of the Republick of Holland *and* West-Friesland, *with their Lives and Estates.*

THEN since we have already enjoyed such noble Fruits of the present Free Government, notwithstanding the grievous Obstructions beforementioned, and that we are as yet but in the Winter of this happy Change, wherein a great part of the said good and fruitful Seed lies still hid in the Ground, and the other part is but preparing to be sowed in the Spring; who is there that may not easily apprehend, how noble and happy
the

the approaching Spring and Summer will be; but especially the Harvest, when that horrible Burden of one hundred and forty Millions will be paid off and fully discharged, and when the Taxes upon Consumption, Commerce, and immoveable Estates, will be leslened by seven Millions, and yet the Treasure of the Land not one Stiver less.

And if at present under so many intolerable Burdens as are expressed in the 5th Chapter, and what have since the Year 1662 befaln us (of which we might give a large account) our Citys and Inhabitants have under a free Government been visibly enlarged and increased; who will not easily apprehend that by continuing the same Government we shall in time with God's Blessing be the most happy and mighty Country for Strength that is to be found upon the Face of the Earth? And therefore we are oblig'd to pray fervently to God Almighty, that he would be pleased not only to keep us in the same State, but also upon occasion to make us willing to hazard our Lives and Estates, and that joyfully, to maintain the same, that so our Children may at least possess that full Happiness, and that compleat worldly Felicity which they cannot fail of, (without God's Extraordinary Judgment) unless we should by our Revolt to a Stadtholder, Governour or Captain-General, pull up the stately Foundations which have so prudently been laid by the present Free Government, and which without such defection will the more easily by continuance be kept up, yea and may from time to time be improved.

All the Inhabitants of Holland ought to support their Free Government.

With this general Conclusion, I might now end the said Part of this Book, were it not that the great Weight of this Affair presseth me to say further, That upon this foregoing Argument, illustrated by Antient and Modern Histories, and also by our own Experience of the many Mischiefs of the former compulsive Government, and of the many good Fruits of the present free Government, we might well hold it for an unchangeable Maxim, That a Country having such Interests or Advantages as *Holland* now hath, ought in all respects to be governed by a Free Republick and States: And that all the good Rulers of this Land, and especially all the Inhabitants that are in any measure concerned in the prosperity of Manufactury, Fishery, Commerce and Shipping, ought to maintain the present Free Government with all their might, and by no means to suffer, and much less to occasion that any Inhabitant, of what Quality soever, do under any specious Title or Denomination acquire so great a Power, that the Gentry and Citys of *Holland* should submit unto, or truckle under him, or not dare by their Deputys at their Assemblys to speak out, and declare that which tends to the true Interest of the Country, and the respective Citys of *Holland*, when it thwarts the Interest of a Political or Military Head; or when they having declared it, dare not maintain it without running into eminent Danger.

And above all we may conclude, That the Ecclesiasticks, who in any wise regard the true Interest of the Reformed Religion, that do not impiously trample upon the Honour of God, and shamelesly sell the Reverence due to them themselves for a mess of Pottage, ought to support this Free Government, and with their Spiritual Weapons defend it against the Incroachments of such a Ruler, considering that the Reformed Religion will be surer and better preserved by the prudent, immortal, and almost immutable Sovereign Assembly of the States of *Holland* and *West-Friesland*, and other Colleges subordinate to them, than by those Voluptuous, Lavish, Transitory and Fickle Monarchs and Princes, or their Favorites, who alter the outward Form and Practice of Religion as may be most consistent with their Pleasures or Profits, and besides, when they die, do often bequeath their Lands to Inheritors of others, and especially of the *Romish* Religion, who by their high Places, Politick Conduct, and the Eminency of their Ecclesiastical Honour and Extraordinary Riches, attract to themselves Great Persons, and especially the surviving poor Daughters and younger Sons, who by them may easily arrive to great Inheritances, as we have often seen in this and the foregoing Ages, in *France, England, Germany, Orange*, &c. And seeing the Consistorys, Classes, and Synods being in some measure inclined to obey this Lawful Government as the Sovereign Power set over them by God himself, have a plenary and ample Freedom allow'd them in all their Ecclesiastical Determinations, and are likely so to continue, pursuant thereunto each Minister doing his duty during Life, and presiding or voting among the yearly Elders, Deacons and Members that depend upon him; and he himself being subject to none save the Sovereign Power, is in effect a little Bishop,

Because a Republican Government can hardly alter, but a single Person may change the Religion of the Place he lives in.

and so will continue, and moreover the said Ministers will retain the due freedom of expounding God's holy Word sett us in the Writings of the Old and New Testament, in sound solid Truth, and may frame their Expositions and publick Prayers according to the Occasion, Time and Place, to the greater furtherance of God's Honour, and the Edification of the Church, wherein the greatest Comfort, and highest Praise of an upright Reformed Minister does consist. Whereas on the other side, a Monarchical Governour, tho not acknowledging the Pope of *Rome*, must and would necessarily then off, and discharge such a Church-Council, to make way for the Ruling of Bishops, or a Political Church-Council, to curb them, and all other Preachers to depend on himself as Head of the Church. And moreover, a single Person would for his greater Security, and Quiet in his Government, deprive the Ministry of their freedom to expound the Word of God according to the best of their Skill, and to frame their publick Prayers to the Edification of the People, and instead thereof give them limited or composed Sermons and Prayers; or if the Prince found himself not strong enough to introduce this Church-Government, and thereby to curb Proud and Seditious Preachers, he would then perhaps set his endeavour to make such Ministers and Clergy submit to the Pope of *Rome*, than if they are to be their own Masters, in hopes of a length of time, and manifold Accidents, and by an Ecclesiastical Government in some measure regulated by a Foreign Head, it would be more tolerable

to

to him than these upstart Seditious People, whom no Body knows how much Power they will pretend to, and of whom, as of a hidden Distemper, and a secret Enemy, the Sovereign is always in jealousy and fear.

Lastly, We may well conclude, That all the forementioned Evils would certainly befal these Lands, as soon as any one single Person, under what specious Pretence or Title soever, shall have the command of our Forces, either during Life, or for a long time. We must consider, that in these unfortified Provinces, where Foreign hired Souldiers are continually entertained in all the adjacent strong Holds, such a Souldiery will not only obey him in despite of the Civil Magistrates who are their Directors and Pay-Masters, and in despite of the honest Ministry, and to the ruin of such as live on their Rents, Trades and Husbandry, but likewise all other ill-disposed Inhabitants, as well as the Rabble, will always be ready, tho not stirred up by any wicked and seditious Preachers, to join themselves with the Party of such a Courteous, Liberal, and Valiant Captain-General. So that the most honest, and virtuous Rulers and Magistrates must be forc'd by constraint to demit, and others to prevent the losing of their Lives, Honors and Estates, or else, to gain more Wealth and Honour and Authority, must concur with him, and dissolve such a Government.

The matter being thus, we must say, that all Persons, who for their particular Interest do wilfully introduce such a Monarchical Government into our Native Country, will *The Contrary hereof would be Treason.*

commit a Crime which afterwards can never be remedied, but the *Adam's* Original Sin be derived from Father to Son to perpetuity, and produce such pernicious effects, that all the good Orders and Laws of these Provinces, whether Civil or Ecclesiastical, must at length be subverted. And seeing Crimes are most properly committed against the Laws of the Sovereign Power, namely either to usurp the Legislator himself, or to endeavour to alter the Sovereign Government, we must therefore conclude, that the said Innocents will by so doing make themselves guilty of *Crimen Majestatis* or *... Perduellionis*, in attempting a most durable and manifest Treason against their Country.

To conclude. We must grant that this Republick of *Holland* and *West-Friesland*, being deprived of their Free Government by erecting a Stadtholder or Captain-General for Life, would in a few Years lose both the Name and Essence of a Free Republick, and be changed into a downright Monarchical Government, which the Merchants perceiving, would leave our Country as they have done others, that they might be under a free Government. Let God forbid such a thing, that losing the greatest worldly Blessing could befall us; for this Country consisting of Traders, Manufacturers, Fishermen, Merchants, Owners of Ships, and others depending on them, who by this means must be bereft of their Livelihood, will become a Land desolate and uninhabited, a Body without a Soul, and a lamentable Theatre of unspeakable Misery.

CHAP.

CHAP. VIII.

The Conclusion of the whole Book, with a Declaration of the Author's Design, and a Caution both to the ill and well affected Readers.

THESE my Remarks upon the three premised Parts of the True Political Maxims of the Republick of *Holland* and *West-Friesland*, hapning to be made Publick, tho very imperfect, under the Titile of *the Interest of Holland* in the Year 1662; and afterwards in the Years 1667, and 1668, being more carefully perused, and more maturely deliberated upon, the Reader ought to be forewarned, that sometimes the Affairs of those respective Years ought to be adverted to in the reading. And that my intent was, both in general and particular, to shew briefly wherein the Interest of *Holland* consists, *viz.* That as in all Countrys of the World, the highest perfection of a Political Society, and in a Land by accident labouring under Taxes, and naturally indigent, as *Holland* is, there is an absolute necessity that the Commonalty be left in as great a natural Liberty for seeking the Welfare of their Souls and Bodys, and for the Improvement of their Estates, as possible. For as the Inhabitants of the most plentiful Country upon Earth, by want only of that natural Liberty, and finding themselves every way encumbred and perplexed, do really inhabit a Bridewel or House of Correction, fit for

The Whole concluded with this Affirmation,

none

... none but miserable condemned Slaves, and consequently, a Hell upon Earth. Whereas ... ... of using their Natural Rights and Properties for their own Safety, provided it tends not to the Destruction of the Society, will be to the Commonalty, tho in a barren and indigent Country, an earthly Paradise: ... to be ... of a Man's own Mind, especially ... Matters wherein all his Welfare consists, is to such a one as acceptable as an Limited Kingdom.

I have Likewise shewn, that such a Liberty and Property of the subject does very well consist ... with the present uncontroled Power of the free Government, and with none other.

So that all good Patriots, and true Lovers of our Native Country, who peruse this Book are earnestly intreated to consider carefully whether the two most weighty Points before mentioned are not strongly and fully to be asserted.

However ... when, and how the particulars ... treated of, may all at once or at several times be set about, or perused, was not ... in the least to direct. For the ... Powers, whom it only concerns in a Republic to conclude of these Matters, and ... to know that such things as ... be born with less inconvenience than ... ever changed, ought to continue, and ... . And when such wise and good Patriots will make any alteration, they

---

... facta tenent. Mul-...

must

must go by degrees, and as far as they conveniently may; yet they must rather stand still, or remain as they are, than run their Heads against a Wall.

And indeed Reformation in Political Affairs depends on so many, and such various Circumstances, namely Customs, Times, Places, Rulers, Subjects, Allys, Neighbouring and Foreign Countrys, that such a Reformation is either proper, or improper to be undertaken, according as the several Circumstances are well weighed, such especially in a free Republick, which is govern'd and managed by prudent Assemblys of the States, venerable City Councils, and reputable Colleges, in which it would be a great Presumption and Self-conceit, yea indeed a Crime for a private Person to dare to conclude any thing, and in so doing to arrogate it to himself, or to put a Hand to that Work which properly and of right belongs only to the States of *Holland*, and those that are thereunto Authorized. *For that would be worthy of a severe punishment.* *Especially in this Country, where are so many Sage and Prudent Rulers.*

If any Man should object by way of Reply, That throughout the whole Book I use no doubtful Proposals, but positive Reasonings, and a conclusive cogent way of Argument: I answer, That all matters which not only consist in knowing something, but also and chiefly in desiring or opposing any thing, and which moreover thwarts the Prejudices and Interests of many Men, neither can, nor ought to be otherwise handled. For if an Angel from Heaven should propose to Mankind such matters doubtfully and faintly, he would have but little audience upon Earth, and

and gain no Credit by People that have imbibed such Prejudices beforehand. So that being desirous of having what I write of such matters to be read with consideration, and not only weighed, and to make some impression on the Reader, I have been necessitated to use this manner of writing. And therefore I find my self likewise obliged at the end of this Book, when I presume all hath been read, and duly weighed, to declare this much, and to give this Caution, that the same may be made use of for the good, and not for the hurt of our Native Country.

I shall add, That such a circumspect Censure of the Readers is the more requisite, because I shall have done much, if in proposing matters which relate to the Prosperity of *H* and my Judgment hath in the general been rightly directed: For it would be incredible, and almost above humane Power, not to have err'd and mistaken in proposing and relating so many several Particular matters. But since notwithstanding my Aim hath been to set nothing before you but Truth, which might tend to the Benefit of my Native Country, I hope, I have not often strayed, and run into mistakes. And I hope that in the Judgment of my serious Readers, and especially those of the lawful Magistracy, and true Fathers of their Country, I may have come so near the mark in many things, that my Errors which in such a Case I renounce, may be so overlooked by them, as they may commend my laudable Zeal, and be excited to greater matters them-

themselves, or may imploy others that have more Ability and Leasure; that by such Countenance and Favour they may be encouraged to write something necessary for the Service of their Native Country, and that more Amply, Methodically and Solidly than I have done. If this be effected, I have my principal End and Design.

But in case any Reader be so ill minded, tho neither willing nor able to effect such a commendable Work himself, as to oppose and despise what I have here laid down, let him remember, that I desire nothing of him but to judg of mine and other Writings with consideration and circumspection; and that I shall be far from such foolish Ambition as to write an Answer which would neither be serviceable to my Country, the Reader, nor my self. For I intend to follow this perpetual Maxim during my short and transitory Life, To make no Man Master of my Time and Repose but my self, and particularly never to grant or yield so much to any ill designing Person, as for their sakes to fall into troublesom, contentious and unprofitable Scribling. For whether my Errors be truly discovered, or peevishly and falsely laid to my charge, the several Readers must be the Judges.

Farewel, and remember this saying, * It

---

* Boni Civis est liberum Reipublicæ statum tueri, nec eum mutatum velle.

is

is the Duty of a good Citizen, to preserve and defend the Common Freedom of his Native Country, as far as in him Lies.

FINIS.